James Joyce's fiction constantly engages with an Ireland whose present and past are marked by the long struggle to achieve full independence from Britain. *Semicolonial Joyce* is the first collection to address the importance of Ireland's colonial situation in understanding Joyce's work. The volume brings together leading commentators on the Irish dimension of Joyce's writing, such as Vincent J. Cheng, Seamus Deane, Enda Duffy, Luke Gibbons, David Lloyd, and Emer Nolan, to present a range of voices rather than a single position on a topic which has had a major impact on Joyce criticism in recent years. Contributors explore Joyce's ambivalent and shifting response to Irish nationalism and reconsider his writing in the context of the history of Western colonialism. The chapters both draw on and question the achievements of postcolonial theory, and provide fresh insights into Joyce's resourceful engagement with political issues that remain highly topical today. This book represents a major contribution to Joycean and postcolonial studies.

Derek Attridge is Leverhulme Research Professor at the University of York and Distinguished Visiting Professor at Rutgers University. He is author or editor of several books on Joyce, including the *Cambridge Companion to James Joyce* (1990) and *Joyce Effects: On Language, Theory, and History* (Cambridge University Press, 2000).

Marjorie Howes is Associate Professor of English at Rutgers University. She is author of *Yeats's Nations: Gender, Class, and Irishness* (Cambridge University Press, 1996).

EDITED BY DEREK ATTRIDGE
AND MARJORIE HOWES

Semicolonial Joyce

CAMBRIDGE
UNIVERSITY PRESS

PUBLISHED BY THE PRESS SYNDICATE OF THE UNIVERSITY OF CAMBRIDGE
The Pitt Building, Trumpington Street, Cambridge, United Kingdom

CAMBRIDGE UNIVERSITY PRESS
The Edinburgh Building, Cambridge CB2 2RU, UK   www.cup.cam.ac.uk
40 West 20th Street, New York, NY 10011–4211, USA   www.cup.org
10 Stamford Road, Oakleigh, Melbourne 3166, Australia
Ruiz de Alarcón 13, 28014 Madrid, Spain

First published 2000

Printed in the United Kingdom at the University Press, Cambridge

Typeset in Monotype Fournier 11/13.5   *System* QuarkXpress®   [SE]

A catalogue record for this book is available from the British Library

Library of Congress Cataloguing in Publication data

Semicolonial Joyce / edited by Derek Attridge and Marjorie Howes.
    p.   cm.
    Includes bibliographical references.
    ISBN 0 521 66179 X (hardback) – Political and social views. 2. Political fiction,
English – Irish authors – History and Criticism. 3. Nationalism and
literature – Ireland – History – 20th century. 4. Joyce, James, 1882–1941 – Views on
nationalism. 5. Imperialism in literature. 6. Ireland – In literature. I. Attridge, Derek. II.
Howes, Marjorie Elizabeth.
    PR6019.O9 Z79447 2000
    823'.912–dc21   99-051422

ISBN 0 521 66179 X hardback
ISBN 0 521 66628 7 paperback

Contents

List of contributors [vii]
Acknowledgments [ix]
Note on references to Joyce's works [x]

Introduction [1]
MARJORIE HOWES and DEREK ATTRIDGE

1 Dead ends: Joyce's finest moments [21]
SEAMUS DEANE

2 Disappearing Dublin: *Ulysses*, postcoloniality, and the politics of space [37]
ENDA DUFFY

3 "Goodbye Ireland I'm going to Gort": geography, scale, and narrating the nation [58]
MARJORIE HOWES

4 State of the art: Joyce and postcolonialism [78]
EMER NOLAN

5 "Neither fish nor flesh"; or how "Cyclops" stages the double-bind of Irish manhood [96]
JOSEPH VALENTE

6 Counterparts: *Dubliners*, masculinity, and temperance nationalism [128]
DAVID LLOYD

7 "Have you no homes to go to?": Joyce and the politics of paralysis [150]
LUKE GIBBONS

8 Don't cry for me, Argentina: "Eveline" and the seductions of emigration propaganda [172]
KATHERINE MULLIN

9 "Kilt by kelt shell kithagain with kinagain": Joyce and Scotland [201]
WILLY MALEY

10 Phoenician genealogies and oriental geographies: Joyce, language, and race [219]
ELIZABETH BUTLER CULLINGFORD

11 Authenticity and identity: catching the Irish spirit [240]
VINCENT J. CHENG

Index [262]

Contributors

DEREK ATTRIDGE is Leverhulme Research Professor at the University of York and Distinguished Visiting Professor at Rutgers University, New Brunswick. His books include *Peculiar Language: Literature as Difference from the Renaissance to James Joyce* (1988), *Joyce Effects: On Language, Theory, and History* (2000), *Post-structuralist Joyce: Essays from the French* (1984), and *The Cambridge Companion to James Joyce* (1990).

VINCENT J. CHENG is the author of *Joyce, Race, and Empire* (1995), *Shakespeare and Joyce: A Study of "Finnegans Wake"* (1984), and *"Le Cid": A Translation in Rhymed Couplets* (1987), as well as many articles on modern literature; and coeditor of *Joyce in Context* (1992) and *Joycean Cultures* (1998). He is the Shirley Sutton Thomas Professor of English at the University of Utah.

ELIZABETH BUTLER CULLINGFORD is Professor of English at the University of Texas at Austin and author of *Yeats, Ireland and Fascism* (1981) and *Gender and History in Yeats's Love Poetry* (1993). She is working on a collection of essays on Irish literature, film, and culture.

SEAMUS DEANE is Keough Professor of Irish Studies at the University of Notre Dame. Among his publications are: *Selected Poems* (1988), *The Field Day Anthology of Irish Writing* (editor, 1991), *Reading in the Dark* (1996), and *Strange Country: Modernity and Nationhood in Irish Writing since 1790* (1997).

ENDA DUFFY is the author of *The Subaltern "Ulysses"* (1994). He is Associate Professor of English at the University of California, Santa Barbara. He is writing a book on speed in modernity.

LUKE GIBBONS is Director of the MA program in Film and Television Studies at Dublin City University. He is the author of *Transformations in Irish Culture* (1996), coauthor of *Cinema and Ireland* (1988), and a contributing editor for *The Field Day Anthology of Irish Writing* (1991).

MARJORIE HOWES is Associate Professor of English at Rutgers University, New Brunswick. She is the author of *Yeats's Nations: Gender, Class, and Irishness* (1996).

DAVID LLOYD is Hartley Burr Alexander Chair in the Humanities at Scripps College, Claremont. He is the author of *Nationalism and Minor Literature:*

James Clarence Mangan and the Emergence of Irish Cultural Nationalism (1987) and *Anomalous States: Irish Writing and the Postcolonial Moment* (1993), the coeditor with Lisa Lowe of *The Politics of Culture in the Shadow of Capital* (1997), and the coauthor with Paul Thomas of *Culture and the State* (1997). His *Ireland after History* was published in 1999.

WILLY MALEY is Professor of English Literature at the University of Glasgow. He is the author of *A Spenser Chronology* (1994) and *Salvaging Spenser: Colonialism, Culture and Identity* (1997), and the coeditor of *Representing Ireland: Literature and the Origins of Conflict, 1534–1660* (1993), *Postcolonial Criticism* (1997), and *A View of the Present State of Ireland: From the First Published Edition* (1997).

KATHERINE MULLIN is a doctoral student at St. Hugh's College, Oxford, working towards a thesis on Joyce, surveillance, and the social purity movement.

EMER NOLAN is Lecturer in the Department of English, National University of Ireland, Maynooth. She is the author of *James Joyce and Nationalism* (1995).

JOSEPH VALENTE is Associate Professor of English, Interpretive Theory, and Women's Studies at the University of Illinois. He is the author of *James Joyce and the Problem of Justice: Negotiating Sexual and Colonial Difference* (1995) and the editor of *Quare Joyce* (1998). His current book projects include "Interview with the Irish Vampire: Bram Stoker, *Dracula* and the Question of Blood," and "Contested Territory: Manhood and Race in Modern Irish Literature," for which he has received a Mellon Fellowship.

Acknowledgments

We gratefully acknowledge the Bettmann Archive for permission to reproduce the photograph used in chapter 2, and the Bodleian Library, University of Oxford, for permission to reproduce three images from Clifford G. Roe, *The Horrors of the White Slave Trader*, 1911, shelfmark 24728 e. 39, used in chapter 8.

An earlier version of the essay by David Lloyd appeared in Rosemary Marangoly George, ed., *Burning Down the House: Recycling Domesticity* (Boulder, Co.: Westview Press, 1998).

Derek Attridge acknowledges the assistance of the Leverhulme Trust in completing this book.

Note on references to Joyce's works

CW   *The Critical Writings*. Ed. Ellsworth Mason and Richard Ellmann. New York: Viking, 1959; reprinted Ithaca: Cornell University Press, 1989.

FW   *Finnegans Wake*. London: Faber & Faber, 1939. References are in the form of page number.line number (e.g., *FW* 318.24). All editions have the same pagination.

Letters I   *Letters*, vol. I. Ed. Stuart Gilbert. New York: Viking, 1957, 1966.

Letters II   *Letters*, vol. II. Ed. Richard Ellmann. New York: Viking, 1966.

U   *Ulysses: The Corrected Text*. Ed. Hans Walter Gabler with Wolfhard Steppe and Claus Melchior. London: Bodley Head and Penguin, 1986; New York: Random House, 1986. References are in the form of episode number.line number (e.g., *U* 13.950)

Other works by Joyce are quoted in the editions listed in the works cited at the end of each chapter.

Introduction

MARJORIE HOWES AND DEREK ATTRIDGE

Semicoloniality

In the sixth chapter of *Finnegans Wake*, Shaun appears in the guise of one Professor Jones, delivering a lecture on the superiority of space to time. To gain his audience's attention for the fable of The Mookse and The Gripes by which he means to exemplify this hierarchical opposition, he announces:

> Gentes and laitymen, fullstoppers and semicolonials, hybreds and lubberds!
> (*FW* 152.16)

With his customary brilliance, Joyce here articulates in a single phrase a variety of binary oppositions that divide human communities. A gender opposition is obvious in the half-heard phrase "Gentlemen and ladies" and class distinction is present in the appeal to "high-breds and low-breds," the latter conflated with the equally derogatory "lubbers." Religious difference is evoked in the allusion to "Gentiles" and "laity," the first suggesting a Jewish classification, the second a Christian one – and both terms implying exclusion from a defined religious group, and thus the contrast between insiders and outsiders. Working in concert with all these is a categorization disguised under the familiar distinction between full stops and semicolons: the opposition between permanent and temporary inhabitants of a colonized country, or "stoppers" and "colonials."

At the same time as oppositions multiply, suggesting the interconnectedness of all these ways of dividing social groups into exclusive compartments, the very structure of opposition is questioned, in a move that is typical of *Finnegans Wake*'s method. In the opening phrase, for instance, "men" is switched from its normal place in the first word to the second word, thus producing gender confusion instead of polarity. What is more, while the natives are "full"-stoppers, the expatriates are only "semi"-colonials; and the members of the high-bred upper class are also – Joyce here seems to have foreknowledge of current discussions of colonialism – "hybrids." (Another punctuation mark is implied here too, this time, appropriately enough, one that registers simultaneous connection and division: the hyphen.) We might note also that Joyce raises the issue of nations and nationality at the very beginning of the announcement: for the Romans, *gens* signified a people or a country, and its plural, *gentes*, could be used to mean "foreign nations."

This strategy of evoking and simultaneously complicating oppositions is entirely characteristic of Joyce's writing and of his attitude to political and ethical issues. Philosophically he could be said to have been both a separatist and a unionist, thinking constantly in terms of oppositions and that which dissolves (or reverses) oppositions. He even extended this preference for undecidability or hybridity to the very opposition between separation and union as distinct principles of thought (as well as practical policies), so that even these terms cannot finally operate in isolation from each other. To identify points of difference, for Joyce, is to articulate a kind of connection. Political (and, more specifically, Irish) separatism and unionism, nationalism and anti-nationalism, therefore, are not for Joyce entirely separable, but neither can they be conflated; to identify wholly with one side is as stultifying as it is irresponsible to make no distinction at all. Joyce's lectures and articles on Ireland dating from his time in Trieste – a constant reference in recent commentaries on his politics – evince the same doubleness, and have been read as both strongly supportive of Irish nationalism and highly critical of it. Emer Nolan, in articulating her position on these writings in *James Joyce and Nationalism*, perhaps speaks for all the contributors to this volume when she says that "his writings about Ireland may not provide a coherent critique of either colonised or colonialist; but their very ambiguities and hesitations testify to the uncertain, divided consciousness of the colonial subject, which he is unable to articulate in its full complexity outside his fiction" (130).

In the Wakean sentence above, the opposition between native and colonizer is both strongly articulated and decisively challenged, and this remains true of the fable that follows. The Mookse (Aesop's fox, and another manifestation of Shaun) is, in historical terms, a conflation of King Henry II of England and Pope Adrian IV, the Englishman Nicholas Breakspeare, who represent the early colonization and domination of Ireland by England and the Roman Catholic Church. The bunch of grapes desired by the fox is associated with Shem and called – in continuation of Shaun's attack on his brother as beggar and complainer – the

Gripes. In terms of the opposition between invader and native, he stands for the Irish population (he is called the Mookse's "Dubville brooder-on-low"), but he is by no means the hero of the story, which ends with the falling of dusk and the transformation of the protagonists to humble articles of clothing carried away by two women, at once Valkyries bearing off the dead in battle and Dublin washerwomen at their daily work. The initial opposition between English and Irish, invader and native, colonizer and colonized, upper class and lower class, space and time, dissolves in the murk of evening, and a different (and equally temporary) opposition structures the conclusion of the story: that between, on the one hand, the warring oppositional males, now impotent, and, on the other, the preserving female community.

This passage reveals one of the reasons why Joyce's writings can be called "semicolonial": in their dealings with questions of nationalism and imperialism they evince a complex and ambivalent set of attitudes, not reducible to a simple anticolonialism but very far from expressing approval of the colonial organizations and methods under which Ireland had suffered during a long history of oppression, and continued to suffer during his lifetime. The allusion to punctuation, furthermore, reminds us that Joyce's handling of political matters is always mediated by his strong interest in, and immense skill with, language: the two domains are, finally, inseparable in his work. The fable of the Mookse and the Gripes demonstrates, as would any passage from *Finnegans Wake*, the way in which language's potential for multiple suggestiveness is used to make connections between the political and historical domain and the domains of, among many others, myth, religion, popular culture, high culture, and philosophy. To write in this way is not to reduce politics to language, but to use linguistic forms to stage political issues with an openness to manifold outcomes that is impossible in the purely pragmatic sphere.

Our title also invokes the disciplinary field of postcolonial studies, in recent years one of the most productive areas of literary and cultural criticism. The adjective "semicolonial" signals our sense of a partial fit between this set of approaches and Joyce's writing. Rather than claiming that the issues raised and models offered by postcolonial studies can illuminate every element of Joyce's works or supersede other interpretive or theoretical frameworks, we believe that it is precisely from the limited compatibility between them that the most interesting lessons can be drawn – for both readers of Joyce and theorists of colonialism.

Another – related – justification for the use of "semicolonial" lies in the fact that Joyce's writings emerge from, and take as their major historical subject, a country whose status *vis-à-vis* the imperial power, although it can be illuminated by the colonial model, cannot be understood straightforwardly in its terms. Ireland's relation to current theorizations of imperialism and postcoloniality is a problematic one, and we take up this issue in more detail below. Other reasons for the caution expressed in our title include the way in which Joyce's encyclopedic appropriations of the material and textual worlds around him exceeded the boundaries of Ireland, and the importance of historical factors other than imperialism in shaping his literary production. Joyce spent by far the larger part of his life out of Ireland, which also contributed to the semidetached nature of his relationship to its national politics, and any literary *œuvre* as complex and inexhaustible as Joyce's will always offer alternative avenues of reading to pursue and interpretive knots that refuse to be untied. Finally, in its evocation of the hilarity of *Finnegans Wake*, the term "semicolonial" reminds us that Joyce, however weighty his concerns, is nothing if not a comic writer, and that critics forget this at their peril.

"Semicolonial Joyce" could also name a series of recent debates among Joyceans. The rise of postcolonial perspectives in Irish studies has generated a good deal of controversy, nowhere more so than in Joyce scholarship; in a 1996 review, Colm Tóibín quipped that "the battle for the soul of Joyce has become almost as intense in recent years as the battle for the GPO in Easter Week" ("Playboys of the GPO," 15). Our volume is not intended to mirror this battle; we have chosen to collect work that finds it useful to engage, however critically, with postcolonial paradigms, instead of simply rejecting them. In this introductory chapter, we offer, as background to the chapters that follow, a brief account of the debates in Irish studies and Joyce studies that center on questions of colonialism and postcoloniality.

Irish studies meets postcolonial studies

Postcolonial studies is perhaps most usefully defined as a series of intractable but productive problems or tensions, rather than as a set of propositions or conclusions. Examining its exchanges with Irish studies and Joyce scholarship can make these problems yield fresh insights, and produce new, but fruitful, difficulties. One set of issues confronting any effort to establish how postcolonial studies might offer appropriate conceptual and methodological frameworks for the study of Joyce lies in the now notorious imprecision of the field's major terms. While "colonial" and "postcolonial" are ubiquitous in much current scholarship, one of their most obvious features is that no one is really sure what they mean. The term "postcolonial" in particular has generated a multitude of definitional difficulties and critiques.[1] While it apparently begs to be defined temporally, efforts to characterize the relationship between the colonial and the postcolonial in terms of sequentially occurring historical periods rarely produce satisfactory results. If Ireland can be said to have been a British colony (a question to which we shall return), when can colonialism in Ireland be said to have ended? With the treaty of 1921? The 1937 constitution? The 1949 repeal of the External Relations Act? The recent peace accord? Or some future final resolution?

The question of when a postcolonial Ireland might emerge, of course, is inseparable from the question of what such an Ireland might look like. Postcolonial studies negotiates between two temporal concepts of the postcolonial-as-after-colonialism, one emphasizing change and the new departures of the "post," the other emphasizing continuity and the aftermath of the "colonial." The first has been criticized for being naïvely, prematurely celebratory and for obscuring the ways in which the legacy and effects of colonialism continue to shape former colonies. The second has been taken to task for conceptualizing the complex and varied political, social, and cultural life of newly independent nations primarily in terms of the lingering impact and issues of the colonial relationship, thus repeating the reductive tyrannies of the colonial project. Would a postcolonial Ireland have its face turned towards the past? Would it be best characterized through the ways in which the ghosts of colonialism haunt it? Or would a postcolonial Ireland look towards the future, defining itself by finding colonial paradigms and their nationalist counterparts outmoded? Of course, these options need not be mutually exclusive, but articulating some combination of them often proves difficult in practice.

---

[1] For critiques of the term "postcolonial," see McClintock, "The Angel of Progress," and Shohat, "Notes on the 'Post-colonial.'" For a more wide-ranging discussion of the definitional issues and conceptual categories involved, see Parry, "The Postcolonial."

The connection Tóibín draws between the Post Office and the post-colonial indicates his assumption, which is fairly widely shared in some Irish studies circles, that much work informed by postcolonial studies represents a continuation of the nationalist tradition in Irish cultural criticism.[2] Irish revisionism is arguably as difficult to define as postcolonial studies (see Boyce and O'Day, *The Making of Modern Irish History*, 4). But it often seeks to critique nationalist mythologies and to decenter the relationship between Britain and Ireland, and it conducts various critiques of postcolonial Irish studies. These critiques often invoke a contrast between a (postcolonial) preoccupation with defining Ireland in relation to Britain and a (revisionist) ability to move beyond the outmoded centrality of the colonial relationship to think in more varied terms (Tóibín, "Playboys of the GPO," 16). What they fail to see is that both approaches are proper to postcolonial studies, and that the tension between them is an important feature of much postcolonial scholarship.

In response to the aporias generated by efforts to conceptualize the postcolonial as a phase of history after colonialism, other scholars have defined the postcolonial as following the *beginning* of colonialism, collapsing any temporal distinction between the colonial and postcolonial. This way of thinking often treats the postcolonial as a resistant element within colonialism, by identifying anticolonial opposition as postcolonial and/or by designating the instabilities and contradictions within colonialism itself as postcolonial.[3] Obviously, such work transfers the problem of periodization rather than solving it; it is no easier to tell when colonialism began than when it might end. When did Britain first colonize Ireland? During the invasions of the twelfth and thirteenth centuries? Those of the sixteenth and seventeenth centuries? The dissolution of the Irish parliament under the 1800 Act of Union? For many scholars in the generation after Edward Said, whose foundational *Orientalism* was criticized for treating colonialism as monolithic and virtually omnipotent, this version of the postcolonial is attractive because it seems to offer a more enabling, and more accurate, view of colonialism as internally ambivalent and conflicted, and as potentially vulnerable to the various

---

[2] See, for example, Foster, "The Lovely Magic," 6. For a critique of this assumption, see Graham, "'Liminal Spaces.'"

[3] For example, the general introduction to *The Post-Colonial Studies Reader* argues that "post-colonialism is a continuing process of resistance and reconstruction" (Ashcroft, Griffiths, and Tiffin, 2).

forms of resistance with which colonized peoples combat their oppression. It has its potential dangers as well, however: a certain fetishizing of "resistance," whose recovery can become the reductive goal of every reading, a related and equally limiting dependence on an opposition between resistance and complicity, and a relative neglect of the massive material power and effects of imperial structures in favor of an overly textualist reading of their instabilities.[4]

Neither of these temporal approaches to the postcolonial addresses what is widely regarded as the most central and contentious question in contemporary Irish studies: in analyzing the centuries-long relationship between Ireland and Britain, is it appropriate and useful to call that relationship "colonial" in any or all periods of its history?[5] One reason for the intensity of this debate is that defining the postcolonial in spatial terms also produces conflicts between equally problematic alternatives. Some critics use "postcolonial" more or less as a replacement for the now unfashionable term "Third World." This usage usually includes a number of characteristics – poverty, underdevelopment, a non-European culture and language exposed to the depredations of a globalized Eurocentric and/or American culture – which are arguably the consequences of Western global capitalism's dominance of the world in the twentieth century. But these characteristics are not dependent upon a specifically colonial or imperial form of domination, though they are often connected to it.[6] Other scholars foreground the sheer fact of colonial domination, a move whose confusing results include a potential characterization of the United States as postcolonial. One version of the postcolonial rests upon a dichotomy between the West and the non-West, and the other invokes an opposition between the colonizer and the colonized. For the former, Eurocentrism is all-important; for the latter, it

---

[4] For critiques of the textualist model, see Parry, "The Postcolonial" and Kaul, "Colonial Figures."

[5] For example, Smyth begins *Decolonisation and Criticism* by observing that "the most contentious debate in contemporary Irish studies concerns the establishment of the proper basis upon which to address the political and cultural activity of the modern period" and by setting out his claim that "a model of *decolonisation*" provides that basis (9).

[6] For this reason, Dirlik, in "The Postcolonial Aura," criticizes postcolonial criticism for repudiating capitalism's foundational role in history, and even suggests that current postcolonial studies reflects the logic of late capitalism in a Third World context.

means very little. There is also a debate between scholars who insist on the material and methodological centrality of such binary oppositions and those who focus on troubling and complicating them.[7]

A further reason for controversy over Ireland's relation to the postcolonial is that Ireland clearly belongs on both sides of each dichotomy. While Ireland under British rule was underdeveloped and deindustrialized compared to England, twentieth-century Ireland has far more in common with Europe than Africa or Asia in terms of economic performance and living standards. And in social, cultural, and religious terms Ireland is clearly of the West rather than opposed to it. Ireland did wage a lengthy and ultimately at least partially successful struggle to free itself from British control, and numbers of people involved in or affected by that struggle saw it as an anticolonial one. On the other hand, Ireland, particularly Protestant Ireland, helped build and maintain the British imperial system, and Catholic Ireland enthusiastically pursued the civilizing and christianizing missions that were an important part of the empire. The "anomalous state" of Ireland, to borrow David Lloyd's suggestive phrase, has been variously characterized as that of "a 'first world' country with a 'third world' colonial history" (Foley, *et al.*, eds., *Gender and Colonialism*, 8), internal colonialism (Hecter, *Internal Colonialism*), and a metropolitan colony (McCormack, *Dissolute Characters*). Instead of a colonial model for British–Irish relations, some revisionist history offers an "archipelago" model which casts Ireland as one of several peripheral regions that gradually became absorbed into the centralizing state (Dunne, "New Histories," 11). Liam Kennedy has suggested the word "secession" rather than "decolonization" as a term for what happened when Ireland broke away from Britain ("Modern Ireland," 116), and Ireland's resistance to the center–periphery models that many postcolonial scholars now find increasingly unsatisfactory does indeed suggest its potential connections to studies of emancipatory movements within Europe. Kennedy, who simply equates the postcolonial with the Third World and then offers evidence to demonstrate Ireland's membership in the First World, cites these connections as a way of rejecting postcolonial paradigms for Ireland in favor of the archipelago model. However, one

[7] The tendency to destabilize binary oppositions is perhaps most closely associated with the work of Homi Bhabha. Critics who insist on the continued importance of the opposition between colonizer and colonized include Benita Parry and Abdul JanMohamed.

could just as logically pursue them under the aegis of postcolonial studies, which has learned much from feminist, African-American, labor, and gay studies, and whose contiguities with those fields remain important areas of scholarly investigation.[8] Investigating such connections further will help scholars to articulate colonialism and modernity together, and to think about the extent to which the fractures, losses, and contradictions that individuals and cultures experience under colonialism are versions of or are related to the dislocations attendant upon modernity itself.[9]

Its terminological difficulties aside, another way of defining postcolonial studies is through its intense, ambivalent engagement with nationalism. Postcolonial scholarship conducts a thorough critique of the category and ideology of the nation on several grounds. One is the now well-established argument that nationalism is derivative of imperialism, and that its intellectual structures simply invert and mirror those of imperialism. For some scholars this derivativeness represents a pernicious complicity with imperial power, while for others it merely reveals the necessary and historically determined predicament of anticolonial resistance. Another mode of critique emphasizes that nationalism, particularly cultural or ethnic nationalism, is often homogenizing; it neglects or seeks to erase various kinds of difference among members of the nation. Subaltern, feminist, and Marxist critiques point out that nationalism usually articulates the political grievances and aspirations of the ruling classes, rather than of that fiction, the "nation as a whole."[10] They concentrate on recovering the specific histories and subjugated knowledges of people whose sufferings and desires are neither addressed by nor included in bourgeois nationalism's field of vision, such as women and the working classes.[11] In Irish studies, such work sometimes appears or is claimed as one of revisionism's modes.[12] These last two kinds of

---

[8] On the relationship between postcolonial and African-American studies, see MacLeod, "Black American Literature."

[9] For examples of work in Irish studies that pursues this project, see Eagleton, *Heathcliff*, Gibbons, *Transformations*, and Kiberd, "Romantic Ireland's Dead and Gone."

[10] For a sustained Marxist critique of the field's preoccupation with the national, see Ahmad, *In Theory*.

[11] The most prominent examples of such work include the writings Gayatri Spivak and the work of the Subaltern Studies group.

[12] For example, Murphy offers the writing of women's history as the truly revolutionary revisionism ("Women's History," 21).

critique also generate a tension between the impulse to critique identity thinking in general and the urge to unearth and assert those subaltern identities that trouble the national.

Despite such criticisms, postcolonial studies remains obsessed with the nation, for several reasons. Because historically, most (though not all) anticolonial struggles have been versions of nationalism, nationalism is an important aspect of the conditions and aspirations that postcolonial scholars take as their objects of study. As a result, the nation tends to migrate from the category of the historically contingent to the category of the historically inevitable; as Graham observes, the nation has a "teleological aura" ("'Liminal Spaces,'" 32). An additional reason for the continuing centrality of the nation lies in the culturalism of postcolonial studies, which is often based in literature departments. Such work tends to privilege culture (rather than, for example, economics or military force) as both an instrument of imperial domination and a vehicle of resistance to it. It usually appeals to a semianthropological conception of culture as cultural difference, and demarcates "national" cultures, literatures, and identities as its objects of investigation, however unstable and hybrid they turn out to be.[13] In postcolonial Irish studies, a preoccupation with the nation can lead to various forms of Irish exceptionalism, which in turn are contested by revisionism's interest in regional particularity within Ireland and in Ireland's similarities to and relations with Europe. They are also countered within nation-centered work in calls for a new comparativism which traces the similarities and exchanges between Ireland and other peripheral or colonized regions.[14]

Postcolonial studies has not simply clung naïvely to the nation; it has generated increasingly sophisticated ways of thinking about it. The field has learned much from scholars who study the meaning and process of nation-building in Europe, such as Benedict Anderson and Eric Hobsbawm. Rather than a spontaneous or naturally occurring form of collectivity, the nation is, in Anderson's famous phrase, an "imagined community," and imaginative styles vary considerably. While some forms of nationalism are narrow, intolerant, and demand conformity, others are more open and pluralistic; some are allied with the state, others

---

[13] For an extended critique of this trend and an elaboration of an alternative paradigm see Gilroy, *The Black Atlantic*.

[14] See the last chapter of Kiberd, *Inventing Ireland*, and the last chapter of Gibbons, *Transformations*.

resist it. Some think in terms of ethnic qualifications and national culture, others in terms of civic citizenship and republican ideals. Some are hostile to the claims of groups like women and the working classes, but others work to articulate their goals with and through those of feminism, Marxism, or humanism. Postcolonial studies also draws on the work of scholars who theorize the origins and shape of non-European, anticolonial nationalisms such as Franz Fanon. While scholars were limning the features of the many different nationalisms that have arisen in Ireland some time before the rise of postcolonial studies, such endeavors have gained additional vitality and depth through their contact with postcolonial perspectives.

Postcolonial studies also distinguishes clearly between nationalism and attachment to tradition. While nationalism may selectively invent and appeal to traditional values, practices and culture, all the major theorists of the nation agree that it is a thoroughly modern phenomenon.[15] There is of course some debate about which aspects of modernity are the crucial ones for the rise of nationalism – industrialization, print capitalism, modern communications and transportation systems – and about nationalism's precise relation to other, earlier forms of attachment and community – racial, ethnic, kinship, religious.[16] Nationalism, then, is not a simple nostalgia for the past or a straightforward defense of tradition. Nor is it solely a response to colonialism. Nationalism is also an ambivalent response to modernity, like modernism, a connection that scholars of modernism have also begun to make.[17] While postcolonial studies has brought to light aspects of Joyce's works that are usually neglected or obscured by a focus on his modernism, this approach also provides the tools for rethinking modernism itself through its relation to imperialism. The critical practice of contrasting Joyce's tolerant, cosmopolitan modernism with the narrow Irish nationalism he rejected is reaching the limits of its usefulness; in its place postcolonial studies offers ways of articulating nationalism, both imperialist and anti-imperialist, and modernism as interdependent rather than opposed phenomena.

[15] For a counterargument by a medieval scholar, see Davis, "National Writing."

[16] Some recent additions to these debates can be found in Balakrishnan, ed., *Mapping the Nation.*

[17] See, for example, Tratner's *Modernism and Mass Politics*, which argues that the modernism of Joyce, Yeats, and Woolf was preoccupied with collective rather than individual phenomena, and Nolan, *James Joyce and Nationalism*, ch. 1.

Postcolonial studies' engagement with the nation occurs in conjunction with a simultaneous critique and embrace of Enlightenment universalism. In many respects, one might think of Enlightenment universalism as the opposite of nationalist thought; rather than difference and particularity, it emphasizes sameness and the abstract, and its ideals and goals – reason, progress, equality, and human rights – all, in theory, transcend national boundaries. But this opposition collapses if pushed. Jacques Derrida has argued that nationalism presents itself as an exemplary philosophical universalism ("Onto-theology") and Robert Young (in *White Mythologies*) and others have revealed Enlightenment universalism as a covert European nationalism. Young characterizes the postcolonial era as the period when the West could no longer think of itself as the unquestioned center of the world, when it was forced to acknowledge the culturally specific and Eurocentric nature and origin of the ideals it had held up as universal. A related point is that historically, in practice, the Enlightenment's universals turn out not to be truly universal at all – they involve various hierarchies and exclusions. This aspect of postcolonial studies builds upon poststructuralism's critique of Western concepts like reason, history, and the subject, and upon the related work of feminism and African-American studies, which have demonstrated the racialized and gendered nature of those supposedly universal concepts. Finally, postcolonial studies views all universals and totalizing theories with suspicion because they have scant respect for difference, locality, and particularity, a view it shares with both revisionism and postmodernism (Eagleton, *Crazy John*, 324). Postcolonial scholars also criticize transcendent categories and master narratives because they pose as objective, obscuring their own ideological and partial – in both senses of that word – nature (a pose postcolonial work often finds and critiques in revisionism).[18]

For many postcolonial scholars, however, this apparently damaging critique does not lead to a simple rejection of the Enlightenment heritage. Universal discourses like human rights still look promising politically, even if they generally fail to realize themselves fully in particular instances, and they represent potential alternatives to the exclusionary

---

[18] For this formulation of revisionism's affinities and differences with colonial and postcolonial studies, see Graham, "Liminal Spaces." For a more sympathetic treatment of revisionism's difficulties with the fact or appearance of claims to disinterestedness and objectivity, see Dunne, "New Histories."

and divisive politics often generated by nationalism. In addition, the conjunction of Eurocentrism and colonialism has meant that Western political thought found its way to the colonies and became part of their cultures and political struggles. While some of the ways in which Enlightenment thought entered these societies may have indicated the retrograde influence of imperialist discourses, others reveal that Enlightenment ideals are also available for truly useful and liberatory appropriations. To see them as foreign to decolonizing cultures simply because they are not indigenous is to deny the complexities of how cultures actually exist and work – namely, in contacts and exchanges with other cultures. It is also to demand an indigenous culture that is timeless, static, and pure – a conception of indigenous culture that was important to imperialism. Like any academic endeavor, postcolonial scholarship needs to use generalizations and abstract categories; it is constantly in danger of creating its own theoretical universalisms. Thus various universalizing tendencies – political and theoretical – sit uneasily alongside critiques of universalism and a preoccupation with the local and particular. And postcolonial studies vacillates between two ethical imperatives – the advocation of universal rights and the injunction to respect the other. The first can simply replicate imperialism, the second can lapse into an ethically rudderless relativism.

Postcolonial studies has not solved the difficulties described above, or even resolved them into manageable dialectics. Nor is its usefulness to Irish studies a matter of sorting through conceptions of the postcolonial to find the "right" one for Ireland. In this respect, the conclusion of a recent review article that "the version of post-coloniality appropriate to an analysis of the Irish case has not yet been found" is accurate but inappropriate (Livesey and Murray, "Post-colonial Theory," 461). It is postcolonial scholarship's struggle with the issues raised here, and the difficulties presented by the Irish case, that make the crossroads between these lines of inquiry and Joyce's works, which famously favor questions over answers, a rich ground for further investigation.

Joyce criticism and the Irish turn

The chapters in this volume reflect a shift in Joyce criticism that occurred in the 1990s as the intellectual development discussed in the previous section – the reconstitution of Irish studies in the light of postcolonial theory – made itself felt. The two elements in this shift cannot be separated: increasing attention to the Irish dimension of Joyce's writing (often by Irish critics, whether living in Ireland or abroad), and a reconsideration of that dimension in the light of postcolonial theory. Although the place of Ireland in Joyce's work had always been acknowledged as important, it was usually seen in terms of material at the disposal of the great craftsman rather than a deep and continuing political concern – a view which Joyce's exile seemed to support. This, for example, is the impression one takes away from Ellmann's biography; and Ellmann's own interpretive method, although it includes discussion of biographical origins, offers very little threat to formalist approaches, as his readings in *Ulysses on the Liffey* (1972) – notwithstanding its reference to Dublin in the title – reveal; and one might say the same of another influential study with a similar reference, *Dublin's Joyce* (1956) by Hugh Kenner.

During the period of New Critical ascendancy that had been initiated by Pound and Eliot and that set the terms for the critical reception of Joyce's work for several decades, Irish literary criticism (when it was not ignoring Joyce) made no especially distinctive contribution to the understanding of his work, although a number of valuable studies were published. A representative text here is the 1970 collection edited by John Ryan, *A Bash in the Tunnel: James Joyce by the Irish*, which included several essays reprinted from a 1951 special issue of the Irish journal *Envoy* for which Ryan had secured Brian O'Nolan's services as guest editor. Although Ryan in his introduction stresses that "Joyce was quintessentially an Irishman" and that this is "a book by *Irish writers* about an *Irish writer*" rather than a contribution to the "formidable corpus of Joycean scholarship and pseudo-scholarship . . . much of it of excruciating abstractness" (14), there is little reflection on the importance of Ireland's political situation for Joyce's creative endeavors. Indeed, Arthur Power's contribution is called "James Joyce – The Internationalist," and Power takes delight in quoting derogatory comments on Ireland made by Joyce to him – such as, "Ah, the bloody nonsense that has been written about Ireland! – parish froth! I intend to lift it into the international sphere and get away from the parish pump" (181). Power does, however, foreshadow later developments in noting that "Ireland at that time, still under British rule, was a country of frustration" (182).

As Power's comment suggests, it would be a mistake to claim that no critics until the 1980s paid attention to the Irish political context of

Joyce's work. In fact, Pound himself had commented in 1922 that in *Ulysses* "Ireland is presented under the British yoke" – though he made nothing of this fact, adding in the same sentence a familiar Poundian obsession: "the world under the yoke of measureless usury" ("James Joyce and Pécuchet," 17). But it was not until the very end of the 1970s that Ireland's historical relationship to Britain began to be a widely examined issue in Joyce studies, thanks partly to the critical rethinking being stimulated by new theoretical approaches. Thus Colin MacCabe's collection of essays reflecting the emerging paradigms, *James Joyce: New Perspectives* (1982), included along with linguistic, psychoanalytic, and deconstructive commentary, Seamus Deane's essay "Joyce and Nationalism" (later reprinted in his *Celtic Revivals*). MacCabe himself had made a pioneering attempt to combine the poststructuralist with the political in *James Joyce and the Revolution of the Word* (1979), and included in his own piece in *New Perspectives*, taking off from Joyce's insistence on the heterogeneity of the Irish "race," a call for a criticism that would "delineate those moments, historical and symbolic, in which fictional forms produce the language and identity of a nation" (126). The book by Dominic Manganiello published the following year, whose title – *Joyce's Politics* – might have suggested a response to MacCabe's call, was in fact informed more by Ellmann's biographical methods (Manganiello was a student of Ellmann's) than by those of the incipient field of cultural and colonial studies, and its usefulness lies more in its presentation of the factual evidence for Joyce's continuing engagement with political issues than in any critical or theoretical (or, indeed, political) arguments.

The community of Joyce scholars seems to have needed some considerable time to digest MacCabe's book, in which an attachment to Lacanian psychoanalysis is as evident as an interest in Ireland's colonial situation. At first, it was the former dimension of his work that attracted most attention, but gradually the picture changed. The 1980s saw the appearance of a few essays which placed Joyce in the context of Irish history and Irish nationalism, like Deane's in *New Perspectives*, Fredric Jameson's "*Ulysses* in History," and Tom Paulin's "The Irish Presence in *Ulysses*," but the surge of interest in these questions did not make itself felt until the following decade, when historical issues were very much back on the agenda. Deane's chapter on "Joyce the Irishman" in *The Cambridge Companion to James Joyce* (ed. Attridge, 1990) and the discussions of Joyce by Deane, Eagleton, and Jameson in the Field Day collection entitled *Nationalism, Colonialism, and Literature* (Eagleton *et al.*,

1990) were followed by a series of books that pursued issues of Irish nationalism, colonialism, and postcoloniality: Enda Duffy's *The Subaltern "Ulysses"* (1994); Vincent J. Cheng's *Joyce, Race, and Empire* (1995); Emer Nolan's *James Joyce and Nationalism* (1995); and the volume in the European Joyce Studies volume entitled *Joyce: Feminism / Post / Colonialism*, edited by Ellen Carol Jones (1998). Joyce also featured in a number of other books and collections on Irish culture. In addition to those mentioned above in connection with the conjunction between Irish studies and postcolonial studies – Lloyd's 1993 *Anomalous States*, Eagleton's 1995 *Heathcliff and the Great Hunger*, Kiberd's 1995 *Inventing Ireland*, and Gibbons's 1996 *Transformations in Irish Culture* – there were discussions of Joyce's relation to the Irish colonial situation in Joep Leerssen's *Remembrance and Imagination* (1996), Deane's *Strange Country* (1997), and Richard Kearney's *Postnationalist Ireland* (1997). Several books on Joyce in the 1990s touched on these issues from other perspectives, including Joseph Valente's *James Joyce and the Problem of Justice* (1995), James Fairhall's *James Joyce and the Question of History* (1993), and a collection edited by Mark Wollaeger, Victor Luftig, and Robert Spoo, *Joyce and the Subject of History* (1996).

Although these works deal with different aspects of Joyce and of colonial and postcolonial studies, and do not all start from or arrive at the same place, they have in common a conviction that the full measure of Joyce's achievement cannot be understood without relating it to the Irish struggle for independence – regarded not merely as a storehouse of images, characters, and narrative possibilities, but as a bitter, complex, and protracted conflict, with a history still alive in Irish political memory, a constantly changing course during Joyce's lifetime, and an unforeseeable future. Joyce's own engagement with this unfolding political, social, economic, and cultural history was, as we have stressed and as most of the authors we have cited also argue, ambivalent and shifting; but it is precisely the subtlety of the judgments implicit in the twists and turns, the referential uncertainties, and the narrative experiments of his fictional writing that we may locate the value of his involvement with the contest for Irish national independence and political freedom.

The high quality of much of this writing, and the illumination which it has provided and continues to provide, indicate that the posing of questions about Ireland's status in relation to Britain makes it possible to understand, and gain pleasure and insight from, aspects of Joyce's work occluded by previous approaches, however acute and perceptive they may have been. The contributors to this volume, who include many of the most distinguished participants in the continuing discussion of Joyce's responses to the Irish anticolonial struggle and to its postcolonial potential, bring to bear on these questions a wide variety of special interests and particular knowledges. They do not form an entirely harmonious chorus; however, we take it to be significant – and a hopeful augury for the interconnectedness of the chapters – that when we first issued invitations to them, a large proportion responded to our title with immediate enthusiasm, even though different individuals saw it pointing at different aspects of Joyce and of Ireland. Though we invite readers to pause over these arguments and readings, and we encourage a retrospective evaluation of the body of work which they represent, our main aim is to propel the discussion forward with renewed vigor and enlarged scope; and we therefore offer this collection not as a full stop but as, at most, a semicolon.

Works cited

Ahmad, Aijaz. *In Theory: Classes, Nations, Literatures*. London: Verso, 1992.

Anderson, Benedict. *Imagined Communities: Reflections on the Origin and Spread of Nationalism*. London: Verso, 1991 (1983).

Ashcroft, Bill, Gareth Griffiths, and Helen Tiffin, eds. *The Post-Colonial Studies Reader*. London and New York: Routledge, 1995.

Attridge, Derek, ed. *The Cambridge Companion to James Joyce*. Cambridge: Cambridge University Press, 1990.

Balakrishnan, Gopal, ed. *Mapping the Nation*. London: Verso, 1996.

Bhabha, Homi K. *The Location of Culture*. London: Routledge, 1994.

Boyce, George, and Alan O'Day, eds. *The Making of Modern Irish History: Revisionism and the Revisionist Controversy*. London: Routledge, 1996.

Cheng, Vincent J. *Joyce, Race, and Empire*. Cambridge: Cambridge University Press, 1995.

Davis, Kathleen. "National Writing in the Ninth Century: A Reminder for Postcolonial Thinking about the Nation." *Journal of Medieval and Early Modern Studies* 28 (1998): 611–37.

Deane, Seamus. *Celtic Revivals: Essays in Modern Irish Literature*. London: Faber & Faber, 1985.

"Joyce and Nationalism." *James Joyce: New Perspectives*. Ed. Colin MacCabe. Brighton: Harvester Press, 1982. 168–83.

Strange Country: Modernity and Nationhood in Irish Writing Since 1790. Oxford: Oxford University Press, 1997.

Derrida, Jacques. "Onto-theology of National-Humanism (Prolegomena to a Hypothesis)." *Oxford Literary Review* 14.1 (1992): 3–23.

Dirlik, Arif. "The Postcolonial Aura: Third World Criticism in the Age of Global Capitalism." *Critical Inquiry* 20 (1994): 328–56.

Duffy, Enda. *The Subaltern "Ulysses."* Minneapolis: University of Minnesota Press, 1994.

Dunne, Tom. "New Histories: Beyond Revisionism." *Irish Review* 12 (spring/summer 1992): 1–12.

Eagleton, Terry. *Crazy John and the Bishop and Other Essays on Irish Culture.* Cork: Cork University Press, 1998.

  Heathcliff and the Great Hunger: Studies in Irish Culture. London: Verso, 1995.

Eagleton, Terry, *et al. Nationalism, Colonialism, and Literature.* Minneapolis: University of Minnesota Press, 1990.

Ellmann, Richard. *James Joyce.* New York: Oxford University Press, 1959, 1982.

  Ulysses on the Liffey. London: Faber & Faber, 1972.

Fairhall, James. *James Joyce and the Question of History.* Cambridge: Cambridge University Press, 1993.

Fanon, Franz. *Black Skin, White Masks.* New York: Grove Weidenfeld, 1967.

  The Wretched of the Earth. New York: Grove Weidenfeld, 1963.

Foley, Timothy, *et al.*, eds. *Gender and Colonialism.* Galway: Galway University Press, 1995.

Foster, Roy. "The Lovely Magic of its Dawn: Reading Irish History as a Story." *TLS*, 16 December 1994: 4–6.

Gibbons, Luke. *Transformations in Irish Culture.* Cork: Cork University Press, 1996.

Gilroy, Paul. *The Black Atlantic: Modernity and Double Consciousness.* Cambridge, Mass.: Harvard University Press, 1993.

Graham, Colin. "'Liminal Spaces': Post-Colonial Theories and Irish Culture." *Irish Review* 16 (autumn/winter 1994): 29–43.

Hecter, Michael. *Internal Colonialism: The Celtic Fringe in British National Development.* Berkeley: University of California Press, 1975.

Hobsbawm, Eric. *Nations and Nationalism Since 1780: Programme, Myth, Reality.* Cambridge: Cambridge University Press, 1990.

Jameson, Fredric. *"Ulysses* in History." *James Joyce and Modern Literature.* Ed. W. J. McCormack and Alistair Stead. London: Routledge, 1982. 126–41.

JanMohamed, Abdul. "The Economy of Manichean Allegory." *The Post-Colonial Studies Reader.* Ed. Bill Ashcroft, Gareth Griffiths, and Helen Tiffin. London and New York: Routledge, 1995. 18–23.

Jones, Ellen Carol. *Joyce: Feminism / Post / Colonialism.* European Joyce Studies 8. Amsterdam: Rodopi, 1998.

Kaul, Suvir. "Colonial Figures and Postcolonial Reading." *Diacritics* 26.1 (spring 1996): 74–89.

Kearney, Richard. *Postnationalist Ireland: Politics, Culture, Philosophy.* London: Routledge, 1997.

Kennedy, Liam. "Modern Ireland: Post-Colonial Society or Post-Colonial
    Pretensions?" *Irish Review* 13 (winter 1992/3): 107–21.

Kenner, Hugh. *Dublin's Joyce*. Bloomington: Indiana University Press, 1956.

Kiberd, Declan. *Inventing Ireland: The Literature of the Modern Nation*.
    Cambridge, Mass.: Harvard University Press, 1996.

    "Romantic Ireland's Dead and Gone." *TLS*, 11 June 1998: 12–14.

Leerssen, Joep. *Remembrance and Imagination: Patterns in the Historical and
    Literary Representation of Ireland in the Nineteenth Century*. Cork:
    Cork University Press, 1996.

Livesey, James, and Stuart Murray. "Review Article: Post-colonial Theory and
    Modern Irish Culture." *Irish Historical Studies* 30.119 (May 1997):
    452–61.

Lloyd, David. *Anomalous States: Irish Writing and the Post-Colonial Moment*.
    Durham: Duke University Press, 1993.

MacCabe, Colin. *James Joyce and the Revolution of the Word*. London:
    Macmillan, 1979.

MacCabe, Colin, ed. *James Joyce: New Perspectives*. Brighton: Harvester, 1982.

MacLeod, Christine. "Black American Literature and the Postcolonial Debate."
    The Yearbook of English Studies 27 (1997): 51–65.

McClintock, Anne. "The Angel of Progress: Pitfalls of the Term 'Post-
    Colonialism.'" *Colonial Discourse and Post-Colonial Theory*. Ed.
    Patrick Williams and Laura Chrisman. New York: Columbia
    University Press, 1994. 291–304.

McCormack, W. J. *Dissolute Characters: Irish Literary History through Balzac,
    Sheridan Le Fanu, Yeats and Bowen*. Manchester: Manchester
    University Press, 1993.

Manganiello, Dominic. *Joyce's Politics*. London: Routledge & Kegan Paul,
    1980.

Murphy, Cliona. "Women's History, Feminist History, or Gender History."
    Irish Review 12 (spring/summer 1992): 21–26.

Nolan, Emer. *James Joyce and Nationalism*. London: Routledge, 1995.

Parry, Benita. "The Postcolonial: Conceptual Category or Chimera?" *The
    Yearbook of English Studies* 27 (1997): 3–21.

Paulin, Tom. "The British Presence in *Ulysses*." *Ireland and the English Crisis*.
    Newcastle-upon-Tyne: Bloodaxe Books, 1984. 92–100.

Pound, Ezra. "James Joyce and Pécuchet." Trans. Fred Bornhauser.
    Shenandoah 3 (autumn 1952): 9–20.

Power, Arthur. "James Joyce – The Internationalist." Ryan, ed., *A Bash in the
    Tunnel*, 181–88.

Ryan, John, ed. *A Bash in the Tunnel: James Joyce by the Irish*. Brighton: Clifton
    Books, 1970.

Said, Edward. *Orientalism*. New York: Random House, 1978.

Shohat, Ella. "Notes on the 'Post-colonial.'" *Social Text* 31/32 (1992): 99–113.

Smyth, Gerry. *Decolonisation and Criticism*. London: Pluto Press, 1998.

Tóibín, Colm. "Playboys of the GPO." *London Review of Books*, 18 April 1996: 14–6.

Tratner, Michael. *Modernism and Mass Politics*. Stanford: Stanford University Press, 1995.

Valente, Joseph. *James Joyce and the Problem of Justice: Negotiating Sexual and Colonial Difference*. Cambridge: Cambridge University Press, 1995.

Wollaeger, Mark A., Victor Luftig, and Robert Spoo. *Joyce and the Subject of History*. Ann Arbor: University of Michigan Press, 1996.

Young, Robert. *White Mythologies: Writing History and the West*. New York and London: Routledge, 1990.

Dead ends: Joyce's finest moments

SEAMUS DEANE

Many readers share the recognition that the highly specified world of *Dubliners* threatens, in subtle and disturbing ways, to fade into ghostliness. The twilit, half-lit, street-lit, candle-lit, gas-lit, firelit settings are inhabited by shadows and silhouettes that remind us both of the insubstantial nature of these lives and also of their latent and repressed possibilities. These people are shades who have never lived, vicarious inhabitants of a universe ruled by others. Highly individuated, they are nevertheless exemplary types of a general condition in which individuality is dissolved. The city of Dublin – not just the place but also the cultural system that constitutes it – exercises an almost dogmatic authority over the people who inhabit it, yet what individuality they have best expresses itself in collusion with that authority. Determined by or derived from sources and resources they do not control, Dubliners have acclimatized themselves to a servitude they affect to resist. Their "identity" may be second-hand, but they are sufficiently meek to be glad of it. Like the sight-seers of "After the Race," the cheer they raise is that of "the gratefully oppressed" (*Dubliners*, 35), one cheer for the systems of autocracy, timocracy, or plutocracy (but never democracy) by which they are ruled.

The monotonous grammar of these stories accentuates the sense of infantile repetitiveness that is the abiding feature of Dublin's condition, although the repetition involved also reminds us that immense psychic as well as rhetorical energy has to be expended on the production of stasis. One of the most obvious effects of Joyce's elaborate stylizations is to convert or pervert stories of imagined adventure, escape, heroism or fame into studies in a cultural pathology, often by making the central figure a plaster cast version of a great original. First there was Parnell, then there was Edward VII; there was Nietzsche, then Mr. James Duffy. Repetition is most woundingly effective when it takes the form of the echo, the epigone, the parody. This extends beyond persons to wider ranges of reference: there was the Eucharist, then there was sherry and biscuits; there was the sacred, now there is the secular. Even where there is revival, of the Fenian-Phoenix or of the Celtic Twilight sort, it too repeats itself in a fall into bathos or into the diminuendo of bad verse or even of that falling faintly, faintly falling snow in "The Dead."

Joyce often indicates how radical and yet elusive the state of being "gratefully oppressed" can be by the strategic repetition of words that gain weight inexorably as they feed on their surrounding contexts and associations. In "After the Race," we are told that Jimmy Doyle, while at Trinity College, "had money and he was popular; and he divided his time curiously between musical and motoring circles" (36). On this day of the race, as he tries to guess and answer what the Frenchmen in the front of the car are saying, Jimmy is confused by the humming of Villona, the Hungarian pianist who is very poor, and by the noise of the motor car belonging to Ségouin, who *appears* to be very rich (he "was reputed to own some of the biggest hotels in France" [36]; "he had managed to give the impression that it was by a favour of friendship the mite of Irish money was to be included in the capital of that concern" [37]; he "had the unmistakable air of wealth" [38]). Rapid motion, notoriety and the possession of money, we are informed, are "three good reasons for Jimmy's excitement" (37). After Ségouin had introduced Jimmy to one of the competitors, who had rewarded Jimmy's "confused murmur of compliment" with a smile, Jimmy found it pleasant "after that honour to return to the profane world of spectators amid nudges and significant looks" (37). The world of the actor (Continental) is sacred, that of the spectator (Irish) profane. Confusion makes the connection between them impossible to clarify. To be seen with Continentals, to be permitted the opportunity to invest in Ségouin's proposed motor establishment in Paris, to be smiled upon is sufficient reward in the hazy world of Jimmy's Dublin that "hung its pale globes of light above them in a haze of summer evening," and whose submissive people "collected on the footpath to pay homage to the snorting motor" (38).

Later, at dinner, Jimmy's two interests, music and motoring, the source of confusion by day, first dominate a discussion in which Jimmy is out of his depth; drink further blurs his capacity to see what is going on. Earlier, Jimmy had been introduced to the French competitor at "the control," meaning the place from which the race had been conducted and overseen. Only a few lines later Jimmy thinks, "he really had a great sum under his control" (37). Unlike Ségouin's reputation for having money, this money is "real"; but it is not under Jimmy's control. Amid all the confusion, we are to see that the investment is, like the card game, a gamble Jimmy has lost, despite the fact that he is "the inheritor of solid instincts" and is "conscious of the labour latent in money" (37). It has disappeared in that vaporous world of paper IOUs, of Ségouin's apparent wealth, of hazy light and alcoholic fume, perhaps even of prearranged deceit.[1] As with the money, so with the politics. His father, once an "advanced nationalist," has become so successful a butcher that he has modified his politics in order to become the "merchant prince" (36) who has won contracts for supplying the police with meat. At the dinner, Ségouin leads the conversation from motoring and music – including ridicule of the pseudo-romantic revival of old English music, an ironic glance at the role and function of so-called cultural revival – into politics. It is then the "buried zeal" of his nationalist father is wakened to life within Jimmy to the point that he "aroused the torpid Routh at last" (39) – the Englishman who is later to scoop the winnings at cards – and the same transformation occurs. The little local difficulty of Irish-English politics is dissolved by Ségouin, who proposes a toast to "Humanity" and "threw open a window significantly." In the next sentence we learn that "That night the city wore the mask of a capital" (39). The city, the money, the mask of disguise and deceit are all related in a manner too complex for Jimmy to control. The bland cosmopolitan world has duped him into believing in humanity, in glamour and style; it has taken his money with his political opinions. What really matters in this world is not the friendship that Jimmy or his father might feel for Villona and the others; it is, precisely, the control of capital which Jimmy is surrendering to these "jovial fellows" (41).

What we see here is the Joycean method of counterposing that which is undeniably real (money, again related to food and feeding) to something which is undeniably fake and then, rather than ratifying the "real," showing that it can be swallowed up in the illusory world, surrendered to it, by those who are, like the Dubliners, hungry for illusion, grateful to be oppressed by something "magical" that somehow dissolves or seems to dissolve the squalor of the actual. Two kinds of capital are involved here, capital investment and a capital city that allows itself, is indeed grateful, to surrender control over its own capital (both the money and the city), bewitched by the glamour of a fake culture of Humanity, having surrendered its own "advanced nationalism" in a haze of incomprehension. Jimmy cannot decipher the world he has entered; to motoring, music,

---

[1] This is suggested by Adams, "A Study"; see also Cheng, *Joyce, Race, and Empire*, 101–27, and Nolan, *James Joyce and Nationalism*, 28–30.

alcohol, crowds, hazy lights, foreign languages and glamour he pays his "confused murmur of compliment" and a considerable part of his inheritance. Still, he does get that smile from one of the real competitors in the race which involves so many races.

Every story has some account of or reference to eating or drinking, the cost involved, the difficulty of getting the money for either, especially for those who overindulge in drink. Yet the (usually squalid) details of these rituals, emphasized for a rancorously secular effect, actually provoke a recognition of their insufficiency. They belong to a world that has committed the sin of simony (the first sin, so-called, in the volume), has exchanged spiritual for material values and yet is still haunted by the afterimage of the spiritual.

In "A Painful Case," Mr. Duffy, in his usual eating-house in George's Street, catches sight of the newspaper report of Mrs. Sinico's death as he is about to put a morsel of corned beef and cabbage in his mouth. His first reading takes place there, in the full squalor of a "secular" setting (108). The second reading has a faint aura of the sacred. It takes place in his bedroom "by the failing light of his window," and he reads "moving his lips as a priest does when he reads the prayers *Secreto*" (109). The two readings are separated by Duffy's return walk home which includes the section from Parkgate to Chapelizod, where he and Mrs. Sinico had finally parted four years before. Here, Duffy slackens his pace, and "His stick struck the ground less emphatically and his breath, issuing irregularly, almost with a sighing sound, condensed in the wintry air" (109).

As at several other points in the story, Joyce takes a moment in which gross physical detail indicates spiritual and emotional stupefaction and etherealizes it into one where the detail is cleansed of its grossness to indicate a spectral emotional or spiritual apprehension. After the second reading, particularly "After the light failed"[2] again, Duffy flees to the pub at Chapelizod and drinks his hot punch as a group of working men down their pints, spit on the floor and drag the sawdust over the spit with their heavy work boots. This moment is designed to remind us of Mr. Duffy's earlier political affiliation, when he had "assisted at the meetings of an Irish Socialist Party" (106) which he had abandoned in despair at the

---

[2] There may be an echo of Kipling's story *The Light that Failed* (1891) here, although there is no evidence that Joyce read it. But there is a similarity in the account of a rejection – in this case of a man by a woman – that leads to a tragic death and is much preoccupied with the demands of common life and high art.

coarse materialism of his comrades. Here is the counterexample to the previous instance of etherealizing. Mr. Duffy neither sees nor hears the men and their conversation about money and a gentleman's estate in County Kildare. But all the detail reinforces the contrasts between the physical and the refined, the worker and the intellectual, respectability and scandal, egoism and love, that the story is elaborating. Subsequently, in the last four paragraphs, the system of repetition that had marked the routine and obsessive nature of Duffy's life intensifies to the point where the goods train from Kingsbridge station, like the slow train from Kingstown that killed Mrs. Sinico – in six lines we have the repetitions of "winding out," "winding through," "winding along," "obstinately and laboriously," "the laborious drone" – is finally "reiterating the syllables of her name" (113). In those final paragraphs Duffy again feels "her hand touch his"; once realizes "he sentenced her to death"; once that "he sentenced her to ignominy, a death of shame"; twice sees himself as "outcast from life's feast" and "gnawed the rectitude of his life" (113), the ritual of eating now transposed into an entirely different register from that of the corned beef and cabbage meal in George's Street. But his pseudo-Nietzschean solitude reasserts itself. The noise fades and Mrs. Sinico with it. The last paragraph is composed of eight anaphoric sentences, each beginning "He . . ." Routine has been reestablished. The closed, repetitive structure of Mr. Duffy's inhuman life has resumed. There is no other in his world, no responsibility for the other. This is a style that excludes ethics, by the intensification of repetitive rhythms that betoken morbid self-obsession. It is the opposite of an ethical condition, the fleeting prospect of which disappears as the serried ranks of final sentences close up in their neat, neurotic repetitions.

It may be that Mr. Duffy considers himself to be a good Nietzschean in ultimately defending his solitary integrity against the decadent feelings of a Mrs. Sinico whose behavior is very much like that of the despicable herd. It hardly matters whether he has molded himself upon a well- or ill-judged version of Nietzsche's thought as it is expounded in *Thus Spake Zarathustra* or *The Gay Science*. The point is that it is a derived identity, based on alienation from himself and from others. Mr. Duffy is not someone deprived of modernity; he embodies it. His provincialism and alienation are integral to it, not its opposite.

Jimmy Doyle's condition is similar. He has been expensively educated to admire all that is not provincial, all that bespeaks money, development, cosmopolitanism, Humanity. This is not only in its derivativeness and complicated slavishness a colonial condition; it is also, because of its profound alienation from its own past and its seduction by the siren appeal of transnational capital, a modern condition. For Joyce, the matter is both simple and involved. To be colonial is to be modern. It is possible to be modern without being colonial; but not to be colonial without being modern. Ireland exemplifies this latter condition and presents it in such a manner that the "traditional" and the "modern" elements seem to be in conflict with one another, like two competing chronologies. But in fact there is little of the traditional in Joyce's Ireland. Everything that has or had deep roots in the country's experience has become decayed or has been tarted up, like the Gaelic kitsch of Mrs. Kearney's world (in "A Mother"), or the Catholicism-for-businessmen that Father Purdon supplies in "Grace." Modernity wears the mask of capital because capital comprises both underdevelopment and development, not as opposites, but as contiguous conditions. With the entry of modernity in this form, nationalist politics is sidelined as a provincial matter, and a cosmopolitan liberalism, armed with the doctrine of Humanity, is substituted for it.

This encourages the separation of the private from the public life. But "A Painful Case" makes it clear that the so-called separation is really a desertion. Mr. Duffy gives us the benefit of his considered opinion on these matters. He is much given to quoting himself. He has "a little sheaf of papers held together by a brass pin" ready for the inscription of his best efforts, although "the headline of an advertisement for *Bile Beans*" (103) is pasted on to the first of these, a wicked exercise in irony, we are to understand, by one who wishes to see banality counterpoint his searing insights, among which are the following:

> No social revolution . . . would be likely to strike Dublin for some centuries. (107)

> We cannot give ourselves . . . : we are our own. (107)

> Every bond . . . is a bond to sorrow. (108)

> Love between man and man is impossible because there must not be sexual intercourse and friendship between man and woman is impossible because there must be sexual intercourse. (108)

The denial of the possibility of human intimacy and of social revolution is central. Duffy can no more be a socialist than he can be a lover; both socialism and love are snares that would violate the integrity of his "heroic" solitude. They would also, of course, introduce an ethical element that is otherwise entirely absent from an authoritarian and sexless narcissism. Love or socialism would deprive Duffy of the pathological alienation that has him in the habit of writing of himself in the third person and in the past tense, of living "at a little distance from his body, regarding his own acts with doubtful side-glances" (104). He is a third person, derived from a first person; his practice is the one Joyce famously adopted for Stephen Dedalus in *A Portrait of the Artist as a Young Man* and Stephen's final possession of the first-person pronoun at the close of that novel is all the more dramatic when we remember the hinterland that contains Mr. James Duffy and his ilk, all condemned to a third personhood from which no escape is possible.

Duffy betrays the possibility of sexual love or of social brotherhood; one is a version of the other. In stories like "Grace" and, most memorably, in "Ivy Day in the Committee Room," betrayal assumes other forms, well-known and much-discussed. Here I want to confine my attention to one feature of the "Ivy Day" – its system of naming or, rather, of misnaming and nicknaming. The key names are those of Parnell and Edward VII, the two kings, one uncrowned and Irish, the other crowned and English, both of them associated with sexual scandal for which Parnell was destroyed and for which, a decade later, Edward earns a celebratory address from the citizens of Dublin. From the outset, the story famously arranges its chiaroscuro effects, from the cinders spread over the dome of coals and the shadow of old Jack giving way to his illumined face, the cigarette lit by Mr. O'Connor which catches the gloss of the ivy leaf in his lapel, the candles lit from the fire, the candlestick used by Henchy to light Father Keon's exit, to the fire that heats the porter and pops the corks of the bottles in mock-salutes. Neither do the cardboard that old Jack uses to tend the fire, nor the pasteboard cards bearing the name of "Mr. Richard J. Tierney, P.L.G." (116) that O'Connor uses to light his cigarettes fail to remind us of the inferior quality of the world and the people surrounding this dozy fire, people whose political commitment and wealth is measured in bottles of porter.

But a listing of the sequences of namings also adds to the effect: "Old Jack" opens the story; thereafter he is referred to as "Jack" (five times), once as "the old caretaker" but repeatedly (thirty-eight times) as "the old man." Mr. Tierney, the nationalist candidate, is first given his full formal name on the pasteboard card; thereafter he will become "Tricky Dicky Tierney" (twice: 119, 120), "the little shoeboy," "mean little tinker,"

27

"Mean little shoeboy of hell," "Tricky Dicky" (120), "that little shoeboy," "little hop-o'-my-thumb" (124). After the drink arrives, we hear that "he's not so bad after all," "as good as his word," "not a bad sort," that he "means well . . . in his own tinpot way" (126), and then Henchy reports himself as saying that Tierney is "*a respectable man*," "*a big rate-payer*," "*a prominent and respected citizen*" and "*a Poor Law Guardian*" (128). It is "the old man," Jack, who refers to his son as "the drunken bowsy" (117) and to Colgan (not *Mr.* Colgan, since he is the labor candidate), before he is named, as "the other tinker"; whereupon Mr. Hynes, who repeats the phrase as a question ("What other tinker?"), refers to Colgan as "a working-man," "a good honest bricklayer," "a plain honest man," and then refers three times to the generic type of "the working-man" (118) of whom Colgan is obviously the particular example. This leads him on to mention "a German monarch" who then becomes "Edward Rex," "a foreign king" (118) and then, later, "King Eddie" (121), "the King" (twice, 128), "the King of England," "this chap," "the man" (three times), "a man of the world," "a jolly fine decent fellow," "King Edward," "an ordinary knockabout," "a bit of a rake," "a good sportsman," "a man like that," "Edward the Seventh" (129). Mr. Hynes retains his name for the most part, although he is "Joe" first to Mr. O'Connor, then "our friend," "poor Joe," "a man from the other camp," "a spy of Colgan's," "a decent skin," "not nineteen carat," "Joe Hynes" (121), "a straight man," "a clever chap," one of these "hillsiders and fenians," one of those "little jokers," "castle hacks," is "a stroke above that" (122), is "one of them . . . that didn't renege him" (130), is then, in counterpoint, "Joe" (seven times) and "Mr. Hynes" (four times, 130–31). Hynes is allowed to have had a father who "was a decent and respectable man," "Poor old Larry Hynes" (121), although this is merely a ploy on Henchy's part to throw the son's failings into relief, one he also uses against Tierney, by reminding his audience of how the "little old father" (120) sold illegal liquor on Sunday mornings in his second-hand clothes shop in Mary's Lane. Father Keon appears first as "a person resembling a poor clergyman or a poor actor" (122). Henchy names him and he remains as "Father Keon" for three mentions before the inquiries begin. Then "he's what you call a black sheep," "an unfortunate man of some kind" (123), "travelling on his own account" and was mistaken for "the dozen of stout" (124). Parnell is initially "this man" (119), "a gentleman" (130), "the only man," once he is "the Chief," otherwise he is "Parnell" (130), except for the title "Our uncrowned King" in Hynes's poem (131).

The vicious and slithery Mr. Henchy is the most prolific name-caller. He is the one to accuse his fellows of betrayal, the chief apologist for the English King, the chief sponger who accuses others of sponging, the most antilabor and antifenian voice, the one to praise Hynes, whom he has condemned in his absence as a spy, for having remained loyal to Parnell and he is, above all, the chief mimic, the star performer in rendering other people's voices. Of course much of what Henchy says bears upon himself. He is the Pilate figure who is forever rubbing his hands "as if he intended to produce a spark from them" (119), rubbing them over the fire "at terrific speed" (120) and, on the arrival of the bottles of porter, "to rub his hands cheerfully" (125). His mimicry of others, like his naming of them, reminds us that this is a story that is, in a double sense, about imitation. With Henchy as master of ceremonies, everything will be brilliantly and degradingly represented and misrepresented. This is a pale imitation, a ghostly version, of the world of Parnell and yet it is also an accurate representation of that imitation. Insofar as representation in such a context can only be a misrepresentation, then betrayal is much more than a theme or preoccupation. Its status is ontological.

The namings are of two kinds – formal and demotic. Some stories sustain the chill of distance by exploiting formal titles and formal versions of names. In "A Painful Case" the newspaper report is fastidious in its attribution of title – "Deputy Coroner" (109), "Captain Sinico," "Police Sergeant Croly," "Constable 57E," "Dr. Halpin," "Mr. H. B. Patterson Finlay" (110) – and the steady repetition of "Mr. Duffy" throughout sustains this official formality, which is disturbingly internalized for a time when the train engine in its "laborious drone" reiterates the syllables of Mrs. Sinico's name (113). "A Mother" and "Grace" also exploit the formal modes of naming and of address for the sake of registering both social chilliness and of ironizing the pomposity of the people involved. But in "Ivy Day," the exchange between the different kinds of naming is much more intense.

Calling Tierney "Tricky Dicky" is meant to demean him, not only by implying that he is dishonest and untrustworthy, but also by diminishing him to a junior level – Richard reduced to Dicky to provide the "natural" rhyme with "Tricky." He is also "a shoeboy," "a little tinker," "a hop o'my thumb." Small in stature, low in status, dismissable, barely respectable, Tierney is also of low origins and therefore should not be allowed to forget these in his aspirations to high elective office. By the same token,

Hynes's father was decent, but the son has not inherited this stalwart virtue, one which is grudgingly restored to Tierney after the porter arrives. Hynes is canvassing for Colgan, who is also "a tinker," in the phrase of "the old man," Jack the caretaker. Hynes's predictably angry and routine defense of "the working-man," who is, unlike his class enemies, not looking for a job, but is honest, conscientious, the producer of the wealth that others enjoy, is not sufficient to impress Old Jack who, first, asserts that Hynes gets no "warm welcome" (121) from him, and second, tells the story – culled from another in a lowly position, Keegan, the porter – about the working-class mayor who has demeaned his office by not entertaining on a grand scale, and then by sending out for a pound of chops for his dinner (125). Jack is a classic example of one of the gratefully oppressed; he admires authority when it is assumed by those who are of a higher class (and in Jack's world, only a "tinker" could be of lower class). Any usurpation of authority, like that by his own so – refigured in the boy who delivers the porter and drinks a bottle of it at the invitation of Mr. Henchy – is to him a sign of the changing times, when natural authority is being challenged and all seems topsy-turvy. In short, the various name-callings indulged in by Jack and Henchy in particular, indicates a perverted class consciousness. Any one of their own class or family is demeaned and criticized for aspiring to either rebellion or leadership.

On the other hand, since King Edward is, in Henchy's view, a decent fellow, like himself, like one of us, he deserves to be received warmly; in his wake will come what Ireland needs – capital. Male camaraderie is offered here as an alternative to or as something that transcends class. It involves drinking, sport and sexual dalliance (including adultery), although the sexual behavior, which is critical in highlighting the "analogy between the two cases" (129) as Lyons calls it – and which Henchy cannot see at all – is very delicately addressed by all concerned. No woman is mentioned, no woman is present. But gender *is* invoked to provide an ideology of the decent fellowship between men of the world, one that does not dwell on fine moral discriminations or indeed on any political discriminations, relying instead on practical business and capital development. King Edward has "no damn nonsense about him" (129) and Mr. Tierney, in Henchy's reported canvass for him, is essentially a businessman who *"doesn't belong to any party, good, bad, or indifferent"* (128).

The Henchy view of King Edward and the imperial monarchy is very like the Father Purdon view of Christ and Christianity in "Grace." Based on the principle of making friends "out of the mammon of iniquity" (173), it requires a reconciliation between spirituality and accountancy, Christianity and capitalism and, in Henchy's case, nationalism of the Parnellite era and Edwardian imperialism. But those who would resist such a maneuver – the hillsiders and fenians and socialist-nationalists in particular – have to be renamed as traitors, Castle hacks, spies, spongers, people of low origin. Those who would wish to challenge or replace traditional English or unionist authority with self-government, democracy, Home Rule or anything of that ilk are to be decried either as traitors interested only in money or as caricatures of what real authority is like. Hynes had identified the type when he spoke of "shoneens that are always hat in hand before any fellow with a handle to his name" (118) and Henchy had later responded with his mock version of himself as Lord Mayor (qualified by virtue of being in debt to the City Fathers), Old Jack as his footman, O'Connor as his private secretary and Father Keon as his private chaplain (124). Betrayal and caricature are the techniques adopted to defend the status quo against any kind of political or social advance or change. A modernizing democracy is the enemy of the plain-speaking decent fellows who are anxious for reconciliation with their imperial masters, these fellows who are ready to identify themselves in Mr. Henchy's words as members of *"these wild Irish,"* or as "we Irish": "Can't we Irish play fair?" (129). After all, this is not really, in the Henchy view, a carefully judged state visit and political act; it's just an impulse on the part of Eddie – "He just says to himself . . ." (129).

But that begs, on this day of all days, and with this king of all kings, the question of Parnell. He cannot be recruited to the decent fellows' club; nor can his origins be impugned; nor can his career be caricatured as that of someone too diminutive in personal qualities to deserve respect. "Respect" is the key word, first introduced by Mr. O'Connor and taken up by the conservative-unionist Crofton, who allows Parnell was a "gentleman," a word that undergoes an immediate transformation by Henchy, who exclaims that Parnell "was the only man that could keep that bag of cats in order. *Down, ye dogs! Lie down, ye curs!* That's the way he treated them" (130).

This is the snarling Henchy imitation of Parnell's leadership of the members of the Irish Parliamentary Party who had met to betray him in that fateful committee room in Westminster in 1890. At that moment, Hynes, the faithful Parnellite and working-man's defendant appears, to be called in by Henchy and congratulated for having stuck to "the Chief," in Henchy's highest term of praise, "like a man" (130). As preface to Hynes's poem, the idiom of class has reappeared, associated benignly now both with unionist and with nationalist politics and also with fidelity, the very element that is lacking in people of meaner status. But it has also made its necessary peace with the idiom of "manliness" and "decency," all the more important in relation to Hynes, the defender of the workingman, and *his* particular form of unmercenary decency. Hynes's formerly specific class allegiance is now blurring into the potent, depoliticized and gender-based ideology that Henchy promotes. There remains only the political nationalist element to be blended into this moist fellowship, an effect nicely achieved by "that thing" that Hynes wrote (122, 130), that "splendid thing" (130) as Henchy calls it, "O that thing is it . . . Sure, that's old now" (131), as Hynes pretends to strain to remember it. "The Death of Parnell" is a wonderful display of kitsch that manages, more than anything previously, "To befoul and smear th'exalted name" (132). Henchy appeals to Crofton and the conservative-unionist gives it his blessing by saying that "it was a very fine piece of writing" (133).

It is not entirely to the point to say the poem is bad from an aesthetic point of view, although the aesthetic view is important here. For it is just that very "fineness" of the writing and of the judgment of the audience that counts. By the time the poem is over, every class position, every political conviction, every version of "decency" has been abandoned. Easy sentiment, greed and amnesia, the features of the cultural world of capitalism, have taken over and the heroic world of Parnell has been incorporated into it, as a form of entertainment, a thing. We might at this moment remember the missing Father Keon, the priest who may have been silenced because he was a political "extremist," an out-and-out supporter of Parnell, or who may have been and may still be an alcoholic, a hanger-on like so many of the men in the room (Joyce's father was both those things). It is the linkage between a political conviction that does not or cannot in these circumstances endure and the consequent and subsequent addictive consumerism which these marginalized canvassers crave to indulge, through alcohol, tobacco, political oblivion and "manly" sentiment, that Joyce dwells upon here, as he also does in several episodes of *Ulysses*. Like the priest, the linkage is silenced, although indubitably there.

In *Ulysses*, the contrast between the abstract and speculative Stephen and the physically immersed Bloom is one of the governing features of the opening episodes. Eating, drinking, urinating, defecating, burping and farting, bathing, luxuriating in sensations of warmth and taste, scent and odor, sexual fantasy and longing, Bloom is grounded to a comically extravagant degree in the world of the body, of the city-world and its streets, of the stereotype of *l'homme moyen sensuel*. With a comparable emphasis, Stephen belongs to the world of theorist-intellectual who longs for a world disembarrassed of the physical and the sexual, where the self can achieve a purity of origin that radically distinguishes it from the common or dominant forms of sociality. The effort to contrast these and to transform one into the other is already visible and even central in *Dubliners*. It is one of the signs of Joyce's conversion of realism into what seems like its opposite, an etherealized world that has been released from standard limitations and constraints. Such a world is often represented as final or ultimate – the snow at the end of "The Dead," the ironic/not ironic boast at the end of *A Portrait*, the Molly soliloquy at the end of *Ulysses*, or that of Anna Livia Plurabelle at the close/beginning of *Finnegans Wake*. But these endings are ambiguous or at least indecisive in themselves, and all the more so when we remember that this is also a characteristic way of ending the stories in *Dubliners*. The unionist Crofton is a warning to all who applaud an ending that is "a fine piece of writing."

In effect, the Joycean drama whereby the world of the actual is processed into the world of consciousness is, of necessity, always incomplete, since the process is never-ending and it is never entirely persuasive. The place might dominate, producing paralysis; the consciousness might dominate, producing fantasy. What certainly dominates is the writer's capacity to represent both, either separately or in a series of complex ratios one to the other. But I am suggesting here that Joyce's political critique of this condition as one that arose out of colonial conditions, involving derivativeness, economic backwardness, internalized submissiveness to established external authority, a *ressentiment* directed towards oneself and one's own culture, and various other modes of alienation, has the great virtue of pointing up how characteristic this also is of the condition of modernity, whether that be understood in Ibsenite, Arnoldian, Weberian, or Nietzschean versions. What the Dubliners suffer from is not the inability to enter into modernity; it is the inability to escape from it and from its emblematic place – their politically marginalized capital that is also on the margins of capital development.

Further, I want to suggest that this Joycean critique effectively comes to a close with "Grace." "The Dead" inaugurates the second and more enduring phase of Joyce's work, wherein he surrenders critique for aesthetics and, in doing so, becomes a characteristically modernist writer. The triumph of form over content, of vocation over life are the catch-cries of the new semisubsidized bohemian for whom art is a religion and anything other than a select audience an embarrassment.[3] Thus, the famous endings of the fiction from "The Dead" forward are examples of "fine" writing that have, as a consequence of that fineness, the capacity to be understood either as moments of final liberation from routine and fate or as moments of final incarceration within these. Rather than say that this is an admirable and rich ambiguity, we should perhaps recognize that this is what happens when critique is aestheticized into a form of writing that has the ambition to be entirely autonomous and that, in pursuit of this ambition, will refine to an unprecedented degree Joyce's favored technique of repetition – even to the point where the repetition merely becomes echoic lyricism. It is not surprising that these finales have so often been taken as celebrations of some essentialist position that is deemed to be "universal" and transcendent of all the local positions that precede them. This is the toast to "Humanity" that Ségouin offers in "After the Race" and to which international modernism, the cultural companion of transnational capitalism, has regularly drunk. Even the "feminine" (but hardly feminist) closures, which parade the sovereignty of the fluid over the fixed, the candidly sexual over the prudishly discreet are, in their politics, still repeating early Ibsen; but in their aesthetics they have become exemplary of the twentieth century's vision of humanism, in which the individual and the archetypal are related by a profoundly elegiac feeling for the future.

In "The Dead," Dublin faces a West which is past and future, undergoing two revivals, one involving Michael Furey, the other Molly Ivors and Irish native culture. Two versions of the dead, locked away for years, now give promise of a rebirth. But there are other deaths – actual, impending, symbolic. The great opera singers of the past have gone (199–200), the grace and hospitality of the old generation is going (204), the monks sleeping in their coffins at Mount Melleray rehearse daily their symbolic death to redeem the world (202). Every item in the story accentuates the contrast between a deep past and a shallow present. But so too does the idea of revival. Gabriel knows that Gretta has lost her beauty,

---

[3] For a sociological analysis of the new field of cultural production associated with figures like Flaubert and Joyce, see Bourdieu, *Cultural Production*, 192–266.

that her face is "no longer the face for which Michel Furey had braved death" (223). His image has remained fixed while all else has changed. His devotion to Gretta is, perhaps, a deal more impressive than Gretta's devotion to him. Here is a center of paralysis in the story, although it is usually read as an exemplary instance of the passion that other Dubliners are unable to feel. Gretta has been devoted all her married life to the memory of a dead seventeen-year old. What is buried in the past can only rearrive in the present in a spectral form – Furey, the Irish language, love, the idea of community. It is at the very least insinuated that the Gretta–Furey relationship, whatever its ostensible glamor might be, has another and less healthy aspect to it.

Then there is the other version of the West, the insulting "West Briton" phrase with which Miss Ivors wounds Gabriel. This is the first revival Gabriel is faced with; Furey has yet to come. Both are potent and yet each has an ersatz quality, deriving perhaps from the immemorial nature of the claim the dead make upon the time-bound living. With his notions of literature's autonomy, his anxiously nursed cosmopolitanism, his refusal of his own nation and culture, Gabriel has many of the features of the colonial dependent. Still, although he is yet another Dubliner who lives a second-hand existence, he is, in that respect, very much like his wife, and like Miss Ivors, both of whom depend upon the reawakening of a buried life to give meaning to their own.

With this story, we have begun the journey out from Dublin to the West to all of Ireland and thence to the universe. The expansion of the final paragraphs of "The Dead" is continued thereafter in all of Joyce's fiction. The key to the journey is repetition. The repetition may appear to be vicious when it brings the traveler or escapee back to the beginning, but it has many other forms. A revival is a repetition, as is an echo, or a memory, or an analogy, or a parallel. Joyce's prose incorporates all these variations, although it never entirely loses the love of monotony that he first discovered and exploited in *Dubliners*. However, repetition indicates the presence of a system of interrelated parts, of a destiny almost. It is this form of repetition that the close of "The Dead" inaugurates. It is not the system of capital, or of the world-spirit; it is not a system that belongs to "History" or to "Humanity." It belongs only to writing. Repetition, used in this fashion, aestheticizes the political. It provides a safety net of correspondences into which any apparently random element might fall and find its place in the universal scheme. In all the stories in *Dubliners* other than "The Dead," repetition has a critical and disturbing function.

It has analytic and polemical power. In this final story, all that is surrendered for lyricism.[4]

When the snow begins to tap upon the window pane, as Furey's gravel had danced years before upon Gretta's window, and as Gabriel had tapped his finger upon the window pane before his speech, Gabriel's identity and the "solid world" are fading and dissolving. He tracks the snow westward, through the seven repetitions of the word "falling," from the Dublin lamplight to Furey's grave and beyond that to its "falling faintly through the universe" and, in the famous chiasmus, "faintly falling, like the descent of their last end, upon all the living and the dead" (225). This is a marvelous instance of the universalizing impulse in Joyce, the conversion, through highly cadenced repetition, of something solid into something spectral. That has been an obsessive concern and technique throughout *Dubliners*. In this, its most self-consciously fine moment, everything is dissolved into writing, into an evocation of a world elsewhere, that of the aesthetic moment, in which conflict is annulled and the distinction between deathly paralysis and total liberation is designedly and with great virtuoso skill canceled. It is one of Joyce's finest fine moments. There were at least three more to go between 1907 and 1939.

Works cited

Adams, Robert M. "A Study in Weakness and Humiliation." *James Joyce's "Dubliners": A Critical Handbook*. Ed. James R. Baker and Thomas F. Staley. Belmont, Calif.: Wadsworth, 1969. 101–4.

Bourdieu, Pierre. *The Field of Cultural Production*. New York: Columbia University Press, 1993.

Cheng, Vincent J. *Joyce, Race, and Empire*. Cambridge: Cambridge University Press, 1995.

Derrida, Jacques. "Ulysses Gramophone: Hear Say Yes in Joyce." *James Joyce: The Augmented Ninth. Proceedings of the Ninth International James Joyce Symposium*. Ed. Bernard Benstock. Syracuse: Syracuse University Press, 1988. 27–75.

Joyce, James. *Dubliners*. Ed. Terence Brown. Harmondsworth: Penguin, 1993.

Nolan, Emer. *James Joyce and Nationalism*. London: Routledge, 1995.

Ziarek, Ewa. *The Rhetoric of Failure: Deconstruction of Skepticism, Reinvention of Modernism*. Albany: State University of New York Press, 1996.

[4] In this regard, I am very far from the political optimism of Derrida's "Ulysses Gramophone." He finds affirmation in rhetorical instability. I find neither. But see Ziarek, *Failure*, 103–16.

2

Disappearing Dublin: *Ulysses*,
postcoloniality, and the politics of space

ENDA DUFFY

The book of stone, so solid and so durable, would give way to the
book of paper, even more solid and more durable.
VICTOR HUGO, *Notre Dame de Paris*

Is it possible to imagine a nationalism without the primal scene of space,
of national territory? I propose that this is the question which *Ulysses*, in
what I will describe as its derealization of the space and setting of Dublin
in the novel, suggests to its readers. This is a chapter about how the
specific spaces of *Ulysses'* Dublin are both fetishized and derealized in
the novel; I wish to understand the possible political effects of such an
inscription of the spaces of the city. Even the most cursory look at Irish
nationalism proves that the extent of the national territory, and the
related matter of its border, have been at the crux of that ideology in this
century. *Ulysses*, dealing with Dublin and not the whole island, educates
us, I suggest, in how to think our way out of the territorial imperative
that nationalism demands.

For a politically interested reader who considers the setting of
Ulysses, perhaps the most poignant images from the archive of modern
Irish history are the photographs of ruined streetscapes in Dublin after
the 1916 Easter Rising (see figure 1). In the very years that Dublin was
being represented with an intense attention to detail in *Ulysses*, swathes
of the real city center itself were being destroyed. In Easter week a
gunboat in the Liffey lobbed shells at real and presumed rebel holdouts:
the General Post Office was left an empty shell, while Liberty Hall, to
British eyes a nest of revolutionaries, was left with gaping holes in its
façade. This occurred in the same year that Joyce was writing some of his
most evocative passages on Dublin streetscapes, in the "Wandering
Rocks" episode. Streets that were hardest hit were north of the Liffey,
where much of *Ulysses* is set: O'Connell Street, at the end of which
Bloom walks in "Lestrygonians" and up which the funeral cortège moves

in "Hades"; the streets near the newspaper office of "Lestrygonians"; and towards Little Britain Street, the setting of "Cyclops."[1] Rising in fiction, being destroyed in fact: this grim difference between the cityscapes described in *Ulysses* and the reality that had been wrought in the very years the book was being written bears witness to how history chases Joyce down in what might appear as the underpoliticized Dublin of the novel.

How can we read these photographs of a destroyed Dublin? In them, Dublin presents itself as a chaos of ruins, and ruins, as Hofheinz has shown in his study of how cartography and early modern Irish historiography inflect *Finnegans Wake*, have been crucial artifacts in the development of the preeminent modern Irish historical narrative. In brief, it was in the attempt to weave a narrative about the ruins – megalithic, medieval, or more recent – dotting the Irish landscape that modern Irish historiography was born, notably in the work of such eighteenth-century antiquarians as Charles O'Connor and, from 1820, by the Ordinance Survey with such figures as Petrie and O'Donovan. Although this latter work was a ferocious colonial project of anglicization, nevertheless, focused first upon ruins as the tangible evidence of a vanished past, these surveyor-antiquarians could not help but see the ruin as totem for a vanquished order and a rebuke to the colonizer who had left the ruin as sign of his oppression. This antiquarian nostalgia translated easily into late colonial resentment, whether genteel, as in the work of Francis Ferguson, or more declamatory, from *The Nation* onwards. A history predicated on a topography of ruins was equipped to see every ruined cottage as a signifier of British perfidy: it was partly because Irish nationalists had learned to find ruins so eloquent that the cabins of evicted tenants struck so poignant a chord in the "Land War." Dublin's ruined streetscapes of 1916 could, therefore, be read in this tradition: here was the culminating example of colonial repression through topographical ruination, that left its traces as ruined memorials throughout the cityscape.

Yet the post-independence government of 1922 did not preserve any of these ruins as a memorial (although bullet holes on the pillars of the Post Office remain as an unofficial monument): these new urban ruins, even of the anticolonial struggle, were seen from the start to be of a

---

[1] For a discussion of the relevance of this destruction to *Ulysses*, see my own *The Subaltern "Ulysses."*

Fig. 1 Demolished buildings along lower Sackville Street in the aftermath of the Easter Rising of 1916.

different order. This was the order of collateral war damage, often associated with terror against civilians. Dublin in this light became one of the first of what would be a long line of bombarded cities in the wars of this century, from Rheims in the First World War to Dresden in the Second. In this other context, the gaping windows of Henry Street become an early augur of Hiroshima. Given its modernity, the image of the bombarded metropolis came to be read less as a testimony to specific kinds of political aggression than as evidence of the tragedy of warfare in general. The shelled, ruined city was read as a vivid example of the gross alienation and dark horror that permeated modern urban reality, a stark flash of the intense urban anomie which a dominant strand of modernist writing, from Kafka to Eliot, had characterized as the death-pervaded terrain of modern streetscapes. In this perspective, Dublin's ruins testify to its status as a modern metropolis, whose alienating realities are laid bare by war.

Reading these photographs of Dublin's 1916 ruins, then, proves a complicated process: in the Irish tradition of topographical historiography, they could be seen as the most recent testimony to British colonial brutishness; within a cosmopolitan tradition developed in this century of reading bombarded cities as the epitome of modernist nightmare, they imply that Dublin was taking its place as a modern metropolis, scene of the alienation thus implied. If you judge modernism and nationalism to be opposing forces, then you will consider these readings contradictory. If, however, as such political readers of Joyce as Emer Nolan[2] and others have striven to do, you see nationalism and modernism as congruent, then the question becomes more interesting: how do alienation and defamiliarization, which modernist representations discern most often in modernist landscapes, gibe with the sense of community and allegiance apparently fostered by nationalism?

Here, to comprehend the politics of *Ulysses'* confrontation of nationalist sentiment and a modernist aesthetic, I will consider what is at stake politically in the way in which the Dublin of 1904, still unshelled and unruined, is represented in the novel. The novel, set in 1904 in a late colonial city, was written in 1914–21 in the very years when the city became the center of the anticolonial struggle that would lead to Irish

---

[2] Nolan uses, among others, the work of Ernest Gellner as her starting point. For a recent example of Gellner's work in an excellent anthology of theoretical debates on nationalism, see "The Coming of Nationalism."

independence. In these years of *Ulysses'* composition, Dublin, with the shelling and fires of 1916 would be "changed utterly" (in Yeats's term) to the extent that insurgency and counterinsurgency had even erased part of the cityscape that Joyce's novel had described. With history, then, creeping up to alter even the physical cityscape being described in the text, *Ulysses* too can seem to the politicized reader to lend itself precisely to the two kinds of readings which the photos of burned-out Dublin suggest. That is, it may be read partly as a record of nationalist desires, as a litany of the varieties of *ressentiment* that are the stock-in-trade of late colonial national movements; at the same time it can be seen also as a kind of pattern book of the manifold varieties of the metropolitan "blase attitude" that Georg Simmel described as key to the anomie of Western urban existence and teased out in texts by such modernists as Kafka, Musil, and Döblin as well as Joyce.[3]

Nationalist *ressentiment* might seem to fit well alongside modernist anomie; yet recent debates about how Joyce's texts represent the trajectories of postcolonial power reveal an anxiety on this score. Such doubts are exacerbated by the fact that *Ulysses* is characteristically read as an exception to Eliotian modernist dourness; Joyce's metropolitan imagery is celebrated for tending towards the heteroglossia of carnival as a means of sidestepping versions of morbid urbanism. The critics' anxiety swirls around the suggestion that while it would be wonderful if Joyce's text provided the model of a broad-minded Irish nationalism, the grim reality might be that the atavism, insularity, and self-centeredness of Irish nationalist ideology cannot find favor in a novel that, minutely concerned with the Irish capital, is famously ambiguous, heteroglossic, and tolerant of all comers. Regardless of the problematic bases for this fear, it seems to be the case that it will only be overcome if we can measure the political value of the wily Joycean aesthetic against a verifiable measure of the material – and the most verifiable measure of such materiality is the urban landscape of the city itself, from which Joyce picked and chose in order to represent Dublin. In other words, the political impact of *Ulysses* can only be judged in the final instance when we understand the political trajectory underlying the text's specific representation of the physical reality of Dublin. By limning the novel's hieroglyphics of the spatial we can take the measure of the political economy of the work.

We need to pitch a political reading of *Ulysses* at the horizon of its

<hr>

[3] For a recent comparative study, see Barta, *Bely, Joyce and Döblin.*

materialist representations because, in its diverse narrative strategies, heteroglossic modernism adroitly undercuts ideological readings. In Joyce studies, initial steps to understand the *œuvre* politically focused on authorial ideology: the question was posed as "What did Joyce believe?" These readings radically recast the ways Joyce can be read; their recourse to the author's professed beliefs, nevertheless, is idealistic, if only because Joyce's own overt ideological commitments (except on religion) were seldom sustained sufficiently to be taken wholly seriously. The second wave of Joycean political readings, pioneered by Cheryl Herr, worked to establish homologies between cultural forces operating in modern Ireland and aesthetic strategies, bolstered by references, in Joyce's texts. Such readings offer a fuller account of how formal strategies homologize ideological forces, but can get trapped in accounts of how textual strategies either supported or subverted such forces.

If Joyce's work is ever to be viably considered more than semicolonial, therefore, I suggest that beyond overt ideology, subversive references, and possibilities of innovative narrative forms that homologize discourses in the culture, one must grasp specific relations between materiality and its modernist representation. I have in mind here Fredric Jameson's still-resonant call, in *The Political Unconscious*, for a materialist criticism capable of providing a totalizing critical account that would subsume the rest. Since that call, however, Jameson's own anxiety about the limits of such a materialism has centered on two interrelated issues: the space of geopolitics, and the space of cities. Thus he has followed such theorists as Henri Lefebvre in understanding that for a full definition of the material in materialist criticism, the category of space must be added to those of labor, commodities, and value. Following this insight, I will examine *Ulysses'* spatial politics here.

Lefebvre's initial insight is summed up as follows: "When Marx in *Capital* showed how the capitalist mode of production opposed (dialectically) capital to labor, the bourgeoisie to the proletariat, and profits to wages, he ignored the question of land, property and its ownership" (*Production of Space*, 234). Correcting this oversight, his thesis is that capitalism relentlessly rationalizes space, that is, expunges its peculiarities and reminders of earlier forms of production to render it serviceable to exploitation, production, consumption, and the generation of profits. Capitalist controlled space tends to be abstracted space – which means spaces as bland as possible to facilitate the traffic in goods and workers, a space marked by prohibitions, and, in ways Foucault delineated, pervasive surveillance. Abstracted space is compartmentalized by functions such as work and play, where, notes Lefebvre, "Desires and needs are uncoupled, then crudely cobbled back together" (*Production of Space*, 308). It is space that, because it is featureless, functional, and replicable in various cultural contexts, advertises itself as an agent of freedom for the individual subject. This new featurelessness and lack of ornament allies rationalized space to the kinds of living and work spaces championed by modernist architects from Loos to Le Corbusier, and relates it to the fractured spaces, and the downfall of Euclidean, perspectival space, in modernist art and literature from Picasso to Joyce. Indeed, Lefebvre uses the evidence of modernist arts' post-perspectival estranging of represented spaces as inspiration for his observations on capitalist spatiality.

The initial question raised by Lefebvre's theory is this: what kinds of spaces did the capitalist abstraction of space obliterate? Even the rules of perspective, for example, might be read as the visual encoding of an early modern, not necessarily less ruthless regime of capitalist spatial organization, where the viewer seems all-powerful because he or she becomes the center of the compositional focus. Another means by which to think about a lost order of spatial interest would be to invoke Benjamin's concept of the "aura." This however would lead us, *via* Benjamin's mysticism, into the post-Heideggerianism of Bachelard (author of *The Poetics of Space*), and elaborated in Heidegger's own meditation on the *heimlich* in "Building Dwelling Thinking," – and ultimately to a nostalgia-bedeviled utopianism. In conceptualizing the spatial abstraction effected in modernity, we must avoid placing it in a narrative predicated on a nostalgia for any imagined 'whole' spatial order; it is utopian to think that rationalized spaces simply obliterated what Foucault (influenced both by Lefebvre and Bachelard) called "sacred spaces" ("Of Other Spaces," 22). Likewise, Benjamin's "aura" is a concept focused on the commodity, that is, an object in circulation, rather than on evocative fixed spaces. Rather, if one surveys the disciplines that have grown up to systematize the observation of spaces, it is clearly anthropology that derived intellectual capital from the work of considering how a space evidences cultural formations. Such work was the intellectual arm of late imperialism; as such, the issue of colonial senses of place and their relation to identity, particularly relevant to Ireland, enters with a vengeance all debates about the representation of space in the modern period.

To briefly explore the implications of anthropology's contribution to the understanding of spatial symbolics, I will focus on the work of one anthropologist, Marc Augé. In *Non-places: Introduction to an Anthropology of Supermodernity*, Augé, without mentioning Lefebvre, deploys the latter's notion of spatial abstraction to characterize postmodern spatial experience. He speaks of the contemporary proliferation of what he calls "non-spaces," that is, airports, freeways, chain hotels, and so on which are the same everywhere in the world regardless of the cultural specificities of their settings; in them, spatial abstraction serves transnational traffic. Defining these new spaces without character leads him to suggest that "place," that has been the subject of anthropology, "can be defined as relational, historical and concerned with identity" (*Non-places*, 77–78), a space where time has been encoded as reminders of the shared history of the community that occupies it. As examples, Augé proffers some French villages; he probably has in mind also the villages of a vast body of ethnographic description.

While one needs to question the political–scientific nexus that marks the origins of Augé's science of "place," his work, in conjunction with that of Lefebvre, provides us with the rudiments of a dialectics of spatiality useful in understanding the distortions prevalent in much of postcolonial modernism's spatial defamiliarizations. Insisting that the hegemony of non-spaces is a "supermodern" phenomenon, Augé cites the critic Jean Starobinski's observation that modernist representations of space, from Baudelaire to Proust to Joyce, while attending to contemporary spatial variety, still note the presence of the past in their polyphonies. As an example, Starobinski quotes the first spoken words in *Ulysses*, "*Introibo ad altare Dei*": we are to understand, he suggests, that while the novel, by dealing with a single day, will devote itself to showing spaces rather than dwelling on past time, it still begins by sounding out (even if ironically) the intonations of past ritual (*Non-places*, 75–76). Following Starobinski, Augé implies that modernist fiction was much more wholly pre-postmodern than the avant-garde of anthropology of the same period: while the discipline devoted itself to discerning signs of culture in a given space and thus denoting it a "place," modernist fiction was presumably offering a spatial dialectic in which "placedness" was relegated to the status of vestige.

Starobinski's resort to Joyce takes us to the question of how "place" and "non-place" (this latter operating as the realization of Lefebvre's "abstracted space") are represented in *Ulysses*. One might consider Augé's distinction between "place" and "non-place" to be mappable on to the distinction I made at the outset between the two ways to read the photographs and the two aspects of a political reading of Joyce's modernism: that the atavistic, resentful, historicist traces of past oppression in the text could be found in *Ulysses* around representations of place, while readings that focused on metropolitan modernist anomie could search in the text for images of drab urban nonplaces. The reality, however, turns out to be more complex and interesting, for reasons that have to do with the political subtexts of the anthropologists' project, and the specific political trajectory of Joyce's work. For a start, observe that while the anthropologist works to give to a particular space a culture without a politics, *Ulyssean* representation cannot fail to suggest the political implications of its representation of Dublin, whether as "place" or "non-place."[4] Nonetheless, politics – the politics of state and colonial power of which the village, even when limned by the anthropologist as a governing unit unto itself, turns out to be a microcosm – may be said to *haunt* every anthropologist's account of an African village. It is by fetishizing the monuments to communal life in the village that the anthropologist decrees the space a "place"; in doing so, she both occludes and brings to our attention the possibility of larger political communities in which the village exists.

On the issues of how Dublin as a built environment, and Dublin as a community, are represented in *Ulysses*, the critical record is incomplete. The objection that Dublin in the novel simply does not represent any larger political entity such as late or postcolonial Ireland is commonly advanced to outmaneuver postcolonial political readings of *Ulysses* altogether. On the novel's representation of the physical city one finds mostly a focus on symbolic geographies – as in Robert Adams Day's fine "Joyce's AquaCities." The critical tradition of minute attention to the text's allusions, however, has fostered the impression that Joyce's ability to defamiliarize was matched with a scrupulousness about exact details of locations, shop names, and every detail of the physical city. Hugh Kenner, for example, rejoices in noting that Joyce wrote home to discover how deep was the area drop down which Bloom would have to jump to enter through the basement door of 7 Eccles Street, as he does in "Ithaca."[5] Behind this is Joyce's own claim (deeply ironic given the 1916 destruction) that if Dublin were destroyed it could be rebuilt using

---

[4] On the politics of anthropological travel and writing, see the interesting work by Karen Kaplan.

[5] See Kenner, *Ulysses*, especially ch. 13, "Lists, Myths," 144–45.

Ulysses as a guide, and his later habit of asking Irish visitors to name every shop and pub up one side of a Dublin street and down the other. Such evidence of a drive for mimetic specificity should not, however, be confused with the achievement of some kind of totalizing mimeticism. Although the mass of detail may appear to provide even an excess of data on Dublin, it can also divert us from how much of the physical city is omitted from the text. And the politics of this vast unsaid can be as eloquent as what gets included in the novel.

Moreover, recent historicist approaches to Joyce have almost unanimously followed a Bakhtinian approach to his heteroglossic style – that is, to stress the excessive, the massed accumulation of detail as a shoring of fragments that exceeds realist representation. In such a light, the successor to the Joycean aesthetic is the magic realism of the Americas – Borges or Pynchon. Remember, however, that a more immediate successor to Joyce was Samuel Beckett, the author of pared-down minimalist works in which the physical setting was mostly elided. Reading Joyce through Beckett's radical refusal to stage a place even though his plays were by necessity performed in physical settings, teaches us that Joyce's work, despite its detail-obsessed carnival, achieves its effects not only through the collage of minutiae, but even more by a ruthless editing that comprehends the value of the unrepresented and the undeclared. Just as, for example, a Cubist composition by Georges Braque can suggest the dishevelment of a tabletop through the composition of a relatively few deft strokes, which can still have the painting seem busy, so too *Ulysses* contrasts a busy mimeticism about specific details on the one hand with a relentless strategy of omitting most of Dublin from the novel on the other. Thus the space represented is at once uncannily hyperrealized in parts and ignored in others. The cornucopia of detail is counterpoised with an equally eloquent missing *Ulysses*. This dual strategy twists the actually represented "real" spaces of Dublin into premonitions of the surreal, presenting the reader, I suggest, with a late colonial milieu where the spatial real is never simply what it appears. The excessive detail about selected aspects of the city shows the novel outdoing the anthropologists, so that the city's character as "place" in Augé's sense is equaled, and then exceeded – and the peculiar politics of such a designation is uncannily suggested. By eliding so much at the same time, however, Joyce also renders Dublin as a nonplace, or rather, makes evident the way in which the political implications of what Augé takes to be the destiny of nonplacedness of Western modernity was incipient in

Dublin, as a late colonial and would-be postcolonial city, at the beginning of the twentieth century.

This modernist Dublin, so strangely lost and found in *Ulysses*, is made possible because the novel is a *flâneur* text, that is, primarily a record of the observations of the roving eyes of pedestrians. As Bloom, in particular, wanders about, his eye is inevitably in thrall to the various ideologies that have interpellated him: thus, for example, he pays a moment's more attention to the statue of the temperance preacher Fr. Matthew than he does to the much grander statue of Daniel O'Connell, "The Liberator" (*U* 7.250, 7.319) in the same street. At the same time, as *flâneur*, he is subject to the myriad shocks-as-sights that, as Sherlock Holmes, another, more purposeful *flâneur* of a few years earlier in the imperial capital put it, "will happen when you have four million human beings all jostling each other within the space of a few square miles" (Doyle, "The Blue Carbuncle," 279–80). For example, Bloom even makes a stab at what Benjamin calls "love at last sight" (*Illuminations*, 169) when he watches for the flashing ankle of the "well heeled" (his term) woman climbing up on an "outsider" in front of the Grosvenor Hotel (*U* 5.112–30). The Holmes reference is apt, because every feature seen by the *flâneur* Bloom and the rest becomes a clue, and the collation of thousands of such clues is what would render Dublin a "place" – a site characterized by relations, history, and a concern for identity – for the reader of the text.

Yet the interplay for Bloom himself in the collation of these clues between his ideological disposition, his previous knowledge, and his absorption of the continuous barrage of minor shocks in navigating the urban scene is exacerbated for the reader by the way in which the stream of consciousness technique preempts any description of the setting or its significance besides what surfaces in the characters' thoughts. Hence, the ideal reader of the novel would have been a Dubliner well versed in the physical aspects of the city in 1904. What this achieves is to alienate other readers from the setting: to continually insist that the reader (who is not a 1904 Dubliner) is an outsider, and that the work of collating these clues into a sense of familiarity with the cityscape is a matter of lifelong interpellation that cannot be provided at second hand to provide a false sense of recognition in the text. In refusing to act as a guide, the novel implies that such a sense of unearned recognition would be false: it implies, too, the existence, in some sense, of a local community bound by, if nothing else, this shared learning experience that allows, for example, recognition of a streetscape merely by its name. Through the constant reiteration of this ruse, the novel suggests, therefore, that the *flânerie* of Dubliners is different to the *flânerie* of, for example, Aschenbach in Mann's *Death in Venice*. In the Dublin of *Ulysses* to be a *flâneur* – even a comic one like Cashel Boyle O'Connor Fitzmaurice Tisdall Farrell (10.919) – is not to declare oneself a cosmopolitan, at ease in any Western metropolis; rather it is to display one's almost secret knowledge of the urban labyrinth which is exclusive to those who inhabit it.

This is a knowledge that, as the novel makes clear, is superficially accessible to all comers, but from which the outsider is in fact always already excluded, in an ignorance about which she is increasingly taunted – if only in the parade of street names – as the novel progresses. Joyce harnesses the representational potential of a classic trope of metropolitan modernism in order to enact, by naming but not telling, how shared, secret knowledge of the cityscape can be the basis of a shared, however tenuous, sense of community. The physical city, then, is the key to the imagined community. For Augé, the *flâneur* might seem the ideal modernist citizen-in-training for the alienating encounters of the non-place: in *Ulysses*, rather, he often seems to be enacting rituals of shared recognition where the processing of clues becomes less a Holmesian fictive version of semiofficial surveillance than the declaration of a shared common knowledge embodied in the cityscape.

This however is by no means to say that Dublin as represented in *Ulysses* is a "place" in Augé's terms; rather I suggest that it throws the very idea of anthropological "place" on its head. When critics have tried to think of the embodiment of "community" in *Ulysses'* Dublin without considering the interaction of the people and the urban landscape – without realizing that the physical city, in the same way that the commodity exists in Marx's theory of commodity fetishism, actually mediates the relations between the various members – they have come up with some startling formulations. Most persuasive may be Fredric Jameson's, when in his Field Day essay "Modernism and Imperialism" of 1988 he decided that because all the male bourgeois and petit-bourgeois scroungers of Joyce's Dublin appear to know each other, then the city seems more like what he terms a "classical city" or a medieval conclave of burgers and guilds than a modern Western metropolis (*Nationalism, Colonialism*, 61–64). Jameson here touches on one of the book's most interesting problems regarding the alignment of city and community:

that is, although even a cursory look at Thom's Dublin Directory for 1904 will convince you that only the merest fraction of Dublin's population is included in the novel, it still manages to suggest to the reader that the rag-tag group it assembles somehow hovers near the heart of the city's civic life.

In fact, that effect of hovering close, with all the pathos it involves, is precisely the point: just as Bloom is on the margins of the newspaper office and of every group he encounters from the funeral mourners to the men carousing in the brothel, so too are the members of those groups themselves on the margins of any presumed centers of power – hangers-on at the National Library or lackeys at Dublin Castle, for example – or downplaying their absolute marginality, as in the case of Ben Dollard, who is now in the Iveagh Home. The pathos of this distance from power is, however, invariably counterpointed by drolly disrespectful images of the powerful: the newspaper editor is a shrill drunkard, the "Quaker librarian" purrs, and the solicitor John Henry Menton has "oyster eyes" (*U* 7.1031). The "vice-regal party" of "Wandering Rocks" is likewise nothing but show. Dublin in *Ulysses* is a place without any center of viable political power and hence (as no real alternative sites of contestation are suggested in the novel) without any real possibility that the city could exist as the site of a viable community. In this light Bloom's self-cultivated marginality is a normalizing, rather than an othering strategy: his ostracized solitariness is the condition of every citizen in the city.

Given this structural inability to foster unmediated personal relations into a sense of community as such, the knowledge of the physical city and its features shared by the citizens assumes greater importance in fostering anything approximating to an "imagined community." Yet without the existence of some viable civic communal relations, the link that the ethnologist claims to discern between the built environment and the community relations it memorializes, the memorializing factor which makes a given space for Augé a "place" in the anthropological sense, can scarcely exist either. This accounts, I think, for the short shrift that official monuments are given in the Dublin of *Ulysses*. Monuments that are mentioned testify not to community but to its impossibility. In "Hades," for example, Bloom's eye lingers on the "Foundation stone for Parnell" (6.320), that is, on the base of the Parnell monument, as yet unbuilt. Later Hynes and Power consider visiting Parnell's grave, but seem reticent because the dead leader may not be buried there at all, and they have heard that "the coffin was filled with stones" (6.923). Later,

Bloom spots the hero's brother, a part of the Dublin cityscape (just as houses have ghosts) whom Bloom thinks of as the "Ghost of Parnell" (8.502). Thus this city boasts a monument that draws attention to its absence, a grave that may not be a grave, and a living ghost, all to commemorate (while denying commemoration to) a failed attempt at forming a community under a parliamentary leader. *Ulysses'* Dublin is a place where the memorialization of community (which the anthropologist demands to decree a settlement a "place") is signaled only by markers of its failure. While the community cannot cohere, no monument to such a community can be in evidence. Even the statue of the proto-nationalist poet Thomas Moore, Bloom notes, is over a urinal.

Yet this is not to imply that Dublin as invoked in *Ulysses* is a city lacking in physical character. On the contrary, what the novel gives its readers are the masses of occasional shocks where city meets citizen, shocks which in *Ulysses'* Dublin are often transformed into moments that denote recognition. Often these appeal to a sense other than sight, as with the pealing bells of St. George's Church heard so differently by Bloom and Stephen, or show Bloom engaged in some de Certeau-like work of everyday resistance, offering obsequies before his own secret landmarks — as when he slips into the national museum to eye the bottoms of the Greek statues. What we are left with, then, whether we accept Bloom's "cognitive map" of the city or use the novel in general to piece together our own map of the metropolis, is a city marked by landmarks which seem somewhat uneasily strange and other-worldly: together as a dense web of sounds, smells, and uncanny sights from the makeshift unintended memorial to Emmet in the junk shop window to the Sacred Heart statue at Glasnevin (7.730), they suggest a city marked by a strangeness to be sensed everywhere but never quite adding up to a defined whole. Augé jokes that Durkheim would have a hard time reading Roissy airport (*Non-places*, 94), as it is so banal; he might have had an even harder time reading the Dublin of *Ulysses*. For Joyce uses a collage of the shocks of the kind shown in modernist and postmodernist representations of anonymous metropolitan milieux, in order to characterize a more uncanny environment, which refuses the ethnographic reading of community-centered "place" but likewise is too feature-laden, and too often secretly apprehended as their own place by its denizens, to generate much of the anomie-laden vacancy of the nonplace. To understand the sources of this dialectical apprehension of the novel's setting, which results in the hyperrealization of some details and the elision of others, we must, I propose, remember Dublin's status in 1904 as a late-colonial city.

Just as Bloom is both an "other" in the novel and the character who epitomizes the marginality of all his peers, so sites such as Glasnevin cemetery are not only another "heterotopic" space, but figures of the city itself. Foucault, in "Of Other Spaces," theorizes that space in our era is characterized by real lived space and heterotopias, closed marginal spaces that actually exist but also have a quasi-sacred role as the repositories of the fantasies of those who inhabit the more mundane real spaces (22–23). My hypothesis is that Dublin, which in *Ulysses* is rife with heterotopic spaces – the cemetery on the edge of the city, the strand at Sandymount, the Ormond Hotel and Nighttown, a heterotopia which has taken over the city's heart – is itself a city as heterotopia. Its status as heterotopia was inevitable because Dublin as a colonial capital was an "other place" in relation to the imperial metropolis.

To theorize the reality of power and emplacement in the colonial city we may turn to Franz Fanon. In *The Wretched of the Earth* Fanon describes how any colonial city will be a bifurcated place, with the "modern" town of wide streets for the colonial administrators, and the native old town as a crowded and (in the eyes of the colonizer) "teeming, stench-filled, dangerous" (38–39) enclave. The colonist town can be described, matching the levels of consciousness and occlusions of its inhabitants, using forms – detective fiction, *flâneur* text, modernist montage – developed to characterize any conventional Western metropolis. The natives' town could be left to the Western anthropologists to read its "sense of place" in a self-serving way. When a modernist text takes on the native quarter, however, its strangeness in contrast to the mundanities of the metropolis, its heterotopic quality, is foregrounded. Hence the uncanny strangeness of many of the details of place that go into making the cognitive map of *Ulysses'* Dublin.

Specifically, this strangeness of the physical setting of Dublin as represented in *Ulysses* is a phenomenon experienced by the reader. It is the reader who, brought into the unfamiliar streets and treated as if she should know them already, is asked to enact the experience of the colonist experiencing the colonial city for the first time. As if to accentuate this point, Haines is cast as a crucial third figure at the opening of the novel: he is our representative, the one we follow, even as we are invited to condescend to him while being made suspicious of his own preposterous imperial condescension, into the labyrinth of Dublin as a colonial "native" enclave. Haines is a tourist – and the reader's own experience of Dublin in *Ulysses* has a tourist quality as that experience has been described by Dean McCannell and others. Just as the tourist seeks to endow the unfamiliar with a simulacrum of significance but merely fetishizes strangeness all the more, so the reader of *Ulysses*, following Haines, smiles benignly at strange and possibly significant details but cannot pick out the significant monuments among them. "This is real Irish cream I take it," Haines tells Mulligan in the DBC, "I don't want to be imposed on" (10.1094). Also in "Wandering Rocks," where the form most directly corresponds to tourist sightseeing, we glimpse some actual tourists to Dublin: "Two carfuls of tourists passed slowly, their women sitting fore, gripping the handrests. Palefaces. Men's arms frankly round their stunted forms. They looked from Trinity to the blind columned porch of the Bank of Ireland" (10.340–43). Here, an apparent example of direct narrative is mediated by Stephen's contemptuous gaze. Calling these (presumably British) tourists "palefaces" comically invokes the colonial analogy – from the native standpoint. The adjective "blind" then strikes off Stephen's "native" consciousness of *his* gaze upon these colonist-tourists' gaze upon his city. The bank of Ireland, at which they stare, until 1800 the seat of Ireland's own parliament, is windowless: among Dubliners it is still known colloquially as "the blind bank." As a taunting monument to a disillusioned nationalism, it was also "blind," that is, disabled. Here, however, this blindness is deflected on to these tourists. And they may be the group in the novel most like us as readers: for the reader who arrives "blind" to *Ulysses*' Dublin is close to a tourist sightseer herself.

Even though the reader may be more adrift than the local population, the native characters, note, are alienated from the city also. And the tourist-reader's and native character's sense of alienation from the city have similarities; hence the reader can share the character's sense of being a little lost in his own city. But the reasons for the alienation are different: the reader, nonnative metropolitan, is placed in the role of tourist-colonizer, while the local character, not wholly part of a realized community, is not going to feel attached to any monuments or markers that would symbolize such a noncommunal identity. It is the tourists, and not the locals, who seek for significance by looking at the bank. Hence Dublin is not, at least in *Ulysses*' representation of it, a "place" in Augé's terms: whereas his places were "relational, historical and concerned with identity" (*Non-places*, 77), Dublin in *Ulysses* is a city without real relations, whose history is denied it, and whose identity in its own terms is unclear.

At the same time *Ulysses'* depiction of Augé's "non-place," or of the capitalist abstraction of space described by Lefebvre, also takes their concepts, in advance, to their logical conclusion: as both writers' notions pinpoint a tendency of modernity to deny the physical reality of space altogether, so Joyce, in advance, erases such spaces from his work. If we follow Fanon in his characterization of a colonial city, then next to the native quarter, in the airier suburbs, should be the colonists' own enclave. Similarly, following Lefebvre, one would expect that in any modern metropolis, and particularly in a colonial city where exploitation is even more blatant, the abstraction of urban spaces, the relentless erasure of cultural forms for profit-making, should be fully in evidence. Yet the milieu of the colonist ruling cadres, whether in the Phoenix Park, Dublin Castle itself, or in the posher south Dublin suburbs, and the zones of the poorest workers, where Lefebvrian abstraction might be most in evidence, are *both* absent from the novel.[6] True, numerous characters from both of these parts of Dublin flit across *Ulysses*, from the impoverished boy with the offal bucket whom Bloom sees by Brady's Cottages at the opening of "Lotus Eaters" (5.5) to the viceregal party parading in "Nausicca." Further, the attention that *Ulysses* gives to all kinds of thresholds, as figures appear over them or disappear behind them – the viceregal cavalcade that emerges from the lower gate of the Phoenix Park (10.1175), the grim bookseller who disappears behind his curtain (10.633), the plump arm that appears at a window to throw a coin at the old soldier (10.251), all in "Wandering Rocks" alone – constantly reminds us that there are numerous spaces that are left unexplored and undescribed in *Ulysses*. Just as Braque, in for example his painting of La Roche-Guyon of 1909 (Hughes, *The Shock of the New*, 28), makes clear, despite the edited version of the hilltop chateau he supplies, that it is a real landscape he is representing, and thus encourages the viewer to dwell on the differences between this composition of a few lines and a (presumed) version of the landscape itself, so too *Ulysses*, I suggest, would have us attend to all of the untold, unsaid spaces of Dublin that do not appear but are suggested in the text. Despite its love of detail, and its "encyclopedic" quality, the novel, I propose, actually strives for a condition which is only achieved in some works of Beckett, where any sense of

---

[6] On the treatment of womens' spaces in *Ulysses*, see Garvey, "City Limits."

place is erased altogether. This erasure of whole swathes of its setting is, I think, one of *Ulysses'* supreme political strategies.

Reading modern works, critics tend to consider the unsaid a negative entity: the secret the text pushes into its unconscious. This is appropriate for texts that bolster existing hegemonic powers. When, however, a subaltern text is in question, then the unsaid may exist as the unarticulated possibility of a utopia. By refusing to map out in the novel the full cityscape of colonial might, with its monuments on the one hand and its degrading effects, the slums it has created, on the other, while always annotating the intrusive realities of their existence, *Ulysses* leaves these spaces as imaginatively blank cityscapes that might therefore be filled with some other more hopeful version of governance, of community, and of the features that would memorialize it. This eloquent subaltern unsaid marks, therefore, the trace of *ressentiment*, where the abject refuses to acknowledge the monuments, and scars, of the master's dominance. It posits a cityscape as yet unmarked by monuments of any community it finds acceptable. It suggests that spaces, as yet undiscerned, exist in the city for any community that may come into being. "Nonplace" is not in *Ulysses* what it is in Augé or Lefebvre; rather, it is truly absent space, whose absence, at all times reiterated, leaves blank a sign of a community to come.

"When Ireland takes her place among the nations of the earth," said Robert Emmet, "then, and not till then, let my epitaph be written." Emmet understood that without a viable community no acceptable monuments, no symbolic cityscape, were possible. Yet Bloom's farting before these very lines (which might even show that he agrees with them, that he will indeed refuse Emmet the respect that the insurgent said he should not yet be given) is often cited as evidence of Joyce's own disdain for Irish nationalism. Whatever the author's own antipathy[7] to the various strands of Ireland's nationalist ideology, I suggest that the strategies used to represent the cityscape in *Ulysses* bear similarities to the representational impetus of nationalism itself.

In much of the writing about nationalism as a kind of magic for modernity, an imaginary but powerfully interpellative glue that hails subjects into "imagined communities," it is easily forgotten that the first principle

---

[7] Among the recent books on Joyce and postcoloniality, those by Nolan and Cheng in particular, following the work of Manganiello and others, stress that the issue of what ideological stances Joyce himself professed is still an open one.

of nationalism is the inviolability of territory – i.e., of space. Every modern nationalism is premised on the idea that the community corresponds to the given territory, and that it is this land that gives the subject citizenship. Perhaps no nationalism, despite much competition, has, since the gaining of Irish independence even more than before, enacted the consequences of this awareness more than that of Ireland. The representational choices of *Ulysses* portray a heightened, perverse sense of Augé's "place" in the anthropological sense, and use as its foil the nonsaid that suggest the abstracted spaces of the Dublin the novel represents, spaces which left unsaid might suggest future utopian community. Likewise, the Ireland which the Anglo-Irish treaty of 1921 inaugurated was split in two, between the Irish Free State in the south, and the "six counties" of the north. Ireland, from the ultra-nationalist perspective, could not exist as a "place," that is, as a community that could represent itself viably in relation to a territory, in the twenty-six county south, while it existed alongside a split-off, heterotopic nonplace of Northern Ireland, half colony and half capitalist abstracted space in the north. The possibility, from that nationalist perspective, has always been that this northern nonspace, incorporated into the Irish Republic, would render the nation as some utopian union of territory and citizenry. As an advance cartography of how these preoccupations regarding territory and community got evoked through an exploration of how its inhabitants saw the space of what was about to become the new (half-)nation's capital, *Ulysses* may have been prescient.

In sketching a local allegory of the effect of nationalism's contradictory dreams of place and space, Joyce in *Ulysses* supplied a map of Ireland's future as a site where the nationalist desire for an ideal conjunction of territory and "imagined community" was destined to remain unfulfilled. In focusing only on how some of the middle-class males of Dublin develop their cognitive map of the city, however, the novel reminds us of the bourgeois origins and effects of modern nationalism itself. Crucially, the novel's portrayal of Dublin's spaces might suggest to us that while nationalism's obsession with territory may like to think of itself as descended from the territorial wars of warrior princes, it has more in common with modern capitalism's drive for property as wealth. Nationalism dreams of communities possessing territory; capitalism, of individuals possessing wealth. Nationalism's obsession with territory is a grander version of bourgeois capitalism's obsession with possession: nationalists, appropriately, saw the Irish as "the dispossessed." It is this territorial, spatial imperative that continues to generate political impasses on the island of Ireland. Perhaps *Ulysses'* utopia of the elided spaces of official and impoverished Dublin, and its drive to elide the matter of a spatial setting in the way that Beckett would later achieve, should challenge us to imagine a national community that could exist without land as the basis of its right to existence. *Ulysses* might be challenging us to imagine a national community without the possession of land as the guarantor of its legitimacy. When nationalism overcomes the need for a community to correspond to a land mass, only then will the power of Ireland's imagined community come into its own.

Works cited

Augé, Marc. *Non-places: Introduction to an Anthropology of Supermodernity*. Trans. John Howe. London: Verso, 1995.

Bachelard, Gaston. *The Poetics of Space*. Trans. Maria Jolas. Boston: Beacon Press, 1969.

Barta, Peter. *Bely, Joyce and Döblin: Peripetics in the City Novel*. Gainesville: University of Florida Press, 1996.

Benjamin, Walter. "On Some Motifs in Baudelaire." *Illuminations: Essays and Reflections*. Ed. Hannah Arendt. Trans. Harry Zohn. New York: Schocken Books, 1969. 155–200.

Cheng, Vincent. *Joyce, Race, and Empire*. Cambridge: Cambridge University Press, 1995.

Day, Robert Adams. "Joyce's AquaCities." *Joyce in the Hibernian Metropolis: Essays*. Ed. Morris Beja and David Norris. Columbus: Ohio State University Press, 1996. 3–20.

Doyle, Arthur Conan. "The Blue Carbuncle." *Sherlock Holmes: Selected Stories*. London: Oxford University Press, 1951. 279–304.

Duffy, Enda. *The Subaltern "Ulysses."* Minneapolis: University of Minnesota Press, 1994.

Fanon, Franz. *The Wretched of the Earth*. Trans. Constance Farrington. New York: Grove Weidenfeld, 1963.

Foucault, Michel. "Of Other Spaces." Trans. Ian Miskowiec. *Diacritics* 19 (1986): 87–92.

Garvey, Johanna. "City Limits: Reading Gender and Urban Spaces in *Ulysses*." *Twentieth Century Literature* 41.1 (1995): 108–23.

Gellner, Ernest. "The Coming of Nationalism and its Interpretation: The Myths of Nation and Class." *Mapping the Nation*. Ed. Gopal Balakrishnan. London: Verso, 1996. 98–145.

Heidegger, Martin. "Building Dwelling Thinking." *Poetry, Language, Thought*. Trans. Albert Hofstadter. New York: Harper & Row, 1975. 143–61.

Herr, Cheryl. *Joyce's Anatomy of Culture*. Urbana: University of Illinois Press, 1986.

Hofheinz, Thomas C. *Joyce and the Invention of Irish History: "Finnegans Wake" in Context*. Cambridge: Cambridge University Press, 1995.

Hughes, Robert. *The Shock of the New*. New York: Alfred A. Knopf, 1991.

Jameson, Fredric. "Modernism and Imperialism." *Nationalism, Colonialism and Literature*. Ed. Terry Eagleton *et al*. Minneapolis: University of Minnesota Press, 1990. 43–66.

The Political Unconscious. Ithaca: Cornell University Press, 1981.

Kaplan, Karen. *Questions of Travel*. Minneapolis: University of Minnesota Press, 1997.

Kenner, Hugh. *Ulysses*. Baltimore: Johns Hopkins University Press, 1987.

Lefebvre, Henri. *The Production of Space*. Trans. Donald Nicholson-Smith. Oxford: Basil Blackwell, 1991.

Manganiello, Dominic. *Joyce's Politics*. London: Routledge & Kegan Paul, 1980.

Nolan, Emer. *James Joyce and Nationalism*. London: Routledge, 1995.

Simmel, Georg. "The Metropolis and Mental Life." *Images of Man: The Classical Tradition in Sociological Thinking*. Ed. C. Wright Mills. New York: George Braziller, 1960.

3

"Goodbye Ireland I'm going to Gort": geography, scale, and narrating the nation

MARJORIE HOWES

> This locality is more *around* temporality than *about* historicity: a form
> of living that is more complex than "community"; more symbolic
> than "society"; more connotative than "country"; less patriotic than
> *patrie*; more rhetorical than the reason of state; more mythological
> than ideology; less homogeneous than hegemony; less centred than
> the citizen; more collective than "the subject"; more psychic than
> civility; more hybrid in the articulation of cultural differences and
> identifications – gender, race or class – than can be represented in any
> hierarchical or binary structuring of social antagonism.   *Bhabha,*
> *"DissemiNation," 292*

> A nation is the same people living in the same place ... Or also living
> in different places.   *U 12.1422–28*

I

Geography has always had an important place in Irish political thinking, whether in British arguments for the inevitability of colonization, republican patriotism, unionism, moderate or militant nationalism. As Oliver MacDonagh has observed, "In one sense, the Irish problem has persisted because of the power of geographical images over men's minds" (*States of Mind*, 15). Irish studies shares with postcolonial studies an interest in the multifarious transactions between material and symbolic geographies that enable this wide range of discourses. My epigraphs organize the problematic of defining or narrating the nation around the confusions and complexities of place that arise from such transactions. Homi Bhabha claims that the nation is "a ubiquitous and obscure form of living the *locality* of culture" ("DissemiNation," 292) that can only be defined through a potentially endless recitation of what it is distinct from, yet related to. Leopold Bloom appeals to an apparent tautology whose central comparative term is missing – the "same people" – and whose spatial elements appear to cancel each other out: "the same place" or

"different places." There is a long tradition in Joyce scholarship of delin-
eating Joycean geographies (see, for example Seidel, *Epic Geography*)
and more recent critics have offered various fruitful approaches to the
issues surrounding the nation in Joyce's works (Cheng, *Joyce, Race, and
Empire*; Duffy, *The Subaltern "Ulysses"*; Nolan, *James Joyce and
Nationalism*; Kiberd, *Inventing Ireland*). Here I will argue that Joyce takes
up the issue of narrating the Irish nation in a kind of geographical representation that has received scant attention from either critical tradition.
These representations foreground spatial scales – the local, regional,
international – which are sometimes thought to represent alternatives to
the category and/or ideology of the nation.[1] In contrast, I will argue that
it is precisely through these alternative scales, and the opportunities and
obstacles they pose for imagining the scale of the national, that Joyce's
engagement with the problematic of the nation appears most vividly.

Although I will focus on "The Dead" and *A Portrait of the Artist as a
Young Man*, this particular geographical approach to narrating the nation
appears in *Ulysses* and *Finnegans Wake* as well. In "Cyclops," just after
Bloom utters his definition and the Citizen challenges his right to be
included in any conception of the Irish nation, Joe's handkerchief swells
into an "intricately embroidered ancient Irish facecloth" (*U* 12.1438–39).
The cloth parodies (among other things) a nationalist geography of
Ireland. It is inscribed with a diverse collection of places, some of which
would be natural fodder for nationalist sentimentalizing, like the lakes of
Killarney and Croagh Patrick. Others remind us of how colonialism
shaped Ireland, like the three birthplaces of the first Duke of Wellington
and Tullamore jail. The absurdity of still other places undercuts any
dream of an Irish nation that claims to encompass them, like Fingal's
Cave, which is actually in Scotland, and Kilballymachshonakill, which
isn't a place at all. One could read the cloth as an illustration of Joyce's
much-quoted claim in "Ireland, Island of Saints and Sages" that "our
civilization is a vast fabric, in which the most diverse elements are
mingled" (*CW* 165). But if the cloth represents the hybridity of the Irish
nation, it also indicates how persistently and thoroughly Joyce thought
through national issues in spatial and geographical terms.

If we focus on the geographical imagination at work here, its critique

---

[1] For a recent collection of essays in geography in which investigations of
regional particularity or international connection in Ireland often present themselves as critiques of the national, see Graham, ed., *In Search of Ireland*.

of naïve nationalist equations of the nation with its physical territory points in two related directions. On the one hand, the imagined community of the nation is far too complex and dispersed to be metaphorized as a space, with its suggestions of contiguity, wholeness, and fixed boundaries. On the other, the actual physical spaces over which nation-states exercise sovereignty are far too complicated to be analyzed solely through reference to that sovereignty, as integrated and natural national territories. One thing that is lacking in both cases is an appreciation of the importance of, and the relations among, different spatial scales. The nameless narrator of "Cyclops," who displays equal scorn for the conceptions of the nation offered by Bloom and the Citizen, brings up this issue when he announces his intention to step outside to urinate: "Goodbye Ireland I'm going to Gort" (*U* 12.1561). The usual form of this colloquial phrase is "Goodbye Dublin I'm going to Gort" (Gifford, *Ulysses Annotated*, 366). The narrator's humorous revision of it, which suggests that Gort somehow isn't "in" Ireland, is in keeping with the parody of nationalist geography on Joe's handkerchief. Gort lies in County Galway, near Augusta Gregory's Coole, and the phrase represents one of Joyce's many assertions that the idealized West offered by the cultural nationalism in which she was a central figure is not to be found anywhere in the real Ireland. It also crosses geographical movement westward, between two comparable material locations, with two other kinds of movement, from the scale of the national to a more local scale, and from the material to the metaphorical. Joyce's rendition of the problematics of narrating the nation repeatedly organizes itself around this combination.

While my epigraph from Bhabha's influential essay appears to insist on the specificity of locality, the essay displays the tendency common to much postcolonial and poststructuralist work to employ a myriad of spatial metaphors but to treat the materiality of space as fairly transparent and unproblematic. Bhabha approaches the complexity of the nation, metaphorized consistently, though not exclusively, as the "space of the nation" (Bhabha, "DissemiNation," 303), through time, most notably in his widely cited articulation of the contradictory "double-time" of the nation (297). Bhabha wants to show that "the space of the modern nation-people is never simply horizontal" (293), to investigate its "irredeemably plural modern space" (300), and his theoretical vocabulary of terms like "enunciatory position" (298), "space of cultural signification" (299), and the "site of writing" (297) relies heavily on spatial metaphors.

At the same time, the essay often characterizes the conceptions of the nation it critiques as forms of spatial thinking that naïvely equate people, territory, and nation. The crude, and crudely spatial, conception of the nation is disarticulated through an analysis of the complexities of temporality. Thus while narrating the nation is rendered wonderfully, helpfully problematic, the materiality of national space and the category of space itself remain fairly inert, naturalized, and abstract.

Neil Smith's *Uneven Development* offers a useful counterexample which approaches the complex materiality of space through scale. For Smith, space is "deep space," which is "the space of everyday life in all its scales from the global to the local . . . quintessentially social space" (160–61). He argues that geographical space, including nature itself, is produced in a particular way under capitalism; uneven development is the "geographical expression of the contradictions of capital" (152). Uneven development is organized through the "continual determination and internal differentiation of spatial scale" (136). Each scale – the urban, the nation-state, and the global – is determined as "an integrated space-economy" (135–36), a geographical unit which represents an identifiable and separate scale of social activity. At the same time, it is also subject to internal differentiation and shaped by its relation to larger scales, factors which both enable and threaten each scale's drive towards realizing itself as "absolute space." This contradictory structure in which the drive towards equalization and the drive towards differentiation confront each other at various scales is the central feature of the production of space under capitalism, and the contradictions of capitalism appear in the problematic doubleness assigned to scale.

Bhabha's and Smith's approaches are complementary. Together they suggest ways of examining relationships that are at the center of the problematic of the nation: relationships between material and metaphorical space, and between capitalist modernity and the modernity of the nation. A number of scholars have argued that Ireland's entry into a specifically colonial modernity was especially traumatic and uneven (Hechter, *Internal Colonialism*; Gibbons, *Transformations*; Eagleton, *Heathcliff and the Great Hunger*, 273–319). However "belated" Joyce might find the Irish (*CW* 70), colonial Ireland was not simply backward or underdeveloped in relation to Britain, whatever one might mean by that. Instead, through colonial intervention, it became a disorienting mixture of the archaic and the modern. The beginnings of the economic and social transformations of the nineteenth century – the extermination of the cottier class, the rise of the strong farmer, the establishment of high rates of celibacy and late marriage age, the hemorrhage of emigration – preceded the Great Famine of the 1840s. But they were greatly accelerated by it, and the Famine constituted, among other things, a sudden, disastrous, and incomplete transition to modernity, especially in agricultural production and the social organization of rural life. If the relative indifference and ineptness with which the British handled the catastrophe of the Famine provided one source of the juxtaposition between the archaic and the modern, a highly modernized state apparatus and a willingness to intervene in Irish society provided another. Historians have often argued that Britain treated Ireland as a "social laboratory in which Englishmen were prepared to conduct experiments in government which contemporary opinion at home was not prepared to tolerate" (Lyons, *Ireland Since the Famine*, 74). Ireland had a national school system before England did, and, as Terry Eagleton observes, "[by] 1850, Ireland had one of the most commercially advanced agricultures in the world, and was fast developing one of the world's densest railway systems" (*Heathcliff and the Great Hunger*, 274).

Thus the uneven development that expresses the contradictions of European capitalist modernity was especially acute in Ireland. Some of Benedict Anderson's work since *Imagined Communities* offers a way of tying the material geography of uneven development to the rise of specifically national forms of consciousness and culture. Anderson metaphorizes the displacements of modernity – geographical and otherwise – as forms of exile. He argues that in the nineteenth century the migration of populations, the standardization of print languages, and the establishment of national school systems represented forms of exile from local origins and affiliations, and that nationalism constituted a compensatory "project for coming home from exile" ("Exodus," 319). It was "the essential nexus of long-distance transportation and print capitalist communications" (316), a nexus that was well developed in largely pre-industrial Ireland, rather than industrialization *per se*, that first prepared the ground for the rise of nationalism. For Anderson's exile, geographical movement (and the other displacements for which it stands in) provokes a nostalgia for a local scale which is eased when the individual transfers some of his or her energies and affections upwards, to the scale of the national: "It was beginning to become possible to see 'English fields' in England – from the window of a railway carriage" (318). Anderson's theory fits well with the long-standing observation of historians that modern Irish nationalism took hold first in the modernizing, relatively prosperous agricultural regions and small towns that experienced these changes earlier than the poor and underdeveloped Gaeltacht (Boyce, *Nationalism in Ireland*). However, because Ireland's modernization was inextricably bound up with the uneven development of colonialism, highly modernized communications and transportation systems, and the forms of exile they generated, occurred in conjunction with archaic or residual social, economic, and cultural formations. In addition, emigration, the decline of the Irish language and the imperial origin of national schools were traumatic, much discussed, and specifically colonial issues. And the nationalisms that emerged were revolutionary rather than state nationalisms. Both materially and symbolically, the specifically colonial nature of Ireland's capitalist modernity helped produce a national imaginary related to but distinct from European statist nationalism.

In nineteenth-century Ireland, the transfer of loyalties to a national scale was an uncertain and incomplete process, and other supposedly regressive responses to the exilic dislocations of modernity were available. For example, part of Daniel O'Connell's unprecedented success in mobilizing and nationalizing the Irish masses was due to his genius for tapping into specifically local grievances and loyalties and tying them to a nationalist project. At the same time, however, he worked hard to discourage the agrarian disturbances and secret societies whose motives and targets were regional rather than national, and which were an attempt to enforce the traditional social and economic structures and values that were being destroyed by agricultural modernization (MacDonagh, *The Hereditary Bondsman*; *The Emancipist*). The notion of a "transfer" is itself somewhat misleading; local issues and affiliations operated simultaneously within a wider national framework without necessarily ceasing to be (problematically) local (Gibbons, *Transformations*, 134–48). With this caveat, Smith's attention to the complex materiality of geographical space and Anderson's metaphorical use of geographical movement demonstrate, in very different ways, that the national is to be grasped most fully in its relation to other scales, rather than in opposition to them. Both differ from the standard observations that some nationalisms are more cosmopolitan or more respectful of regional and local difference than others because they insist that these other scales are structurally, simultaneously, both necessary and inimical to the national.

Seamus Deane has acutely observed that Joyce's civilization was "the civilization of Catholic Dublin, related to but distinct from that of Catholic Ireland" (Deane, "Joyce the Irishman," 40), and much current Joyce scholarship understandably focuses on Joyce's Dublin as exemplary of Ireland's uneven development or the relationship between the national and more local scales (Jameson, "*Ulysses* in History"; Duffy, *The Subaltern "Ulysses,"* 53–92; Leerssen, *Remembrance and Imagination*, 224–31; Fairhall, *Joyce and the Question of History*, 64–79). Certainly, during the nineteenth century Dublin underwent various forms of industrial decline that made equating progress, modernity, and urban life impossible, and well into the twentieth century the city experienced massive backwardness in terms of housing and public health in comparison to other cities in the United Kingdom (O'Brien, *Dear, Dirty Dublin*). But Dublin's incomplete and uneven colonial modernity had a counterpart in what we might call the perverse modernity of the Irish countryside. Rural villages in post-Famine Ireland were not modern anonymous collectivities. But they were also not the kind of totalizable, knowable, face-to-face community that some scholars associate with precapitalist forms of social life. The main reasons for this were Ireland's uniquely high rate of emigration, driven in part by agricultural modernization, mostly (during this period) to the United States, and the specific cultural meanings attached to emigration in Irish culture. Every village, virtually every family, had sons, daughters, or other relatives over the water. They remained absent yet active members of the community – they wrote letters, sent money home, financed the emigration of siblings or other relatives, and followed events in Ireland through the Irish-American press. The anthropologists Arensberg and Kimball observe that often many members of the same family or village emigrated to the same place, even over several generations, a practice that forged lasting international connections with specific foreign localities. These diasporic relations between emigrants and those at home were quite continuous with local affiliations; they were "part of the general 'friendliness' by which the Irish countryman sums up the family obligations" (*Family and Community*, 144) and were expressed in the same terms. There were also various uniquely Irish cultural traditions organized around the departures of emigrants, many of whom viewed themselves as unwilling exiles, such as American wakes, the all-night parties resembling wakes that were often held before a boat sailed (Miller, *Emigrants and Exiles*, 556–68). The sheer size of the international Irish diaspora and its intimate incorporation into everyday social and cultural life in Ireland meant that rural communities did not coincide with the local territories they occupied. We might call them communities of mourning or melancholy, or see in them something resembling an Irish Atlantic.[2]

The ambiguous modernity of rural Ireland and the concomitant porousness of local and regional geographical scales posed a problem for the cultural nationalism that appropriated the Irish countryside, and especially the West of Ireland, symbolically, as an ahistorical and antimodern repository of Irishness. In many ways a bourgeois, modernizing movement, cultural nationalism sought less to return to or recreate this version of the West than to unify the Irish people around the idea of its (safely distanced and enclosed, both temporally and geographically) worth. In Joyce's works, the geographical mode of inscribing the problematic of the nation that I am tracing centers on characters like Gabriel Conroy and Stephen Dedalus, who reject the conventional forms of national belonging offered to them by cultural nationalism only to find themselves drawn in some manner into alternative narratives of the nation. The narrator of "Cyclops" is, in a minor way, another such figure. This paradigm is well-established in Joyce studies, and represents a dominant view of Joyce himself. Here I will try to show that Joyce organizes his alternative narratives of the nation around a series of distinctions enabled by the recognition of rural Ireland's perverse partial modernity: material versus metaphorical geographical movement, the complex materialities of spatial scales versus their symbolic appropriation or metaphorization, and movement over space versus movement from one scale to another.

II

"The Dead's" much-debated engagement with questions of national ideology and community is organized around two related regions – the West of Ireland and "that region where dwell the vast hosts of the dead" (*Dubliners*, 224) – and their crucial, ambiguous role in the versions of the national to which various Dubliners subscribe. Much of the story does what the imagination of the cultural nationalism Joyce overtly scorned

---

[2] Paul Gilroy's *The Black Atlantic* offers a model that is suggestive for the Irish experience, though of course it is by no means strictly analogous to it.

also did: merge the two regions into one, a conflation that Joep Leerssen has described as "one of the dominant modes of nineteenth-century Celticism" (*Remembrance and Imagination*,188). Each region represents something that Gabriel feels able to reject or master early in the story, but that threatens to overwhelm him at its close. Gabriel's resolution not to "linger on the past" (*Dubliners*, 205) in his speech gives way to his help-less subordination to the dead, and he resists the critical but flirtatious Molly Ivors' invitation to "come for an excursion to the Aran Isles" (189), only to "swoon" (225) before the ominous seductions of another "journey westward" (225), this one associated with Gretta and Michael Furey. Gabriel's self-conscious cosmopolitanism is, in Bernard Benstock's words, "mere window-dressing" (*Undiscover'd Country*, 5); in his worship of things foreign, Gabriel is simply the last and most sympa-thetic in a series of provincial Dubliners. Molly looks west, Gabriel looks east, and they are linked through their competing versions of Irish pro-vincialism, as well as through their commensurate educations, profes-sions, and superior intellectual status (in Gabriel's mind, at any rate).[3]

Molly's nationalism and Gabriel's cosmopolitanism represent equally undesirable relations to the national. Much critical debate has revolved around what Emer Nolan calls "a revivalist sub-text" in the story (*James Joyce and Nationalism*, 29), which raises the question of what, if any, alternative relation to the national Gabriel establishes or is forced into by his "journey westward." Nolan's provocative reading of "The Dead" incorporates a number of competing interpretations by appealing to formulations of the nation's doubleness suggested by Anderson and Bhabha. She argues, following Anderson, that Gabriel's final epiphany represents both death and immersion in the community because it is the job of nationalism to transform mortality into continuity (36). Nolan also asserts that readings which claim that Gabriel capitu-lates to the communal or Irish lures of the West and those that claim he achieves a self-realization that isolates him from any larger community are in fact complementary because "national belonging is an enabling illusion for individuals who, in spite of it, live in real social isolation"

---

[3] The text emphasizes the parallels between Gabriel and Molly in this passage: "He wanted to say that literature was above politics. But they were friends of many years' standing and their careers had been parallel, first at the University, and then as teachers: he could not risk a grandiose phrase with her" (*Dubliners*, 188), marking an obvious contrast to the superiority Gabriel feels in relation to all the other guests.

(34). Gabriel's "intensely solitary, but yet shared experience" (36) is his incorporation into the community-in-anonymity of the nation, symbolized by the reference to the unifying snow in the newspapers, one of the cultural forms that Anderson uses to exemplify the homogeneous, empty, clock-time of the modern nation.

Nolan's reading synthesizes elements in the ending that had often appeared as alternatives to critics: death and continuity, isolation and national belonging, the West as social or literal death and the West as Ireland. She focuses on Gabriel, while other analyses emphasize that the West signifies a diverse and even conflicting constellation of entities and concepts for different characters. Luke Gibbons suggests that "The Dead" presents a struggle, which Joyce outlined in his 1907 essay on Fenianism (*CW* 188), between two competing forms of nationalism: constitutional nationalism and a "dissident, insurrectionary tradition" (Gibbons, *Transformations*, 146). This struggle is "articulated through the competing strategies of the newspaper, and the popular ballad" (146); the former is allied with Gabriel's symbolic appropriation of the West, the latter with "The Lass of Aughrim" and the meanings the song and the West have for Gretta. In a similar vein, Cóilín Owens claims that "To Gretta [the West] is that which she can never recover; to Gabriel, it is that which he can never know; to the reader it is a radically ambiguous symbol of the differences between Gretta's and Gabriel's temperaments, and of the differences between Gaelic Ireland as a cultural ideal and the impossibility of a reconciliation between it and the 'thought-tormented age' into which modern, urban, bourgeois Ireland is being assimilated" (Owens, "The Mystique of the West," 84–85).

Nolan, Gibbons, and Owens all read the West as embodying the national, whether as a vehicle of reconciliation or of division. But there is another, related set of ambiguities surrounding the West in "The Dead," one that is organized through competing geographical scales and the perverse modernity of rural Ireland. This set of ambiguities resists the conflation of the West with the dead. To the aporias about what the West *means*, the text adds a related series of uncertainties about what it *is* as a physical region. Joyce crosses the complexities of the movement over space – the journey westward – with the problem of scale in defining the region that represents the destination. The West is a shifting, semimodern, marginal set of regions that both enables and defies the fantasies that Gabriel, Molly, and Gretta construct, and the text carefully renders it ambiguous in geographical and scalar terms.

Molly combines her invitation to the Aran Isles with an observation about Gretta's origins: "She's from Connacht, isn't she?" (*Dubliners*, 189). Voicing her enthusiasm for the trip, Gretta says "I'd love to see Galway again" (191). Terence Brown's note to Gretta's remark comments, "Presumably she means Galway city, the principal city of County Galway and of the province of Connacht" (311). The slippage in these exchanges between the particular places and geographical scales that stand in for the West – a set of islands, a city, a county, a province – gives the West a physical ambiguity which is related but not reducible to its symbolic richness. Other elements of the story give the region a further geographical complexity. Michael Furey's people live in Oughterard, a small village seventeen miles north of Galway city, and he works in the gasworks of Galway city, a typical rural–urban migrant in a semideveloped region. Gretta lived in a district of Galway city called Nuns' Island, which suggests both the inner differentiation of the city-scale and a Catholic alternative to supposedly pagan, primitive Aran. And, as Vincent J. Cheng has argued, the town of Aughrim in County Galway evokes two catastrophic Irish military defeats in the face of British imperialism: the Battle of the Boyne and the Battle of Aughrim (*Joyce, Race, and Empire*, 143–44). Various private and public histories – imperial, industrial, romantic, nationalist – are embedded in competing scales and geographies.

Five years later, Joyce again combines a consideration of the West's relation to the past and the dead with an analysis of its ambiguous and uneven modernity. In his 1912 essay on Galway, he begins by invoking the ideas, which he describes as both right and wrong, of "the lazy Dubliner, who travels little and knows his country only by hearsay" (*CW* 229), and who thinks of Galway as the exotic "Spanish city." Joyce goes on to offer his own blend of fantasy and reality, lamenting the city's decline from a vibrant international trading center and cultural contact zone to its current isolated, decaying modernity: "Outside the city walls rise the suburbs – new, gay, and heedless of the past, but you have only to close your eyes to this bothersome modernity for a moment to see in the twilight of history the 'Spanish city'" (229). What we might call the true modernity of Galway, with its surprising and energizing contradictions and juxtapositions of the archaic and the modern, regional particularity and international connection, in contrast to its current backward modernity, Joyce finds in a sixteenth century travel narrative, "in which the writer says that, although he had travelled throughout the world, he had never seen in a single glance what he saw in Galway – a priest elevating the Host, a pack chasing a deer, a ship entering the harbour under full sail, and a salmon being killed with a spear" (230).

One might be tempted to read the inclusion of so many actual western locations in "The Dead" as an instance of the kind of Joycean referential mapping that means, for example, that contemporary readers who visit Dublin can retrace Lenehan's walk in "Two Gallants" and that the route and landmarks of this walk assemble a fairly coherent set of references to English domination, or that Leopold Bloom and Stephen Dedalus can be read as versions of the *flâneur* (Duffy, *The Subaltern "Ulysses,"* 53–92; Wills, "Joyce, Prostitution, and the Colonial City"). In contrast, the point in "The Dead," with its emphasis on different scales, rather than on streets, buildings, and monuments, is to portray the region as rich, problematic deep space, rather than to define it as something readily mappable or easily traversable. The West as Molly's Aran may be that clichéd embodiment of Irishness worshipped by cultural nationalism. But Gretta's reference to Galway, which introduces a tension between the city and the county, is ambiguous; it signifies cultural nationalism's idea of the primitive rural heartland, the perverse modernity of its material space, an idealized, cosmopolitan past for the "Spanish city," and the backwardness of Ireland's industrial centers.

Taken together, these references to different material features of the region's uneven modernity, embodied in different geographical scales, both multiply the possible nationalist appropriations of the West and highlight the obstacles that the area in question presents for them. Similarly, the last paragraph of "The Dead" accomplishes the unifying, symbolic journey westward, but at the same time it suggests a material journey by including the "dark central plain," "the treeless hills," and the "Bog of Allen" (*Dubliners*, 225), all of which belong to the supposedly uninspiring midlands that travelers from Dublin to the West must cross. Joseph Valente has suggested that Gabriel's failure of vision at the end of "The Dead" springs from "his inability to identify with *the otherness* of the other" ("Cosmopolitan Sublime," 73) and his penchant for revivalist myth-making, arguing that the primitive and self-immolating Michael Furey is not an alternative to such myth-making but a symptom of it (69–73). Furthermore, Gabriel is "humiliated" (*Dubliners*, 220), not simply by Furey's romantic, archaic death, but by the contrast between that death and Furey's mundane, modern working life.[4] The conflict Joyce stages between the symbolically freighted journey westward and the material, geographical ambiguities of its destination indicates that the real otherness of the other is symbolized, not by the fiery depths of Furey's passionate heart, but by the flames of the gasworks where he earned his living.

III

In *A Portrait of the Artist as a Young Man*, Stephen, like Gabriel, rejects conventional Irish nationalism and finds himself engaging with an ambiguous and sometimes threatening alternative mode of narrating the nation. Rather than emphasizing the scalar ambiguities of the West or the local as material regions, *A Portrait* highlights the role different conceptions of scale play in different versions of the nation. And instead of focusing primarily on a largely symbolic journey to the West, *A Portrait*'s analysis of the impulses and obstacles to the formation of Stephen's national consciousness foregrounds the importance of his mundane travels between home and school. Stephen is a complex version of Anderson's exile, struggling with competing ways of transforming the local affiliations he has lost into membership in a national community. This process depends upon two major factors: first, Stephen's geographical movement, other displacements, and the homesickness they produce, and, second, fantasized but threatening constructions of rural Ireland.

Early in the novel, Stephen, unable to learn the geography lesson that maps the spatial divisions of the New World in straightforward topographical terms – through "the names of places in America" (*A Portrait*, 12) – thinks about a different conception of space. In the flyleaf of his geography book he has written:

---

[4] His exchange with Gretta makes this clear:
  – He is dead, she said at length. He died when he was only seventeen. Isn't it a terrible thing to die so young as that?
  – What was he? asked Gabriel, still ironically.
  – He was in the gasworks, she said.
    Gabriel felt humiliated by the failure of his irony and by the evocation of this figure from the dead, a boy in the gasworks. (*Dubliners*, 221)

> Stephen Dedalus
> Class of Elements
> Clongowes Wood College
> Sallins
> County Kildare
> Ireland
> Europe
> The World
> The Universe (12)

Stephen's alternative geography involves an extensive but incomplete list of different scales; he wonders "What was after the universe?" (13). It also signifies one potential avenue for Stephen's incorporation into a conventional nationalist community. Stephen's list of scales does not include Great Britain; instead he places Ireland in Europe. His formulation offers a model of the relations among scales as orderly and commensurate, with each scale neatly enfolding the smaller ones, something it has in common with the explicitly nationalist verse that Fleming has written on the opposite page:

> *Stephen Dedalus is my name,*
> *Ireland is my nation.*
> *Clongowes is my dwellingplace*
> *And heaven my expectation.* (13)

Fleming's verse harmonizes the individual and national scales through a narrative of salvation that links the individual's affiliation with the national – his recognition of Ireland as his nation – with a projected movement from home – his dwelling place – to heaven. Both inscriptions figure the individual climbing the geographical scales from himself to the Irish nation (and beyond) according to the dictates of conventional nationalism.

This process takes place at school, and is catalyzed by the kinds of exile school represents. Torn from his home, which is associated with the maternal and the local, Stephen is encouraged to transfer his loyalties to the protonationalist male community who express their resentment of authority through a parody of insurrection: "Let us get up a rebellion, Fleming said. Will we?" (44). As critics have often noted, this change involves his incorporation into a related set of discourses succinctly described by Vicky Mahaffey as "the necessity of homosocial bonding, homophobia, and misogyny" (Mahaffey, "Père-version and Im-mère-sion," 124). The fact that there is no right answer to the question "Do you kiss your mother before you go to bed?"[5] indicates that local affiliations are both mandated and forbidden by nationalism; they acquire a problematic doubleness or ambivalence, the experience of which binds the members of the national community together. Stephen is interpellated into the community, not by answering correctly, which is impossible, but by "try[ing] to laugh with them" (11) at his own newly created discomfort with his maternal origins.

The forms of transportation that brought Stephen to school – trains and hired cars – figure heavily in the first chapter of *A Portrait*, and are associated with his feelings of exile. When Stephen feels that he is "sick in his heart if you could be sick in that place" he consoles himself by alternately covering and uncovering his ears, comparing the resulting auditory changes to those that occur when a train enters and leaves a tunnel (10). They are also connected with the vehicle that enables Stephen simultaneously to reject and reconstitute his local, maternal loyalties as part of his membership in a nationalist community: a fantasized construction of rural Ireland. This fantasy revolves around a vision of the women another boy has seen in the village of Clane "as the cars had come past from Sallins" on the way to Clongowes: "he had seen a woman standing at the halfdoor of a cottage with a child in her arms" (15). Stephen finds the rural Ireland they represent both appealing and frightening. While he thinks "It would be lovely to sleep for one night in that cottage before the fire of smoking turf," he also feels afraid, and his fear focuses on the road that enables his transportation from home to school, from the local to the national, by way of such rural areas: "But, O, the road there between the trees was dark!" (15). The roads, signs of rural Ireland's perverse modernity, of Stephen's exile from home, and of his partial return home via national identification, are dark and threatening because they do not resolve the conflicts of scale, between the local/maternal and the national, that they initiate.

Such resolution is only possible at a further remove of fantasy, in the context of imagined rather than actual geographical movement homeward. Anticipating the holidays, Stephen imagines the cars carrying him past the same emblematic women at Clane, and the journey creates an image of community through geographical movement:

[5] I do not agree with those critics (for example, Williams, *Reading Joyce Politically*, 106–7) who claim that "I do not" would have been a correct initial answer; when Stephen does give that answer, it is wrong.

> The cars drove past the chapel and all caps were raised. They drove merrily
> along the country roads. The drivers pointed with their whips to Bodenstown.
> The fellows cheered. They passed the farmhouse of the Jolly Farmer. Cheer
> after cheer after cheer. Through Clane they drove, cheering and cheered. The
> peasant women stood at the halfdoors, the men stood here and there.   (17)

Bodenstown is where Wolfe Tone is buried, and in his note to this passage
Deane speculates that the drivers are pointing their whips towards his
grave (282). This vision includes the peasant women of Clane, but their
threat has been neutralized, the drive is merry, and the nationalist community is based more on the reciprocal (masculine) cheering and the unifying memory of a nationalist hero than on the attractive but disturbing
female figures.

The topographical geography that the exiled Stephen rejects in favor of
an ambiguous journey from the local to the national scale is allied with the
stridently anti-Parnellite Dante: "A little boy had been taught geography
by an old woman who kept two brushes in her wardrobe. Then he had been
sent away from home to a college" (98). It also displays imperialism's preoccupation with the mapping and territorial conquest of exotic places:
"She had taught him where the Mozambique Channel was and what was
the longest river in America and what was the name of the highest moun-
tain in the moon" (7). Of course, a major lesson of Stephen's actual visit
home (and of chapter 1 generally) is that nationalist politics are more about
division and ambivalence than they are about the kind of cheery, unproblematic unity figured in Stephen's imagined journey. In addition, Stephen
later rejects the nationalism fostered at schools and other institutions while
groping his way towards some alternative exilic relation to the Irish nation.

When an older Stephen contemplates his ambivalent relation to the
category and ideology of the nation – his rejection of nationalism, his
separation from the national community, his desire to learn "the hidden
ways of Irish life" (196) and to "hit their conscience" (259) to help revive
his nation – his imagination returns to the women of Clane, now remembered in the context of his own geographical movement, and associated
with the woman who tries to seduce Davin:

> The last words of Davin's story sang in his memory and the figure of the
> woman in the story stood forth, reflected in other figures of the peasant women
> whom he had seen standing in the doorways at Clane as the college cars drove
> by, as a type of her race and his own, a batlike soul waking to the consciousness
> of itself in darkness and secrecy and loneliness and, through the eyes and voice
> and gesture of a woman without guile, calling the stranger to her bed.   (198)

It has become possible for Stephen to see the "peasant women" of villages like Clane as representatively Irish figures and himself as part
(however problematically) of the national community they embody –
from the window of a car or train. His conflation of these women and
Ireland consistently involves versions of a contrast between a stationary
rural woman and a traveling man: "A woman had waited in the doorway
as Davin had passed by at night" (259). Stephen's actual travel through
the space of rural Ireland has helped him produce an imaginary and
specifically national geography, in which a national male subject performs the integration of the local into the national by his movement
through space and his symbolic appropriation of the peasant women as
national types.

But the country roads that link rural and urban areas, carry the displaced into exile, and create the modern, traveling national subject continue to frighten Stephen: "I fear many things: dogs, horses, firearms, the
sea, thunderstorms, machinery, the country roads at night" (264). The
processes they represent are ambiguous and incomplete; Stephen cannot
complete a "project for coming home from exile" (Anderson, "Exodus,"
319) by embracing a national scale and narrative. The other regions and
scales such a narrative seeks to integrate are not as commensurate as
Stephen once believed. As in "The Dead," the West emerges as both necessary and recalcitrant to a national narrative, a problematic embodied in
a different representatively Irish figure: the Irish-speaking old man with
red eyes. Critics usually assume that the old man represents the cultural
nationalist ideal of primitive Irishness that Joyce rejected. But he also
signifies an alternative, and problematic, conception of scale to match
Stephen's ambivalent alternative to conventional nationalism:
"Mulrennan spoke to him about universe and stars. Old man sat, listened,
smoked, spat. Then said: – Ah, there must be terrible queer creatures at
the latter end of the world" (274). Mulrennan's remarks, so to speak, give
the old man a chance to repeat Stephen's earlier trip up-scale from his
own individual being, through the nation to the universe. But the old
man refuses, and his reply figures space in terms of immense, mythic
geographical distance and utter alienation, rather than in terms of
linkage and commensurability. What the young Stephen, along with
conventional nationalism, imagined as a progression of ever-widening
frameworks, each one neatly enclosing the smaller ones, has become the
radical incommensurability of scales. Like the country roads, the old
man represents something that is both enabling and crippling for a

74

national narrative, and, like them, he is ambiguous and threatening. Stephen's initial claim, "I fear him" (274), and his conclusion that he means the old man "no harm" (274), indicate that his famous resolution to narrate the Irish nation, to forge in the smithy of his soul the uncreated conscience of his race, must incorporate or acknowledge these contradictory elements.

Both Gabriel and Stephen fail to arrive at coherent visions of the Irish nation or, more precisely, arrive at visions of the nation notable for their ambiguity, in part because the real rural landscape both supports and resists the imagined national geography they attempt to project on to it. The material geographies of Ireland's uneven development, and their various possible relationships with imaginative appropriations of space, form a basis for Joyce's critique of cultural nationalism as well as for his alternative narratives of the nation. Both "The Dead" and *A Portrait* combine a focus on the materiality of space and physical journeys with an investigation of the metaphorical uses of geographical movements, regions, and scales. They figure versions of the "double-time" of the nation, not by simply metaphorizing the nation as a space, but by teasing out the complex relations between metaphorical and material space, between the Gorts that are in Ireland, and the Gorts that aren't.

Works cited

Anderson, Benedict, "Exodus." *Critical Inquiry* 20 (1994): 314–27.
  Imagined Communities: Reflections on the Origin and Spread of Nationalism.
    London: Verso, 1991.
Arensberg, Conrad M., and Solon T. Kimball. *Family and Community in Ireland.*
    1940. Cambridge, Mass.: Harvard University Press, 1968.
Benstock, Bernard. *James Joyce: The Undiscover'd Country.* New York: Barnes
    & Noble, 1977.
Bhabha, Homi. "DissemiNation." *Nation and Narration.* Ed. Homi Bhabha.
    London: Routledge, 1990.
Boyce, D. George. *Nationalism in Ireland.* London: Routledge, 1991 (1982).
Cheng, Vincent J. *Joyce, Race, and Empire.* Cambridge: Cambridge University
    Press, 1995.
Deane, Seamus. "Joyce the Irishman." *The Cambridge Companion to James
    Joyce.* Ed. Derek Attridge. Cambridge: Cambridge University Press,
    1990. 31–54.
Duffy, Enda. *The Subaltern "Ulysses."* Minneapolis: University of Minnesota
    Press, 1994.
Eagleton, Terry. *Heathcliff and the Great Hunger: Studies in Irish Culture.*
    London: Verso, 1995.

Fairhall, James. *James Joyce and the Question of History*. Cambridge: Cambridge University Press, 1993.

Gibbons, Luke. *Transformations in Irish Culture*. Cork: Cork University Press, 1996.

Gifford, Don. *Ulysses Annotated*. Berkeley: University of California Press, 1988.

Gilroy, Paul. *The Black Atlantic: Modernity and Double Consciousness*. Cambridge, Mass.: Harvard University Press, 1993.

Graham, Brian, ed. *In Search of Ireland: A Cultural Geography*. London: Routledge, 1997.

Hechter, Michael. *Internal Colonialism: The Celtic Fringe in British National Development*. Berkeley: University of California Press, 1975.

Jameson, Fredric. "*Ulysses* in History." *James Joyce and Modern Literature*. Ed. W. J. McCormack and Alistair Stead. London: Routledge & Kegan Paul, 1982. 126–41.

Joyce, James. *Dubliners*. New York: Penguin, 1993.

  A Portrait of the Artist as a Young Man. New York: Penguin, 1976.

Kiberd, Declan. *Inventing Ireland*. Cambridge, Mass.: Harvard University Press, 1996.

Leerssen, Joep. *Remembrance and Imagination: Patterns in the Historical and Literary Representation of Ireland in the Nineteenth Century*. Cork: Cork University Press, 1996.

Lyons, F. S. L. *Ireland Since the Famine*. 1971. London: Fontana, 1982.

MacDonagh, Oliver. *The Emancipist: Daniel O'Connell, 1830–47*. New York: St. Martin's Press, 1989.

  The Hereditary Bondsman: Daniel O'Connell, 1775–1829. London: Weidenfeld & Nicolson, 1988.

  States of Mind: A Study of Anglo-Irish Conflict, 1780–1980. London: Allen & Unwin, 1983.

Mahaffey, Vicki. "Père-version and Im-mère-sion: Idealized Corruption in *A Portrait of the Artist as a Young Man* and *The Picture of Dorian Gray*." *Quare Joyce*. Ed. Joseph Valente. Ann Arbor: University of Michigan Press, 1998. 121–38.

Miller, Kerby. *Emigrants and Exiles: Ireland and the Irish Exodus to North America*. Oxford: Oxford University Press, 1985.

Nolan, Emer, *James Joyce and Nationalism*. London: Routledge, 1995.

O'Brien, Joseph V. *Dear, Dirty Dublin: A City in Distress, 1899–1916*. Berkeley: University of California Press, 1982.

Owens, Cóilín. "The Mystique of the West in Joyce's 'The Dead.'" *Irish University Review* 22.1 (spring 1992): 80–91.

Seidel, Michael. *Epic Geography: James Joyce's "Ulysses."* Princeton: Princeton University Press, 1976.

Smith, Neil. *Uneven Development: Nature, Capital and the Production of Space*. Oxford: Basil Blackwell, 1984.

Valente, Joseph. "James Joyce and the Cosmopolitan Sublime." *Joyce and the Subject of History*. Ed. Mark A. Wollaeger, Victor Luftig, and Robert Spoo. Ann Arbor: University of Michigan Press, 1996. 59–82.

Williams, Trevor. *Reading Joyce Politically*. Gainesville: University of Florida Press, 1997.

Wills, Clair. "Joyce, Prostitution, and the Colonial City." *Ireland and Irish Cultural Studies*. Ed. John Paul Waters. Special issue of *South Atlantic Quarterly* 95.1 (winter 1996): 79–96.

4

State of the art: Joyce and postcolonialism

EMER NOLAN

"I cannot," Joyce told Nora Barnacle, "enter the social order except as a vagabond."[1] Joyce's evident hostility towards all political state forma-tions – including both the British state in Ireland, and the twenty-six county independent Irish state which emerged after 1922 – has long been acknowledged but seldom articulated with much analytical force. This situation has changed in recent times as critics such as Luke Gibbons and more especially David Lloyd have addressed the question of Joyce's rejection of anticolonial nationalism and of the state. Their analyses are clearly influenced by (among others) Fanon and the Indian Subaltern Studies group.[2] This account of Joyce, as we shall see, offers a powerful theoretical framework for the increasingly widespread view of Joyce as a postcolonial writer.[3] I will initially be concerned with an explication of this notion of Joyce "against the state," and with some of the conse-quences this has for Irish cultural theory and for postcolonial criticism.

All nationalists, it can be argued, seek to attain or control state power.[4] But the universalist claims of the modern liberal state create a contradic-tion for the exponents of anticolonial nationalism. For, in embracing the modern state form, nationalists demand an end to what Partha Chatterjee calls "the rule of colonial difference": the state should be culture-blind just as it should be color-blind – all its citizens must be treated as equals.[5] In this, nationalism demands that the colonial state be transformed so that the ethnic or sectarian differences upon which it is founded are abolished and replaced by the principles of equality that legitimate the normalizing mission of the modern state. But, as in India, nationalism's claim for state power is generally posited on spiritual *difference* from (and superiority to)

[1] Letter from Joyce to Barnacle, 1904. Quoted by Manganiello, *Joyce's Politics*, 218.
[2] See Gibbons, "Identity Without a Centre," and Lloyd, "Adulteration and the Nation" (in *Anomalous States*) and "Nationalisms Against the State."
[3] See, for example, Cheng, *Joyce, Race, and Empire,* and Duffy, *The Subaltern "Ulysses."*   [4] See Breuilly, *Nationalism and the State*, 1–2.
[5] See Chatterjee, *The Nation and its Fragments*, 10.

imperial or Western culture. The private, spiritual, or inner realm – this anticolonial version of civil society – indeed constitutes anticolonial nationalism's "own domain of sovereignty within colonial society" (Chatterjee, *The Nation and its Fragments*, 6).

But this inner realm must be defined and molded by the largely bourgeois élites who are generally the leaders of nationalist opinion. They face the task of unifying the disparate "subaltern" groups (such as women, peasants, and outcasts) who typify this spiritual sphere – in Chatterjee's words, "the fragments of the nation." Their discrete stories and struggles are in effect co-opted by the nationalists, and ultimately absorbed into the essentially bourgeois history of state-directed nationalism. Such subaltern groups and their histories recede from the official narrative of nationalist history and are consigned to being no more than the irrational cultural substrate of the rationalizing modern state. The task of the radical postcolonial historian or critic, according to Chatterjee and the "Subaltern" school of Indian historiography, is to brush the history of the nation-state against the grain, and to recover these fragments of tradition and of the people's history, while resisting the temptation merely to incorporate them into grand historiographical metanarratives, be they of the imperialist, nationalist, or Marxist variety. The appropriate subjects of a postcolonial history are neither the emerging self-conscious citizens of the modern nation, nor the working class, but the "people-nation," which Chatterjee (optimistically enough) believes still subsists in the margins of the nation, as a site of potential excess over the official nation-state, "struggling in an inchoate, undirected and wholly unequal battle against forces that have sought to dominate it."[6] So, as Lloyd writes, the possibility of a progressive nationalism depends on our "recognition of the excess of the people over the nation and in the understanding that that is, beyond itself, the very logic of nationalism as a political phenomenon" ("Nationalisms Against the State," 276). Hence, "the critique of nationalism is inseparable from the critique of post-colonial domination" (Lloyd, *Anomalous States*, 115) – a genuinely emancipatory politics must supersede the old politics of the nation-state.

Lloyd's essay on "Adulteration and the Nation" (*Anomalous States*, 88–124), which is centrally concerned with the "Cyclops" chapter of

---

[6] Chatterjee, *Nationalist Thought*, 170. See also Guha, "Historiography and Colonial India."

Ulysses, provides some telling examples of the insights that such a post-colonial approach may yield in relation to Joyce. It would seem that Lloyd regards the milieu of Barney Kiernan's pub as strikingly at odds with, even subversive of, the imagined milieux of a Gaelic nationalism which promoted cultural purity, a closed and repressive view of native tradition (together with a disdain for urban or "Anglicized" culture), and an ideology of the modern (male) subject as at least potentially coherent, autonomous, and equal to the demands of capitalist self-discipline. Hence, the dereliction of these future citizens of the Irish state – their idleness, drunkenness, and hopeless economic indebtedness – together with the medley of heterogeneous styles which Joyce deploys in writing the episode, deliver a riposte to Irish nationalism's demand for a uniform civic purity.

The dominant conceptions of both the cultural and political realms in Joyce's society were drastically limited by their preoccupation with various forms of bourgeois individualism. This is a feature of both capitalist and postcolonial nations. In particular, the notion of *representation* is central to both modern aesthetics and democratic politics – demonstrated by a persistent stress on the "representativeness" of the artist and of the artifact, and on the capacity of the political representative to stand in for others, and to speak on their behalf (including, of course, the leaders of anticolonial "national" movements, as Chatterjee and others have demonstrated). Lloyd has explored the alliance between culture and the politics of representative democracy in a number of contexts, arguing that modern conceptions of the arts as supposedly cultivating the "common humanity" of their audiences are in fact implicated in the production of obedient citizens for the state. Therefore, Joyce's repudiation of the aesthetics of national art is in itself a potent political gesture, given that "culture is seen to provide the ground for political citizenship" in the modern state (Lloyd and Thomas, *Culture and the State*, 1). As we shall see, Lloyd maintains that Joyce's texts enact a decisive break with representation, in all of these senses.

But, of course, what distinguishes such a reading of "Cyclops" from more familiar liberal accounts of Joyce's rejection of Irish nationalism is its quest to disclose the "people-nation" (or the subaltern), resistant then to the ideology of the Irish national bourgeoisie which assumed control of the state in 1922 and still resistant to it today. Lloyd emphasizes the importance of "the attempt to recover subterranean or marginal practices which have been variously understood as aberrant, pre-modern and

residual, or incoherent." As he insists: "Without the recovery and interpretation of such occluded practices as an expansion of the field of possibilities for radical democracy, the critique of representative national
democracy and state formation remains more or less formalist"
(*Anomalous States*, 7).

It remains, that is to say, at the level of form or style, as opposed to the
level of content or structure: we will go on to investigate how well
Lloyd's analysis fulfills his own exacting requirements. Of course, his
critique also ranges beyond Joyce, and in the Irish context alone, considers other texts from "low" cultural sources, such as street ballads, and
relates these to actual political movements, such as agrarian secret societies, and to socialist and feminist campaigns. Hence, merely to counter
specific aspects of Lloyd's reading of "Cyclops" may seem to involve the
repression of the larger implications of his project. He is not, after all,
primarily an exegete of Joyce, and essays such as "Adulteration and the
Nation" may usefully illuminate neglected aspects of Joyce's texts by
pointing out their resonances with popular or "resistant" cultural forms.[7]
The examples Lloyd deploys from "high" culture, popular culture, and
the history of popular agitation are all integral to the development of his
theory of "subaltern" culture, but I will argue that Joyce has an especially privileged position within this interpretative paradigm. It is in this
context that Lloyd's reluctance to engage with certain important dimen-
sions of Joyce's texts – as we will see – is significant.

As Robert Young observes, whereas for Gramsci "the subaltern is the
state in emergence," for Lloyd, "the subaltern is redefined not as the one
who desires the state but as the one who resists it . . . who is inassimilable
to the state."[8] So, although in "Cyclops," the drinkers consciously

---

[7] This is also true of Luke Gibbons's essay, "Identity Without a Centre."
Gibbons's critique of "the mutant that passes for modernization in Ireland," and
of policies of industrial modernization which lacked any "commitment to
social, political or cultural modernization" (*Transformations in Irish Culture*, 89,
91), also reveal a cautious commitment to Enlightenment thought – or to a
theory of universal emancipation that could usefully be broadened to include
serious engagement with questions concerning history, local tradition, imperialism, etc. This would appear to distinguish his position from Lloyd's. See also
Gibbons's "Alternative Enlightenments."

[8] Young, "From Gráinne to Gramsci," 108. For Lloyd's comments on Gramsci,
see *Anomalous States*, 9. The term "subaltern" – as adopted from Gramsci by
Guha and others – has come into widespread use, influenced in particular by

espouse nationalism, they are nonetheless clearly subaltern. The most obvious "practice" in which they engage is talking, but their speech, despite their aspiration towards an ideal discourse which would be specifically Irish, belongs to the realm of Babel, with Joyce's mixed and decentered styles. As Lloyd argues, "For while the citizen is militant against the hybridization of Irish culture, *the chapter itself* dramatizes adulteration as the condition of colonial Ireland at virtually every level" ("Adulteration," 107; my emphasis). This bears out the case that in this period "Both the popular and the literary forms [e.g., *Ulysses*] map a colonial culture for which the forms of representational aesthetics and politics required by nationalism begin to seem entirely inadequate, obliging *us* to conceive of a cultural politics which must work outside the terms of representation" (89; my emphasis). "Resisting the state" is here, then, primarily an *unconscious* practice, revealed in slips and contradictions, which subsequently become available for the reader's interpretation. The subaltern *can* talk, but in this instance, he *cannot* speak, or cannot truly know what he is saying.

This is not to suggest that the critic is dependent on realist discourse in seeking to analyze the politics of *Ulysses* – "representative" as its cast of characters may be of a class which was not notably "resistant" to the politics of nationalism. For "Cyclops" is, to be sure, much more than simply a realist portrayal of a specific historical situation. A complex relationship exists between its stylistic practices (vividly described by Lloyd as "the adulteration of interpenetrating discourses" ["Adulteration," 107]) and those of the pub's clientele. Yet it seems excessive to imply that the whole aim or effect of Joyce's extraordinary recreation of a significant historical moment of Irish political consciousness is to represent it as thoroughly *false* consciousness.[9] Lloyd's insistence on Joyce's absolute break with realism precludes the possibility that the voices in this episode can wittingly testify to the range of possibilities open to them; instead, in making the already overdetermined

footnote 8 (*cont.*)

> Spivak's "Can the Subaltern Speak?" and other essays. For an account of the controversies generated by Spivak's use of the word, see Moore-Gilbert's *Postcolonial Theory*, 97–113. Of course, some critics nevertheless reserve the right to use the term "subaltern" fairly loosely in relation to Joyce; see Duffy, *Subaltern "Ulysses,"* on the notion of "subaltern sensibility" (5 *et passim*).

[9] I offer something of an apologia for the citizen in my *James Joyce and Nationalism*, Chapter 3.

choice of nationalism and of the state formation which it is nationalism's ambition to achieve, these voices attempt to speak in unison. But what we hear is in fact a discordant chorus in which many other possibilities are audible.

So, Joyce's practice of writing, as Lloyd understands it, reflects the multiple possibilities for future development which belonged to the colonized Irish by virtue of the cultural damage, or hybridization, that they had suffered. Although betrayed by the likes of the monological citizen and his real historical counterparts, potentially renewable political energies can evidently be apprehended in this episode. It is these which we can glimpse through the varied and competing styles of the kaleidoscopic lens of "Cyclops." But what, more precisely, are they? What can we, as readers and critics (and as ourselves citizens of the modern state) learn from them?

The problems surrounding the condition of subalternity can be highlighted by contrasting it with the condition of the proletariat as it was presented in the great Marxist classic, Lukács's *History and Class Consciousness,* published the year after *Ulysses.* The proletariat's emergence as a class "means the *abolition of the isolated individual*"; it is only in the proletariat that the process of commodification "leads to a revolutionary consciousness" (171). Little of this historical destiny remains for the subaltern. What does remain, however, is the notion that the subaltern, like the proletariat, is always beyond or in excess of the processes of economic or political development – and development will always be incomplete until that group is incorporated within it. But the subaltern should not be figured as the emerging subject of a future universal history, and cannot benefit from the benign attentions of the enlightened intellectual. Indeed, the intellectual, because of his or her disciplinary formation, is likely to be on the side of the state rather than on the side of the people-nation, and therefore will tend merely to assimilate subaltern history into the history of modern citizenship (Lloyd, "Adulteration," 115). [10] Lloyd stresses the importance of the historian's or critic's search for forms of resistance that have been consistently occluded by the records of official history, and the need to attend to present-day forms of

---

[10] Chakrabarty argues that "Nation states have the capacity to enforce their truth games, and universities, their critical distance not withstanding, are part of the battery of institutions complicit in this process" ("Postcoloniality and the Artifice of History," 384–85).

protest that are equally inassimilable to the logic of nation-state politics and to the procedures of the academic disciplines that, knowingly or not, are complicit with that logic. He asserts that Fanon's "zone of occult instability where the people dwell" *has* a history, albeit one which is unreadable to canonical historiography (*Anomalous States*, 11). The question of how legible this history can be rendered by a *new* practice of historiography is regularly and eloquently addressed by Lloyd; yet it is not, in my view, successfully resolved.

Lloyd offers this summary of his argument in relation to Joyce:

> Irish street ballads and folk songs are read, against nationalist refinements of them, as being vital representations of the hybridity of a colonial culture. That these songs, while stylistically and tonally inassimilable to nationalist representations, were nonetheless sites of resistance and possibly even means of popular instruction, illuminates the politics of style in *Ulysses* in relation to a popular rather than aesthetic consciousness. Both *Ulysses* and this popular tradition are recalcitrant to the emergent nationalist as to the imperial state formation precisely in refusing the homogeneity of "style" required for national citizenship.
>
> (*Anomalous States*, 11)

How did these popular texts operate as "sites of resistance and possibly even means of popular instruction?" The ballad "Father Murphy," Lloyd suggests, may have served "exactly the same function in terms of tactical knowledge as John Mitchel's regular military lessons in the *United Irishman* of 1848, themselves adapted from a British military handbook" (*Anomalous States*, 96). This, however, is a solitary example of the possibility of "popular instruction" taking place through these means. And, in this case, the end of such action would apparently be a military attack on the British state: not a "practice" clearly distinct from those practices which are legible to official historiography. Moreover, how is the significance of this information changed by being coded in this cultural form, rather than say (as in the case of Mitchel's lessons), being printed in a newspaper? *Ulysses*, in the lines quoted above, is illuminated only by the reflected glory of what is itself a rather insubstantial link with popular insurrection. Nor is this "insurrection" obviously "subaltern" in complexion. In effect, the juxtaposition of *Ulysses* with the ballads does not seem to me to be an advance on Lloyd's original point that *Ulysses* departs from the unitary style sponsored by official nationalism. So once more, the subaltern critic announces that in this novel we encounter the *other* voices of Irish modernity. These are not the voices of modern "individuals," but of the remnants and fragments which are the by-products of centralizing, statist modernization, whether that be driven by the colonial or the postcolonial (national) state.

The "subaltern" critic is condemned to dwell over and over on that (albeit important) moment in Joyce's text when the residual, or the voiceless, are granted speech. Unquestionably, *Ulysses* is committed to lending articulation to those who were previously inarticulate or unheard. This is surely the meaning of the displacement of the young male intellectual, Stephen, by others not so privileged – by Bloom, the Dublin Jew, and his petit-bourgeois entourage, and by women, especially Molly. (But certainly, we would hunt in vain in *Ulysses* for any trace of the so-called subaltern *groups*, or forms of organization – for example, socialist nationalist, agrarian, or women's movements.) But it does not necessarily follow that Joyce believes that these voices could never be – or should not be – assimilated into a notion of national community. Indeed, the fact that Joyce himself represents and includes them may even suggest otherwise – that *Ulysses* is as much at ease with a liberal vision of inclusiveness, as it is with a supposedly radical idea of absolute heterogeneity. And certainly Joyce's engagement with the subaltern is not immune to the kind of objections that have already been leveled by feminist commentators at his adoption of feminine voices, especially those of Molly and Anna Livia.[11] Joyce may present a polyphony of voices – translating this into a politics is by no means straightforward.

In this way, "subaltern" historians may be charged with what Francis Mulhern describes as the failure to recognize the necessary "discrepancy" between culture and politics. Mulhern argues that both culture and politics

> can be understood as encompassing the totality of social relations but they do so in distinctive ways . . . Cultural practices may treat any and all differences as absolute . . . Politics, in seeking to bring about or to forestall some particular state of affairs, to secure this or that general condition of existence, cannot treat difference in the same way. It must be able to bridge the kind of difference that cultural practices may regard as absolute, to create solidarities in pursuit of specific ends.
>
> ("The Politics of Cultural Studies," 38–39)[12]

---

[11] For an account of feminist controversies about Joyce's depiction of women, see my *James Joyce and Nationalism*, chapter 6.

[12] Lloyd, on the other hand, describes the division of culture and politics "as the hallmark of liberal ideology"; see "Cultural Theory and Ireland," 87.

I will argue, however, that *Ulysses*, as a document of culture, in its staging of argument, contradiction, and conflict between different voices in the text, itself acknowledges this discrepancy. It acknowledges politics, that is to say, in the narrower sense of that term, as well as in the broader sense of "cultural politics," as understood by many of Joyce's contemporary "cultural" critics. Firstly, however, I want to comment on Lloyd's remarks about the articulation of state-directed nationalism with other political and social movements, in order to question whether "subaltern" criticism succeeds in mapping out a new role for the critic or intellectual.

In order "to envisage the progressive moment in nationalisms," Lloyd states, we must "do historical justice to the complex articulation of nationalist struggles with other social movements" ("Nationalisms Against the State," 257). In the context of twentieth-century Ireland, he points to "the broad ideological spectrum of social and political movements," encompassing, among others, socialist and feminist republicans such as Constance Markievicz and James Connolly: "Each movement has a distinct history and a distinct tempo which may be occluded but is not terminated by the consistent focus of subsequent history, nationalist or revisionist, on political institutions and state apparatuses" (267). But the various critiques (including the self-critique) of nationalism since 1916 or 1922 do not really answer the question that throws an oblique shadow on Lloyd's analysis. Were the alliances between nationalism and the various other emancipatory movements necessary or were they accidental? In other words, does nationalism represent the essential preliminary step along the path to a fuller emancipation? This remains the central question for what we would now call postcolonialism since it was first raised by Fanon's *The Wretched of the Earth*. But while Fanon still believed in the possibility of a radical popular movement involving the intelligentsia,[13] Lloyd's vision of forms of subaltern or nonstatist resistance to capitalist modernity – whether modernity presents itself in the guise of the colonial or the national state – does not shed light on the strategic choices a participant in these struggles should make. For example, the Irish women's movement in the early years of the twentieth century was split over how to regard the nationalist movement. Those prepared to struggle for the right to vote in elections for Westminster stood accused of being content to accept the legitimacy of the imperial state;

[13] See Lazarus on Fanon in "National Consciousness."

those who were prepared to defer the question of women's voting rights until the establishment of an Irish state were regarded as political innocents by their suffragist comrades – and sadly deluded as to the feminist sympathies of their republican brothers-in-arms.[14] According to Lloyd, republican feminists evidently "saw no contradiction between their distinct but articulated affiliations" ("Nationalisms Against the State," 267). But real historical actors *must*, after all, decide to ally themselves with one side or another of a particular question. How would a *conscious* opposition to the state-form as such have advanced either nationalism or feminism in this context? The Olympian vision of "the complex articulation of nationalist struggles with other social movements" offers no assistance. Having surrendered the arrogance of "knowing better," the critic is obliged to avoid any retrospective intervention on the question of what should or might have been done; instead, he or she has to take a fundamentally quietist and contemplative attitude towards those who have embodied "subalternity" in the past. For, as Madhava Prasad argues, "The subaltern historian therefore finds him/herself in the self-effacing role of a facilitator unwilling to articulate a counter-hegemonic project that is 'extraneous' to the histories unearthed . . . And since new conceptual frameworks are to be avoided . . . celebration of others' struggles becomes the only option" ("Theory of [Third World] Literature," 64, 67).

The "subaltern" view appears to be predicated on the existence of the state, just as subaltern resistance is predicated on the nationalist aspiration towards the state. What, then, is the political end of such a critique? Placing the critical emphasis on the "people-nation" co-opted by nationalism tends to serve the assumption that the victories of anticolonial forces were inevitable. Thus the struggle against imperialism is downplayed by the radical commentator to make way for a proleptic critique – which is, nonetheless, retrospectively uncovered – of the successful nation-state in popular or avant-garde forms. Postcolonial critics rejoice that the state cannot finally overcome resistance, for such resistance marks the constitutive failure of the state to encompass or "represent" the entirety of the people's culture, or of the emancipatory impulses which gave birth to the state. Chakrabarty evokes those "other narratives of human connections that draw sustenance from dreamed-up pasts and futures," which will inevitably recur, "for these dreams are what the

[14] See Ward, *Unmanageable Revolutionaries*, 70–74.

modern represses in order to be" ("Postcoloniality and the Artifice of History," 388). In a similar vein, Chatterjee writes of "the narrative of community, relegated to the primordial zone of the natural, denied any subjectivity that is not domesticated to the requirements of the modern state, and yet persistent in its invocation of the rhetoric of love and kinship against the homogenizing sway of the normalized individual" (*The Nation and its Fragments*, 238). But can "resistance" overtake the state, any more than the state finally overcome "resistance?" Chakrabarty and Chatterjee would seem to suggest that it cannot, and to accept this with melancholy resignation.

This subaltern theory of the state bears a striking formal similarity to the social contract theory generally associated with Rousseau, whereby a radical "natural" freedom is surrendered for the sake of civil liberty. But that "natural" state is always in excess of what the actual state can realize. Postcolonial theory wears this classical rue with a difference. Chakrabarty, for instance, calls for a new history which makes visible "the part it plays in collusion with the narratives of citizenships in assimilating to the projects of the modern state all other possibilities of human solidarity. The politics of despair will require of such a history that it lays bare to its readers why such a predicament is necessarily inescapable" ("Postcoloniality and the Artifice of History," 388). The intellectual can only elucidate lost possibilities – which can only surely have been *possibilities*, properly speaking, if they *could* have developed into powerful realities. Benita Parry has outlined the relationship between the rejection of nationalism and the exorbitation of the intellectual in postcolonial theory, especially in Spivak's work. Yet as Neil Lazarus points out, Spivak's emphasis, and certainly the emphasis in a certain strain of "postmodern" postcolonial theory, in fact falls far too heavily on the side of circumscribing and limiting the intellectual.[15] It is Lloyd's optimistic departure from the epistemological and political pessimism of much postcolonial theory, in his exploration of "the zone that does *not* lack a history," that make his work so appealing. Yet he, too, has recently offered the following characterization of the function of the intellectual:

> What we come to comprehend is that as intellectuals we do not stand before, as examples representing a fuller capacity or as epigones of progress. We come

[15] See Parry, "Problems in Current Theories of Colonial Discourse" and "Resistance Theory/Theorising Resistance," and Lazarus, "National Consciousness," 209.

after. We come after a whole repertoire of possibilities, of counter-hegemonic
strategies and alternative imaginations, that we cannot claim as our inheritance.
In the debris of their passing we find nothing to develop and nothing to mourn
as foregone. For in the present, in the gradual collapse of our own inherited
spaces and practices, we find alongside the specter of a consolidating and
homogenizing capitalism, alternative openings and fluidities that are in no way
"exemplary," so specific are they to their given historical moment and its
indeterminacies. Precisely in that different relation to the "ends" of humanity,
in the negation of universal claims by contemporary social movements, we
discover an unexhausted repertoire of renewed possibilities.

(Lloyd and Thomas, *Culture and the State*, 30)

But these renewed possibilities cannot be named, and must not be assimilated to the universalizing, statist habits of intellectuals. How is the sense
of belatedness and humility which we are enjoined to feel in the first sentence, and the counsel here against generalization or abstraction, to be
squared with any sense of renewed hope – or certainly, with optimism in
any activist or interventionist sense? Against this, Lazarus defends the
capacity of the intellectual to represent others, and to speak for them. Or,
as Bruce Robbins adds, the sense of intellectual vocation may even
"*require* accepting the task of analyzing, understanding and representing
the experience of others"; Robbins thus speaks up for "a professionalism
which, without presumption of ultimate totalizing certainty, believes in
its own power of generalization, abstraction, synthesis and representation at a distance" (*Secular Vocations*, 156, 188).

To continue in this vein is perhaps simply to repeat the by now familiar exchanges between critics who, in short, offer a qualified defense of
enlightenment, and those who condemn it. For example, Terry Eagleton
describes current quarrels in Irish studies as:

a reproduction *in parvo* of a more global altercation between those for whom
modernity is still alive if unwell, and those who believe themselves to be
confidently posterior to it. The political discourse of modernity is one of rights,
justice, oppression, solidarity, universality, exploitation, emancipation.
Nationalism, along with liberalism and socialism, belongs with this world-view.
The political language of postmodernity is one of identity, marginality, locality,
difference, otherness, diversity, desire . . . There are those for whom the former
language is now effectively bankrupt, and there are those for whom the second
way of speaking is no more than a disastrous displacement of the first, one
consequent of the failure of that discourse to realise itself politically in our
time.

Moreover, these two registers, Eagleton argues, are incommensurable; and "cusped as we are between modernity and postmodernity, there is no satisfying theoretical resolution of these questions historically available to us" ("Revisionism Revisited," 326–27). Nonetheless, the current fixation of postcolonialism on what might ultimately appear to be philosophical games – about representation, the subaltern, can the subaltern speak? – is both understandable and the more to be regretted in the current global situation, in which people find it easier to imagine the end of the world than the breakdown of the capitalist system.[16] It is surely disappointing to note the healthy state of "postcolonial theory" as an academic field in, say, Ireland, in the context of the lamentable standard of political debate about, for example, the Good Friday Agreement (1998), or the issues of state politics involved in removing articles 2 and 3 from the constitution of the Irish Republic. In this respect, it is hard not to sympathize with Aijaz Ahmad when he calls for radicals to desist from characterizing nations and states simply as coercive entities. Rather, he asserts, "one struggles not against nations and states as such but for different articulations of class, nation and state" (*In Theory*, 11). For intellectuals are surely not confined to either a passive acceptance of the existing forms of the state or its utter repudiation.[17] Otherwise what Edward Said describes as "the immense cultural shift from the terrain of nationalist independence to the theoretical domain of liberation," which he, too, traces to Fanon, seems to represent not a step towards greater freedom, but its final displacement (*Culture and Imperialism*, 324).

If *Ulysses* accords with the paradigm of subaltern history, it already illustrates the irony of such a history – in announcing that articulation has been denied to some, we necessarily articulate their case on their behalf. This is the difference between writing about subalternity (criticism) and being subaltern. Can a subaltern be aware of being so and remain subaltern? Or, more precisely, can such an awareness be articulated without the loss of the condition which is defined by inarticulacy? Is Joyce merely writing about subalternities, speaking for them, or do his subalterns speak for themselves? If the historical relevance of the

---

[16] As Jameson remarks in *The Seeds of Time*, xii.

[17] For an example of such a critical project, see Cleary, "Partition and the Politics of Form." While acknowledging the nation-state as a "historically contingent form of political organisation," Cleary nevertheless argues for the importance of studying "the variety of processes that go into the continual making and remaking of the Irish border" (230).

political opinions actually held by the characters in the novel is denied, then such a reading is concentrated on subaltern *energies* rather than subaltern *subjects* – and energies which are, as Lloyd's essay demonstrates, difficult to relate to Irish history except in the most general "cultural" sense. His analysis cannot be based on some "authentic" colonial/subaltern subject presenting him- or herself at the bar (in this case, *in* the bar) of history. What must be labeled as "inauthentic" here is the "desire for the state" actually expressed by the community. Hence, according to Lloyd's analysis, we ratify the cultural forms of the citizens' pronouncements, rather than the content.

On the other hand, such a reading may usefully deconstruct the critical history of reading the episode as a clash between nationalism (the citizen) and internationalism (Bloom). It emerges that the so-called antimodernity of nationalism is intimately related to its modern antonym in ways that exhibit their codependence rather than their opposition. For all their heated disagreement, the citizen and Bloom basically accept the same international system of nation-states. Bloom evidently acknowledges what he believes to be the inevitable coercive violence of any established state: "I mean wouldn't it be the same here if you put force against force?" (*U* 12.1360–1). And no matter how fiercely the citizen may desire an independent Ireland, he can conceive of this so-called Irish "autonomy" only in the context of the international systems of commerce, diplomacy and war, as he looks forward to the time when "the first Irish battleship is seen breasting the waves with our own flag to the fore, none of your Henry Tudor's harps, no, the oldest flag afloat, the flag of the province of Desmond and Thomond, three crowns on a blue field, the three sons of Milesius" (12.1306–10).

Nationalists may talk about the coming to national self-consciousness of their own nations, but historically, nationalism has served to create and consolidate a system of states, whose underlying logic is that of the development of international capitalism. In this sense, the cosmopolitan Bloom and his Gaelicist antagonist represent two sides of the same coin. For all his patriotic bluster, the citizen wants Ireland to enter the capitalist world; but Bloom is already an apologist for that "music of the future" (15.1368). Indeed, Bloom's acceptance of "discipline" and, more generally, of punishment, is significant, tied as it is both to his own masochism, and the symbolic castration which in fact has been described as the hallmark of the modern, self-regulating, self-denying subject – of which he ("the prudent member") furnishes *Ulysses'* best (indeed perhaps sole) example. And while the citizen's militant, physical-force patriotism may seem antithetical to Bloom's pacifism, his defense of commerce, and his hopes for Irish economic development throughout *Ulysses*, it is also true that one of capitalism's great ideological victories is its capacity for presenting itself as "natural" and essentially pacific. Moreover, Bloom (himself the victim of racism) has not understood how the modernizing ambitions of his fellow Irish citizens have been thwarted by the colonial state – that in the larger political unit of the United Kingdom, they are the victims of discrimination.

But neither is it possible to interpret "Cyclops" as a clash between modernity (nationalism) and antimodernity (subalternity). In effect, both of the main protagonists in "Cyclops" have decisively entered modernity. The range of political options presented in this episode, and in the novel at large, is predetermined by the dominance of nationalism in the Ireland Joyce remembers, although he also depicts its attendant ironies and contradictions. But this episode dramatizes in itself – and has dramatized for generations of readers – the most important possibilities with which the whole text engages; freedom through commercial enter-prise/the bourgeois project, and freedom through collectivist national-ism. These are both essentially modern, however, although they are haunted by other narratives of connection, by kinship, by "the agenbit of inwit," of a lawless sexuality, by "what the modern represses in order to be" (Chakrabarty, "Postcoloniality and the Artifice of History," 388). Joyce's Dublin is a village *and* a city, a place of traditional relationships and practices, and a place in which these are disappearing. Nationalism is the dominant agency in creating this transition; in Žižek's terms, "it is precisely the new suture effected by the nation which renders possible the 'desuturing,' the disengagement from traditional organic ties" (*For They Know Not*, 20). But in this transition, or in the various collisions that punctuate that process, no harmonious resolution is offered. We are not speaking here of a transition from an archaic to a modern condition. Instead, the transitional nature of the condition in which the archaic and the new intermingle uneasily is itself the modern. No radical individual-ity of the subject can be established (either for Bloom, or for Stephen in his version of the search for autonomy and a radically pure lineage), nor is there a wholly unified and unifying communal discourse of the kind that characterized the realist novel, nor of the kind that stimulates nationalism's ambition to collect all competing discourses into one. The struggle between what Said calls the terrain of nationalist independence and the theoretical domain of liberation is not resolved. We see the official faces of these ideologies and in "Circe" we see what their unconscious represses – the claims of the past, of family, the countering anarchic force of sexuality. We do not see, even as an emergent possibility, a modernity totally free from domination. That radical democracy, in which heterogeneity and emancipation would be realized, is a vision shared between postmodernity and postcolonial theory. But it has as yet had no historical realization. *Ulysses* consistently addresses the issue of the bearing of the imagined or even the remembered upon the actual. How can a vision of liberation be distinguished from a fantasy of it? Molly's soliloquy is of course a moment often captured for the various theologies of liberation that modernity has bred. But she herself is the afterthought to the nonclimax of "Ithaca"; her discourse of liberation is incommensurable with what went before. For *Ulysses* is grounded in real states, in real possibilities, real outcomes, even though it recognizes how subtly these are interwoven with dreams of possibilities that have not been and may never be realized.

Works cited

Ahmad, Aijaz. *In Theory: Nations, Classes, Literatures.* London: Verso, 1992.

Ashcroft, Bill, Gareth Griffiths, and Helen Tiffin, eds. *The Post-colonial Studies Reader.* London and New York: Routledge, 1995.

Barker, Francis, Peter Hulme, and Margaret Iversen, eds. *Colonial Discourse/Postcolonial Theory.* Manchester: Manchester University Press, 1994.

Breuilly, John. *Nationalism and the State.* Manchester: Manchester University Press, 1993.

Chakrabarty, Dipesh. "Postcoloniality and the Artifice of History." Ashcroft *et al.*, eds., *The Post-colonial Studies Reader*, 383–88.

Chatterjee, Partha. *Nationalist Thought and the Colonial World: A Derivative Discourse.* Minneapolis: University of Minnesota Press, 1986.

The Nation and its Fragments: Colonial and Postcolonial Histories. Princeton: Princeton University Press, 1993.

Cheng, Vincent J. *Joyce, Race, and Empire.* Cambridge: Cambridge University Press, 1995.

Cleary, Joe. "Partition and the Politics of Form." *Ireland and Irish Cultural Studies.* Ed. John Paul Waters. Special issue of *South Atlantic Quarterly* 95.1 (winter 1996): 227–76.

Duffy, Enda. *The Subaltern "Ulysses."* Minneapolis: University of Minnesota Press, 1994.

Eagleton, Terry. "Revisionism Revisited." *Crazy John and the Bishop and Other Essays on Irish Culture.* Cork: Cork University Press, 1998. 308–27.

Gibbons, Luke. "Alternative Enlightenments." *1798: 200 Years of Resonance*. Ed. Mary Cullen. Dublin: Irish Reporter Publications, 1998. 119–27.

"Identity Without a Centre: Allegory, History and Irish Nationalism." *Transformations in Irish Culture*. Cork: Cork University Press, 1996. 134–47.

Guha, Ranajit. "On Some Aspects of the Historiography of Colonial India." Spivak and Guha, eds., *Selected Subaltern Studies*, 37–43.

Jameson, Fredric. *The Seeds of Time*. New York: Columbia University Press, 1994.

Lazarus, Neil. "National Consciousness and the Specificity of (Post) Colonial Intellectualism." Barker *et al.*, eds., *Colonial Discourse/Postcolonial Theory*, 197–220.

Lloyd, David. *Anomalous States: Irish Writing and the Post-colonial Moment*. Dublin: Lilliput Press, 1993.

"Cultural Theory and Ireland" (a review of Terry Eagleton's *Heathcliff and the Great Hunger*). *Bullán* 3.1 (spring 1997): 87–91.

"Nationalisms Against the State: Towards a Critique of the Anti-nationalist Prejudice." *Gender and Colonialism*. Ed. Timothy P. Foley *et al.* Galway: Galway University Press, 1995. 256–81.

Lloyd, David, with Paul Thomas. *Culture and the State*. London: Routledge, 1998.

Lukács, Georg. *History and Class Consciousness*. Trans. Rodney Livingstone. London: The Merlin Press, 1971.

Manganiello, Dominic. *Joyce's Politics*. London: Routledge & Kegan Paul, 1980.

Moore-Gilbert, Bart. *Postcolonial Theory: Contexts, Practices, Politics*. London: Verso, 1997.

Mulhern, Francis. "The Politics of Cultural Studies." *Monthly Review* 47.3 (July–August 1995): 31–40.

Nolan, Emer. *James Joyce and Nationalism*. London: Routledge, 1995.

Parry, Benita. "Problems in Current Theories of Colonial Discourse." Ashcroft *et al.*, eds., *The Post-colonial Studies Reader*, 36–44.

"Resistance Theory/Theorising Resistance or Two Cheers for Nativism." Barker *et al.*, eds., *Colonial Discourse/Postcolonial Theory*, 172–96.

Prasad, Madhava. "On the Question of a Theory of (Third World) Literature." *Social Text* 10.2/3 (1992): 57–83.

Robbins, Bruce. *Secular Vocations: Intellectuals, Professionals and Culture*. London: Verso, 1993.

Said, Edward. *Culture and Imperialism*. London: Chatto & Windus, 1993.

Spivak, Gayatri. "Can the Subaltern Speak?" *Marxism and the Interpretation of Culture*. Ed. Cary Nelson and Lawrence Grossberg. Chicago: University of Chicago Press, 1988. 271–313.

Spivak, Gayatri, and Ranajit Guha, eds. *Selected Subaltern Studies*. Oxford: Oxford University Press, 1988.

Ward, Margaret. *Unmanageable Revolutionaries: Women and Irish Nationalism.*
    London: Pluto Press, 1983.
Young, Robert. "From Gráinne to Gramsci" (review of Lloyd's *Anomalous
    States*). *Bullán* 1.2 (autumn 1994): 107–8.
Žižek, Slavoj. *For They Know Not What They Do: Enjoyment as a Political Factor.*
    London: Verso, 1991.

5

"Neither fish nor flesh"; or how "Cyclops" stages the double-bind of Irish manhood

JOSEPH VALENTE

The "Cyclops" episode of *Ulysses* has proven perhaps the happiest of hunting grounds for those scholars anxious to explore Joyce's critical anatomy of contemporary masculinity in its relation to Irish cultural and political nationalism. Shifting the focus of this on-going investigation, this chapter proposes to look instead at Joyce's interrogation of the more dominant late Victorian/Edwardian construct of *manhood*, its supportive – even constitutive – role in the delineation of ethnic differences between colonizing and colonized peoples, and the disabling ambivalence it tapped, almost by design, in the semicolonial space of Ireland, where nationalist resistance grounded itself in many of the gender and racial attitudes of imperialist rule.

I

The normative construct of manhood or manliness in the late Victorian/Edwardian period should not be equated or confused with the current feminist and psychoanalytic construction of masculinity: a narrowly gendered subject formation animated by oedipalized tendencies towards strongly repressive ego defense, correspondingly fetishistic and aggressive modes of desire, and a pronounced will to social mastery rationalized as moral or intellectual transcendence. While closely related to this structure of subjectivity, the dominant "muscular" conception of late Victorian manhood unfolds rather in a dialectical logic or syntax of hegemony, irreducible to any positive set of psychic properties or propensities. In this regard, its most appropriate theoretical analogue is not the popularly disseminated notion of the phallus as an obtrusive index of social authority, but the properly Lacanian notion of the phallus as an assumed phantasmal latency conferring social authority as a recursive or "retroversive" effect (Lacan, *Ecrits*, 288). In the words of David Rosen, "One cannot enter [the lists of manhood] simply by behaving in a 'manly' fashion . . . no particular behavior but something *in* men makes them manly. 'Masculinity' became the expression and perfection of that something" (Rosen, "The Volcano and the Cathedral," 21–22). The indeterminability of that "something" and the resulting contingency of its performative guises enabled manhood to function as an intellectual vortex in which the vectors of gender and sexuality coalesce, commingle, and agitate with those of race, nationality, and class. On one side, manhood served as a vehicle for injecting the figures and forms of gender hierarchy into these apparently distinct social registers; on the other, manhood served to reveal how gender categories always harbored determining elements drawn from those registers. That is to say, if the imperative to be a man regularly intervened in the negotiation of class and ethno-national differences, the definition of manliness itself incorporated and conjured with such differences as a part of its hegemonic function.

The late Victorian/Edwardian logic of manhood bears a strategic and inverse correlation with the dichotomized stereotype of femininity that was enshrined during the same period and drawn from the same bourgeois metropolitan milieu. Woman had of course long been defined on a disjunctive basis, as either virgin or whore, spiritual ideal or bodily abject, maternal nurturer or dangerous virago, the fetishized sum or the fearful subversion of all cultural values. But during the late nineteenth century, this bipolar profile took a specific bio-sexological inflection: normative (upper-/middle-class) British women were understood to be emotionally centered yet comparatively delicate or muted in their desires, and therefore passive and reserved in their sexuality, the vessels of an idealized "passionlessness" (Adams, *Dandies and Desert Saints*, 7). Active or aggressive female desire counted as not only immoral but abnormal, a mark of psychic disturbance or pathology, but one which seemed to betoken, like hysteria or neurasthenia, the *intrinsic* weakness of women's rational faculty and the instability of their affective constitution.

"Manly" men, a category similarly restricted in class and ethnic terms, were understood to be rationally capable, yet strong, even violent in their passions, and therefore active, aggressive, and sometimes errant in their sexuality. But the normative (gentle)man was also seen to be invested with great and effective moral energy for the restraint, discipline, and redirection of his urgent and brutish desires. A muscular ideal of manhood consisted precisely in the *simultaneous* necessity for and exercise of this capacity for rational self-control – in strong passions strongly checked – from which the virtues of conventional "masculinity" (fortitude, tenacity, industry, candor) were assumed to derive. Thus Samuel Smiles asserted "energy of will . . . to be the very central character in a man – in a word, it is the man himself" (Smiles, *Self-help*, 254). The doyen of the "muscular" doctrine, Charles Kingsley, famously declared "[t]he *prerogative* of a man is to be bold *against* himself" (*Life and Works*, v, 19). His disciple, Thomas Hughes, author of *Tom Brown's Schooldays*, *the* novel of Victorian manliness, held that "a man's body is given him to be trained and brought into subjection" (*Tom Brown*, 99).

As these sentiments indicate, the Victorian middle class defined the normative man on a *conjunctive* basis, thereby extending to him a superior capacity of self-integration, self-possession, self-command, and self-reliance. In so doing, the masculine ideal not only engages the feminine ideal in a relation of complementary opposition where each gender properly completes the other, but a metonymic relation of whole to part, where the masculine itself is self-sufficient in a way the feminine never can be. Normative manliness comprehends and commands the very property that normative femininity *properly* lacks. On this basis, the ideal of manhood garnered its exponents and clients an extraordinary measure of socio-symbolic capital.

Given how supple an instrument of male sovereignty and supremacy the muscular paradigm provided, it is not surprising that it became the virtually universal norm of European manhood well into the twentieth century (see Mosse, *The Image of Man*). What is perhaps surprising, however, is that the symbolic capital comprehended in manhood seems to have been grounded in a lower rather than a higher order of being: the manly man was construed as having a much closer commerce with the bestial dimension than the womanly woman. Kingsley, in particular, celebrated the inherence of plentiful "animal spirits" to biological maleness and their importance in the production of genuine manliness. Having proclaimed, "[m]an is not a mere animal – he is *the* spirit animal," Kingsley pronounced "manly *thumos* [animal passion] the root of all virtue" (*Letters* I, 161; II, 62). In an analogous fashion, Hughes declared courage "the foundation of manliness and yet its lowest or rudest form . . . not exclusively a human quality at all, but one which we share with other animals" (*The Manliness of Christ*, 21). On this dialectical model, man's primordial bestiality represents the very cause of the self-disciplining spirituality that sublates, dignifies and subsumes it. As Hughes put it, "self-restraint is the highest form of self-assertion" (23). It is not, therefore, the attributes that make the man, but the logic of their arrangement.

At this point, the strategic advantage of this seemingly abject appurtenance of manhood begins to come into focus. To conceive the character of manhood as this sort of *discordia concors*, a closed-circuit self-referring tension between its own component energies, was to guarantee it in advance the traditionally male-identified attributes of autonomy and integrity, self-containment and self-determination. Every act of obedience stood to be recuperated as self-government, every act of obeisance as self-restraint, every act of compromise as fidelity to higher principal or more rational interest. The state of manhood could, as a result, effectively pose as the essential ground for possessing in full the rights and privileges of liberal democratic citizenship. Moreover, as the condition of self-contained independence, manhood could and did emerge as a defining trope of ethno-national enfranchisement and was specifically contrasted in this regard with the "ideal feminine character," which consisted, as J. S. Mill opined, in "submission and yielding to others" (Adams, *Dandies and Desert Saints*, 9). In the political code of the time, individual and collective manhood equaled "fitness for freedom"; individual and collective womanhood carried the dubious prerogative of "protection," hence of being a protectorate.

Typed on the one hand as passive, passionless, delicate, and ethereal, the womanly woman bore a more than passing resemblance to the spirit animal's purely spiritual side. In this respect, the Victorian woman's fabled role as "angel of the house" chimed with her idealization as the manly man's "better half," his aerial fragment. On the other hand, however, her characteristic spirituality coexisted and conflicted with her characteristic heteronomy, a predicate that has served as the very mark of a being's immersion in the material world. Since *pure* spirit, God, has long been identified in Western religious and philosophical thought with pure autonomy and unmoved movement, and the animal (animate materiality) has been correspondingly identified with behavior patterns exhaustively determined by material laws and instinct, the ideal lady's supposed heteronomy gave her rarefied stature the kind of reversibility that has persistently defined the Woman in patriarchal society (madonna/whore, nurse/witch, babe/bitch, etc.). Accordingly, each of the archetypal woman's rarefied angelic traits housed an innate liability to pass into its appetitive or overembodied opposite: passionlessness into emotional incontinence, passivity into hysterical frenzy or paralysis, sensibility into irrationality.

In this light, of course, manhood's external other also bore a more than passing resemblance to manhood's internal other, its own animal substratum, which it likewise opposed in a metonymic relation of whole to part: in Kingsley's terms, "spirit animal" to "mere animal." Here again, a reversibility in its constituent parts showed manhood to be a true *discordia concors*. The visible unleashing of *thumos* or animal passion, whether in vehement words or violent deeds, registered a certain disjunction of manhood's component energies and so a breakdown in its distinguishing faculty of rational self-control and containment. That is to say, the *actual* of manifestations of manhood's animal aggression evinced a lapse into emotional excess and heteronomy – hysteria at the extreme – which bore the unmistakable imprint of the feminine. By the same token, this spasm of emotional excess resulted in self-display and dramatization – histrionics at the extreme – which, however aggressive, likewise betrayed a feminine streak. Thus, as a flexible logic rather than a fixed content, manhood not only amounted to more than the sum of its parts, those parts did not even build upon one another, but proved finally interchangeable, in contradistinction to "the divineness of the whole manhood."

This immanence of the "whole manhood" to itself, in turn, its transcendence of any positive attributes, lent manhood a tremendous political malleability, which materialized in the strategic play of its descriptive and prescriptive aspects, its role as symbolic capital and symbolic mandate respectively. As symbolic capital, the category of manhood designated and enriched or bypassed and impoverished individual or corporate subjects on politically contingent grounds, thereby introducing into the texture of gender identity apparently extrinsic factors like class or racial origin. Thus, true manhood could and did take shape as the ontological essence of a very limited and specialized type of subject, the metropolitan gentleman, whose defining virtues could be indexed, but never *proven or achieved*, through exemplary displays of conventionally virile qualities. As a symbolic mandate, manhood helped to extend the forms of male privilege and the dynamic of gender hierarchy beyond their immediate frame of reference and into wide ranging contests over class enfranchisement, colonial rule, and national independence. Inasmuch as manliness enshrines an explicitly gendered mode of subjectivity as "fit to be free" and so worthy of emulation by all aspirants to democratic forms of life, manliness inevitably accrued the normative authority and hierarchizing power that exceeded its narrowly coded range of secure applicability. So comprehensive was this authority that it passed directly into the political lexicon of the time; promoting the claims of any group to greater self-determination became synonymous with summoning, expressing, or defending their collective manhood.

For the caste of metropolitan gentleman, the de- and pre-scriptive functions align themselves *conjunctively*, so that their possession of its dignified moral status and the accompanying symbolic capital might paradoxically seem *natural* and yet *earned*. Thus, the cultural stipulation of metropolitan bourgeois manliness served to invest the attributes, attitudes, and exploits of the pertinent subject class with an aura of manly attainment, so that these attitudes, attributes, and exploits could, in turn, vindicate the initial cultural stipulation. For subdominant castes of subject, conversely, the de- and pre-scriptive functions of manhood were arranged *disjunctively* (the mark of feminization, as we have seen), so that the acquisition of its dignified moral status and accompanying symbolic capital might paradoxically be *compulsory* and yet *impossible*. The cultural stipulation of subaltern unmanliness or premanliness invested the attributes, attitudes, and exploits of the pertinent subject class with a sense of inveterate deficiency that both demands and defies remedy. In this way, manhood functioned as the ideological engine of "flexible positional superiority," wherein the hegemonic group legitimated their power and privilege by manipulating either side of a given, politically charged binarism to their advantage (Cairns and Richards, *Writing Ireland*, 47–48). The particular suitability of manhood for this task rests in its *discordia concors* of animality and spirituality, which enabled subaltern claims on manhood to be undermined by referring any positive evidence of manly bearing or accomplishment to whatever notional equilibrium of these contrary elements seemed best defined to refute it. Subdominant groups could be classified as embodying a hypertrophy of some component part of manhood, its internal or external other, while "the divineness of the whole manhood" remained the preserve of metropolitan gentlemen. The Chartists, for example, were bestialized thus (Hall, "The Making and Unmaking of Monsters," 51–55), while the colonial subjects of the East were feminized (Said, *Orientalism*, 113–201).

The semicolonial Irish found themselves successively and simultaneously on the receiving end of both typological barrels: on one side, the discourse of simianization; on the other side, the feminizing discourse of Celticism. Literary and cultural critics, myself included, have addressed Irish feminization and simianization from a variety of perspectives, which limitations of space compel to assume in evidence rather than reviewing in detail.[1] What the accounts to date have generally failed to delineate, however, is the dialectical interplay of these racial figurations over time, the concerted action that gave the Irish stereotype its "stereo," self-ratifying effects. The ideological formation orchestrating these contrapuntal tropes and lending them their hegemonic power of containment was precisely the compulsory norm of manliness. For this reason, it is important to notice that many of the exponents of Irish simianization (Carlyle, Froude, Kingsley) and Irish feminization (the Arnolds, Thomas and Matthew, Acton, Tennyson) were among the leading theoreticians of (Anglo-Saxonist) manliness. Their alternating allegories of imagined Celtic deficiencies in virile self-possession and mastery circulated, in turn, among the mass cultural media of Victorian Britain and Ireland: popular novels and melodramas, newspaper articles, humor and opinion magazines, political cartoons (see L. P. Curtis, *Apes and Angels*).

Drawing upon contemporary sexological and Darwinian preoccupations, this ideological assemblage unfolded the logic of manhood in a manner calculated to manipulate semicolonial conflicts and anxieties and thus to disable the culture of Irish resistance. Here enlisted as footsoldiers of empire, participating *de facto* in the ethos of manliness; there reduced to inmates of empire, relegated *de jure* to the status of manhood's other – most politically articulate Irishmen internalized the broad Eurocentric ideology of gendered racial stereotyping, in which narrow Anglo-Saxon supremacism quickened and flourished. The contradictory semicolonial inscription of the Irish national subject often translated into a contradictory semi-imperial attitude on the part of the Irish nationalist subject, the most conspicuous manifestation of which was a masculinized identification with the colonial aggressor. But because the norm of aggressive passions aggressively checked presupposed the subject formally, if not fully, empowered to dispose of himself,

---

[1] For general accounts of Irish feminization and simianization see L. P. Curtis, *Anglo-Saxons and Celts* and Liz Curtis, *Nothing But the Same Old Story*. For more particular and ramified arguments concerning Irish feminization see Valente, "The Myth of Sovereignty" and Howes, *Yeats's Nations*; and concerning Irish dehumanization see L. P. Curtis, *Apes and Angels*, and Deane, "Civilians and Barbarians."

and because its accompanying code of social conduct was tailored to
serve as moral justification of this existing entitlement, manliness posed a
decisive double-bind for the (semi)colonial subaltern, who could only
secure the "quiet grandeur" (Mosse, *Image of Man*, 56) of its symbolic
mandate through vehement, even violent opposition to the status quo.
Feminization and simianization figured and implemented either side of
this double-bind in late Victorian/Edwardian Ireland.

No sooner did the metropolitan ethnologies of the Celt take hold in
the 1840s than the nationalist vanguard of the time, Young Ireland,
began urging its adherents to a collective display of manliness centering
on the traits of resolute endurance, self-discipline and respectability (see
Duffy, "The Young Men" and "Advice to the People"; Davis, *Literary
and Historical Essays*, 104–7). In this reaction, they anticipated the inaugural posture of subsequent moral force movements including Home
Rule and Sinn Fein. Each found itself confronted with the first side or
phase of the double-bind.

(1) If the semicolonial subject, individual or collective, elected to enact
the manly ideal and to demonstrate thereby his capacity for self-
control and respectable self-government, he had to restrain and
regulate his conduct in conformity with the received canons of
gender and social practice. But by pursuing this regimen, he would
perforce testify to his potential (gentle)manliness at the price of
abiding the order of his oppression and so lending at least tacit
support to its legitimacy and the correlative legitimacy of his own
exclusion from the rights and liberties of manhood. For the Irish
subaltern, observance of the manly norms of self-regulation
amounted to an acquiescence in the womanly norm of
submissiveness to others, evincing to all appearances the core
properties of the feminine stereotype – passivity, pliancy, a
willingness to yield – that British opinion regularly invoked as proof
of the essentially Celtic desire to be ruled.

Inevitably, Irish nationalists responded to the eternally returning specter
of feminization by asserting those part values of manliness best suited to
exorcise it. From this agenda evolved the compensatory posture that
Ashis Nandy has named "colonial hypermasculinity," the effort to
reverse the military-political success of the conquerors by mapping onto
the aggressive principles and practices animating that success (*The
Intimate Enemy*, 9–10). This ideological turn, from the promotion of

dignified self-control to the celebration of aggressive militancy, characterized the political itinerary of each of these moral force movements, as they gradually came into league with the physical force wing of the nationalist struggle: the progress of Young Ireland, from the pre-Famine alliance with O'Connell to the Rising of 1848, which ushered in the Fenian era of violent separatism; the progress of the Home Rule campaign, from the genteel suppliancy of Isaac Butt through the New Departure covenant, which tacitly included a new, highly volatile strain of agrarian Fenianism; and the progress of Sinn Fein, from the principled nonviolence of Griffith's original conception to its adventitious yet decisive identification with the martyred Volunteers of 1916.

That this common trajectory sketched a series of unconsciously defensive responses to the hegemonic ideal of manhood may be deduced in part from the rhetorical practices of Fenianism, with which these movements dovetailed. Leaders of the Irish Republican Brotherhood and its political and cultural confederates (the Land League, the Gaelic Athletic Association) sought to *nominally* attach the militarized, hypermasculine ethos they promulgated to the socially dominant mandate of manliness from which it *substantially* diverged. At the same time, however, men like James Stephens, O'Donovan Rossa, Michael Cusack, Joseph Roche, and Michael O'Doherty, deployed the vocabulary of manhood in a partial or synecdochic fashion that reversed its logic and thus belied its very essence.[2] Instead of marshaling aggressive force to the ends of self-discipline and mastery, their rhetoric of manhood marshaled forms of discipline as a means of enhancing aggressive force. So whereas the efforts of moral force nationalism to appropriate the symbolic capital of an assumed manliness tended to vitiate their agenda of practical resistance, the Fenians' attempt to appropriate the manly code to their practical agenda tended to vitiate their claim on its symbolic capital. This then triggered the other side of the double-bind.

(2) If the semicolonial subject, individual or collective, elected to assert his masculinity in defiance of the self-regulatory norm or the political regime that it served – if he sought, for example, the violent overthrow of the forces subordinating him – his course of action

---

[2] See Toby Joyce, "'Ireland's Trained and Marshalled Manhood.'" Joyce completely fails to recognize the motivated misreading involved in the Fenian use of the concept of manhood because he takes account of no other cultural context.

would indicate an inability to keep his passions in check, an absence of the self-control that was the hallmark of normative manliness and hence the fitness for freedom. By this path too, the Irish could only testify to the legitimacy of their marginalization. Now this supposed failure of self-possession could be referred to a range of predicates – hysteria, instability, irrationality – signifying a less acceptable but no less recognizable mode of racial and cultural femininity. But that which *went* uncontrolled in this sort of lawless aggression was, from the "muscular" standpoint, an excess of "animal spirits," bespeaking a racial and cultural subhumanity.

In the wake of Darwin's discoveries, the anthropoid afforded the readiest figure of a racial barbarism now attributed to the Irish largely in response to Fenian style risings and outrages. Indeed, the degree and frequency of Irish simianization varied in direct and uncannily exact proportion to the real or perceived threat of Fenian aggression (Curtis, *Apes and Angels*, 29–58). At the same time, the effort to controvert Calibanesque stereotypes of Irish belligerence and brutality with proclamations of the innate idealism and incomparable spirituality of the Celtic race – a staple of revivalist nationalism – was appropriated from the start to an Arnoldian framework of Celtic femininity, whose central tenets it recalled and reinforced. Just as the resistance of Irish *political* nationalism to racial feminization tended to ratify the concomitant imperialist discourse of racial simianization, so the resistance of Irish *cultural* nationalism to simianization tended to ratify the concomitant imperialist discourse of feminization.[3] With this closure of the ideological circuit, finally, the slippage I posited at the outset between late Victorian manhood and masculinity reveals its hegemonic import in yet another version of the gendered

---

[3] By this point it will be seen how significantly my sense of the sexual ethnologies of colonial Ireland differs from that addressed in Deane's "Civilians and Barbarians." Contra Deane, the Irish were not *primarily* feminized *qua* barbarians, but rather masculinized to the point of bestiality and denied their collective manhood on that basis. Nor were they feminized *precisely* as "civilians" or fully assimilated members of the metropolitan *socius*, but rather as semicolonials whose controlled resistance to empire took forms consonant with submission if not exactly loyalty to it. It will be seen, more importantly, that a complexly normative gender construct like manhood implies a far more supple and dynamic relationship between categories of ethno-colonial difference than a static dichotomy like civilians and barbarians. See ibid., 33–42.

double-bind we have been discussing. On one side, the British élite could deny the Irish their collective manhood for failing to meet the fundamental standard of virile masculinity, that is, for being insufficiently courageous, powerful, and unyielding in their resistance to colonial rule; on the other side, the British élite could deny the Irish their collective manhood for exceeding the fundamental standard of virile masculinity, for being excessively violent, aggressive and refractory in their resistance to colonial rule. One of the crueler effects of the Union, with its forced conversion of the Irish from colonial to metrocolonial subjects, was the way it facilitated their internalization of these strictures, in this disabling configuration, so that the Irish trauma of manhood would be reproduced, at least fractionally, in every attempt to overcome it. With all of its historical contingency, this dynamic most closely approximates the theoretical paradigm of colonial power known as "mimicry," wherein the subaltern inevitably confirms his or her difference from metropolitan norms in the compulsory approximation thereof (see Bhabha, *The Location of Culture*, 91).

II

It is one measure of Joyce's uncommon and imperfectly understood grasp of the commerce between gender and colonial politics that he seems to have compassed not only the overdetermined anxieties besetting Irish masculinity, but also the second-order, still more intractable aporia of semicolonial manhood. His renowned critical anatomy of the Dublin *parade virile* in the "Cyclops" episode of *Ulysses* attests as much. The brutish portrait of "the citizen" in the testosterone-soaked atmosphere of Kiernan's pub has repeatedly been read, not unjustly, as an interrogation of the embattled will to dominance fundamental to the patriarchal construction of masculinity. I myself might argue that the same portrait, whose model was Michael Cusack, the founder of the Gaelic Athletic Association, asks to be glossed in more historically specific terms as an indictment of colonial hypermasculinity, the ultimately self-betraying identification of the conquered with the phallic aggression of the conqueror. Each of these lines of interpretation restricts its own scope, however, by exempting the novel's protagonist, Leopold Bloom, from the episode's gender critique; each tacitly translates his subjection to xenophobic racism *within* the narrative frame into a kind of immunity from the duelling parodic voices that articulate the frame.[4] Once this error is corrected, however, and the unforgiving sweep of the satirical perspective acknowledged, one can see that the epicenter of the chapter is not finally the citizen as obtrusively phallicized index of a problematic (Irish) masculinism, but the underlying *logic* of his relationship to Bloom, which demarcates with astonishing precision the double-bind of Irish manhood.[5]

The introduction of the principals establishes the symbolic register of manliness as the framework of their growing antagonism. The citizen, who comes to figure hypermasculinity as dehumanizing, an overflow of animal spirits, first appears in a *tête-à-tête* with his animal "spirit" or "familiar": "having a great confab with himself and that bloody mangy mongrel, Garryowen" (*U* 12.118–20). The interchangeability of man and beast suggested by the formulation reasserts itself in a pointedly comprehensive pattern throughout the episode. Man and dog share a diseased outward appearance, the citizen "puffing and blowing with the dropsy" (12.1784–85) and the dog "growling and grousing and his eye all bloodshot from the drouth . . . and the hydrophobia dropping out of his jaws" (12.709–11). They likewise share a mendicant lifestyle: "getting fed up by the ratepayers and the corporators. Entertainment for man and beast" (12.754–55). They appear to share an inner life as well. The citizen's irrepressible animosity toward Bloom repeatedly finds its counterpart in Garryowen's hostility: "and the citizen scowling after [Bloom] and the old dog at his feet looking up to know who to bite and when" (12.1161–62); "Don't tell anyone, says the citizen, letting a bawl out of him . . . And the bloody dog woke up and let a growl" (12.1765–66). Finally, man and beast share a mode of expressing that inner life: "He starts . . . talking to him in Irish and the old towser growling, letting on to answer, like a duet in the opera. Such growling you never heard as they let off between them" (12.705–7). That the Irish language is specifically marked as the medium for this unification of the higher and lower orders situates the citizen's bestial associations as a

---

[4] One exception is Emer Nolan's reading, whose impetus, very different from my own, is to rehabilitate the citizen to some degree. See Nolan, *James Joyce and Nationalism*, 102–12.

[5] Enda Duffy reads Bloom and the citizen in terms of Deane's dichotomy of civilians and barbarians (*The Subaltern "Ulysses,"* 111–14). Taking the ideological stake of manhood shifts and volatizes the grounds of his literary interpretation in much the same way that it does Deane's historical interpretation.

function of his being a stereotype, both living and literary, of the "wild" Irishman (Duffy, *The Subaltern "Ulysses,"* 112).

The parodic excursions attached to Garryowen and his master serve to ratify and extend the citizen's stereotypical role, while simultaneously lampooning the Revivalist movement for reinforcing such stock images of Gaelic savagery in the very attempt to dispel them. The "duet" triggers an hilarious parody of Gaelicist propaganda, in which the growlings of the "old Irish red setter wolfdog" are celebrated for their approximation of "the ranns of ancient Celtic bards" and "the satirical effusions of the famous Raftery" (12.722–23, 729–30). Not only, the passage intimates, does such promotion of "the spread of human culture among the lower animals" emulate the self-styled, British imperialist mission of soul-making, but the Revivalist enthusiasm for conferring significant cultural interest or value on the most dubious if distinctively Irish excrescences of the soul enacts a refusal of aesthetic discrimination and decorum consonant with imperialist preconceptions of native barbarism. The Irish beast-as-man, Garryowen as "Owen Garry," cannot be dissociated from the (stage) Irishman as beast, the citizen as Caliban. To emphasize this point, Joyce redoubles the narrative "duet" at the level of the parodic set pieces. This entire passage answers to an earlier pastiche of Revivalist mythography that casts the citizen as an idealized specimen of Irish manliness:

> broadshouldered deepchested stronglimbed frankeyed redhaired freelyfreckled shaggybearded widemouthed largenosed longheaded deepvoiced barekneed brawnyhanded hairylegged ruddyfaced sinewyarmed hero. From shoulder to shoulder he measured several ells and his rocklike mountainous knees were covered, as was likewise the rest of his body wherever visible, with a strong growth of tawny prickly hair in hue and toughness similar to the mountain gorse (*Ulex Europeus*). The widewinged nostrils, from which bristles of the same tawny hue projected, were of such capaciousness that within their cavernous obscurity the fieldlark might easily have lodged her nest.
> (*U* 12.152–61)

Like the canine poet, this primordial figure of the citizen parodies not just a cultural discourse but a cultural dynamic, how the need to affirm Irish worth in the teeth of colonial ambivalence and abjection induces modes of exaggeration, both verbal and behavioral, which violate the canons of stalwart moderation informing the metropolitan ideal of manhood.

Bloom, by contrast, enters on to the "Cyclops" stage as something of a paragon of self-control. Joe Hynes calls him "the prudent member"

(12.211), and the ensuing parody of Irish legend turned this epithet into an epitome of Bloom's character: "O'Bloom, the son of Rory: it is he. Impervious to fear is Rory's son: he of the prudent soul" (12.216–17). The mock-heroic bathos of the final and defining phrase prepares the reader for the received Dublin interpretation of Bloom's signature trait as an infraction of the homosocial code that shapes immediate judgments on gender normativity and compliance. Whereas the citizen's own narrative associations with the generic hero, Rory – "doing the raparee and Rory of the hill" (12.134) – betokens an attitude of spurious hypermasculine bravado, Bloom's parallel association here comes increasingly to adumbrate an effeminate or *hypo*masculine attitude of circumspection.

First, Bloom's prudence-as-wariness around the growling Garryowen raises suspicions in both the citizen and the "nameless" narrator as to his physical courage, a baseline requirement of masculine and therefore manly self-presentation. Next, Bloom's prudence-as-discretion in refusing the offer of drink – "he wouldn't and he couldn't and excuse him no offense and all to that" (12.435–36) – not only violates local notions of sociability but also local notions of intestinal fortitude (literally), which involve the willingness to submit to homosocial rituals of self-abandon. The derision with which the nameless one greets Bloom's demurral – "Gob, he's a prudent member and no mistake" (12.437) – subtly modulates the key sense of the term "member," bringing in a punning phallic connotation that qualifies Bloom's disposition as the opposite of, say, raging virility. In a decisive paradox, which virtually defines the larger ideological matrix we are examining, the very mark of élite metropolitan *manhood*, unaffected self-restraint, counts as a lack or deficiency in lower-class subaltern *masculinity*. This normative slippage, in turn, allows for what we might call a ruse of (gendered) reason: in placing an emasculating construction upon Bloom's temperate habits, the barflies not only radiate their unconscious anxiety over their own colonial emasculation, they simultaneously testify to their misapprehension of and thus their incapacity for manhood proper.

Finally, there is the credited rumor of Bloom's prudence-as-calculation in his campaign to propitiate a wealthy dowager (Mrs. Riordan) at the City Arms Hotel. Both the manner and the matter of the nameless one's representation of Bloom's conduct speaks to its perceived effeminacy: "and Bloom trying to get the soft side of her doing the mollycoddle playing bézique to come in for a bit of the wampum in her will and not eating meat of a Friday because the old one was always

thumping her craw . . ." (12.505–8). From the narrator's perspective, the
unmanly quality of Bloom's oblique, self-serving scheme reveals itself in
the contrivances to which he resorts: participating in female-identified
entertainment like "bezique" and submitting to an alien female authority
in matters like dietary regulation. The effeminate gloss given Bloom's
course of action is brilliantly telescoped in the phrase "doing the mollycoddle." Molly is, of course, the name of Bloom's wife, so that the phrase
suggests performing as a Mrs. rather than a Mr. Bloom. But "molly" was
also current slang for male homosexuality, a preference then predomi-
nantly construed on the model of sexual inversion, what Karl Ulrichs
famously encapsulated as "a feminine soul enclosed in a man's body"
(Sinfield, *The Wilde Century*, 110). The phrase "doing the mollycoddle,"
accordingly, also suggests revealing one's inner feminine/homo sexuality. These various associations subsequently crystallize in the nameless
one's sudden memory of yet another page from the City Arms chapter of
Bloom's legend: "Lying up in the hotel Pisser was telling me once a
month . . . like a totty with her courses" (12.1659–60). While this report
and others like it in "Cyclops" chime with the novel's many indices of
Bloom's gender mobility, their local ideological purport is just the opposite of Joyce's overall design, not to build up a character whose rounded-
ness might exceed the sex–gender system of classification, but to reduce
a character to a fully and narrowly classifiable abnormality. Bloom, like
the citizen, functions *in this episode* less as a psychologized subject than as
a discursive effect, a particular moment in the circulation and consolida-
tion of ethno-gender stereotypes.

   With this in mind, it is worth noting that the particular nexus constel-
lating Bloom's reputation for prudence with his gender status centered
on certain stock preconceptions of the ethnic differences between
Jewishness and Irishness, preconceptions that Bloom shares, in
significant respects, with his anti-Semitic interlocutors. Thus, the nameless one opposes a clichéd image of the clever and devious Jew to the likewise familiar stereotype of the ingenuous and simple-minded Irishman,
finding the latter to be inevitably bested by the former. "Never be up to
those . . . Jerusalem . . . cuckoos," he says (12.1571–72). But at the same
time he tacitly transposes these conventional ethnic affiliations into the
register of late Victorian gender assumption, where (Jewish) sophistica-
tion and overcultivation were signifiers of racialized femininity, while
the racially inflected norms of masculinity included a straightforward
and uncorrupted vigor. Recounting his experience in Kiernan's pub to

Stephen in "Eumaeus," Bloom invokes a cognate if transvalued racial dichotomy. Driven "from some bump of combativeness or gland of some kind" (16.1112), Bloom's Irish type repeats the nameless one's ethno-ego ideal with a difference: in its bodily overdetermination, his masculinity shades into bestiality on one side ("bump of combativeness") and femininity on the other ("gland of some kind"). "Practical and...proved to be so" (16.1125), Bloom's Jewish type likewise registers the nameless one's anti-Semitic construction with a difference: his feminized caginess and carefulness shades into the manly public virtue of economic rationality – what Bloom, in aptly metropolitan tones, calls being "imbued with the proper spirit" (16.1124). For Bloom, finally, as for the narrator, the Jew inevitably bests or surpasses the Irish Catholic, the former bringing prosperity wherever he goes, the latter condemned to poverty by his sedulous adherence to Catholic "dogma" and clerical authority (16.1129). The nameless one builds his typological framework on the popular ethnological classification of the Jews as bearers of feminine traits of mind and culture.[6] By this means he moves to displace or preempt the no less prevalent ethnological thesis that the Celto-Irish possessed an "essentially feminine" racial cast (Cairns and Richards, *Writing Ireland*, 42) most clearly evidenced in the culture of defeat that the narrator himself repeatedly invokes. The narrator does not, that is to say, treat Bloom as an Irish Jew, a hybrid and doubly feminized identity formation, but as a Jewish negation of Irishness, feminized in its stead. In so doing, he works to counter the gender allegory of British imperialism *while and by* affirming its basic principles and presuppositions: the absolute disjunction of gender categories; the essential congruence of racial or gender identity; the derogation of the feminine as inferior, properly subject to male command, and, in its racial dimension, humiliating. For the subaltern who internalizes these attitudes, like the narrator, the ideological aim is typically to enforce his claim to a rugged and aggressive masculinity. But this objective just as typically turns out a foil or decoy for the real exclusionary standard of entitlement (privilege/desert), metropolitan manliness.

Bloom's corresponding typological framework supplies, or at least implies just this sort of critique. Although Bloom proclaims himself "as good an Irishman as that rude [citizen]" (16.1132), he no more frames his

---

[6] For Joyce's conversance with these Semitic ethnologies, see Valente, *James Joyce and the Problem of Justice*, 84.

subject position in the hybrid terms of Irish Jewry than the narrator does. He too, in fact, represents Jewishness as something of a negation of Irishness, but he sees the object of that negation as the improvident passion that defines the Irish to their detriment. So whereas for the narrator, the Jew constitutes the feminized other of the Irish colonial, a scapegoat of his own masculine anxiety, for Bloom the Jew forms the pragmatic, rational other of the Irish colonial, a necessary supplement to his present, unmanly condition.

Taken in combination, these racial paradigms reveal how the double-bind of manhood can and perhaps must come to exacerbate the interracial stresses *within* the colonial society and to reproduce itself along the faultlines thus engendered. Because the norm of proper manliness evolved under the aegis of imperialism and as a mechanism for confining the subaltern to a position of flexible inferiority, the claims of subdominant groups to such manliness could only be sustained relative to one another and through an internecine struggle of mutual abjection. In "Cyclops," the barflies on one side, noisily, and Bloom himself on the other, more quietly, exemplify this dynamic. By having Bloom answer the explicitly gendered anti-Semitism of the citizen *et al*. with a "reverse" but no less racialist discourse, Joyce elaborates the problem of Irish racial antipathy as a structural effect of the colonial predicament in general and the trauma of Irish manhood in particular.

Nowhere did this vise of semicolonial manhood pinch to more constraining effect than in the explicitly political arena of national resistance, and no debate topic, "Cyclops" shows, could more readily expose and sexualize Ireland's interracial division and hostility. In order to emphasize, once again, the systematic nature of the problem, Joyce stages the political disagreement between Bloom and the citizen as a thinly mediated expression of their opposed styles of colonial "mimicry." To this end, he initially leaves the gravamen of their dispute unspecified, while foregrounding their differently gendered mode of address. Bloom's politics of "moderation and botheration" seems an effect of his genteel, reasonable, and consensus-oriented cast of mind and argument – "with his *but don't you see?* and *but on the other hand*" (12.1195, 513–14). The citizen's politics of forcible separatism seems an effect of an immediately confrontational and ferociously polarizing demeanor. In either case, the mode of address signals a fundamental link between the frustrated strain of nationalism avowed and the failed synecdoche of manhood personified.

As befits his embrace of hypermasculinity, and his correlative fall into troglodytism, the citizen (over)embodies the cause and principles of physical force nationalism. He is given out, first of all, to be the founder of the Gaelic Athletic Association which, as Joyce well knew, had from its inception served as a satellite, front, and recruiting arm of the Irish Republican Brotherhood. Hence, Joe Hynes's otherwise inexplicable identification of the citizen with the founder of modern Fenianism: "There's the man . . . that made the Gaelic sports revival. There he is sitting there. The man that got away James Stephens" (12.880–1). Of course, little pragmatic correlation exists in the modern age between martial and athletic prowess; to paraphrase Stephen Dedalus's mockery of Davin, a Cusack disciple, one cannot "make the next revolution with hurling sticks" (*A Portrait*, 202). The strategic connection between the movements, accordingly, must be seen to lie elsewhere (as Stephen comes to recognize in "Nestor"), specifically in the *symbolic* equivalence of martial and athletic endeavor as competitive mechanisms for asserting and reproducing a certain fantasy of masculinity and as dynamic signifiers of the masculinity thus asserted and reproduced: masculinity as strength, as energy, as brute mastery. For this very reason, however, the valorization of sport, like the adherence to violent political methods, opened itself to the charge of debasing the ideal of manhood to its most visceral denominator, of confusing manliness with "mere" animal spirits.

Thus, even as British journalism had begun to press this claim with respect to simianized Irish freedom fighters, the *Dublin Review* stated much the same case with respect to athleticized British public school culture, where the higher values of religion and morality were allegedly being "strangled by the luxurious overgrowth of animal vigour" (Mangan, "Social Darwinism and Upper Class Education," 145–46). Even the most famous chronicler and exponent of public school athleticism, Thomas Hughes, exclaimed against the fetishism thereof. His later work, *The Manliness of Christ*, explicitly pairs feats of martial daring and feats of athletic skill as "tests of animal courage" that "have come to be very much overpraised and overvalued amongst us" as "tests of manliness," which would be more appropriately fashioned in accordance with the cerebral and spiritual attributes displayed by Jesus Christ (24–25). His position finds an allusive echo in that adopted by Bloom himself, in his role as standard-bearer for the spiritual and cerebral component of Irish manhood. Within a parody of the sport's society, *Slaugh na h-Eireen*, Bloom demurs at the jingoistic aggrandizement of "Gaelic sports and pastimes" as being "calculated to revive the best traditions of manly strength and prowess" (12.909–11). And shortly thereafter he seeks to affirm the value of sport, including the English game of "lawn tennis," on a more temperate and rational basis, that is, in proportion to such pragmatic benefits as "the agility and training the eye" and "the circulation of the blood" (12.945–46, 952–53). It is this infringement on the hypermasculine fantasy space that elicits the first overt rebuke of Bloom ("a mixed reception of applause and hisses," 12.912–13) and helps to trigger the group dynamic leading to his mock crucifixion, a "test of [his] manliness" conformable with "the manliness of Christ."

Initially, the gripe against Bloom focuses on his apparent lack of patriotic fervor. Thus, the group answers his skeptical comments on the Gaelic Athletic's Association by exhorting the citizen to a "stentorian" rendition of "A Nation Once Again," an anthem whose apotheosis of the "ancient freemen of Greece and Rome" (Davis, *National and Other Poems*, 27) serves, in this context, to center an identification of Gaelic sports with Irish freedom upon the exercise of aggressive masculine power. By these lights, Bloom's questioning of the sports revival is seen to betray the nationalist cause in and through a failure of personal virility. But in what proves a characteristic rhetorical gambit in "Cyclops," Joyce undercuts this easy patriotism in advance by showing hypermasculine Irish athleticism to be already caught in a web of ideological self-betrayal.

An immediately antecedent parliamentary parody conjoins the program of *Slaugh na h-Eireen* and the government-mandated slaughter of suspect animals:

> Mr. Cowe Conacre (Multifarnham. Nat.): ... may I ask ... whether ... these animals shall be slaughtered though no medical evidence is forthcoming as to their pathological condition? ...
> Mr. Orelli O'Reilly (Montenotte. Nat.): Have similar orders been issued for the slaughter of human animals who dare to play Irish games in the Phoenix park?
> (*U* 12.860–67)

The Irish Nationalists' question for the government not only underscores the phantasmatic linkage of athletic struggle and military discipline but, more importantly, hints at how the double valuation of these activities – as manly by certain lights and bestial by others – could be mapped onto the metropolitan–subaltern dichotomy to ludicrous yet deadly effect. So long as the Irish can simply be deemed "pathological" human animals, the parody stresses, casual imperialist bloodletting remains a conceivable and even respectable treatment for inherently bar-barous native sport. The satiric thrust, which reflects back on the citizen/Gaelic Athletic Association's displaced admiration for such naked masculinized coercion, is enhanced on all counts by a sly proleptic allusion to the Croke Park Massacre, where English soldiers responded to a savage Irish Republican Brotherhood outrage with the arbitrary "slaughter of human animals" out for a Gaelic Athletic Association sponsored football match. Joyce thus adumbrates a vicious semicolonial circle in which hypermasculine identifications with the aggressor return as unmanly, in this case bestialized, self-aggression.

The same semicolonial loop delimits the citizen's more direct promo-tion of the physical force movement, with opposed yet strictly correla-tive typological effects. In keeping with his symbolic role, the citizen apparently awaits any stray opportunity to recite the Fenian litany of failed Irish risings: "So of course the citizen was only waiting for the wink of the word and he starts gassing about the invincibles and the old guard and the men of sixtyseven and who fears to speak of ninetyeight and . . . all the fellows that were hanged, drawn, and transported for the cause." In this case, the "wink of the word" arises out of speculation on the "philoprogenitive erection" of one Joe Brady, "Invincible" assassin, on the event of his hanging (12.479–83). As the barroom discussion unfolds, the Brady anecdote comes to emblematize not only the eroti-cization of political violence as a desperate assertion of colonial virility, but also the eroticization of political violence *suffered*, at the hands of a mightier foe: indeed, it literalizes the notion of "having a hard on" for defeat and death. Fortified by the ensuing parody of Robert Emmet's hanging, which features the *homocolonial* transfer of Emmet's fiancée to a "young Oxford graduate" (12.658–62), the Brady anecdote hints at the hidden complicity of the citizen's position with the imperialist regime. This critique specifically turns upon the profound reversibility of the colonial hypermasculine ethos into a feminized cult of (self-)sacrificial loss, which Celticists like Matthew Arnold had long established as the grounds of Irish subordination.

As the citizen unpacks his rhetorical store, the deadlock at the heart of his political faith presses to the surface of the collective awareness of his bar mates, where it is ultimately disavowed (acknowledged yet denied) through a transferential group dynamic that gives his debate with Bloom its distinctive trajectory. A couple of related factors enable this dawning awareness, neither of which is fully accessible nor even admissible to it. First, for many of the characters, the hybridized subject position of semicolonialism makes for a dehiscent political sensibility we might call seminationalism. Doubly/divisively inscribed in both the metropolitan and colonial orders, interpellated by the antagonistic yet structurally complicit discourses and value systems that bind these orders abrasively together, such subjectivities take shape through split institutional dependencies, split ethno-gender identifications, split adherences to empire and to decolonization, all operating across multiple layers of express and repressed motivation. On the terms of this highly particular psychic agon, where affective divisions cross lines of geopolitical generality, support for local modes of cultural separatism, like playing "Irish games," does not translate into support, nor even signify robust desire for a more violent separation (in all senses) from the metropolitan marriage. To the contrary, such support often obscures and allays – in the manner of a compromise formation – the ambivalence that the prospect of outright divorce arouses. Like Irish anti-Semitism, with which it is connected, the familiar Joycean motif of Irish (self-)betrayal finally answers less to moral judgments on national character than to structural analyses of the metrocolonial condition of subjectivation.

It is precisely to highlight this circumstance that Joyce punctuates the proceedings with the arrival of that most politically compromised caste of Dubliners, the "Castle Catholics" (Cunningham and Power), whose seemingly benign appearance in "the castle car" occasions a medieval romance parody targeting the utterly venal privilege of their official position (12.1588–1620). Their characteristically latitudinarian brand of politics, already articulated at this point by their colleague, J. J. O'Molloy, primarily consists in the guarded "moderation" associated with Bloom and involves the affectation of a metropolitan style of gentlemanliness, what the narrator calls "doing the toff" (12.1192). Whereas the citizen tropes British imperial civilization as "syphilisation," a foreign contagion vitiating the manly properties of the native body politic, O'Molloy seems to honor that same imperial civilization as an offspring of "the European family," a wholesome form of incorporation in which Ireland shares (12.1197, 1202). A very different sort of identification with the colonizer underlies this viewpoint (which is shared by most of the more vocal characters of the episode), an identification not with the brute strength of his aggression but with the sublimated and legitimated fruits of that aggression.

This alternative identificatory perspective, secondly, is especially prone to apprehend the self-defeating impetus of the citizen's violent separatism and to focus thereon as a way of defending itself against a full recognition of its own conflicts, complicities, and irresolution. When the citizen grandly imagines Ireland recovering her place as a center of European trade, he is immediately reminded of the overpowering impediment posed by the British navy. When the citizen moves to belittle the navy, by adducing the homoeroticized cruelty of its disciplinary rituals, Bloom turns the imputation back upon his own hypermasculine agenda: "But . . . isn't discipline the same everywhere. I mean wouldn't it be the same here if you put force against force?" (12.1361). Most pointedly, when the citizen proceeds to call for armed rebellion ("We'll put force against force" [12.1364]), he immediately finds his message read back to him, as the Lacanians say, "in reverse order." He stakes the success of the coming revolution on the might of "our greater Ireland beyond the sea," now populated with valiant and vengeful Irish expatriots, "the sons of Granuaile, the champions of Kathleen ni Houlihan" (12.1364–65, 1374–75). But his interlocutors, Lambert and Nolan, are quick to indicate that Ireland's foreign dependence has always proven the flip side of its colonial corruption, figuring no less heavily in the feminized Celtic tradition of romantic expenditure without return. They reiterate the citizen's own familiar roll of Irish defeats and disappointments, not for the purpose of ennobling a thwarted past, but of discouraging a self-immolative future. ("We fought for the royal Stewarts that reneged us . . . We gave our best blood to France and Spain, the wild geese. Fontenoy, eh? And Sarsfield and O'Donnell . . . But what did we ever get for it?" [12.1379–84].) If, as Emer Nolan notes, the citizen's list of historical grievances (12.1239–57) derives from Joyce's "Ireland, Island of Saints and Sages," the others' dissent from his position seconds the same essay's conclusion, that it is "past time for Ireland to have done once and for all with failure" (*CW* 174).

The perceived futility of the citizen's posture, in turn, feminizes the man himself in his very troglodytism, for it exposes his hypermasculine potency as mere pose or show, the kind of self-advertising performance associated in the late Victorian Imaginary with feminine *heteronomy*, woman's inherent being-for-others. If, as Lacan has argued, the phallus can only function when veiled, it is in part because phallic display always admits of feminine construction *qua* display, particularly when, as in this case, the display reveals the phallus to be myth or fraud. Thus the nameless one sneers that the citizen is "all wind and piss like a tanyard cat" (12.1311–12), a formulation that neatly synthesizes the animal with the feminine. He goes on to remark how, owing to the citizen's breach of Land League solidarity, the Molly Maguires wanted to answer his phallic pretensions, "his tall talk," by putting a hole in him (12.1312–16).

Strangely unremarked in *Ulysses* criticism, this concerted yet subterranean resistance to the citizen's agenda neither originates nor terminates with his designated adversary, Leopold Bloom. Bloom does, however, crystallize the resistance in simultaneously symbolic and narrative terms. Consistent with his personification of the "prudent" self-controlled aspect of metropolitan manhood, Bloom stakes out the political necessity of getting beyond the endless cycle of "force against force." In keeping with the nationalist terrain of Edwardian Ireland, this priority inclines him towards an identification with, if not actual participation in, the various constituency groups of the moral force movement. At one point, Bloom sympathetically invokes "the Gaelic League and the antitreating League" and, with the phrase "drink, the curse of Ireland," the temperance movement generally (12.683–4). In addition, he is repeatedly credited with contributing significantly to Sinn Fein's initial nonviolent strategy (12.1574, 1625–37). What these movements have in common in their respective domains – cultural, social, and political nationalism – is a commitment to enhancing Irish self-respect conceived along the lines of social respectability, a project which subscribes closely to the *Weltanschauung* of bourgeois manliness. Thus, while the Gaelic League curriculum venerated peasant culture and folklore, its institutional organization and self-promotion aimed to advance middle class social values and cultural prestige, so that even a sympathetic observer like George Russell could complain of its "boyscoutish propaganda" (Kiberd, *Inventing Ireland*, 157), thereby affiliating the League with the one institution most identified with cultivating middle-class manliness. For their part, the temperance movement and the antitreating league not only held the achievement of bourgeois respectability to be essential to the decolonization of Ireland ("Ireland sober is Ireland free"), they explicitly defined such respectability in terms of self-discipline, self-control, and personal integrity, thus conflating the ethical mandates of *individual* manliness with the political goals of autonomy, unity, and self-determination that had come to delimit *racial* manhood. Sinn Fein drew out this connection with still greater force; it projected the approved manly criteria of self-sufficiency, self-containment, and self-reliance directly into the public political sphere via its signature policy of passive resistance and parliamentary withdrawal. At the same time, insofar as this signature policy envisioned a "shadow government . . . complete with a sort of Parliament" (Tifft, "The Parricidal Phantasm," 320), Sinn Fein's claim to enabling national autonomy could well be judged more rather than less dependent than violent separatism on an on-going act of identification with the colonizer. In either event, the fact that Bloom is "know[n] . . . in the castle" to have outlined precisely this policy to Arthur Griffith accentuates his own political profile in its stark and schematic opposition to the citizen's as an image of Irish manhood (12.1637–38).

As Enda Duffy has remarked, however, by the time Joyce composed and revised the "Cyclops" episode, Sinn Fein had grown identified in the popular mind with the Easter Rising and, in consequence, had become the leading physical force party in Ireland (*The Subaltern "Ulysses,"* 125). The proleptic allusion to this turn of events in "Cyclops," reinforced by the citizen's use of the phrase Sinn Fein as a war cry (12.523), has the effect of undercutting Bloom's political credo in a manner analogous to the parodic undercutting of the citizen's attitudes earlier. It reminds the reader that just as colonial hypermasculinity regularly issued in a feminized cult of defeat and self-immolation, exemplified by the Easter Rising, so the passive gentlemanly resistance of Sinn Fein ultimately mutated into a program of violent guerrilla insurgency in response to its own emasculation, of which a "delirium of the brave" like Easter 1916 was sharp notice.

Bloom's own moment of political advocacy in "Cyclops" epitomizes the gendered dilemma of purely moral intervention. Attempting to parry the citizen's casual anti-Semitic thrusts, Bloom draws a parallel between the Irish and the Jews as victims of persecution:

> And I belong to a race too, says Bloom, that is hated and persecuted. Also now.
> This very moment. This very instant . . . Robbed . . . Plundered. Insulted.
> Persecuted. Taking what belongs to us by right. At this very moment, says he,
> putting up his fist, sold by auction in Morocco like slaves or cattle . . . I'm talking
> about injustice, says Bloom.
> (*U* 12.1468–74)

But when invited to pursue the belligerent course that his clenched fist seems to endorse ("Stand up to it then with force like men," 12.1475),

Bloom declines on principle – Force, hatred, history, all that. That's not life for men and women, insult and hatred" (12.1481–82) – and confesses by his body language to having no other effective solution: "He collapses all of a sudden, twisting around all the opposite, as limp as a wet rag" (12.1478–80). While this image of sudden detumescence and flaccidity undoubtedly proceeds from the narrator's already feminized construction of Bloom ("Gob, he'd adorn a sweeping brush, so he would, if only he had a nurse's apron on him" [12.1477–78], it nevertheless speaks to the fatal weakness of Bloom's colonial impersonation of manhood. Throughout "Cyclops," Joyce manipulates narration, dialogue, and parodic excursion in an effort to discredit without entirely discounting the invidious viewpoint of the nameless one and to achieve thereby a measure of stylistic "binocularity." In this case, Joyce half-participates in the narrator's caustic irony by satirizing the incapacity of Bloom's political sensibility to combat just such a jaundiced perspective. Thus, Joyce carefully juxtaposes the "injustice" of Bloom's complaint with the "force" of Nolan's rejected recommendation so as to craft an allusion to Pascal's famous *pensée*, "Justice without force is impotent" ("La justice sans force est impuissante"),[7] which can be read as articulating metaphorically the practical futility and the personal emasculation encoded in Bloom's limp bodily attitude.

These two forms of impotence ultimately converge in Bloom's facile panacea to the Irish–Jewish question: an abstract notion of "love," defined only as "the opposite of hatred" (12.1485). Having been successively glossed along religious, political, and romantic lines, this unanchored signifier is progressively displaced and debased across one of the episode's most vicious parodies, the "Love loves to love love" interlude (12.143–1501). To acknowledge Joyce's supplement to the barflies' mockery of Bloom here is not to ally him in any simple way with Bloom's tormentors. Whereas they pillory Bloom for a racialized dearth of masculinity, Joyce marks the semicolonial limitations of the mode of manliness, political and otherwise, that Bloom does in fact assume. To disregard Joyce's critique of Bloom on this score, accordingly, is to miss a crucial aspect of Joyce's subtle engagement with mimicry as a technology of imperial power. After all, self-immolation is not the only type of failure with which Ireland "must have done," according to the essay "Ireland, Island of Saints and Sages" (*CW* 174). In the same paragraph,

---

[7] Quoted in Derrida, "Force of Law," 37.

Joyce notes that "Ireland had already had enough of equivocations" as well (*CW* 174). And for the subaltern, equivocation – as between self-possession and self-repression – is the irreducible risk of internalized "prudence" or restraint.

To appreciate this same technology, moreover, it is essential to recognize not just that the episode's anti-Bloomite sentiment is not entirely confined to the barroom community, but also that the barroom sentiment itself is not entirely anti-Bloomite. To the contrary, Joyce takes care to position most of the assembled characters somewhere between the gendered political polarities occupied by Bloom and the citizen. Not, it should be noted, in a site of mediation, but rather along a curve of vacillation and (self-)betrayal, which expresses, in pragmatic terms, the double/divisive interpellation of their semicolonial subjectivity and the psychomachia it engenders. As a function of their understated opposition to the citizen's hypermasculine extremism, many of the symposiasts league themselves with rather than against Bloom at various points in the discussion: O'Molloy in "arguing about law and history" with the citizen (12.1235); Lambert and Nolan in questioning the wisdom of armed revolution; and, most passionately, Nolan once again in adducing Bloom's decisive contribution to Sinn Fein. As a function, conversely, of their sense that this more "prudent" restrained political stance also forsakes virtues essential to national(ist) manhood (strength, valor, fortitude, etc.), these same symposiasts find it necessary to seize opportunities for turning on Bloom and disowning his views. By the same token, the citizen is encouraged to train his nationalist ire entirely on Bloom as a way of binding the others to him in an on-going dissimulation of their differences. Thus, a kind of negative racial transference unfolds: the men identify with Bloom largely in order to project their own Irish inflected shame, anxiety, and vulnerability on to his Jewishness, bringing their structurally determined self-betrayal and their structurally determined anti-Semitism into alignment.

Such a collective dynamic, however, cannot but remain arrested in what Freud called denegation, that is, unconscious affirmation in the very form of categorical denial (Freud, *General Psychological Theory*, 214–17). For the scapegoat figure, in this case Bloom, cannot come to bear the constitutive frailties of the congregation except insofar as he dwells within as well as beyond its borders *in the very form of his expulsion*. He must be a participant-outcast, if you will, performing each of these conflicting offices by way of the other. Joyce fashions Bloom to fulfill this precise role in the secular context of "Cyclops" by giving him the status of social symptom as well as stereotype, and a symptom of the very men who currently stereotype him. A symptom, to paraphrase Slavoj Žižek, is something that encodes the hidden law of any system (personality, institution, community) as its most persistent disturbance (*The Sublime Object of Ideology*, 71–75). It is therefore, like the scapegoat, intensely representative of a given whole in and through its exceptionality, and Bloom occupies just such an internal ethno-gender boundary for Kiernan's patrons. He is, as Žižek would say, in them more than them (76). Accordingly, at just the moment that Bloom's racial and sexual abjection achieve their ultimate articulation, he stands forth as the image of the group in his imposed otherness, quintessentially Irish in the social construction of his Jewishness.

The group's final attack on Bloom begins by pushing beyond his perceived lack of patriotism to his supposed absence, as a Jew, of any proper *patrie*, and as such it clearly acts to displace the trauma of their own undecidable social inscription in the interstice of colony and metropole. Notice that the acid exchange is initiated by Nolan, periodically Bloom's most vocal supporter.

> – But do you know what a nation means? says John Wyse.
> – Yes, says Bloom.
> – What is it? says John Wyse.
> – A nation? says Bloom. A nation is the same people living in the same place.
> – By God, then, says Ned, laughing, if that's so I'm a nation for I'm living in the same place for the past five years. So of course everyone had the laugh at Bloom...
> – Or also living in different places.
> – That covers my case, says Joe.
> (*U* 12.1419–29)

Joyce here arranges the dialogue so that the barflies cannot but reassert in their implicitly anti-Semitic banter the larger parallelism the novel develops between the Irish and Jewish condition. The very mechanism for ridiculing Bloom's Hebraic placelessness underlines the fundamentally self-reflexive nature of the enterprise, insistently returning the muddled question of nationhood to the Dubliners' own place of residence, which is indeed, geopolitically speaking, a *self-different* interspace, at once the capital of Ireland, the center of the English pale and the seat of colonial government.

This decentering of the domestic space of Irish life signals a form of political castration for Irish manhood, a breakdown in corporate autonomy and self-possession. Dublin as gnomon equals the Dubliner as no man. Here again, the linkage must somehow be displaced on to Bloom as Jew. Hence Nolan's admonition to Bloom and his coreligionists, "stand up to [persecution] then with force like men" (12.1475), when not five minutes earlier he had prudently rejected the very same course for Ireland. This particular trauma of dispossessed Irish manhood is so pronounced in fact that its symptomatic expression shows a compulsive tendency to repeat. No sooner do those personifications of semicolonial ambivalence, the castle hacks, appear than the question of Bloom's Sinn Fein nationalism reemerges, closely shadowed by the stigma of his "Jewish" deracination:

> — And after all, says John Wyse, why can't a jew love his country like the next fellow?
> — Why not, says J. J., when he's quite sure which country it is.
>   (*U*12.1628–30)

On this occasion, the analogy of the Irish to the Jewish condition finds explicit affirmation, and in terms which speak to what the double-bind of dehumanizing violence versus feminizing restraint leaves behind as an irredentist option: "They're still waiting for their redeemer, says Martin. For that matter so are we" (12.1644–45). The collective psychic threat posed by this comment can be deduced from the alacrity with which it is made the grounds for emasculating the absent Bloom as an "every Jew" (12.1647):

> — Yes, says J. J., and every male that's born they think it may be their Messiah. And every jew is in a tall state of excitement... till he knows if he's a father or a mother...
> — O, by God, says Ned, you should have seen Bloom before that son of his that died was born... buying a tin of Neave's food six weeks before the wife was delivered.
> — *En ventre sa mère*, says J. J.
> — Do you call that a man? says the citizen.
> — I wonder did he ever put it out of sight, says Joe.
>   (*U*12.1646–56)

The shifting of Bloom's position from father to mother, the mockery of his uxoriousness and maternal solicitude, the skepticism as to his sexual experience, the citizen's pointed question, all of this extends the strategy previously deployed by the nameless one to transpose the double-bind of Irish manhood on to the received stereotype of Jewish femininity. In accordance with the transferential logic of the scapegoat/symptom, however, the details selected for the task harbor points of Irish reference strictly pertinent to the issue at hand, including the matriarchal strain in colonial Irish life, the renowned Mariolatry of Irish Catholicism, the native female iconography of the Irish nation, the imposed feminine typology of the Celtic race, and the sexual repressiveness of modern Irish society, which conduces to expressions equating coitus with castration ("put it out of sight"). The nameless one's summary judgment on this interlude, that Bloom represents "one of those mixed middlings" (12.1658–59), also serves, against the grain of his intent, as a summary, self-reflexive judgment on the assembled Dubliners, articulating the double-inscription of their political estate as an aporia in their gender performance.

The physical assault on Bloom that closes the episode may be seen as an attempt on the citizen's part to dissolve once and for all the antagonistic intimacy of the symptom/scapegoat with his host/subject – to convert, finally, the trauma of collective self-betrayal into a more psychically manageable sense of betrayal by the other. (Indeed, what drives the citizen to actual battery is Bloom's outright assertion of his proximateness to the group: "Your God was a Jew. Christ was a Jew like me," 12.1808–9.[8]) The nature of this transaction, however, only typifies the double-bind that is the informing condition of the symptomatic relationship. Thus, the citizen enacts both sides of colonial hypermasculinity: he translates his athletic strength (he was a shotputter) into an act of patriotic violence (hurling the biscuit tin), only to bestialize himself in the process, "puffing and blowing with the dropsy" like his dog and "shouting like a stuck pig" (12.1784–85, 1845). Bloom enacts both sides of colonial gentlemanliness; he maintains his dignity and self-control, asserts his superior moral and rational strength, only to wind up marked for emasculation in the process, incurring the jeers of "all the ragamuffins and sluts of the nation": "*If the man in the moon was a jew, jew, jew* ... Eh, mister! Your fly is open, mister!" (12.1796, 1801–2). The others collectively enact a paralyzing, multiply fissured affiliation and disaffiliation with both representative figures: either egging the citizen on with laughter, "aiding and abetting" (12.1900), trying to restrain him, mysteriously disappearing (Nolan), endeavoring to protect Bloom, attempting to silence Bloom, and so on. The nameless one epito-

---

[8] For the logic of proximate-ness see Dollimore, *Sexual Dissidence*, 14–17; for this logic in Joyce, see Valente, "Thrilled by his Touch," 48.

mizes this self-division. He begins by criticizing the citizen in words that suggest a preference for a more restrained moral force manliness, "Arrah, sit down on the *parliamentary* side of your arse . . . and don't be making a public exhibition of yourself" (12.1792–93; emphasis added). But he ends by expressing his support for the citizen in words that carefully endorse physical aggression, "Bloody wars, says I, I'll be in for the last gospel" (12.1849). When the same narrator calls Bloom a "mixed middling," unwittingly implicating the other Dubliners in that estate, he is clearly bent on likening Bloom to the pixilated Dennis Breen, whom the citizen has already declared a "half and half," a person of indeterminate gender (12.1052–53). With the riotous "last gospel," Breen emerges as a kind of allegorical limit case of the trauma of Irish manhood. Like the litigious Breen, the bar dwellers prove themselves neither "fish nor flesh" (12.1055–56), but violently torn between the two – between feminized grievance and masculinized aggression, between Bloom ("old cod's eye") and the citizen (a "ravenous brute") – and they grow more than a little hysterical from the strain (12.841, 485).

It will be noted that no path beyond the impasse of (semi)colonial manhood has been adumbrated herein. In fact, Joyce conspicuously avoids the faintest suggestion that such a path exists, and he carefully underlines this decision by emblazoning the beginning, middle, and end of the episode with twinned images of cyclopean blinding and oedipal castration. All of this is to say that Joyce takes the impasse quite seriously. He wishes to dispel the ready assumption that the trauma of Irish manhood can resolved strictly at the level of means, literary or political. The problem lies not in the colonial strategies of gender assumption, but in the imperialist gender construct to be assumed. *The normative structure of metropolitan manhood is in itself the traumatic structure of (semi)colonial castration.* There is accordingly no negotiation of the aporia on the terms given; the terms must be changed. Why the terms must be changed is the lesson written into "Cyclops." How that change must be written is a lesson for later episodes and later works.

Works cited

Adams, James Eli. *Dandies and Desert Saints: Styles of Victorian Manhood.*
    Ithaca: Cornell University Press, 1995.
Bhabha, Homi. *The Location of Culture.* London: Routledge, 1994.
Cairns, David, and Shaun Richards. *Writing Ireland.* Manchester: Manchester
    University Press, 1988.

Curtis, L. P. *Anglo-Saxons and Celts: A Study of Anti-Irish Prejudice in Victorian England*. Bridgeport, Conn.: University of Bridgeport Press, 1968.

Apes and Angels: The Irishman in Victorian Caricature. Newton Abbot: David & Charles, 1971.

Curtis, Liz. *Nothing But the Same Old Story*. London: IoI, 1983.

Davis, Thomas. *Literary and Historical Essays*. Dublin: James Duffy, 1846.

National and Other Poems. Dublin: Gill, 1907.

Deane, Seamus. "Civilians and Barbarians." *Ireland's Field Day*. Field Day Theatre Company. Notre Dame, Ind.: University of Notre Dame Press, 1986. 33–42.

Derrida, Jacques. "Force of Law: The 'Mystical Foundations of Authority.'" *Cardozo Law Review* 11.5–6 (1990): 920–1045.

Dollimore, Jonathan. *Sexual Dissidence*. New York: Oxford University Press, 1991.

Duffy, C. G. "Advice to the People in October '43." Reprinted in *Voice of the Nation*. Dublin: James Duffy, 1844. 182–87.

"The Young Men of Ireland." Reprinted in *Voice of the Nation*. Dublin: James Duffy, 1844. 110–14.

Duffy, Enda. *The Subaltern "Ulysses."* Minneapolis: University of Minnesota Press, 1994.

Freud, Sigmund. *General Psychological Theory*. New York: Macmillan, 1963.

Hall, Donald. "The Making and Unmaking of Monsters." *Muscular Christianity*. Ed. Donald Hall. Cambridge: Cambridge University Press, 1996. 45–65.

Howes, Marjorie. *Yeats's Nations: Gender, Class, and Irishness*. Cambridge: Cambridge University Press, 1996.

Hughes, Thomas. *The Manliness of Christ*. London: Macmillan, 1879.

Tom Brown at Oxford. 1861. London: Macmillan, 1929.

Joyce, James. *A Portrait of the Artist as a Young Man*. New York: Penguin, 1964.

Joyce, Toby. "'Ireland's Trained and Marshalled Manhood.'" *Gender Perspectives in Nineteenth-century Ireland*. Ed. Margaret Kelleher and James H. Murphy. Dublin: Irish Academic Press, 1998. 70–80.

Kiberd, Declan. *Inventing Ireland: The Literature of the Modern Nation*. Cambridge, Mass.: Harvard University Press, 1996.

Kingsley, Francis, ed. *Charles Kingsley, his Letters and Memories of his Life*. London: Macmillan, 1901.

The Life and Works of Charles Kingsley. 19 vols. London: Macmillan, 1902.

Lacan, Jacques. *Ecrits*. New York: W. W. Norton, 1977.

Mangan, J. A. "Social Darwinism and Upper Class Education in Late Victorian and Edwardian England." *Manliness and Morality*. Eds. J. A. Mangan and J. Walvin. Manchester: Manchester University Press, 1987. 135–59.

Mill, James Stuart. *The Subjection of Women*. Collected Works 21. Ed. John Robson. Toronto: University of Toronto Press, 1964–92.

Mosse, George. *The Image of Man*. New York: Oxford University Press, 1996.

Nandy, Ashis. *The Intimate Enemy*. Oxford: Oxford University Press, 1983.

Nolan, Emer. *James Joyce and Nationalism*. London: Routledge, 1995.

Rosen, David. "The Volcano and the Cathedral." *Muscular Christianity*. Ed. Donald Hall. Cambridge: Cambridge University Press, 1996. 17–44.

Said, Edward. *Orientalism*. New York: Vintage, 1979.

Sinfield, Alan. *The Wilde Century*. New York: Columbia University Press, 1994.

Smiles, Samuel. *Self-help*. New York: Harper, 1876.

Tifft, Stephen. "The Parricidal Phantasm: Irish Nationalism and the *Playboy* Riots." *Nationalisms and Sexualities*. Ed. Andrew Parker *et al*. New York: Routledge, 1992.

Valente, Joseph. *James Joyce and the Problem of Justice: Negotiating Sexual and Colonial Difference*. Cambridge: Cambridge University Press, 1995.

"The Myth of Sovereignty: Gender in the Literature of Irish Nationalism." *ELH* 61 (1994): 189–210.

"Thrilled by his Touch: The Aestheticizing of Homosexual Panic in *A Portrait of the Artist as a Young Man*." *Quare Joyce*. Ed. Joseph Valente. Ann Arbor: University of Michigan Press, 1998. 47–76.

Žižek, Slavoj. *The Sublime Object of Ideology*. New York: Verso, 1989.

6

Counterparts: *Dubliners*, masculinity, and temperance nationalism

DAVID LLOYD

I

The man returned to the lower office and sat down again at his desk. He stared intently at the incomplete phrase: *In no case shall the said Bernard Bodley be* ... and thought how strange it was that the last three words began with the same letter. The chief clerk began to hurry Miss Parker, saying she would never have the letters typed in time for post. The man listened to the clicking of the machine for a few minutes and then set to work to finish his copy. But his head was not clear and his mind wandered away to the glare and rattle of the public-house. It was a night for hot punches. He struggled on with his copy, but when the clock struck five he had still fourteen pages to write. Blast it! . . . He longed to . . . bring his fist down on something violently. He was so enraged that he wrote *Bernard Bernard* instead of *Bernard Bodley* and had to begin again on a clean sheet.

He felt strong enough to clear out the whole office single-handed. His body ached to do something, to rush out and revel in violence. All the indignities of his life enraged him . . . Could he ask the cashier privately for an advance? No, the cashier was no good, no damn good: he wouldn't give an advance . . . He knew where he would meet the boys: Leonard and O'Halloran and Nosey Flynn. The barometer of his emotional nature was set for a spell of riot.

(Joyce, *Dubliners*, 86)

In this brief scene from the story "Counterparts," Joyce draws out the complex rhythms of alienated labor in early twentieth-century Dublin, linking the repetitive functions performed by the legal clerk Farrington with his sensation of humiliation, frustration, and rage. Male rage and violence against the conditions of work in an office with which, apparently, his very bodily frame is at odds, are counterpoised with the heterotopic site of the public house, with its odors and sensations and the prospect of homosocial conviviality. In the larger course of the story, Farrington indulges in a brief witticism at the expense of the Northern Irish head of this clearly British firm, in consequence of which he is further humiliated by having to make public apology; later, in the pub, as the story is retold and circulated, the humiliation is erased and the scene becomes one in which Farrington figures as momentary hero. But as the evening progresses, Farrington is again humiliated, this time by an English actor whom the "boys" meet, who sponges off them and then defeats Farrington in an arm-wrestling contest: both his own and the "national honour" he is jocularly called on to defend are tarnished. Returning home, raging, his money spent, his watch pawned, his thirst unslaked, he finds the house dark, his dinner cold, and his wife out at chapel. The story concludes with him savagely beating his son who pleads for mercy with the promise that he will "say a *Hail Mary*" for him.

This spare and desolate story, together with many others in *Dubliners*, is bitterly diagnostic of the paralysis of Irish men in colonial Ireland, of their alienation and anomie which, so often, is counterpointed by drinking. As is so much of Joyce's work, it is also profoundly suggestive as to the disposition and practices of gendered social spaces in early twentieth-century Dublin: spaces of work, leisure, domesticity, and religion. As much as anything, it is indicative of the troubled nature of the intersection of these spaces, of their antagonism and contradictory formations. In what follows, I want to situate "Counterparts" in relation to the gradual and complex emergence of modernity in late nineteenth- and early twentieth-century Ireland and to the sites of "countermodernity" that seem simultaneously to be engendered. In particular, I want to follow the story's suggestions in the exploration of the forms in which Irish masculinity was deliberately and programmatically being reconstituted by Irish nationalist movements at this moment and of the recalcitrance which the performance of masculinity in popular culture presented to such projects. Since this chapter represents a small and early part of an on-going project on the transformation of bodily practices in the modernization of Ireland and on the survival of "nonmodern" forms of cultural difference, I will from the outset make no apology for the speculative nature of the argument at many points. Much remains to be done by way of producing a "gender history" of Irish social spaces and their refiguration within nationalist as well as colonial projects of modernization. What I hope to do here is suggest the singularity and unevenness of the ways in which Irish culture enters modernity and the complexity of the historiographic project that we require in order to grasp the implications of such singularity.

The problematic status of the nationalist project of modernization is in evidence in Ireland as generally among Third World nationalisms. It is evident both in relation to the philosophical foundations of modernity from which largely it derives and in relation to the cultural formations of the colonized society as these emerge in time with but yet athwart modernity. The problematic nature of nationalist projects has been more fully elaborated elsewhere and can be briefly summarized here. Nationalism is deeply informed, and yet simultaneously judged lacking or "secondary," by the twin concepts of autonomy and originality that furnish the regulative norms for virtually every level of the modern socius: for the individual, for culture, as this emerges as a separate or distinct sphere, and in turn for each of the increasingly differentiated social spaces of civil society. In its drive to produce or capture the modern state, the nationalist project in its turn must pass by way of the reproduction of such autonomous entities. At the same time, the legitimacy of the call for independent national statehood must be founded in the establishment of the cultural difference of the nation or people, a difference necessarily derived from the traditions of the people that are distinct from those of the dominant or colonial culture. In this way, the claim to autonomous statehood is founded in the originality of national identity, but in an identity whose configurations derive from the elements of society that have, in some sense, survived the inroads of colonial modernity, that are the formations of nonmodernity. Nationalism proceeds, furthermore, by the direct politicization of cultural institutions: that is, where it is the function of aesthetic culture in dominant societies discretely to form subjects for the state, under the conditions of insurgent nationalism, cultural forms are directly endowed with political significance. Culture cannot be either disinterested or autonomous, but is openly subordinated to the political projects of the nationalist movement.

But nationalism's relation to tradition is no less refractive and problematic. For what, through a rigorous process of selection, canonization, and fetishization, gets called "tradition" in relation to modernity emerges as such in the very recalcitrance of popular practices to colonial modernity. These practices prove to be no less recalcitrant to nationalism insofar as it is itself devoted to modernization as the very condition of state formation. In particular, popular practices tend to be resistant to the cultural disciplines that seek to forge the formal citizen-subjects of political modernity that the nation state requires to constitute its people. Accordingly, in its drive to produce subjects to be citizens of the nation that has yet to come into being, nationalism seeks to refine its own version of national culture out of the heterogeneity of popular cultural practices, modernizing and regulating what survives in the form of cultural difference. This is understood, of course, as an attempt to overcome the damage inflicted by colonialism: it is the function of national culture to produce national subjects as empowered agents against the heteronomy and the paralysis of the colonized culture and to restore the wholeness of a fragmented society. In this respect, the function of the icons selected as representative of tradition – whether national heroes or aestheticized natural or artifactual objects – is not merely inspirational. They are symbols which, by virtue of their participation in the original and – in its occluded depths – continuous life of the people, represent the virtual nation that has yet to be realized. Around these symbols the aesthetic formation of the citizen subject takes place. Tradition becomes, in this refined form, the means by which the nation accedes to modernity. But tradition itself, as Frantz Fanon vigorously argued in *The Wretched of the Earth*, thus becomes the paradoxical enemy of the popular culture wherein the cultural difference of the colonized persists in its embedded resistances, its unevennesses, and its perpetual transformative adaptations.[1] It is this problematic and doubled relation to its own modernity and its traditionalism that makes nationalism, in Partha Chatterjee's memorable phrase, at once "a different discourse, yet one that is dominated by another" (*Nationalism and the Colonial World*, 42).

A principal means by which nationalist movements declare their cultural distinctiveness from the dominant power and engage in the refinement of popular culture is manifest in a certain "transvaluation of values" undertaken generally in the early stages of anticolonial mobilization. This transvaluation involves the reversal of stereotypes by which the colonizer has marked as inferior the signs of the colonized's cultural difference. Perhaps the most famous instance of this process is that of the *négritude* movement among Francophone blacks of which Fanon writes extensively and with some critical sympathy in *Black Skin, White Masks*, and with less sympathy in *The Wretched of the Earth*. The critique of the *négritude* tendency in his later work is what enables Fanon to move beyond the prevalent perception of the paralyzed and historically fixed nature of popular culture under colonialism and towards an

---

[1] Since the literature on nationalism from which I have drawn here is so voluminous, let me cite those from which I have drawn most closely here: Fanon, *The Wretched of the Earth*, especially 223–24; Chatterjee, *Nationalism and the Colonial World*; Gibbons, "Identity Without a Centre," *Transformations*, 134–37, and, indeed, the whole book in which this essay is collected. My own explorations of the discrepancies between official nationalism and popular culture are in *Anomalous States*.

understanding of cultural difference rather than tradition as the foundation for an on-going process of decolonization. As we shall see, this equally entails a different understanding of the temporal rhythms of colonialism than that which, on either side of the anticolonial struggle, subsumes tradition within modernization.

Irish cultural nationalism at the turn of the century engaged in a reversal of stereotypes akin to and in anticipation of the *négritude* movement. Thus, for example, the notion of Irish factionalism, based in an inveterate attachment to clan or family rather than to the abstract forms of law and state, becomes the sign of an indomitable resistance and of a spirit of loyalty capable of attachment to the nation. It forms, no less, the foundations of a masculinity that would be transformed and disciplined through institutions ranging from sports to paramilitary movements. The famous quality of "sentimentality" is recast as the foundation for piety and for an empathetic moral identification with the oppressed, while even the stereotype of a racially determined backwardness becomes the sign of a distaste for mechanical English modes of modernity and the grounds for an alternative conception of the modern. It is important to emphasize this point, since it is rarely the case, even in such ardent defenders of Gaelic tradition as Douglas Hyde, that Irish nationalists seek to go against the current of history: it is an alternative modernity rather than the restoration of old forms that nationalists seek even as they appeal to traditions. The transvaluation of the stereotype at once recognizes it as a form of knowledge, predicated on the apprehension of a difference, and converts its meaning in relation to the possibility for modernization. A Celticist nationalism engages in a revalorization of social or cultural traits whose material conditions of possibility it in fact seeks to eradicate.

But in certain cases, both reversal and eradication are attended with peculiar difficulties. This is evidently the case with that most common and perdurable of stereotypes of the Irish, our propensity for drink and drunkenness. The reasons for the difficulty that nationalism found in dealing with the possibility that drinking represented an engrained ethnic trait are at once logical and cultural. Logically, it is difficult to conceive of a *reversal* of intemperance, though its eradication was all too readily advocable. For, though in different forms, drinking is the effect of a prior cause, whether that cause be seen, as we shall see, as colonialism or ethnic predisposition. Unlike sentimentality, it is not an essential characteristic whose valence only is in question; it is a metonym for Irishness which can be disavowed, suppressed, or denied, but not inverted or transvalued. Even where attempts were made to convert the phenomenon of drinking into a perversion of native "hospitality," drinking remains an ever possible effect of that trait, not its obverse: as Weathers, the English actor in "Counterparts," slyly remarks, "The hospitality was too Irish" (90). Culturally, it remains the case that drinking practices remain a critical site for the performance of Irish masculinity and ethnicity, an actuality so embedded that any national movement that attempted to overlook this phenomenon would have been obliged to disavow a profoundly significant popular mode of articulation of cultural difference. As I shall be suggesting, it is in the attempt to transform the terms of Irish masculinity rather than to transvalue the stereotype that nationalism backhandedly acknowledges the significance of this cultural trait while at the same time necessarily suppressing the counter-modern implications of drinking practices themselves. But this may be because of a third difficulty that attaches to nationalism's relation to drinking, which is that drinking itself may be seen as an allegorical figure for nationalism. That is, like nationalism, drinking represents the imbrication of resistance with dependence: as a practice which refuses the values of the colonial economy, values of labor, regularity, or thrift, in favor of an alternative mode of homosociality, drinking resists the incorporation of the colonized culture into the colonial enterprise; as a practice that entails debt as well as psychic dependence, it is at once the cause and effect of an individual and national lack of autonomy. It is, to paraphrase Partha Chatterjee, a practice of difference, but a dependent one.

We will take up this line of argument again momentarily. But the acknowledgment that drinking practices constitute a mode for the performance of masculinity raises a second stereotype that proved difficult for nationalists to reverse, that is the famous "femininity" of the Celt. The notion of an essentially feminine Celtic nature emerges in the writings of philologists and ethnographers in the nineteenth century and receives its clearest and most widely disseminated formulation in Matthew Arnold's "On the Study of Celtic Literature" (1867): "The sensibility of the Celtic nature, its nervous exaltation, have something feminine in them, and the Celt is thus peculiarly disposed to feel the spell of the feminine idiosyncrasy; he has an affinity to it; he is not far from its secret" (86). But it is important to note that the stereotype of the feminine Celtic nature is constituted within a matrix of stereotypes that intersects, on the one hand, with a corresponding set of stereotypes about the "feminine idiosyncrasy" and, on the other, with the set of stereotypes that constitute the "ungovernable and turbulent" Irish as the proper objects of Anglo-Saxon discipline within the empire. The femininity of the Celt is a function of his "receptivity," of a certain more or less passive submission to impulse, whether the impulse of unreflective personal inclination or the impulse of external influence of nature or society. It is the very foundation of Celtic sensibility, and Arnold's only wish is "that he [the Celt] had been more master of it" (85). The lack of self-mastery explains the possibility for the convergence of apparently incompatible stereotypes, of feminine sensibility with the violent turbulence that, especially in the proliferating caricatures of simian Irish terrorists that stemmed from the Fenian campaigns of the 1860s, dominated popular images of the Irish in late nineteenth century England.[2] An unmastered sentimentality founds the political servility of the Celt no less than his aesthetic hypersensitivity:

> The Celt, undisciplinable, anarchical, and turbulent by nature, but out of affection and admiration giving himself body and soul to some leader, that is not a promising political temperament, it is just the opposite of the Anglo-Saxon temperament, disciplinable and steadily obedient within certain limits, but retaining an inalienable part of freedom and self-dependence... (86)

The Celt's "unpromising political temperament" requires its complement in Anglo-Saxon rule just as, within the gradually consolidating domestic ideology of Victorian Britain, woman's private sentimental morality required regulation by male civic virtues.[3]

For an Irish nationalism seeking to restore a sense of agency to a colonized people, this is a no less unpromising stereotype to confront. Rather than a transvaluation, however, this stereotype requires eradication through a series of projects that are directed at the reconstitution of Irish masculinity. I use the term reconstitution advisedly, in order to suggest that what is at stake here is not merely assertions of Irish manliness in denial of the stereotype, but a more or less systematic attempt to reproduce in Ireland a modern division of gendered social spheres within which the image of a masculine civic or public sphere could be reframed in opposition to a privatized feminine space.[4] The nationalist

---

[2] On the Victorian representation of the Celt, see Curtis, *Anglo-Saxons and Celts* and *Apes and Angels*.   [3] See also Joseph Valente's chapter in this collection.

[4] I use the term also by analogy with KumKum Sangari and Sudesh Vaid's conception of the "reconstitution of patriarchies" that takes place continually both under the British Raj and in the context of Indian nationalism. See their introduction to *Recasting Women*, 1, 25, *et passim*.

modernization of Ireland is inseparable from its project of the masculin-
ization of Irish public culture and the regulation of a feminine domestic
space, a project, as I shall suggest, that to a very large extent runs against
the grain of both cultural and material popular practices. This is so
because nationalism at once accepts the colonial stereotype of "turbulent" Irish masculinity and seeks to respond by transforming Irish masculinity into "governable" forms that would found an independent state
formation.

In the first place, there seems little doubt that we are dealing here with
the emergence of something new in Irish culture. For the apparent self-
evidence of the assumption that masculinity is properly defined and
differentiated in opposition to femininity was by no means predominant
earlier in the century. For Young Ireland nationalists in the 1840s, "manliness" as an ethical and political disposition of the subject was properly
opposed not to womanliness but to slavery as the ultimate index of subjection. The autonomy of the politically free citizen and nation was
opposed to the absolute instantiation of heteronomy, the slave. By the
turn of the century, however, a fundamental shift has taken place in
nationalist discourse such that a major component of its rhetoric
involves the proper distribution of opposed male and female spaces and
practices, a distribution that is, as is well known, finally enshrined in the
constitution of 1937. One condition for this shift is that the intervention
of a new racial discourse on the Irish, which asserts their femininity as
part of the set of characteristics that makes them incapable of self-government, demands a response in the form of a remasculinization of the
Irish public sphere.

We can identify two distinct but interlocked modes of response to the
feminization of the Irish during this period. The first can be seen as a celebration of those elements of Irish culture that could be identified in
certain ways as feminine. In general, the stereotype of femininity attaches to those survivals of a Gaelic culture that are now seen as the domain
of folk or peasant society. As is well known, the Irish Literary Revival
and the Gaelic League's project to restore the Irish language are predicated on a massive effort to collect, catalog, disseminate, and refunction
Irish folklore. This project required the translation of oral cultural elements into the forms of a print culture and in certain senses foregrounded the opposition between the modernity of the collectors and
their public and the premodernity of the folk. But the gathering and
rationalization of a body of materials that include fairy and folk tales,

superstition and rural religious practices, and records of medical and other lore is shadowed equally by an implicitly gendered division. It is not for nothing that, although many of the storytellers and informants were men, the figure of the old woman as repository and transmitter of folk culture dominates the folkloric imaginary. The space of the Irish peasantry is at once premodern and feminine; in its conversion and refinement into a coherent body of tradition, it is subject to the labor of modernizing nationalist men. At the same time, the tone of the collector is elegiac: these are the records of a dying civilization that nationalism itself has displaced, even though that cannot be acknowledged. In the new dispensation, the feminine oral tradition has been absorbed into the foundations of a virile Irish modernity. Yeats's famous distinction between the moon of folk culture and the sun of an aristocratic literary culture is only the most notable expression of such an attitude.[5]

This ambiguous celebration of the "feminine" elements of Irish folk culture is thus both counterpointed by and contained within a vigorous project aimed at the reconstitution of Irish masculinity. Given the current context, wherein it is all too often assumed that anticolonial violence stems from the aberrant "hypermasculinity" of the republican "physical force" tradition, it is important to register that it is not only within the tradition that lays claim to the right to take up arms that this project of remasculinization is expressed. Not only in the paramilitary organizations that found legitimation in the traditions of the United Irishmen, Young Ireland, and the Fenians, but in a whole range of closely articulated civil and paramilitary organizations, institutions, and practices did this project emerge. These political and economic projects are triangulated, and at the moment of the turn of the century explicitly linked, with the cultural projects that found expression in the Literary Revival, the National Theatre, and the Gaelic League. The emergent institutions of cultural nationalism are no less concerned with the production of a new Irish masculinity, and have at their core the project of organizing Irish political desire around feminized symbols of the nation which become the object of a heterosexual male devotion. There is, as I

---

[5] See W. B. Yeats, "Gods and Fighting Men." Marjorie Howes has explored in detail the ways in which Yeats responded to the Arnoldian stereotype by setting his own masculinity over against the femininity of folk culture (*Yeats's Nations*, 16–43). I have discussed Douglas Hyde's need to refine and purify the Irish songs he collected in order to produce a coherent sense of the Irish "spirit" in "Adulteration and the Nation," *Anomalous States*, 101–4.

shall argue more fully later, a profound connection between the symbol-
ist poetic mode, no less present in Patrick Pearse than in the Yeats of *circa*
1904, and the transformations and regulation of social space that a modernizing nationalism requires.

The projects of this modernizing nationalism meet in every domain a
deep material and cultural resistance. The desire to produce an Ireland
whose foundations lay in a feminine domestic space was at best utopic in
a country where a large proportion of the most exploited workforce was
female, both in the industrialized and semi-industrialized cities of Belfast
and Dublin, and in rural areas where much female labor was unpaid and
unacknowledged. It was utopic equally in a country where in urban
centers there was a constantly acknowledged drastic shortage of dwell-
ings, leaving whole families to inhabit single rooms in Dublin's notorious tenements, and where in rural society the stem family system
continued to predominate over any emerging nuclear family unit. It also
came up against an increasingly organized social resistance to the new
post-Famine patterns of both industrial and agrarian labor, especially in
the form of a syndicalist labor movement whose agenda was by no means
always congruent with or subordinated to nationalist mobilization, and
which forged its own version of engagement with capitalist modernity.
These struggles and resistances, of course, produce the contestatory
field within which Irish nationalism takes its shape. But there is another
mode of resistance to official nationalism which I would term recalcitrance, which has less to do either with the difficulties of material conditions in the colony or with alternative modes of organization, and far
more to do with cultural practices that are at once embedded in the
popular imaginary and incompatible with nationalist canons of tradition
and moral citizenship. They are problematic, as I have already suggested,
precisely because they represent, alongside nationalism, significant sites
for the performance of cultural difference that cannot simply be erased or
disavowed.

In what follows, then, I want to focus on the cultural significance of
drinking in Ireland and its rendering within nationalism as a problem of
intemperance. The focus is not on what we would now call alcoholism,
though that is ineradicably one aspect of an anomic culture within which
dependence itself constitutes a form of resistance to incorporation by
antipathetic social norms. I want rather to approach drinking practices
more widely as these are embedded within a whole matrix of behaviors
that are the recalcitrant effects of modernity. That is to say, Irish drinking

is not to be seen as the residue of premodern, preindustrial practices, nor as in any simple way congruent with, for example, working-class drinking in modern industrial societies, but rather as itself transformed and reconstituted in relation to an emergent modernity as an element of unincorporated cultural difference.

II

The work of temperance nationalism becomes inseparable from the production and dissemination of a vigorous domestic ideology which sought to establish the well-regulated feminized home as the counterpart to a reformed masculine labor as the foundation of a reformed and independent nation-state. Its discourse forms part of a larger project of modernization which, in its desire to regulate the feminine domestic sphere, establishes domestic economy as a foundation for the national or political economy. It is not so much a discourse about the repression of an evil, drunkenness, as it is about the reconstitution of the social formation and the establishment of the domestic sphere as the counterpart to an invigorated masculine public sphere of economic and political labor.

Inasmuch as "there is a rivalry between the home and the public-house," we can understand the public house to be no less a rival to the public sphere.[6] It constitutes a third term whose very name marks its ambiguous location. It is a rival to the home in providing an alternative space for male conviviality, leisure, and community, one not yet subordinated to the regulations of private domesticity and accordingly "public." At the same time, it rivals the public sphere insofar as it constitutes a space for the dissemination of news and rumor, for the performance of a heterogeneous popular culture, and, indeed, for the organization and dissemination of dissent, sedition, and resistance. But it is no less a recalcitrant space, the site of practices that by their very nature rather than by necessary intent are out of kilter with the modern disciplinary projects. As a site which is irrevocably a product of modernity in its spatial and its temporal demarcations and regulations, in its relation to the increasingly

---

[6] This phrase comes from Father J. Halpin's *The Father Mathew Reader on Temperance and Hygiene* (23), a tract for schools that emphasizes temperance, labor, and the well-managed domestic sphere as the combined foundations for a modern Irish nation.

disciplined rhythms of work and leisure, it is nonetheless a site which preserves and transforms according to its own spaces and rhythms long-standing popular practices that will not be incorporated by discipline: treating or the round system; oral performance of song, story, and rumor; conversation itself, which becomes increasingly a value in a society ever more subject to the individuation and alienation of the worker within the system of production.[7] It may be seen as a crucial site of countermodernity.

In this respect, then, the pub is no less a rival to the linked set of national institutions which came into being alongside and in relation to temperance nationalism, and often under the auspices of the same figures: the Gaelic Athletic Association, the Gaelic League, the Irish Literary Revival and the National Theatre, and the various paramilitary movements. At the same time as such institutions often expressly seek to provide an alternative to drinking as the predominant form of male recreation, they seek to produce a public sphere cleansed of the intoxicating influence of English culture and commodities. As Archbishop Croke, first patron of the Gaelic Athletic Association, put it: "England's accents, the vicious literature, her music, her dances, and her manifold mannerisms . . . [are] not racy of the soil, but rather alien, on the contrary to it, as are for the most part, the men and women who first imported and still continue to patronise them."[8] Yet it is clear that these various institutions sought equally and no less importantly to constitute an alternative, nationalist civil society alongside the institutions of the colonial state, in the anticipation of an independent national state with its own civic institutions. Their function is not only to propagandize and disseminate nationalist ideology, it is also to produce *formally* a counterhegemonic set of articulated but autonomous spheres that will perform the modernizing functions of education, recreation, political organization, and opinion formation and through which the national citizen will be formed.

The public house not only rivals such institutions, then, it troubles their intents. It is a site of the performance of a profoundly heterogeneous popular culture, one inflected, as the "Sirens" chapter of *Ulysses*

---

[7] Surprisingly, there has been little historical or anthropological work done on the Irish pub or on Irish drinking practices. But for a very suggestive analysis of the cultural significance of the pub, or saloon, which has considerable insight to offer on Irish practices despite examining the context of Massachusetts, see Rosenzweig, "The Rise of the Saloon."

[8] Quoted in Kevin Rockett, "Disguising Dependence," 22.

alone might suggest, by Italian opera, English music hall, nationalist bal-
ladry, gossip, irreverence and humor, all of which is intrinsically recalcitrant to nationalist refinement. At the same time, it is, even in its
demarcation as a distinct space, internally resistant to differentiation: it is
a crucial site not only for the mixing of cultural elements but for the
intersection of functions, leisure and work, politics and religion, literature and orality, public life and a kind of domesticity. It is the locus of cultural differences with which nationalism must intersect but which it
cannot fully incorporate.

Nationalism, as we have seen, requires the establishment of cultural
differences from the colonial power in order to legitimate its own claims
to statehood, but the cultural difference it requires must, in order to fit
with its modernizing drives, be a difference contained and refined into
the canonized forms of tradition. The civil institutions of national modernity work off but also against the grain of popular cultural practices
through which the heterogeneous, unrefined, and recalcitrant modes of
cultural difference are continually constituted and transformed. What is
intended here is not the ideal form of pure and originary difference
towards which an extreme traditionalist and separatist nationalism might
tend; it is rather that mode of constant differentiation, refraction, and
refunctioning that occurs in the encounter between the evolving institutions of colonial modernity and the adaptive spaces of the colonized
culture. What determines cultural difference is not its externality to
modernity, nor the persistence of a premodern irrationality, but rather
the mutually constitutive relation between the modern and the counter-
modern. The temporal structure within which the colonized culture
emerges in its difference is not that of a movement from an origin which
is interrupted by and then assimilated into a more developed, more powerful state, nor that of the recuperation of an authentic and ultimately
unbroken tradition within the revivalist logic of nationalism. It is rather
the structure of the eddy by which Walter Benjamin redefines the processes of origination:

> Origin [*Ursprung*], although an entirely historical category, has, nevertheless,
> nothing to do with genesis [*Entstehung*]. The term origin is not intended to
> describe the process by which the existent came into being, but rather to
> describe that which emerges from the process of becoming and disappearance.
> Origin is an eddy in the stream of becoming, and in its current it swallows the
> material involved in the process of genesis.
>
> (*The Origin of German Tragic Drama*, 45)

The cultural forms of the colonized do not simply disappear; in the turbulence of the encounter with colonization, they become something other which at once retains the traces of the violence of that encounter, preserving it in the very form of a persistent damage, and yet survives. Survival in this sense is a mode of adaptation that is often more resistant to than acquiescent in domination, a "living on" that is not about the preservation or fetishization of past forms but nonetheless refuses incorporation. This unevenly distributed relation of damage and survival forges the recalcitrant grain of cultural difference.

We can situate Irish drinking as one element in a matrix of such historically shifting cultural differences, differences of practice and social form that prove unincorporable either by colonial or by nationalist modernity and that remain accordingly ungathered by history, as a kind of dross or irregularity of which neither sense nor use can be made. At this juncture, I want to touch speculatively on a number of instances through which we might come to understand more fully what survives in the countermodernity of Irish drinking. It is, for example, well known that both the Land League and the Fenians customarily used pubs as sites for meeting, recruiting, and organizing, a fact by no means neglected in the temperance advocates' attempts to introduce stricter licensing hours throughout the latter nineteenth century. Publicans, indeed, seem to have made up a high proportion of the Fenians' local organizers and the pub itself represented a crucial locus for congregation and dissemination.[9] What remains unclear is how the location itself may have inflected the forms and practices of these populist movements and even retained a persistent if officially unacknowledged influence on later nationalist and republican mobilizations. It is at least certain, however, that the use of the pub as a principal organizing center signals ways in which the space of the political was not rigorously differentiated from other social spaces in Irish popular culture.

In fact the problematic status of Irish drinking has over and again to do with what seems to the modernized eye the improper confusion of spaces and practices. One instance of this is evident within the arguments for licensing and regulation of drinking to separate work time from leisure or drinking time, and to end such practices as paying workers in

---

[9] See, for example, Malcolm, "Temperance and Irish Nationalism," 84–90, 98, and *"Ireland Sober, Ireland Free,"* 192–93. One might say that the largely teetotal Fenian leaders knew well how to swim in the water of the people, even if, like fish, they abstained from drinking it.

public houses. This was, as Rosenzweig points out, the ubiquitous concern of industrial societies, but it may be that the uneven penetration of rationalized capitalist modes of labor in Ireland permitted the persistence of mixing labor and pleasure to a greater degree than elsewhere.[10] Similarly, particularly in rural districts, the overlap between public and domestic drinking, between the shebeen and the private dwelling, and the persistence of customs like the wake and the ceilidh, spelt a culture spatialized in ways not only different from those that were coming to be regulated by state law and religious dictate, but in ways increasingly seen to be improper. These spaces of popular drinking were clearly not gendered and indeed could involve whole communities: there is little to suggest the homosociality of drinking practices at least prior to the Famine. At the same time, these were spaces often regarded as giving material expression to the fluctuations of Irish "sentimentality": wakes, in particular, which had always been suspected by English observers, were the object of increasing censure by the Catholic Church as the century progressed, not least because of their improper display and mixing of lament and keening, laughter, social criticism and satiric, often impious, invective, all under the influence of drinking.[11]

What each of these instances figures is the persistence and complexity of a culture of orality, in the fullest sense, alongside, inflecting and inflected by a modern state and print culture. What orality here signifies is not so much the modes of transmission of a nonliterate society – it would be hard to point to any moment at which Gaelic culture was not already chirographic at the least and nineteenth-century Ireland was saturated with writing – as the modes of sociality and bodily practice.[12] Indeed, it would perhaps not be entirely fanciful to suggest that the persistence of forms of orality in Irish culture represents the sublimation and survival of the nonnucleated settlements of pre-Famine Ireland, whose patterns and social relations furnish a material map of contiguity rather than differentiation, a map that underlies like a palimpsest the actual and psychic landscapes of modernized Ireland.[13] What disturbs

[10] See Rosenzweig, "The Rise of the Saloon," 121–26.

[11] I have discussed this more fully in "The Memory of Hunger."

[12] On the imbrication at any historical moment, and especially in modernity, of past and emergent modes of cultural transmission and practice, see Lowe, *History of Bourgeois Perception*, 14–16.

[13] On the pre-Famine landscape and the social forms of the rural Irish poor, see Whelan, "Pre- and Post-Famine Landscape Change."

the modernizing mentality is the confusion of spaces, emotions, and functions that are signified in Irish orality. The improperly differentiated functions of the mouth and the tongue are the indices of that disturbing cultural difference – mouths that imbibe drink and utter sedition, nonsense, lament, and palaver are the figure for an absence of distinction and for the borderless contiguity of social and psychic or emotional spaces. Looseness of the tongue makes of it an insubordinate and virtually separable autonomous organ, one that is closely associated in "Counterparts" with the recalcitrance and pleasures of the drinker:

almost before he was aware of it, his tongue had found a felicitous moment ... (87)

He had made a proper fool of himself this time. Could he not keep his tongue in his cheek? (88)

The bar was full of men and loud with the noise of tongues and glasses. (90)

Within the emergent modernity of Dublin in the early 1900s, the pubs that Farrington repairs to constitute heterotopic sites within which drinking is articulated with a whole set of other cultural practices that function as an Irish mode of countermodernity. It is precisely this fact that makes the public house an alternative space for homosocial conviviality that operates outside the norms and rhythms of alienated labor or the hierarchies of the work space that impinge on Farrington's daily life. Outside, but nonetheless constrained and defined in relation to those rhythms and norms as a transgressive negation. The public house as alternative space is already defined by licensing hours as a space of leisure that no longer intersects with the rhythms of work: the consumption of alcohol during the day has become marked as the sign of indiscipline and anomie; its pleasures are tainted and secretive. The public house, with its traditions of treating and oral exchange, abuts the theatre that has become marked as the domain of English incursions and commodification. The figure of Weathers condenses that displacement and contamination of Irish male pleasure by its rivalrous counterpart, and the English actor's victory over Farrington is doubly humiliating, expressing not only a breach in his performance of masculinity, but his inferiority within a colonial hierarchy and the consequent endangerment of his spaces of pleasure. Within the unforgiving laws of commodity exchange, drinking is only notionally a space of reciprocity: defiant of the logic of the cash nexus as a cultural survival like treating may be, modernity makes of it an accumulation of debt. Pawning his timepiece to subvent the evening's drinking, as if in revolt against the clock that has marked his entrapment, Farrington nonetheless ends his evening penurious and on the edge of a fatal economic dependence that matches as it is produced by his alcoholic dependence. His outlet is to bring home the violence he could not express at work: the story concludes with a violence that, for all its vigor, is no less paralyzed insofar as it is issueless and doubtless the source of its own repetition, generation after generation.

Read in this way, "Counterparts" stages drinking as a dangerous and unstable instance of damage and survival within and athwart the terrain of modernity. To be sure, drinking represents the recalcitrance of an Irish orality against the alienating rhythms of labor, against the regulation and division of time and space that are characteristic of modernity. It is no less opposed in this to the domestic than to the work spaces of modernity, and is by no means the site of a sentimental celebration of hearth and home against economic rationality and calculation that structures domestic ideology as a function of capitalist modernity. Yet its containment within the spaces of modernity makes of it the locus of a damaged masculinity, predicated on the recalcitrance of an anomie that constantly swallows up any articulation of resistance that might emerge there. Shot through with the paralysis of anomie, drinking repeats, at the level of the individual, the violent colonial apparatus of humiliation, with its system of economic and cultural dependence. In this, I have already suggested, drinking is, as Joyce clearly grasped it, the shadowy figure of nationalism's own articulation of resistance and dependence: drink, not temperance, is nationalism's counterpart.[14]

And yet, as so often, something escapes the dismal sobriety of this logic.

Let us return to the scene from "Counterparts" with which we opened. It is a scene of writing in which, as Farrington repetitively, absently, copies over a document, the materiality of the letters ("B . . . B . . . B") separates out from the sense of the phrase. In his very frustration and alienation, and in his mild inebriation, something detaches itself

[14] This is perhaps also allegorized in *Dubliners* through the fate of Jimmy in the story "After the Race," whose attempt to emulate the representatives of more powerful modern nations — England, France, and the USA — leads him into drunkenness and enormous gambling debts. See further Cheng, *Joyce, Race, and Empire*, 101–9.

from sense. In this scene, Farrington is copying a document known in legal parlance as a *counterpart*: a copy torn off from the original in such a way that, when the two are brought together, the copy authenticates the original. The counterpart of the title refers, then, not only to rivalry, but to secondariness, imitation, but in a way that disturbs the hierarchies of originality. If we consider nationalism as a rival of the imperial state, it is also its counterpart in the second sense, its dependent or secondary copy. But its repetition constitutes not simply a difference, capable of rehierarchization, but a deviation of sense. This deviation is, I shall argue, into the space of a cultural difference that is not caught in the logic of opposition.

This deviation is no less a deviation from what were, around 1900, the givens of nationalist aesthetics, with its emphasis on the representative function of the symbol. The counterpart as document is identical to the symbol in its etymological derivation, from the Greek *symbolon*:

> *Symbola* were pledges, pawns or covenants from an earlier understanding to bring together a part of something that had been divided specifically for the purpose of later comparison . . . A coin could be a *symbolon*. Indeed, *symbola* were often "halves or corresponding pieces of [a bone or] a coin, which the contracting parties broke between them, each keeping one piece."[15]

But this etymological derivation highlights the extent to which the contemporary meaning of the symbol deviated from its original. The *symbolon*, like the counterpart, is an allegory: it is in a relation of contiguity to what it represents rather than being a part of it. Precisely what activates the nationalist political possibilities of a post-Romantic definition of the symbol is its conceptualization as a representation that participates in what it represents, as a particular that is part of the whole for which it stands. The landscape may be a symbol of nature or natural process because it is already a part thereof; the national martyr or poet is the symbol of the nation for whose virtual existence he stands. The temporality of symbolism entails the transformation of a merely contingent relation to the nation into a representative function. We might describe this as a series of rhetorical transformations: from the metonymic (Leopold Bloom's "I'm Irish; I was born here") to the synecdochic ("I participate in the nation as a particular instance or member of the whole

---

[15] See Shell, *The Economy of Literature*, 32–33. Internal citation from Liddell and Scott, *A Greek–English Lexicon*.

body politic") to the metaphoric ("I represent the nation because my qualities are those with which an Irish subject should identify"). It is a movement which educes generality out of particularity and contingency and its mechanism is desire, in the sense that Yeats understood his early cultural nationalist work to have sought to "organize" the desire of the nation around certain symbols.[16] In its effort to mobilize a unifying desire, nationalist symbolism is directed against the fragmentation and dispersal of the body and the social space of modernity and towards a suturing of the individual body in itself and with the nation as a whole.

Joyce's *Dubliners* is structured rather around what he describes as the epiphany, an epiphany secularized beyond the account that Stephen Daedalus gives of it in *Stephen Hero*. There, the epiphany appears as a still auratic translation of the religious epiphany, the moment of the manifestation of the divine in the worldly; in effect, as a symbol in which the particular undergoes a transubstantiation into an illumination of the transcendent:

> By an epiphany he meant a sudden spiritual transformation, whether in the vulgarity of speech or of gesture or in a memorable phase of the mind itself . . .
>
> First we recognize that the object is *one* integral thing, then we recognize that it is an organized composite structure, a *thing* in fact: finally, when the relation of the parts is exquisite, when the parts are adjusted to the special point, we recognize that it is *that* thing which it is. Its soul, its whatness, leaps to us from the vestment of its appearance. The soul of the commonest object, the structure of which is so adjusted, seems to us radiant. The object achieves its epiphany.
>
> (*Stephen Hero*, 188–90)

But even within this description, saturated as it is with the young Joyce's Aquinian aesthetic vocabulary, something moves beyond the symbolic, auratic register and closer to the form of the profoundly secular epiphanies that he collected in his notebooks and which came to inform the work of *Dubliners*. For the epiphanies of Joyce's work, as opposed to those of Stephen's theory, are dedicated less to the symbolization of the real, its transumption into representation, but rather to a certain metonymic singularity. They are dedicated to a presentation of the "whatness" of the thing that is achieved by way of what this passage intimates,

---

[16] See W. B. Yeats, *Autobiography*, 119. I have discussed Yeats and the conception of nationalist symbolism more fully in "The Poetics of Politics: Yeats and the Founding of the State," *Anomalous States*, 70–74.

an extreme degree of internal intensification which ensures rather their detachment from than their representation of that of which they are a part. The intensified moment, like Gabriel Conroy's glimpse of his wife standing on the stairs listening to distant music, in fact refuses to be a symbol of something and embeds instead a profound resistance to incorporation, a recalcitrant particularity that refuses to be subsumed into the narrative of representation ("The Dead," *Dubliners*, 211). It is, as a diagnostic moment structured around its internal relations, closer to the "alienation" of Brecht's later tableau or *gestus*.

In Stephen's analogy, what is emphasized in the epiphany is its effulgence of spiritual radiance: an auratic light emanates from and detaches itself from the transubstantiated object. As Joyce writes of the effect of *Dubliners*, it is not so much an aura that detaches itself from the object as an odor:

> It is not my fault that the odour of ashpits and old weeds and offal hangs around my stories. I seriously believe that you will retard the course of civilisation in Ireland by preventing the Irish people from having one good look in my nicely polished looking-glass.
>
> (*Letters* I, 63–64)

Odor is for Joyce the aura that escapes the representation of the object, that is suspended above it as its ineffable trace. Insofar as it is also distasteful, it implies the status of a counteraesthetic. What is implied here is the inseparability of the odor from a project of rigorous mimesis, the juxtaposition of a project of specular revelation, predicated on visibility and illumination, with an unprojected effect of that mimesis, its countersense. The celebrated "scrupulous meanness" of the style of *Dubliners* invokes a naturalism that refuses the incorporative desire of either symbolism or realism that would be the privileged modes of a bourgeois nationalism. It is devoted to the mimesis of a paralysis which suspends action outside the teleological drive of representation: it refuses to redeem colonial paralysis by subordinating it to a transformative sense of history. Instead, the diagnostic mimesis of paralysis produces a suspension of sense which issues in this odor that hangs around these stories. The odor is a countersense made possible by the very rigor of the sense on which Joyce's mimesis of colonial Dublin insists.

We can understand the relation between odor and mimesis as constituting a double track of signification. Within the track of mimesis, which is still subject to a moral and formative intent, narrative itself becomes over and again suspended in paralysis. In that paralysis, we are to decipher the dysfunctional contours of colonial Dublin, the ineluctable determination of material and psychic conditions, repetition, and the inhibition of the will. The sense of the narratives in this register is overwhelmingly that of the vacuity of narrative itself where nothing moves. And yet that very suspension of narrative in paralysis releases an odor whose sense has nothing to do with paralysis, which does not even seek to effect or justify things in the registers of moral or political agency. Odor is a trace which survives the passing of the body as the circulation of stories in the public house detaches itself from the violence and repetition of the narrative to constitute less a determinate engagement with the real than a repertoire and a rehearsal of alternatives. This realm of possibilities is not legitimated by its realization in the actual but sets off eddies in the forward-moving stream of a historicized temporality. Joyce suggests to us, as does Fanon, that in the sites of an apparent suspension of historical motion are the grounds for possible counterhistories. For with the countersenses that these eddies preserve, a materialist historiography must go to work, tracing over and again the alternative resources that are the emanations of the damage taken up in every living on.

Works cited

Arnold, Matthew. "On the Study of Celtic Literature." *On the Study of Celtic Literature and Other Essays.* Intro. Ernest Rhys. London: J. M. Dent, 1910.

Benjamin, Walter. *The Origin of German Tragic Drama.* Trans. John Osborne. London: Verso, 1985.

Chatterjee, Partha. *Nationalism and the Colonial World: A Derivative Discourse?* London: Zed Books, 1986.

Cheng, Vincent J. *Joyce, Race, and Empire.* Cambridge: Cambridge University Press, 1995.

Curtis, L. P. *Anglo-Saxons and Celts: A Study of Anti-Irish Prejudice in Victorian England.* Bridgeport, Conn.: University of Bridgeport Press, 1968.

Apes and Angels: The Irishman in Victorian Caricature. Washington, DC: Smithsonian Institution Press, 1971.

Fanon, Frantz. *Black Skin, White Masks.* Trans. Charles Lam Markmann. London: MacGibbon & Kee, 1968.

The Wretched of the Earth. Trans. Constance Farrington. New York: Grove Press, 1968.

Gibbons, Luke. *Transformations in Irish Culture.* Cork: Cork University Press, 1996.

Halpin, Father J. *The Father Mathew Reader on Temperance and Hygiene.* Dublin: M. H. Gill, 1907.

Howes, Marjorie. *Yeats's Nations: Gender, Class, and Irishness.* Cambridge: Cambridge University Press, 1996.

Joyce, James. *Dubliners.* Intro. Terence Brown. New York: Penguin, 1992.
    Stephen Hero. Ed. Theodore Spencer; rev. ed. John J. Slocum and Herbert Cahoon. St. Albans: Triad/Panther, 1977.

Liddell, H. G., and Robert Scott, *A Greek-English Lexicon.* Oxford: Oxford University Press, 1940.

Lloyd, David. *Anomalous States: Irish Writing and the Post-colonial Moment.* Dublin: Lilliput Press; Durham: Duke University Press, 1993.
    "The Memory of Hunger." *Irish Hunger: Personal Reflections on the Legacy of the Famine.* Ed. Tom Hayden. Boulder, Col.: Roberts Rinehart, 1997. 32–47.

Lowe, Donald. *History of Bourgeois Perception.* Chicago: University of Chicago Press, 1982.

Malcolm, Elizabeth. *"Ireland Sober, Ireland Free": Drink and Temperance in Nineteenth-century Ireland.* Dublin: Gill & Macmillan, 1986.
    "Temperance and Irish Nationalism." *Ireland Under the Union: Varieties of Tension.* Ed. F. S. L. Lyons and R. A. J. Hawkins. Oxford: Clarendon Press, 1980. 69–114.

Rockett, Kevin. "Disguising Difference: Separatism and Foreign Mass Culture." *Circa* 49 (January/February 1990): 20–25.

Rosenzweig, Roy. "The Rise of the Saloon." *Rethinking Popular Culture: Contemporary Perspectives in Cultural Studies.* Ed. Chandra Mukerji and Michael Schudson. Berkeley: University of California Press, 1991. 121–56.

Sangari, KumKum, and Sudesh Vaid. *Recasting Women: Essays in Colonial History.* New Delhi: Kali for Women, 1989.

Shell, Mark. *The Economy of Literature.* Baltimore: Johns Hopkins University Press, 1978.

Whelan, Kevin. "Pre- and Post-Famine Landscape Change." *The Great Irish Famine.* Ed. Cathal Poirteir. Cork and Dublin: Mercier Press, 1995. 19–33.

Yeats, W. B. *Autobiography.* New York: Macmillan, 1953.
    "Gods and Fighting Men." *Explorations.* New York: Macmillan, 1962. 24–26.

7

"Have you no homes to go to?": James Joyce and the politics of paralysis

LUKE GIBBONS

> The vision made him feel keenly the poverty of his own purse and
> spirit . . . He would be thirty-one in November. Would he never get a
> good job? Would he never have a home of his own? *"Two Gallants"*

> — We were waiting for him to come home with the money. He never
> seems to think he has a home at all. *"Grace"*

Returning from a visit to Ireland in 1903, the novelist Filson Young commented on the torpor and listlessness that was endemic to Irish society: "The sands of national life have run very low in the glass; the people are physically and mentally exhausted, apathetic, resigned; the very soil of the country itself is starved and impoverished. So stands Ireland, weak and emaciated, at the crossroads" (*Ireland at the Crossroads*, 15–16).[1] Contrary to de Valera's later comely vision, the view from this crossroads is not very inspiring, for all traces of enjoyment, or even sobriety and work discipline, have vanished from the landscape: "There are no organised amusements; half the prisons and workhouses are derelict; and only three great tumorous growths stand triumphant and alive – the lunatic asylum, the public house, and the Catholic chapel; and into these the life of the remaining population is steadily absorbed" (*Ireland at the Crossroads*, 5–6). This bleak vista is not due to the improving zeal of Puritanism, for Ireland "never knew that austere and spiritual blend of character that has elsewhere been the legacy of the Puritans." Instead, it derives from an unstable alliance between the vestiges of a premodern folk culture and the ornamental allure of the Catholic Church: "For Ireland there can be nothing between paganism and that marvellous superstructure of symbolism which the Roman Catholic faith rears upon an emotional foundation" (*Ireland at the Crossroads*, 31).

[1] Young (1876–1938) was born in Ballyeaston, County Antrim, and spent most of his life as a novelist, critic, and journalist in London.

It is worth speculating whether James Joyce knew Filson Young's book, and whether it played any role in introducing the social aspects of the theme of "paralysis" in *Dubliners*, so notably absent from the earliest publication of the stories. Certainly, the description of the "dull routine" of Irish life in *Stephen Hero* – "a life lived in cunning and fear between the shadows of the parish chapel and the asylum" – evokes Young's characterization above, and echoes of *Ireland at the Crossroads* also appear in *Dubliners*.[2] In any case, the paths of both authors crossed when Joyce sent the manuscript of his stories to Grant Richards, Young's publisher, in 1905.[3] Young was the publisher's reader, and sent a favorable report, on the strength of which Richards signed a contract, ill-fated as it turned out, with Joyce. Young found that Joyce portrayed Dublin "with sympathy and patience which equal its knowledge of . . . its idiom, its people, its streets and its little houses," and, in a turn of phrase echoed in *Ulysses*, praised his "artistic sincerity [which] has been placed above other cries in the street."[4] One of the most interesting aspects of Young's own diagnosis of the ills facing Ireland is that it is not poverty alone which is the cause of the problem, but the dysfunctional forms taken by post-Famine modernization. The restructuring of the economy and the conversion of vast tracts of land into cattle pasture was a recipe for emigration and demoralization in the outlying areas: "Along the whole western Irish

[2] See, for example, Young's discussion of the monks' sleeping practices in Mount Melleray, which is similar to that which recurs during the dinner conversation in "The Dead": the monks, Young informs us, "sleep in their habits, in cubicles partitioned off in the great dormitory; the cubicles are as big as an ordinary grave, and their furniture is simply a raised wooden platform with a mattress laid upon it" (*Ireland at the Crossroads*, 99).

[3] Grant Richards wrote to Joyce on 10 May 1906: "The man who read your stories for us was a man whose work you are likely to know, Filson Young" (*Letters II*, 135–60). Young's novel, *The Sands of Pleasure* (1905), was among the books in Joyce's Trieste library, and, as Kershner suggests, its Ibsenite approach to sexuality and Parisian "low life" must have appealed to Joyce (*Joyce, Bakhtin and Popular Literature*, 272–77).

[4] Cited in Magalaner and Kain, *Joyce*, 65. Young also discerned "an order and symmetrical connection between the stories making them one book." Though Richards claimed that Young agreed with his reservations about printing the book, the fact that Joyce valued his comments is clear from attempts to get him to write an introduction for the eventual publication of *Dubliners* in 1914. Young, however, did not accede to the request, for reasons that are not clear (Ellmann, *James Joyce*, 353).

coast is to be found one great natural influence, unchanging, paralysing, daunting" (*Ireland at the Crossroads*, 53): "No amenities, no festivities; even the family affection – that great and tragic possession of the Irish – fostered and encouraged, not by community of joy, but by community of misfortune, and too often withered and ended by departure and separation" (52–53). Hence the stunted world of *Stephen Hero* and *Dubliners* in which lives are numbed even by the very affections of family and home, the last outposts of intimacy in the disenchanted world of bourgeois private life.

The pathology of post-Famine Ireland

The word "paralysis" is explicitly introduced in the opening paragraph of "The Sisters" in *Dubliners*, but as we have noted above, the earliest version of the story, published in the *Irish Homestead* in 1904, did not employ the term.[5] It first appears in essays and letters written by Joyce during this period,[6] and also surfaces in *Stephen Hero* (1904–6) in a context which accords with Filson Young's indictment of Catholicism, but which also evokes morbid images of social plague and pestilence:

> The deadly chill of the atmosphere of the college paralysed Stephen's heart. In a stupour of powerlessness he reviewed the plague of Catholicism. He seemed to see the vermin begotten in the catacombs in an age of sickness and cruelty issuing forth upon the plains and mountains of Europe . . . Contempt of [the body] human nature, weakness, nervous tremblings, fear of day and joy, distrust of man and life, hemiplegia of the will, beset the body burdened and disaffected in its members by its black tyrannous lice.
>
> (*Stephen Hero*, 198–99)

---

[5] For the introduction of the theme of paralysis, and its sexual connotations, in the early fiction, see Waisbren and Walzl, "Paresis and the Priest."

[6] For the most often cited formulations, see the description of the artist "amid the general paralysis of an insane society" in Joyce's early essay, "A Portrait of the Artist" (*Poems and Shorter Writings*, 211–18); Joyce's letter to Constantine Curran, July (?) 1904, in which he first proposes a collection of stories entitled *Dubliners*: "I call the series *Dubliners* to betray the soul of that hemiplegia or paralysis which many consider a city" (*Letters I*, 55); and the well-known letter to Grant Richards, 5 May 1906: "My intention was to write a chapter in the moral history of my country and I chose Dublin for the scene because that city seemed to me the centre of paralysis" (*Letters II*, 134).

For Stephen's Irish contemporaries, the specter of disease and pestilence was likely to recall the recent catastrophe of the Great Famine rather than the more distant European past: "Potato Preservative against Plague and Pestilence, pray for us," intone the "daughters of Erin" in *Ulysses*, mocking the superstitious trappings of Catholic devotional practices.[7] As Stephen himself drifts through the backstreets of Dublin, the sight of a "burly black-vested priest taking a stroll of pleasant inspection through these warrens" provokes his anger, and he curses the inhabitants of an island "who entrust their wills and minds to others that they ensure for themselves a life of spiritual paralysis," while Christ and Caesar "wax fat upon a starveling rabblement" (150–51).[8]

In the eyes of many observers, the devastation wrought upon Irish society both during and after the Famine was such that the entire culture seemed reduced to the kind of enervation associated with hysteria, what became known as "the great silence." According to W. Steuart Trench, recounting his own harrowing experiences of Kerry:

> Half Ireland was stunned by the suddenness of the calamity, and Kenmare was completely paralysed... The local gentry were paralysed, the tradesmen were paralysed, the people were paralysed, and the squatters and cottiers and smallholders... unable from hunger to work, and hopeless of any sufficient relief from extraneous sources, sank quietly down, some in their houses, some at the relief works, and died almost without a struggle.
>
> (*Realities of Irish Life*, 113, 115)

In a sense, the Famine effected in four years what took over four centuries to achieve on the European mainland, namely, the purging of an unruly premodern culture from a newly constituted bourgeois public sphere. As a number of recent scholars have argued, following the pioneering analyses of Norbert Elias and Mikhail Bakhtin, the early modern era witnessed a concerted effort on the part of liberal reformers in Europe to purge popular culture of its festive or carnivalesque elements, and to

---

[7] As Ellmann notes, one of Joyce's earliest literary efforts, a play entitled *A Brilliant Career*, was described by William Archer as a "huge fable of politics and pestilence" (*James Joyce*, 79). For a particularly insightful account of the impact of the Great Famine on Joyce's writings, see Lowe-Evans, *Crimes Against Fecundity*, 5–31.

[8] See also Stephen's description of bourgeois suburbia as "those brown brick houses which seem the very incarnation of Irish paralysis" (*Stephen Hero*, 216).

release prospective citizens and rational subjects from their dependence on what were considered grotesque communal rituals.[9] Through processes of fragmentation, marginalization, sublimation, and suppression, traditional practices involving bodily excesses such as feasting, violence, drinking, processions, fairs, wakes, superstition, rowdy spectacles, and so on, were brought under scientific observation and subjected to systematic social regulations. These controlling mechanisms sought not so much to eliminate these practices as to sanitize and refine them, in particular redirecting and privatizing the sexual energies associated with carnival within the more manageable confines of the home. Much of the animus against superstition and irrationality was directed against the Catholic Church, and the affront presented by its mystique and medievalism to the "march of intelligence." It is not surprising, therefore, that the Irish were considered to be in particular need of rational enlightenment, if they were to take their place in the modern world. According to the great historian, W. E. H. Lecky, in a character sketch of the Irish preceded by an image of barely literate priests and monks "flitting to and fro among the mud hovels":

> In the absence of industrial and intellectual life, and under the constant pressure that draw men to the unseen world, Catholicism acquired an almost undivided empire over the affections and imaginations of the [Irish] people. The type of religion was grossly superstitious. It consecrated that mendicancy which is one of the worst evils of Irish life. Its numerous holidays aggravated the natural idleness of the people. It had no tendency to form those habits of self-reliance, those energetic political and industrial virtues in which the Irish character was and is lamentably deficient; but it filled the imagination with wild and beautiful legends . . . and diffused abroad a deep feeling of content and resignation in extreme poverty . . . which has preserved it from at least some of the worst vices that usually accompany social convulsions and great political agitations on the Continent.
>
> (Lecky, *Ireland in the Eighteenth Century*, 407–8)

It is not too difficult to see in Lecky's diagnosis the elements of quietism and superstition which, as we have noted, characterized Irish responses to the Great Famine in the eyes of both contemporary and later

[9] See Bakhtin, *Rabelais and his World*, and Elias, *The Civilizing Process*. For a recent Bakhtinian approach, see Stallybrass and White, *The Politics and Poetics of Transgression*, and for a synthesis based on Elias's works, see Spierenburg, *The Broken Spell*.

commentators.[10] Lecky, however, was concerned to link this with the historical absence of other kinds of convulsions in Ireland, those having to do with the social hysteria which attended the witch craze in Europe in the previous two centuries. As the author of the highly successful *The History of the Rise and Influence of the Spirit of Rationalism in Europe* (1865),[11] Lecky's ambitious attempt to demonstrate the triumph of reason over irrationality, and to secularize the public sphere, exerted enormous influence on his European contemporaries, not least the young Sigmund Freud. According to William McGrath, it may indeed have been Freud's reading of Lecky which first stimulated his interest in hysteria (*Freud's Discovery of Psychoanalysis*, 79). Though Freud persisted at one level in construing nervous disorders as the result of purely individual problems, his early psychological researches were part of a general European movement, spearheaded by the great French neurologist Jean-Martin Charcot, which applied scientific, medical explanations to hitherto inexplicable forms of social and religious behavior. This intellectual trend was aligned to a wider political project which sought to liberalize society by challenging the influence of religion, and particularly the Catholic Church, in schools, hospitals, and other areas of public life (see Goldstein, "The Hysteria Diagnosis"). The irony facing social reformers in Ireland, however, was that whereas the Catholic Church was the main target of criticism in metropolitan Europe, the task of modernizing Irish society after the Famine devolved on to the Catholic Church itself, and a debilitated middle class coming out from under both the shadow of catastrophe and the legacy of colonial rule.

Though the Famine had dealt a body blow, quite literally, to the carnality of a wayward folk culture, it was unable to displace these energies on to the home, due to the instability of the family, and the frustration of even the limited pleasures provided by the bourgeois privatization of the erotic, in the post-Famine reorganization of society. As Clair Wills

[10] It is ironical that as the author of four volumes on the turbulent 1790s in Ireland, Lecky persisted in seeing Ireland as missing the great political agitations which convulsed the Continent during this period.

[11] Lecky's remarkably successful book went into eighteen editions and was translated into several languages. See McCartney, *W. E. H. Lecky*, 34. The discussions of modernity and tradition in *Stephen Hero* bear the hallmarks of Lecky, and, indeed, Stephen comes across Moynihan in the National Library, preparing for his inaugural address at the Literary and Historical Society, with "some bulky volumes of Lecky at his side" (154).

observes of the actualities of family life in relation to the new emergent ideologies of faith and fatherland,

> Given the emphasis in conservative rhetoric on the family as the locus and breeding ground of distinct and traditional values, and on the need to protect it from encroachment by the welfare state, the typically open-ended character of the Irish family until quite recently seems ironic. It is not simply, as [Dympna] McLoughlin has argued, that there were alternative forms of familial and sexual relationship – the pauper family, the gentleman's miss, prostitution – but also that because of the dual institutions of emigration and [domestic] service, the family was not bounded in the way that we conceive of today. In effect, family members were always living in one another's households.
>
> ("Rocking the Cradle?," 102–3) [12]

As the incessant campaign against ribald wake amusements shows, the fact that a whole range of popular rituals and practices took place indoors was not sufficient to domesticate them, for they were, like the family structure itself, bound up with communal ties, and with the major festivals and patterns which punctuated the cultural calendar.[13] The most anomalous feature of the disciplinary regimes introduced to curtail the excesses of popular culture in post-Famine Ireland was their ineluctable public dimension, and their inability to fully privatize the communal aspects of culture. Hence, the distinctive character of the "Devotional Revolution" in the Catholic Church, which sought to counter pre-Famine communal religious practices by an insistence on forms of worship centering on mass attendance, Benediction, devotions, and regular confession, which were of an equally public and "associative" nature.[14] As

---

[12] The internal reference is to Dympna McLoughlin's valuable article, "Woman and Sexuality in Nineteenth-century Ireland." Perhaps the crucial factor here is the extensive increase in domestic service as an employment outlet for women, both at home and abroad, in the absence of a strong industrial working class or manufacturing base (except in Belfast). Almost half of all women with stated occupations in 1881 worked as domestic servants (Daly, *Women and Work in Ireland*, 31). As Wills goes on to note: "It is important to remember that the institution of domestic service did not merely change the boundaries for the 'master' family, but also for the family which provided the servants" (103).

[13] For the relationship between unruly conduct at wakes and wider communal concerns bound up with faction fighting and agrarian secret societies, see O'Suilleabhain, *Irish Wake Amusements*, 71–72.

[14] It is difficult not to suspect that the undue importance subsequently attached to the family rosary, and to the Virgin Mary, was an attempt to bring religion into

Filson Young so graphically puts it, it was as if the tawdry ornamental excesses of the new churches – "the sickening images, with their gaudy paintings of pink and blue, the wounds gushing crimson paint, the Virgins under their hideous canopies of Reckitt's blue, the prophets in vermilion and purple, the glare and blaze of cheap and hideous decorations that enshrine the mysteries of the Mass" (*Ireland at the Crossroads*, 73) – were designed as ersatz compensations for the more earthy sensuality of a once thriving vernacular culture.

For these reasons, the conditions prevailing in other parts of Europe whereby the emotional excesses of carnival and popular customs were "interiorized" in domestic space, whether in a bourgeois intimate sphere or the more disruptive eroticism of hysteria, did not exist in Ireland. For one thing, the time scale involved in this fundamental transformation of culture was too short and too abrupt. Lecky, Charcot, and Freud were looking at a process which took centuries to evolve, even if the final convulsive spasms were not manifest until the nineteenth century. In Ireland, however, as we have observed, the Famine concentrated in a few years the work of centuries, so that the cultural devastation which ensued did not have the time, the "long duration," to work its way fully through society. According to Catherine Clément, the hysteric "whose body is transformed into a theatre for forgotten scenes, relives the past" in a manner akin to the "sorceress" or "witch" who "incarnates the reinscription of the traces of paganism that triumphant Christianity repressed" (Cixous and Clément, *The Newly Born Woman*, 5). Instead of being privatized in the domestic sphere in Ireland, however, these "forgotten scenes" maintained a liminal or clandestine existence in public space, the spectral traces of the past cohabiting with the modernity that was supposed to abolish it.

It is in this context that we must view the repeated expressions of outrage and bewilderment over the persistence of premodern culture, both in its sinister and carnivalesque forms, in late nineteenth-century Ireland. In his controversial diagnosis of the ills pervading Ireland at the turn of the century, *Five Years in Ireland, 1895–1900*, Michael J. F. McCarthy includes, along with a chapter on "The Helplessness of the Catholic Peasantry," two further related chapters on "Belief in Fairies

the household, the Catholic equivalent to reading the Bible. Even then, however, it was still "public" in the sense that it involved a shared, participative ritual.

and Witches" and "Belief in Fairies and Devils and the Tortures of Hell."[15] These latter chapters deal with a number of gruesome incidents which, the author reminds us, if not exemplary, at least touch on the lives of the thousands of country people "who, if they do not firmly believe the superstitions which led to such horrible results in these cases, do certainly border on these beliefs" (141–42). The most notorious of these took place in County Tipperary in 1895 when a young woman, Bridget Cleary, was tortured and burned to death in her kitchen by her husband, father, and neighbors on the grounds that she may have been a witch or "possessed by the fairies." Like the Maamtrasna murders in the west of Ireland a decade earlier, this atrocity became part of a protracted national debate on the state of Ireland at the end of the nineteenth century, coinciding, as Angela Bourke has shown, not only with the arrest and trial of Oscar Wilde, but also with the upsurge of interest in folklore and the occult inspired by the Celtic Twilight and the Literary Revival.[16]

The fashionable craze for the occult in metropolitan Britain represented a retreat from traditional religion and the public world, an attempt to fill a spiritual void through a privatization of the supernatural in darkened Victorian drawing rooms. By contrast, the link between the occult and folk culture in Ireland allowed a social élite to renew its contact with the wider community, drawing on an alternative clandestine culture to that of the official public sphere: "I have longed to turn Catholic, that I might be nearer to the people," Lady Gregory confided to Yeats, "but you have taught me that paganism brings me nearer still" (cited in Foster, *Yeats*, 170). Yet the brutality of the Bridget Cleary affair was a harsh reminder to those who dreamed of fairyland that their worst nightmares might be confirmed by venturing into the otherworld of rural Ireland.[17] Agitated by the episode, Yeats sought reassurance that when spirits occupy the body, they seek merely to make it uncomfortable for its tenants, but are "not likely to go too far":

[15] It is highly likely that Joyce was acquainted with McCarthy's anticlerical works, though he would not have sympathized with his imperial leanings. Joyce owned a copy of MacCarthy's *The Irish Revolution*, and Stanislaus Joyce records his own reading of McCarthy's best known work, *Priests and People in Ireland* (1902), in *My Brother's Keeper*.

[16] See Angela Bourke, "Reading a Woman's Death" and *The Burning of Bridget Cleary*.

[17] I develop this point in a related context in "'Some Hysterical Hatred.'"

A man actually did burn his wife to death, in Tipperary a few years ago, and is
no doubt still in prison for it. My uncle, George Pollexfen, had an old servant
Mary Battle, and when she spoke of the case to me, she described that man as
very superstitious. I asked her what she meant by that and she explained that
everybody knew that you must only threaten, for whatever injury you did to the
changeling the faeries would do to the living person they had carried away . . .
The Tipperary witch-burner only half knew his own belief.

("Two Essays and Notes," 360)

So far from being a release from the fallen condition of the modern
world, not least of the unsettling aspects of this manifestation of the
occult was that it did not take place in a hovel, or a remote rural setting,
but in a new laborer's cottage beside the public road in Ballyvadlea,
County Tipperary. Representatives of the emergent bourgeoisie such as
the local medical doctor, the priest, the police, big farmers, and even the
market in the form of an egg salesman, coexisted in the story alongside
the "fairy fort" which brought Bridget Cleary to her doom.[18] This relic
of an irrational culture, according to McCarthy, exercised a pernicious
influence over the inhabitants of the district:

I am informed that people in Ballyvadlea believe that a person being near this
fort at night is liable to be struck with rheumatism, *paralysis* and so forth! Those
accursed unlovely and useless remains of barbarism should be levelled to the
ground by every man who wishes to see Ireland prosper. I myself know a score
of farmers who have these forts on their land: all farmers of the best,
comfortable, rational, hospitable, intelligent, keen men of business: yet, not one
of them has the courage to remove these nuisances from their holdings,
although they continually grumble at the inconvenience they cause.

(*Five Years in Ireland*, 159; italics mine)

These events, he continues, took place "not in darkest Africa, but in
Tipperary; not in the ninth or tenth, but at the close of the nineteenth
century; not among atheists, but among Catholics, with the Rosary on

[18] Bourke notes that "All indications are that the Clearys were a modern couple,
much more upwardly mobile in socioeconomic terms than their neighbours or
Bridget's relatives." Michael was a cooper, and was literate, and Bridget had
been trained as a milliner and dressmaker and also kept hens and sold eggs. "The
Cleary's house alone would have been enough to mark them as different: it was a
new 'labourer's cottage,' a slated, two-bedroom dwelling of the type built only
after the passing of the Labourers (Ireland) Act of 1883" ("Reading a Woman's
Death," 575–76).

their lips, and with the priest celebrating mass in their houses" (173).[19] For all the rigors of the "Devotional Revolution" and the craven pursuit of respectability displayed by the new middle class, the demons of the past had not yet been exorcised.

Joyce and the suburban supernatural

> Out of the material and spiritual battle which has gone so hardly with her, Ireland has emerged with many memories of beliefs ...
>
> (James Joyce, review of Lady Gregory's *Poets and Dreamers*)

That the liminal forces of the otherworld infiltrated not only the countryside but also the city, unsettling the boundaries of the sedate urban household, is clear from Joyce's description of the long-suffering Mrs. Kernan in "Grace":

> Her beliefs were not extravagant. She believed steadily in the Sacred Heart as the most generally useful of all Catholic devotions and approved of the sacraments. Her faith was bounded by the kitchen, but, if she was put to it, she could believe also in the banshee and in the Holy Ghost.
>
> (*Dubliners*, 464)

Though regulated by the tempo and commerce of the modern city, Dublin was subject also to a less frenetic, "sacred" sense of time, marked characteristically by women and punctuated by Church holy days such as the Epiphany or, even more vestigially, by traces of pagan culture and the old Celtic calendar such as Halloween.[20]

---

[19] As Bourke argues, citing the coroner's verdict that "amongst Hottentots one would not expect to hear of such an occurrence," such comparisons with Africa were integral to colonial attempts to primitivize subaltern culture, which, in the particular case of Ireland at the turn of the last century, meant it could not be entrusted with Home Rule ("Reading a Woman's Death," 558–60).

[20] As a writer observes in *Fraser's Magazine*, May 1869, expressing sentiments that drew the ire of the Nun of Kenmare, Mary Francis Cusack:

> Not only is it true that peasants are still capable of believing in witchcraft, but the majority even of the educated classes are ready to listen respectfully to superstitions quite as gross. Now, from this point of view, we must reckon the overwhelming majority of woman as amongst those who, if they do not hold superannuated doctrines, owe their immunity to chance, or to the influence of male relations ... As long as woman are left in their present stage, any decided progress is impossible.
>
> (Cited in Cusack, *Women's Work in Modern Society*, 282)

Halloween, of course, was the season in which witches made their appearance, and if the hysteric's body is a secular counterpart, in however muted a form, of the communal suspicion of old, unmarried women which plagued the Middle Ages, then Maria in "Clay" is indeed one of life's losers. Set on Halloween eve, her physiognomy indicates that all is not well at the outset, as if her body speaks louder than her words, or even her thoughts: "Maria was a very, very small person indeed, but she had a very long nose and a very long chin. She talked a little through her nose, always soothingly: *'Yes, my dear,'* and *'No, my dear'*" (110). On this night above all she is conscious of modern urban time, for she carefully estimates how long it will take her to travel on the tram across the city from Ballsbridge where she works, to the home of Joe Donnelly, whom she once nursed, in Drumcondra: "From Ballsbridge to the Pillar, twenty minutes; from the Pillar to Drumcondra, twenty minutes; and twenty minutes to buy the things. She would be there before eight" (110). The Dublin by Lamplight laundry in Ballsbridge where Maria works is an institution for "fallen women" who, literally, have no homes to go to, but that she is also condemned to this fate by virtue of her lack of marriage prospects is something she can barely contemplate. "Often," she muses in relation to Joe, "he had wanted her to go and live with them; but she would have felt herself in the way (though Joe's wife was ever so nice to her) and she had become accustomed to the life of the laundry" (111). When the coarse inmates of the institution tease Maria over getting the ring in the barmbrack at tea, she "had to laugh and say she didn't want any ring or man either; and when she laughed her grey green eyes sparkled with disappointed shyness . . . till the top of her nose nearly met the tip of her chin and till her minute body nearly shook itself asunder" (112).

It is striking, as Margot Norris notes in her acute analysis of the story, that the term "witch" is not actually mentioned in "Clay," any more than the "soft wet substance" which Maria touches in the party game is named (apart from the title). But it does not follow from this that the appellation of "witch" is simply a projection of a witch-hunting proclivity in the reader's ill-disposed imagination, "a hermeneutical touch as poisonous as that of any witch who ever turned a prince into a toad" ("Narration Under a Blindfold," 215). As Norris herself shows, the whole story is structured around such narrative ellipses, and no more so than in the "semiotic silences," in keeping with the muted condition of the hysteric, which prevents Maria from naming her own experiences. Her repeated involuntary spasms betray rather than express her aching inner life. When she dithers in a shop over buying a plum cake to bring as a present to Joe's house, "the stylish young lady behind the counter, who was evidently a little annoyed by her, asked her was it wedding cake she wanted to buy. That made Maria blush and smile at the young lady" (113–14). On the tram, she is so taken aback by a "colonel-looking gentleman" who strikes up a conversation with her that she forgets the plum cake, and "remembering how confused the gentleman with the greyish moustache had made her, coloured with shame and vexation and disappointment" (115). Her spirits are lifted, however, when the party assembled in Joe's house begin to play Halloween games, of the kind which marked the end of the old Celtic year. As O'Suilleabhain notes, many of these were divinatory in nature, as traditional communities sought to allay the uncertainty of the future.[21] It is one of these which proves Maria's undoing as, blindfolded, her fingers alight not on a prayer book (indicating a religious vocation), water (a sign of emigration), or a wedding ring, but on a portent of death, a saucer of clay substituted as a prank by the children next door. "She felt a soft wet substance with her fingers and was surprised that nobody spoke or took off her bandage. There was a pause for a few seconds; and then a great deal of scuffling and whispering" (117), as those around her tried to shield her from the pain of recognition.

That the truth sinks into her body, however, is clear from her rendering of her party piece, "I Dreamt that I Dwelt in Marble Halls," in which she suppresses the second verse, with its fantasy of noble suitors lining up for her hand, and involuntarily repeats the first verse. For Maria, dwelling itself is the stuff of dreams, and her forgetting is symptomatic not only of her predicament, but of a whole culture's repression of its

---

[21] That the specter of death and famine loomed large at this particular time of year is clear from O'Suilleabhain's observation that Halloween was believed to be a time when "fairy forts" were opened, and the dead might reappear. People stayed indoors "and many games were played, and divinatory acts performed afterwards. The food supply for the winter being very important, hunger and famine were symbolically banished by throwing a cake of bread against the door" (O'Suilleabhain, *Irish Folk Custom and Belief*, 70). By losing the plum cake, Maria is, in effect, leaving the inner sanctum of the home at the mercy of the "otherworld." Stanislaus Joyce notes how James was not immune to a version of this custom, throwing a loaf of bread in through the front door of their house in Cabra on one New Year's Eve.

family romances through the atrophy of late and loveless marriages. Many Halloween rituals directly addressed the threat of famine, and in this connection, as Donald Torchiana observes, the fact "that four children of the same family should receive prayer book and water" in the divination game "suggests the narrowed options in Irish life since the Famine – the church, the marriageless state, and emigration" (*Backgrounds for Joyce's Dubliners*, 157). All rituals are a form of repetition, but whereas many traditional folk practices perform a constructive role, transforming "a passive into an active position which results in a mastery over a disturbing, wounding event," destructive repetition is compulsive, based on sameness, stasis, and ultimately (as the clay in the saucer indicates) death.[22] The equation of desiccated ritual with death, and indeed clay, is seen to telling effect in the abject wake which follows Isabel's death in *Stephen Hero*: no one "can contemplate," muses Stephen, "the network of falsities and trivialities which make up the funeral of a dead burgher without extreme disgust" (173). "The inexpressively mean way in which his sister had been buried" prompts the young Stephen to flout bourgeois propriety by sharing a pint of beer with the grave-diggers rather than the "small specials" more suited to mourners: "He was conscious of his startled father and he felt the savour of the bitter clay of the graveyard in his throat" (173). What we witness in "Clay" is a similar conversion of enabling rituals into their immobilizing opposites, as vestiges of the communal past wither in the emotional sterility of parlor games in bourgeois Dublin. As Kershner describes this process: "Significantly, the game in which Maria chooses the clay is a traditional one; but the folk tradition, with its possibility of brutal honesty, does not fit the bourgeois household in which everyone conspires to conceal from Maria what she has chosen in her life" (*Joyce, Bakhtin and Popular Literature*, 108).[23]

The fact that the disruptive substance in the parlor game is introduced from the outside (the garden), and indeed by members of the wider community (neighbors) rather than the family, attests to the manner in which the occult hovers in the unresolved regions between

[22] See Shlomith Rimmon-Kennan, "The Paradoxical Status of Repetition," *Poetics Today* 1 (1980), cited in Bronfen, *Over Her Dead Body*, 325.

[23] The importance of parlor games in Joyce is perceptively discussed by Alan Friedman in two unpublished papers, "Party Pieces in Joyce's 'The Dead,'" and "Party Pieces: Joyce, Beckett, and Performance." I am grateful to Professor Friedman for providing me with copies of these papers.

the public and private space, in what might be seen as a spectral public sphere. As Bourke contends, part of the underlying animus against Bridget Cleary was that she violated the boundaries between "inside" and "outside," between domestic and communal life. Her crime was that she had allegedly taken to straying from the household, and walking alone in a nearby fairy fort, but it is clear that she had also strayed from her crucial role as mother, by not producing any children in six years of marriage: "Legends of fairy abduction express metaphorically . . . the 'floating' position of women in the status hierarchy" who were unmarried, or who had failed in the reproductive roles allotted to them in the community ("Reading a Woman's Death," 574). Though veiled in the mystique of the otherworld, Bridget Cleary was, in fact, a victim of a form of domestic violence brought to its ultimate tragic denouement.

The tyranny of home

> The subject of the play is genius breaking out in the home and against the home. You needn't have gone to see it. It's going to happen in your own house.
>
> (James Joyce, on the play *Magda*, 1898)

Domestic violence, albeit of a more understated variety, occurs in "Eveline" when a young woman attempts to escape the emotional aridity of the home after her mother's death, to escape with her paramour to far-off Buenos Aires. Home in this case signifies not a haven in a heartless world but the lifeless monotony of domestic routines: "Home! She looked around the room, reviewing all its familiar objects which she had dusted once a week for so many years, wondering where on earth all the dust came from" (*Dubliners*, 37–38). The futility of repetition embraces the tragedy of her mother's death, which presides over the story, as evinced by her unintelligible last words: "saying constantly with foolish insistence 'Derevaun Seraun! Derevaun Seraun!'" (41). It is significant that Eveline's desire to escape is precipitated not only by her mother's death, but also by her father's domestic violence, which is also construed as repetition:

> She would not be treated as her mother had been. Even now, though she was over nineteen, she sometimes felt herself in danger of her father's violence. She knew it was that that had given her the palpitations. When they were growing up he had never gone for her, like he used to go for Harry and Ernest, because

she was a girl; but latterly he had begun to threaten her and say what he would
do to her only for her dead mother's sake.

(*Dubliners*, 38–39)

It may be that Eveline's last-minute change of heart regarding her plans
to emigrate is motivated by a deep-seated fear of more domestic violence, for as Katherine Mullin shows in her chapter in this volume, behind
the smooth talk of her beau Frank, and his promise of "a home waiting
for her" in Buenos Aires, lies the moral panic of white slavery, with its
dismal prospects of seduction, betrayal, and abandonment. In this, as
Mullin suggests, "Eveline" acts as a parody of the kind of uplifting tales
on emigration carried by *The Irish Homestead* which contrasted the
family romances of idyllic Irish homes with the fleshpots of foreign
climes. In one of the canonical homilies on this theme, Revd J. Guinan's
Scenes and Sketches in an Irish Parish, or Priests and People in Doon (1903),
the eve of departure is indeed an American wake, for "it might truly be
said that the parting of many, aye, of most on that [railway] platform,
would be the parting of death":

> Many of these rosy-faced, fair young girls, so pure, so innocent, so pious, were
> exchanging the calm and holy peace of home for an atmosphere of infidelity,
> scepticism and sin. Alas! some of them, now so like unto the angels, might yet be
> dragged down to shame and crime, and to an early and dishonoured grave.

And, as if with Eveline's premonition of her own future in mind, it continues:

> If they could only "forecast the years," how many would choose to live on a dry
> crust at home rather than emigrate . . . One trembled to think of how easily the
> designing wretches – who, 'tis said, haunt American ports – might deceive and
> ensnare these poor, sheepish, unsuspecting country girls, who never wandered
> more than a dozen miles before from the paternal hearth. (43–44)

In Joyce's story, however, home is not where you escape to, but
where you escape from. Though Eveline seeks to reassure herself that
"in her home anyway she had shelter and food" (38), in fact, due to her
father's alcoholism, she "had hard work to keep the house together and
to see that the two young children who had been left to her charge went
to school regularly and got their meals regularly"(39). By the same
token, Fr. Guinan inadvertently exposes the shadow of starvation
lurking behind the family romance of faith and fatherland through his
references to the "dry crust at home": "How blessed would have been
the lot of that Irish girl, the poor, betrayed victim of hellish agencies of

vice, had she remained at home and passed her days in the poverty, aye
and wretchedness of a mud wall cabin – a wife and mother mayhap"
(Guinan, *Scenes and Sketches*, 45). Eveline's predicament is that even
dreams of "outside" and faraway places are intercepted by her domestic
duties, and bring her back to the stasis of home. As she waits by the
window with her farewell letters in her hand, "inhaling the odour of
dusty cretonne":

> Down far in the avenue she could hear a street organ playing. She knew the air.
> Strange that it should come that very night to remind her of the promise to her
> mother, her promise to keep the home together as long as she could. She
> remembered the last night of her mother's illness; she was again in the close
> dark room at the other side of the hall and outside she heard a melancholy air of
> Italy. The organ-player had been ordered to go away and given sixpence.
>
> (*Dubliners*, 41)

As Stephen Dedalus notes in *A Portrait of the Artist*, "home" is one of
the words, along with "ale" and "master," that sound different on
English and Irish lips (205), and we may speculate that the latter two
words, with their associations of alcohol and colonial domination, are
not unrelated to the different resonances of "home" in Ireland.[24] In
Stephen Hero, the young Stephen's determination not to be incarcerated
within the home gives rise to his restless walks through the streets of
Dublin, the wanderings not so much of a modern *flâneur* but of an
outcast from a family whose members were strangers to themselves.[25] As
Stephen "promenaded miles of the streets" with his friend Cranly, it is as
if the ground he covers distances him from his family, allowing him "to
spread out a few leagues of theory on the subject of the tyranny of
home" (130):

> His sister had become almost a stranger to him on account of the way in which
> she had been brought up. He had hardly spoken a hundred words to her since the
> time when they had been children together . . . She was called his sister as his
> mother was called his mother but there had never been any proof of that
> relation offered him in their emotional attitude towards him, or any recognition
> of it permitted in his emotional attitude towards them.
>
> (*Stephen Hero*, 131)

[24] For an insightful discussion of Stephen's rejection of home, see Watt, *Joyce,
O'Casey and the Irish Popular Theatre*, 93–112.
[25] The cultural specificity of the *flâneur* in Joyce's Dublin is the subject of Duffy,
The Subaltern "Ulysses," chapter 2. See also his chapter in this volume.

Such gestures towards intimacy as Stephen experiences take place in public space, as when he caresses Emma's hands on the step of the Rathmines tram (72), or when she "leaned appreciably" on his arm as they walk by the courting couples in dusky corners of St. Stephen's Green (158), or when he tells her that the sight of her "hips moving inside her waterproof" as she walked "proudly through the decayed city" filled him with desire: "I felt that I longed to hold you in my arms – your body. I longed for you to take me in your arms" (202–3). As Jules David Law observes of his wider sense of belonging and attachment: "In Stephen's mind, the integrity of home is preserved . . . by a venture outside the home. The external thus supplements, and is perhaps superior to, the internal" ("Joyce's 'Delicate Siamese' Equation," 203).

The meager enjoyment which Stephen's father draws from life also has its source outside the home, for it was only on his endless social rounds that he "had been accustomed to regard himself as the center of a little world, the darling of a little society." As his alcoholism and profligacy, however, brings increased misery and ruin on his family,

> He consoled and revenged himself by tirades so often prolonged and repeated that he was in danger of becoming a monomaniac. The hearth at night was the sacred witness of these revenges, pondered, muttered, growled and execrated. The exception which his clemency had originally made in favour of his wife was soon out of mind and she began to irritate him by her dutiful symbolism.
>
> (*Stephen Hero*, 115)

Mr. Daedalus could be Eveline's father or, indeed, any of the pathetic figures whose recourse to domestic violence, whether leveled at women or children, runs like a discordant refrain through the pages of *Dubliners*, and, with its attendant chorus of alcoholism and emotional sterility, may be partly responsible for the different sound of "home" to Irish and English ears. In "The Boarding House," Mrs. Mooney arranges a separation from a butcher who "drank, plundered the till, ran headlong into debt" (66) and fought with her in public, before taking a cleaver to her one night. Mrs. Kernan, in "Grace," is more stoical with regard to her husband's binges: "She accepted his frequent intemperance as part of the climate, healed him dutifully whenever he was sick and always tried to make him eat a breakfast. There were worse husbands. He had never been violent since the boys had grown up" (176). In several other stories – "A Little Cloud," "Counterparts," "Ivy Day at the Committee Room," "An Encounter" – children are on the receiving end of domestic rage, social frustration, or sexual abuse, not to mention the pervasive corporal punishment in *A Portrait* which was construed, perversely, as a disciplinary corrective to antisocial behavior.

Some contemporary observers sought to account for the different responses to the idea of "home" in Ireland and England by arguing that the dysfunctions of the family were greater in Ireland, not on account of a racial pathology, but due to the social and economic consequences of a post-Famine colonial condition. In keeping with Filson Young's analysis quoted above, Michael J. F. McCarthy cites the lack of an urban manufacturing base, and the absence of any vision of social reform in the Catholic Church, as being responsible for the breakdown of national character. In particular, he draws attention to the fact that the notorious Mecklenburgh Street (or "Monto") area, the "greatest blot" on public decency in Ireland or Great Britain, was allowed to carry on its immoral traffic in vice in the immediate vicinity of the Catholic Pro-Cathedral. McCarthy links this to the lack of legal protection afforded to women against domestic violence and, in this, both the Catholic Church and the colonial administration were in active collusion. As Elizabeth Steiner-Scott has recently shown, none of the landmark acts in English law, such as the 1853 and 1878 acts giving a wife greater protection against domestic violence, extended to Ireland, nor were the promoters of the sanctity of the home to the forefront of demands for this basic human right ("'To Bounce a Boot'"). To call into question the integrity of the family was to undermine the foundational fictions of the colonial public sphere, and it was perhaps this porousness between public and private life which led Joyce to proclaim in an early letter to Nora: "My mind rejects the whole present social order and Christianity – *home*, the recognised virtues, classes of life, and religious doctrines. How could I like the idea of *home?*" (*Letters* II, 48; italics mine).

In his initial plan for *Dubliners*, Joyce made explicit provision for stories dealing with "public life," but none for private life, as if it had not yet constituted itself as a distinctive affective sphere. Freud's thesis in *Civilization and its Discontents*, that civilization rests on a restriction of the erotic within the confines of the home, makes little sense when the home itself is drained of sexual passion, even by the standards of Victorian or bourgeois morality. It is this failure to fully interiorize paralysis as an ailment of the individual which accounts for its functioning as a "cultural-somatic," and not just a psycho-somatic, condition in Ireland. These links between the public and the private survive in the endangered traces of unofficial street or public culture, and it is perhaps from this recalcitrant border zone that Joyce launched his own powerful raids on the inarticulate.[26] Notwithstanding the jingle in *Ulysses,* more than Plumtree's Potted Meat is required to make a home complete, or "an abode of bliss," in the emotional void of Joyce's Dublin.

Works cited

Bakhtin, M. M. *Rabelais and his World.* Trans. H. Iswolski. Cambridge, Mass.: MIT Press, 1968.

Bourke, Angela. *The Burning of Bridget Cleary*, London: Pimlico, 1999.
  "Reading a Woman's Death: Colonial Text and Oral Tradition in Nineteenth-century Ireland." *Feminist Studies* 21.3 (fall 1995): 553–86.

Bronfen, Elisabeth. *Over her Dead Body: Death, Femininity and the Aesthetic.* Manchester: Manchester University Press, 1992.

Brunsdale, Mitzi M. *James Joyce: A Study of the Short Fiction.* New York: Twayne, 1993.

Cixous, Hélène, and Catherine Clément. *The Newly Born Woman.* Trans. Betsy Wing. Manchester: Manchester University Press, 1986.

Cusack, Mary Francis. *Women's Work in Modern Society.* Kenmare Publications, 1875.

Daly, Mary. *Women and Work in Ireland: Studies in Irish Economic and Social History.* Dublin: Dundalgan Press, 1997.

Duffy, Enda. *The Subaltern "Ulysses."* Minneapolis: University of Minnesota Press, 1994.

Elias, Norbert. *The Civilizing Process.* Trans. E. Jephcott. 2 vols. New York: Pantheon, 1978/1982.

Ellmann, Richard. *James Joyce.* Rev. edn. New York: Oxford University Press, 1982.

Foster, R. F. *W. B. Yeats: A Life*, vol. I, *The Apprentice Mage.* Oxford: Oxford University Press, 1997.

Freud, Sigmund. *Civilization and its Discontents.* 1930. Trans. James Strachey. New York: W. W. Norton, 1961.

Gibbons, Luke. "'Some Hysterical Hatred': History, Hysteria and the Literary Revival." *Irish University Review* 27.1 (spring/summer 1997): 7–23.
  "'Where Wolfe Tone's Statue Was Not': Joyce, Monuments and Mourning in Irish Culture." Paper delivered at Classic Joyce conference, Rome, June 1998.

Goldstein, Jan. "The Hysteria Diagnosis and the Politics of Anticlericalism in Late Nineteenth-century France." *Journal of Modern History* 54 (June 1982): 209–39.

---

[26] I deal with this in relation to other works of Joyce in "'Where Wolfe Tone's Statue Was Not.'"

Guinan, Revd J. Canon ("A Country Curate"). *Scenes and Sketches in an Irish Parish, or Priests and People in Doon*. 1903. Dublin: Talbot Press, 1925.

Joyce, James. *Dubliners*. London: J. M. Dent, 1991.

    Poems and Shorter Writings. Ed. Richard Ellmann, A. Walton Litz, and John Whittier-Ferguson. London: Faber & Faber, 1991.

    A Portrait of the Artist as a Young Man. Harmondsworth: Penguin, 1992.

    Stephen Hero. London: Paladin, 1991.

Joyce, Stanislaus. *My Brother's Keeper*. Ed. Richard Ellmann. London: Faber & Faber, 1958.

Kershner, R. B. *Joyce, Bakhtin and Popular Literature: Chronicles of Disorder*. Chapel Hill: University of North Carolina Press, 1989.

Law, Jules David. "Joyce's 'Delicate Siamese' Equation: The Dialectic of Home in *Ulysses*." *PMLA* 102 (1987): 197–205.

Lecky, W. E. H. *Ireland in the Eighteenth Century*. 1892. Vol. 1. London: Longman, 1913.

Lowe-Evans, Mary. *Crimes Against Fecundity: Joyce and Population Control*. Syracuse: Syracuse University Press, 1989.

McCarthy, Michael J. F. *Five Years in Ireland, 1895–1900*. London: Simkin, Marshall, Hamilton, Kent & Co., 1902.

    The Irish Revolution. Edinburgh: Blackwood, 1912.

    Priests and People in Ireland. 1902. London: Hodder & Stoughton, 1908.

McCartney, Donal. *W. E. H. Lecky, Historian and Politician, 1838–1903*. Dublin: Lilliput Press, 1994.

McGrath, William J. *Freud's Discovery of Psychoanalysis: The Politics of Hysteria*. Ithaca: Cornell University Press, 1986.

McLoughlin, Dympna. "Woman and Sexuality in Nineteenth-century Ireland." *Irish Journal of Psychology* 15.2–3 (1994): 266–75.

Magalaner, Marvin, and Richard M. Kain. *Joyce: The Man, the Work, the Reputation*. New York: Collier Books, 1962.

Norris, Margot. "Narration Under a Blindfold: Reading Joyce's 'Clay.'" *PMLA* 102 (1987): 206–15.

O'Suilleabhain, Sean. *Irish Folk Custom and Belief*. Dublin: Cultural Relations Committee, 1967.

    Irish Wake Amusements. Cork: Mercier Press, 1969.

Showalter, Elaine. *The Female Malady: Woman, Madness, and English Victorian Culture, 1830–1980*. Harmondsworth: Penguin, 1987.

Spierenburg, Pieter. *The Broken Spell: A Cultural and Anthropological History of Preindustrial Europe*. New Brunswick: Rutgers University Press, 1991.

Stallybrass, Peter, and Allon White. *The Politics and Poetics of Transgression*. London: Methuen, 1986.

Steiner-Scott, Elizabeth. "'To Bounce a Boot of her Now and Then': Domestic Violence in Post-Famine Ireland." *Women and Irish History*. Ed. Maryann Gialancella Valiulis and Mary O'Dowd. Dublin: Wolfhound Press, 1997. 125–43.

Torchiana, Donald T. *Backgrounds for Joyce's Dubliners*. Boston: Allen & Unwin, 1986.

Trench, W. Steuart. *Realities of Irish Life*. 1868. London: Longmans & Green, n.d.

Waisbren, Burton A., and Florence L. Walzl. "Paresis and the Priest: James Joyce's Symbolic Use of Syphilis in 'The Sisters.'" *Annals of Internal Medicine* 80 (June 1974): 758–62.

Watt, Stephen. *Joyce, O'Casey and the Irish Popular Theatre*. Syracuse: Syracuse University Press, 1991.

Wills, Clair. "Rocking the Cradle? – Women Studies and the Family in Twentieth-century Ireland." *Bullán* 1.2 (autumn 1994). 97–106.

Yeats, W. B. "Two Essays and Notes." Lady Augusta Gregory, *Visions and Beliefs in the West of Ireland*. 1920. Gerrard's Cross: Colin Smythe, 1979. 302–65.

Young, Filson. *Ireland at the Crossroads: An Essay in Explanation*. 1903. London: E. Grant Richards, 1907.

8

Don't cry for me, Argentina: "Eveline" and the seductions of emigration propaganda

KATHERINE MULLIN

> It finally got to her that Buenos Ayres was her own private prison.
> That's when she decided to run away.
>
> GILDA, *dir. Charles Vidor, 1941*

> Look at the story in the paper The Irish Homestead. Could you write anything simple, rural?, livemaking?, pathos?, which could be inserted so as not to shock the readers. If you could furnish a short story about 1800 words suitable for insertion the editor will pay £1. It is easily earned money if you can write fluently and don't mind playing to the common understanding and liking for once in a way.
>
> (*Letters* II, 43)

Commissioning the first version of "Eveline" for *The Irish Homestead*, George Russell advised Joyce to "play to the common understanding for once in a way" (Ellmann, *James Joyce*, 163). Joyce responded by writing what I will suggest was a particularly intricate and politically loaded perversion of a familiar fiction. His story of thwarted emigration, with its frustrations, ambiguities, and ellipses, writes against the prescriptive narratives more usually published in *The Irish Homestead* fiction sections. *Homestead* emigration stories, as I will show, relentlessly insisted that displacement from Ireland was dangerous, isolating, and disappointing. In particular, the paper articulated contemporary nationalist anxieties over the vulnerability of young female emigrants to sexual dangers abroad. In this context, Argentina, I will argue, acts as the occluded center of "Eveline," its disparate cultural meanings interrogating the *Homestead's* didactic emigration monologue. For, through Argentina's various contemporary notorieties, Joyce brings *Homestead* nationalist propaganda into contest with other, rival propagandas of emigration. "Eveline," I will suggest, is a "semicolonial" story because, through these competing propagandas, Joyce writes his estrangement from the kind of nationalism *The Irish Homestead* expected its stories to dictate. Instead, "Eveline," through its submerged and subversive intertexts, expresses what didactic nationalism has in common with other ideologically irreconcilable fictions of emigration and national identity.

The Irish Homestead led a contemporary nationalist initiative to slow emigration, explaining schemes to "Brighten Rural Life" and holding an annual "Stop Emigration" competition offering a cash prize to "the co-operative society which shall have done the most to make their parish a place from which no Irishman would want to emigrate" (20 October 1900; 8 November 1902). Its proprietor, Sir Horace Plunkett, described emigration as "the symptom of a low national vitality . . . which not only depletes our population, but drains it of those elements which can least be spared" (*Ireland in the New Century*, 41). He argued that "we cannot exercise much direct influence upon the desire to emigrate, beyond spreading knowledge as to the real conditions of life in America for which home life in Ireland is often ignorantly bartered" (40). Plunkett's understanding of emigration as the symptom of a national wasting disease looked to the popular press as part of its cure. Accordingly, the fiction published in *The Irish Homestead* between 1900 and 1904 uniformly insisted that emigration was not a road to self-fulfillment, adventure, or even Eveline Hill's "escape." Rather, it ruptured the natural bonds of lovers, families, community, and nation.[1] If Joyce followed Russell's advice and scanned back issues of the paper for likely stories to reinterpret, then one typical emigration story which might have appealed to his well-documented delight in coincidence was the Reverend Jeremiah O'Donovan's "The Awakening of Brian Joyce."[2] It is set in Galway, home to "generations of the Joyces," on the

---

[1] Examples include Morris, "Monica's Twin Sister," where parental insistence that the hero take a dowered bride rather than the penniless Monica forces the desperate lovers to contemplate "clearing off to the land of Stars and Stripes, aye, and sink or swim" (114). The lead story of the 1904 "Celtic Christmas" supplement, "An American Visitor," similarly tells of a past emigrant who regrets ever leaving Ireland, a theme repeated by Seumas McManus's poem in the same issue, "The Disillusioned," where another repentant emigrant rues the day he saw "a glittering world beyond" the old country, and pleads "With ye I'll find forgetfulness of a world so void and vain / Oh mountains, mountains of my youth, fling wide your arms again." America was repeatedly constructed as a "glittering," but ultimately "void and vain" locus of disappointment and heartbreak.

[2] O'Donovan's life story ironically shadows his commitment to the prevention of emigration through propaganda. He met Plunkett in 1899, and was described in a penportrait in the *Homestead* of 20 January 1900 as "one of the best exponents of the co-operative movement, not only in its idealist, but in its practical aspect." His skill as a propagandist made him a regular contributor of articles and short

eve of Brian Joyce's departure for America. Brian's farewell party is marred by his weeping girlfriend Nora, who laments: "The fever for roaming is in your blood. The people are in Ireland all for America now. I'm not the first girl America put a heavy cross on" (15). That night, Brian dreams of Kathleen Ni Houlihan, who appears "to the sound of harps" and asks "Are you, like the others, going to leave me?" (16). Chastened, O'Donovan's Joyce stays in Ireland to marry Nora, explaining "I've learnt my duty now to God and to you and to Ireland, and I'll do it" (16). "The Awakening of Brian Joyce," "simple, rural and livemaking," contains many of the features which made up a typical *Homestead* emigration story. Firstly, America threatens to lure the protagonist away from his true love and a wholesome, sober, and industrious rural community with (hollow) promises of material gain. Secondly, O'Donovan gestures towards the national cultural inheritance the hero is on the verge of renouncing through smattering the dialogue with Gaelic, and through the Kathleen Ni Houlihan figure. Finally, the protagonist is brought to the realization that emigration is a betrayal of Ireland, and must therefore lead to misery.

This, then, was the kind of story Russell invited Joyce to replicate, where the refusal to board the steamer signifies not paralysis but national awakening. Joyce's story of thwarted emigration instead queries the conventions of *Homestead* emigration fiction. The "love interest" in Joyce's story is disrupted by Eveline's decision to stay at home. She looks out of her window, not at tidy cottages and wholesome peasantry, but at the urban landscape of "little brown houses" and "new red houses," and at that familiar stranger in the city, the "man out of the last house" who daily passes her home (*Dubliners*, 29). Even Joyce's use of Gaelic is subversive of the *Homestead* use of the language to reinforce a sense of nation and encourage those "believers in the language move-ment" studying at Gaelic League classes. Instead, he corrupts Gaelic into "Derevaun Seraun," that nonsensical crux withholding its meaning from

footnote 2 (*cont.*)

stories to the *Homestead* between 1898 and 1903, but in 1904 O'Donovan left the priesthood after a dispute with the church over his political activities and emi-grated to England, where he changed his name to Gerald, married, and found work as a journalist. During the First World War his "energy and enthusiasm" led to his appointment as Head of British Propaganda in Italy under the Ministry of Information, where the novelist and travel writer Rose Macaulay was his sec-retary. They began a clandestine relationship, which continued until his death in 1942. See Ryan, "Gerald O'Donovan," for a fine account of O'Donovan's life.

heroine and reader alike.[3] However, the most obvious, and I will argue the most radical, of Joyce's subversions of the *Homestead* emigration narrative is his positioning of Argentina, rather than the ubiquitous "America," at the center of his story. For, between 1900 and 1904, Argentina was never mentioned as an emigration destination in either *The Irish Homestead* or, as Mary Power has shown, *The Weekly Freeman*. Joyce, I will argue, exploited Argentina's various contemporary reputations to produce a story which is not the emigration propaganda the readers of *The Irish Homestead* might expect.

What, then, was Argentina's reputation in Ireland? As Patrick McKenna ("Irish Migration to Argentina," 79), Andrew Graham-Yooll (*The Forgotten Colony*), and Peadar Kirby (*Ireland and Latin America*) have each shown, the peak period of Irish migration to the Argentine lasted from around 1825 to 1875. Although the precise number who emigrated from Ireland during this fifty-year period is uncertain, the generally accepted estimate is around 30,000 (McKenna, "Irish Migration to Argentina," 80). In Argentina, Irish emigrants could cast off their identity as colonized, and instead take on that of colonizer, mastering the unplanted terrain of the Pampas. As the Irish community prospered during the nineteenth century, Argentina became known in Ireland as a land of opportunity. As the Irish community's newspaper *The Southern Cross* boasted on 6 January 1875, "In no part of the world is the Irishman more respected and esteemed than in the Province of Buenos Ayres, and in no part of the world in the same space of time have Irish settlers made such large fortunes." Argentina, then, was considered to be a country where the Irish emigrant made good, as the journalist William Bulfin noted: "Over the richest sheepruns in the province of Buenos Ayres you may gallop during every hour of the longest day in summer without crossing a single rood of land that is not owned by some son of the Emerald Isle" (*Tales of the Pampas*, 205).[4] Frank, who claims to

---

[3] For a summary of possible interpretations of "Derevaun Seraun," see Jackson and McGinley, ed., *James Joyce's "Dubliners"*, 31.

[4] William Bulfin was an Irish settler in Buenos Aires who wrote from the 1870s until the 1890s about the lives of the Irish migrants under the name "Che Buono," and much of his writing appeared in both *The Weekly Freeman* and *The Southern Cross* around that period. He was better known for his popular *Rambles in Eirinn*, which contains an account of meeting Joyce and Oliver Gogarty at the Martello Tower in Sandycove. Joyce commented scathingly on his contributions to Arthur Griffiths's *Sinn Fein* in several letters to Stanislaus (*Selected Letters*, 129, 145).

Table 1. *Emigration from Ireland to America and to Argentina, 1886–1904*

	Total emigration	To USA	To Argentina
1886	63,416	50,723	41
1887	82,923	69,798	44
1888	78,684	66,906	123
1889	70,477	59,723	1,651
1890	61,313	52,685	65
1891	59,623	52,273	27
1892	50,867	46,550	30
1893	48,147	45,243	12
1894	35,895	33,096	20
1895	48,703	45,298	24
1896	38,995	35,216	7
1897	32,535	28,760	3
1898	32,241	27,855	31
1899	41,232	35,433	18
1900	45,288	37,765	16
1901	39,870	31,942	1
1902	40,190	33,683	0
1903	40,653	33,501	0

Source: Table compiled from Parliamentary Papers, "Emigration: III: Statistical Table: Ireland," 1886–1904.

have "fallen on his feet in Buenos Ayres," and can offer Eveline status and "a home," appears to fit this prototype of the successful Irish emigrant.

However, to read Frank as a successful emigrant smuggled past George Russell oversimplifies the extent of Joyce's subversion. Frank may appear to fit the stereotype of the local boy made good in Argentina, but, as the figures in table 1 imply, such a stereotype had become obsolete. During the two decades preceding Frank's return to Dublin, the rate of migration to Argentina from Ireland had dwindled to zero. These figures suggest that, just as Frank's tales of the terrible Patagonians are tall because the Patagonians became extinct many years before his birth, so he calls upon a distant, half-remembered story of Irish enterprise abroad, rather than its modern reality. He attempts to seduce Eveline, therefore, with an emigration propaganda of his own. "He had tales of distant countries" (*Dubliners*, 32), and his bewitching stories of adventure abroad are in direct contest with *The Irish Homestead's* warning fictions.

Any regular reader of *The Irish Homestead* would, therefore, be inclined to concur with Hugh Kenner's analysis of that tell-tale "He had fallen on his feet in Buenos Ayres [comma] he said [comma]" (*The Pound Era*, 37), and read Frank as "a bounder with a glib line trying to pick himself up a piece of skirt" ("Molly's Masterstroke," 21). Argentina's contemporary reputation in Ireland compromises Frank's credibility further. After 1889, the country became notorious throughout Ireland as the home of Frank's kind of misleading and exploitative emigration propaganda. The British government report on Irish emigration in 1889 commented upon "the exceptionally high number of 1,651 (1,497 who went by one vessel in January) to Buenos Ayres" (Parliamentary Paper 1890: 761), and this sudden surge in emigration resulted from the efforts of the Argentine government to attract immigrants by releasing 50,000 prepaid steamer passages through agents (Kirby, *Ireland and Latin America*, 88). Immigrants were offered free employment bureau services and temporary accommodation on arrival in Buenos Aires, but when on 12 February 1889 the steamer *Dresden* arrived in Buenos Aires, carrying the 1,497 Irish beneficiaries, it became clear the authorities were ill-prepared for them. The immigration hostel was severely overcrowded, and one eyewitness, Michael Dinneen, the editor of *The Southern Cross*, reported: "There were 3,000 people there, all mixed together regardless of sex or nationality. The Irish having come last, many hundreds were sleeping in the courtyard" (Parliamentary Paper 1889: 243). Furthermore, the new recruits were ill-fitted to the kind of work on offer, and there were too many dependent women and children (Parliamentary Paper 1889: 241). The *Dresden* emigrants became the beneficiaries of private philanthropy, rather than the promised state aid.[5]

The *Dresden* episode illustrates a turning point in Argentina's reputation in Ireland. Two weeks before the steamer's arrival, the *Buenos Ayres Standard* reported: "The Argentinean Republic is certainly better

---

[5] See Parliamentary Paper 1889: 241, 256 for details of the Bahia Blanca project, and contemporary tributes to the "unselfish devotion and charity of the Irish community."

known in Dublin now than it was ten years ago, and this is due to the exertions of Mr. O'Meara, the Immigration agent, who is most unceasing in his efforts to promote Irish emigration to Buenos Ayres" ("Memories of Dublin," 24 January 1889). O'Meara was paid commission of between fifteen shillings and £1 per emigrant by the Argentine government, and soon his unceasing efforts were under close scrutiny (Hansard, 15 April 1889: 1712). As George Jenner, the British *chargé d'affaires* in Buenos Aires, complained to the Foreign Office, "The subordinate agents employed in Ireland have proved utterly corrupt and worthless, and have allowed the propaganda to fall into the hands of a class of persons most unfitted for emigration to this country, including prostitutes and beggars" (Parliamentary Paper 1889: 240). Argentina swiftly became perceived as an unscrupulous foreign power intent upon exploiting Irish hardship. When *The Southern Cross* learnt that a further 12,000 Irish were preparing to escape bad harvests in Ireland and sail for Argentina, the paper protested that "Mr. O'Meara has been scattering falsehoods broadcast throughout Ireland" and petitioned the Catholic Archbishop of Dublin to "use his influence to stop all emigration to this country" (*Buenos Ayres Standard*, 17 April 1889). Home Rule MPs repeatedly demanded that the British government take steps to protect its Irish subjects from Argentinean expansionism. John O'Connor and F. A. O'Keefe asked the Foreign Secretary to "issue a warning to poor Irish people to abstain from emigrating to Argentina" (Hansard, 26 March 1889: 841) and when Tim Healy discovered in June 1889 that 3,500 people had been promised free passages, had sold up their property and made their way to Queenstown to board a steamer which never arrived, he protested: "It is a monstrous thing that a foreign government trying to recruit its population here should be allowed to bring ruin upon thousands of people" (Parliamentary Paper 1889: 300). Healy pressed the Foreign Office to make it a penal offence for "Foreign agents to entice emigrants abroad by false promises" and tried to secure compensation (Hansard, 12 August 1889: 1012). In response, Customs officers in all Irish ports were warned to report "any large body of Irish emigrants travelling to the Argentine Republic," and the further distribution of assisted passages was prohibited (Parliamentary Paper 1889: 275, 280).

The *Dresden* crisis therefore places Argentina at the center of the kind of anti-emigration narrative which would not have been out of place in *The Irish Homestead*. Home Rule MPs and the Irish expatriates in

Argentina attempted to counter the dissemination of emigration propaganda by, in Horace Plunkett's terms, "spreading knowledge of the real conditions for which home life in Ireland is often so ignorantly bartered" (*Ireland in the New Century*, 41). Their propagandist counteroffensive succeeded, as O'Meara's offices closed in 1890, unreplaced until 1899, when a M. Jordi opened an "Argentine Republic Consulate" in the back room of his cork and wine business on Ormond Quay.[6] It would seem that Argentina was slow to recover from its notoriety, for, as table 1 shows, in the three years prior to "Eveline's" publication, the country failed to attract a single Irish emigrant, whilst 97,764 traveled to the United States. Buenos Aires' reputation in Ireland as the city of happy-ever-after propaganda imposed upon the gullible has transparent application to Frank's "He had fallen on his feet in Buenos Ayres, he said." What that suspicious "he said" appears to indicate in the context I have outlined is that Frank, like O'Meara and the Argentine government before him, is a propagandist for Buenos Aires whose motives are similarly shady. No wonder, then, that Mr. Hill articulates his disapproval of Frank in terms which insist upon the dangers of participating in Frank's propaganda. Rather than warn Eveline not to have anything to do with him, he forbids her to "have anything to say to him," a nuance which betrays his fear of his daughter's vulnerability to her lover's persuasive and seductive discourse.[7]

What Frank has to say about his adopted homeland forms the crux of "Eveline." What Joyce's many clues to Frank's untrustworthiness – his tales of terrible Patagonians, his reluctance to marry Eveline before the ship sails, his anachronistic claim to have made his fortune in Argentina – indicate is that the propagandist of myths of nation is not to be relied upon. Thus, Joyce provides a further subversion of the *Homestead* fiction writer's role. Rather than contributing to a nationalist drive to halt emigration by producing propagandist fictions celebrating Ireland and warning of dangers overseas, "Eveline" starkly figures its heroine's paralysis in terms of her susceptibility to such fictions. Eveline is caught

---

[6] Information gathered from *Thom's Dublin Directory*, 1886–1904. Neither O'Meara nor any Argentinean emigration agency are listed anywhere in Dublin after 1891.

[7] Joyce altered this line in one of his few revisions to the *Homestead* version of "Eveline" from "have anything to do with him" to "have anything to say to him," effectively casting a heavier emphasis upon the textuality of Frank. See *The Irish Homestead*, 10 September 1904.

between competing propagandas of emigration, one promoted by Frank of "a home waiting for her in Buenos Ayres," with its overtones of glamour, adventure, and escape, and the second of the security and familiarity of her life in Ireland, which she has gathered from another source. Joyce shows this second propaganda to be contained within *The Irish Homestead's* persistent ideological construction of "home" as the locus of retreat, of the Reverend Jeremiah O'Donovan's pretty Galway cottages and convivial peasant communities. Accordingly, the word "home" pulses relentlessly through "Eveline," cumulating in Eveline's deathbed promise to her mother to "keep the home together as long as she could" (33). "Home" is counterpointed with "house," both words appearing six times in a five-page story, and the tension between the two loosely synonymous terms articulates the difference between a physical and an ideological space. "Home," for Eveline, offers no fulfillment: instead, the word signifies an oppressive, paralyzing force Joyce recognized in both the *Homestead*'s name and its emigration stories.[8]

"Home" carries dual ideological overtones of both a national and a gendered space, and, for Eveline, "wondering where on earth all the dust came from" (*Dubliners*, 29), this overlap is particularly potent. Young, single, literate women like Eveline Hill comprised the majority of emigrants leaving Ireland between 1885 and 1910 (Diner, *Erin's Daughters in America*, xvi; Nolan, *Ourselves Alone*, 49). Such women were slamming the door on the "home country" which *The Irish Homestead* promoted as an Irishwoman's proper place. For this large scale migration of young Irishwomen supplied another dimension to emigration anxieties, as nationalist critics predicted what John Verschoyle described as "the moral murder of countless virtuous Irish maidens" ("The Condition of Kerry," 552–53). Nationalist anxieties over the sexual vulnerability of female emigrants were summarized in Agnes O'Farelly's lecture to the Gaelic League in 1900: "Oh, those poor little brown-haired Irish girls – they don't know yet what is before them. No wonder the wisest pinch and scrape for a few years so that they may go home and settle down. But they are not all wise" ("The Reign of Humbug," 10–11). This glimpse of nebulous peril was enlarged upon by *The Irish Homestead*'s own Jeremiah O'Donovan, who was a Gaelic League colleague of O'Farelly:

---

[8] As Luke Gibbons explains, for Joyce, "home is not where you escape to, but where you escape from." See the chapter by Gibbons in this volume, p. 165.

What of the girls? Ask those who know the slums of Chicago, of New York, of Boston. I shall throw no mud at an Irish girl, even when she has fallen. Poor, misguided, trusting girls, innocent even in their guilt, was there no-one to tell them of the whirlpool into which they were being cast adrift?

("An O'Growney Memorial Lecture," 15)

Responding to his own call to propaganda in the *Homestead* later that year, O'Donovan's story "Rose Brolley" offered a guided tour of that "whirlpool" of loose living awaiting the Irish girl abroad.

O'Donovan's heroine Rose, a nineteen-year-old Galway girl, throws over "an honest man's love and a little cottage by the sea" for the temptations of "balls, parties and big wages and theatres and fine clothes" (22) across the Atlantic. Like the *Dresden* emigrants, she too is lured by the seductions of emigration propaganda in the form of letters from her friend Nell, recently settled in New York. Telling her disappointed suitor "I would make a bad wife to you with the longing for excitement that is in my blood" (21), Rose joins Nell to seek pleasure in New York dance halls. There, she is cruelly disappointed: "The men were drunk and the women were encouraging them. Rose was shocked by their coarse talk. The natural refinement of the Irish peasantry clung to her, and her heart sickened at the vulgarity which surrounded her" (22). Soon, Rose succumbs to a mystery illness, and her story closes with her exemplary death in the care of the Sisters of Mercy, lamenting in a letter to her slighted Galway lover, "I was young and foolish and led away by love of excitement. It is hollow and disappointing life is here. The only happy days I have spent are the few with the Sisters, waiting to die" (22). O'Donovan forcefully constructs "home," meaning both the "little cottage by the sea" and Ireland, as his heroine's proper place, calling upon the *Homestead*'s readers' understanding of the "natural refinement" of Irish womanhood to emphasize her displacement. He draws upon a contemporary nationalist insistence upon the innate moral purity of the Irish, a synthesis of national pride and sexual chastity contained in Arthur Griffith's assertion that "all of us know that Irish women are the most virtuous women in the world" (Ward, "Conflicting Interests," 133). In this context, O'Donovan diagnoses Rose's desire to leave her homeland as the symptom of "a longing for excitement" that is, like a congenital and contagious disease, "in my blood." O'Donovan's insistence that Rose's emigration is a fatal act of un-Irish sexual impropriety is underlined by her death-bed association with the Sisters of Mercy, well known throughout

Ireland as the supervisors of Magdalen Asylums for penitent fallen women.[9]

Another of *The Irish Homestead*'s naïve nineteen-year-olds, considering leaving Ireland with a man not yet her husband, is almost lured into a parallel situation of sexual impropriety. Eveline Hill shares Rose Brolley's dangerous innocence, susceptibility to tall tales, and unwholesome "longing for excitement," for she enjoys Frank's attentions because "First of all it had been an excitement for her to have a fellow" and "She wanted to live" (*Dubliners*, 32, 33). Frank, with his tan, stories, theatre tickets, songs about the lass that loved a sailor and, above all, prepaid passage to Buenos Aires, offers Eveline the "excitement" which proved fatal to Rose Brolley and which *The Irish Homestead*, discerning the "exit" buried in "excitement," described as "a dangerous thirst for sensation more easily slaked abroad" ("Recreation in Rural Ireland," 20 October 1900). Contemporary Irish nationalist anxieties over the sexual safety of the Irishwoman abroad can thus be seen to incite a reading of "Eveline" as a seduction and betrayal narrative. Frank's character is informed by the stereotype of the moustache-twirling seducer from overseas, a stereotype to which Mr. Hill, with his "I know these sailor chaps" and Hugh Kenner, with his analysis of Frank as "a bounder with a glib line," are equally susceptible. However, by 1904, the old story of seduction and betrayal had a very contemporary twist in an imperialist narrative of female emigration and sexual danger, produced in England, exported to Ireland, and focused upon Buenos Aires. By submerging this second fiction within "Eveline," and thus smuggling it into the pages of the Irish journal of nationalist self-reliance, Joyce subversively emphasizes the suggestive and contradictory overlap between Irish nationalist and English imperialist fictions of national identity and emigration.

This imperialist fiction of sexual danger abroad was popularly known as the "White Slave Traffic." Its historical coincidence with Irish nationalist anxieties over emigration to Argentina was demonstrated when, in the aftermath of the *Dresden* disaster, the chairman of the British Immigration Society, Grenfell Maxwell, complained to the Foreign Secretary that "I can find places for any number of young girls as housemaids or cooks, but as you know they have been prevented from coming by reports that it is dangerous for girls to emigrate here, as they

---

[9] See Luddy, *Women and Philanthropy*, 110–15, for an account of the Sisters of Mercy's rescue work with Magdalen Asylums.

are kidnapped into houses of ill-fame" (Parliamentary Paper 1889: 288). Maxwell gestured towards a sophisticated propaganda campaign which, from the early 1880s until the 1920s, relentlessly promoted anxieties about an underground sexual danger targeting city-dwelling young working women like Eveline Hill. The campaign against the White Slave Traffic began in 1879, when Alfred Stace Dyer, an English evangelical writer of religious tracts against "self-abuse," rescued Ellen Newland, a nineteen-year-old Brighton maidservant from a Brussels brothel. On New Year's Day, 1880, Dyer broke Ellen's story in the English national press.[10] Like Eveline Hill, Ellen had been courted by "a man of respectable exterior," who she had met one day on the city street. Like Frank, her suitor walked out with her and treated her at the theatre, and eventually promised marriage if she would leave the country with him. The couple traveled to Calais, where Ellen was abducted by her fiancé's accomplice, and taken to Brussels. Speaking no French, she was gynecologically examined, registered as a prostitute, and imprisoned in a brothel. Dyer argued that Ellen's case indicated a cross-channel traffic in young English girls, ensnared in "the confinement and horrors of a licensed hell." He provided an irresistible combination of national outrage and sexual titillation, and a year later his account of his rescue work, *The European Slave Traffic in English Girls*, ran to six editions in nine months.[11] Like Joyce, Dyer constructed a narrative in which a young working woman is accosted by a charming stranger on the streets. After a period of courtship, he offers marriage and a new life abroad. Dyer's heroine leaves to be betrayed and imprisoned. Joyce's heroine is wise enough to stay at home.

By the time "Eveline" appeared in *The Irish Homestead*, social purity campaigners had redrafted the seduction and betrayal narrative. The National Vigilance Association, a London-based pressure group founded in the wake of Dyer's revelations, ensured the white slave scare lasted well into the second decade of the twentieth century (Bristow, *Vice and Vigilance*, 98–125). Dedicated to abolition through publicity and legislation, the National Vigilance Association's propaganda campaigns produced and sustained a narrative which closely shadows Joyce's story. Shop-girls like Eveline were perceived to be particularly vulnerable, as

---

[10] The story ran prominently in the *Daily News*, *Standard*, and *Pall Mall Gazette*. See Pearson, *The Age of Consent*, 123, for publication details.

[11] Publication details of *The European Slave Traffic* listed in Bodleian and British Library catalogues. My quotations are from pp. 25–32.

their positions on the margins of moneyed society combined with their poor wages to render them easy prey to the blandishments of disreputable men.[12] One of the association's pamphlets began with a chapter called "The Shop-girl and the Trafficker," which described a shop-girl who, like Eveline, spends her leisure time in the streets where

> nothing is more natural than that a chance acquaintance should be struck up. A theatre or dinner is proposed, then by slow and certain degrees she is drawn into the inevitable vortex which invariably ends in the same thing – the career of the unfortunate. The procurer has no need to travel far to find his prey – undoubtedly, large numbers of his victims are drawn from the ranks of the shop-girl class.
>
> (*In the Grip of the White Slave Trader*, 21)

The extent to which Frank's courtship uncannily suggests that of the white slave trader is probably most strikingly demonstrated in an extract from Olive MacKirdy's *The White Slave Market* (1912), a book Joyce bought, made notes on, and incorporated into *Finnegans Wake*:

> Some pimps take months and months to gain proper control over his victim who was a good girl [*sic*]. For a long time, the fiend incarnate contented himself with merely "walking out" with the girl, taking her to cheap picture shows, buying her little presents, meeting her as she came home from work and doing everything that would take her mind off his villainy. Once he had taught her to trust him, to love him, he ruined her and ruthlessly "dumped" her into the inferno at Buenos Ayres.   (276)[13]

[12] For an example of this perception, see Jeune, "The Ethics of Shopping," 123. Joyce's participation in the contemporary opinion that the shop-girl was available to a male public is made explicit at several points in his fiction. The bazaar shop assistant in "Araby" flirts with two loitering Englishmen, the "Sirens" barmaids, similarly on display behind a counter, snap garters and stroke phallic beer pumps for the delectation of the regulars, and roguish Blazes Boylan leers down the cleavage of the Thorntons' shop-girl (*Dubliners*, 27; *U* 11.409–18, 1112–17; 10.327–36).

[13] Joyce made notes from MacKirdy, particularly of the slang terms surrounding the White Slave Traffic, which he transferred to *Finnegans Wake*, mainly pages 351–52 (see Joyce, *Index Manuscript*, 121–24). *The White Slave Market*, like many similar books on the subject, summarizes the received wisdom on the traffic built up over the past three decades, and although Joyce obviously read it many years after composing "Eveline," I would argue that his use of MacKirdy as a source for *Finnegans Wake* represents a long-standing fascination with the white slave narrative most strikingly manifest in "Eveline."

Eveline's job, the circumstances of her meeting Frank, the manner of their courtship, and most of all his persuading her to emigrate without marrying her first saturate Joyce's plot with white slave nuances. The courtship ploy recurred many times within the pages of white slave pamphlets, often illustrated by pictures of moustache-twirling rogues luring innocents to their doom (see figure 2).

The National Vigilance Association, then, like Verschoyle, O'Donovan, and O'Farelly, constructed emigration as a state of constant potential peril for unchaperoned young women. In 1897, its women members began to patrol the ports and railway stations of major cities, including Liverpool and Dublin, in order to intercept young women traveling without respectable escorts.[14] They placed "Friendly Warnings" at all British and Irish ports and aboard all passenger steamers, which read, "There is risk to young women when travelling alone from one country to another," and advised women foolhardy enough to travel unchaperoned to contact the stewardess who would direct them to social purity workers at their destinations (*Sixteenth Annual Report*, 19). In Dublin since 1888 "very large posters" displaying this warning had been placed in all train stations and ladies waiting rooms (*Vigilance Record*, March 1888: 15). By 1910 the National Vigilance Association was able to boast "Over the last thirteen years, no fewer than 38,000 cases have been dealt with either at railway stations or ports" (*The White Slave Traffic*, 23). The scale of this surveillance indicates a climate of suspicion where any young woman traveling without a respectable escort was likely to be warned of the dangers of the foreign brothel. The combination of Frank's striking suntan, marking him out as a traveler, and

---

[14] Details of railway and port work of the National Vigilance Association's "International Guild of Service for Women" gathered from Parliamentary Paper 1907: 907 and *The Vigilance Record*, 2 April 1903: 35. The association was imitating the Travellers Aid Society, who since the mid-1880s had been distributing their distinctive pink handbills warning young women of the dangers of travel, meeting women off trains and steamers, and putting up posters in ladies' waiting rooms. This association was active in Dublin from 1886, and was financially supported by large annual contributions from Arthur Guinness (see Annual Report 1890: 18). Information gathered from Travellers Aid Society minutes and annual reports, held in 1/TAS Box 201, The Fawcett Archive, London Guildhall University. In 1887 the Dublin branch of the Travellers Aid Society reported "We have joined the Vigilance Association in placing large placards in Dublin stations" (*Annual Report*, 1887: 14).

THE FIRST MEETING.

The white slave trader, skilled in the arts and wiles of flattery, accosting a young girl on the street.

Fig. 2a Clifford Roe, *The Horrors of the White Slave Traffic* (1911).

THE SECOND MEETING—SHE KNOWS NOT THE DANGEROUS TRAP BEING SET FOR HER.

The smooth tongued villain tells of his affection and undying love for her. He paints a beautiful picture of how happy they will be. She is enraptured and promises to meet him and go to dinner with him.

Fig. 2b Clifford Roe, *The Horrors of the White Slave Traffic* (1911).

THE THIRD STEP—DRUGGED AND LED TO HER RUIN.
Having taken the drugged potion she is now incapable of self-control and is easily led to her ruin. Awaking she will find herself an inmate of a house of shame.

Fig. 2c Clifford Roe, *The Horrors of the White Slave Traffic* (1911).

Eveline's youth, would make the couple a likely target. Emigration with a young man neither relative nor husband was an action that would transform Eveline into the contemporary specter of the foolish shop-girl sweet-talked to her ruin.

One might speculate that Joyce was keenly aware of these "morality police" when writing "Eveline" as, in the summer of 1904 he, like Frank, was persuading a woman to leave Ireland with him without the security of marriage.[15] It is unlikely, given the vigilance activities which I have outlined, that Joyce could have been unaware of the potential difficulties of taking a young woman abroad. Like Frank and Eveline, Joyce and Nora Barnacle fitted the stereotype of procurer and procured too closely. Yet, whereas Joyce took Nora to Paris, Frank offers to take Eveline to Buenos Aires, a riskier destination by far, and it is Buenos Aires' centrality that pushes the similarities between "Eveline" and the white slave narrative beyond coincidence. By 1904 the city was perceived to be the international capital of the White Slave Trade. Eric Partridge explains that the phrase "going to Buenos Ayres" was turn-of-the-century slang for "taking up a life of prostitution, especially by way of a procurer's offices" (*A Dictionary of Slang*, 101). This was no mere figure of speech. From the late 1880s through the first decade of the twentieth century, Buenos Aires displaced Brussels, as it was repeatedly theorized as the center of, and culpable for, the White Slave Trade.[16] In 1889 the National Vigilance Association exposed "the business dealings of an arrangement for taking girls to Buenos Ayres for immoral purposes" (*Fourth Annual Report*, 26), and as we have seen, later that year, partly in response to White Slave Traffic anxieties, and partly in the aftermath of the *Dresden* disaster, the British Immigration Society was set up in Buenos Aires to "transmit accurate information to Britain and Ireland concerning Argentine emigration" and "for the protection of women" (*Vigilance Record*, February 1890: 10). The British Immigration Society met women off boats, and in 1902 they were joined in this work by the Argentine League for the Protection of Young Women, who liaised with the National Vigilance Association to "combat the unworthy traffic which

---

[15] Brenda Maddox outlines the courage of Nora's decision to leave with him (*Nora*, 65).

[16] The first International Conference on the White Slave Traffic stated that "one large branch of the traffic has its destination in South American ports, chiefly Buenos Ayres" (National Vigilance Association, *Fourteenth Annual Report*, 27).

seems unhappily to have taken deep root in this country" (*Vigilance Record*, October 1902: 71). Buenos Aires' notoriety as "the worst of all centers of immoral commerce in women" (*Vigilance Record*, October 1913: 80) was sustained through the first decade of the century. Millicent Fawcett asserted at the first International Conference on the White Slave Trade in 1899 that "there were at least 3,000 European women imprisoned and enslaved in the 'tolerated houses' of Buenos Ayres" (*The White Slave Trade*, 2). In 1902 the second International Conference on the White Slave Traffic, whilst attempting to coordinate international vigilance patrols at ports and railways, identified Argentina as particularly suspicious (Parliamentary Paper 1905: 1027). In 1907, Frederick Bullock, the chief constable at Scotland Yard, regretted that "it is almost impossible in the present state of the law to prevent passengers starting from London to South America, even when suspicion, amounting almost to certainty, may exist as to their character when they are escorting young women" (Parliamentary Paper 1907: 11). The chairman of the National Vigilance Association, William Coote, provided a retrospective assessment of the decade's work in 1910, asserting that "From statistics and other information in our possession, we knew that in Buenos Aires a constant demand existed for the victims of the traffickers, and that a large price was paid for them" (*A Vision and its Fulfilment*, 122). By the time Frank endeavors to escort Eveline to Buenos Aires, the city had thus accrued a fearsome international reputation as, in the words of one campaigner, "The hotbed of this abominable trade in human flesh, the grave of many of England's daughters' hopes" (*In the Grip of the White Slave Trader*, 76).

Once Mr. Hill discovers that his daughter is being courted by a man she has met on the streets and who has made a career from sailing from country to country, he comments "I know these sailor chaps," and forbids Eveline to have anything more to say to him (*Dubliners*, 32). Hugh Kenner has attributed Mr. Hill's mistrust to the sailor's reputation as a footloose ladies' man, but I suggest it might also stem from the darker notoriety the charmer from overseas had more recently acquired. Joyce's familiarity with the white slave narrative can be conjectured not merely from his later purchase of MacKirdy's *The White Slave Market*, or from the way it so closely coincides with "Eveline." In *Finnegans Wake*, the word "frank" is seldom without hints of white slavery: a "counterfeit frank" (183:19) precedes a list of *Dubliners* titles where "eveling" leads to "a protoprostitute" (186:26), Issy is "fatally fascinated

by a fine frank fairhaired fellow of the fairytales" (220:12), "Frank
Shaun," a "cademus" endeavors to complete a "white paper" under the
scrutiny of "Mrs. Grumby" (413:31), and, when endeavoring to place
Issy in the brothel surroundings of "an electric ottoman in the lap of
lechery, simprisingly stitchless with admiration amongst uxoriously fur-
nished appartments," he is "frank and hoppy" (452:15). Above all,
Joyce's fascination with Buenos Aires' notoriety as the destination of the
white slave is confirmed when Shaun warns Issy away from "Autist Algy,
the pulcherman and would do performer, oleas Mr. Smuth, stated by the
vice crusaders to be well-known to all the dallytaunties in or near the
ciudad of Buellas Arias, taking you to the plaguehouse to see the
Smirching of Venus" (434.35–435.03). Autist Algy is a "pulcherman," a
trader in pulchritude under a corruption of the most common British
alias, "Mr. Smith." He is an aspiring "performer," slang for "whoremonger," well known to "vice crusaders" and "dallytaunties," a perversion
of "dilettantes" which compresses the dalliance and the taunting of the
soliciting prostitute.[17] Like Frank, Autist Algy takes girls to the "plaguehouse," where the theatre disguises the brothel. The pun "Buellas Arias"
mediates the city through "puella" and "aria," retrieving "songs" about
"girls" from its name, and implying Joyce's understanding of the city as
the locus of fictions about women. To Joyce, Buenos Aires was a city
synonymous with the sexual betrayal of women, and the ill-wind of its
notoriety blows across "Eveline."

Joyce's translation of Buenos Aires through "puella aria" into a
"song about girls" or fiction of the feminine implies his perception of the
vice crusaders' cautionary tale as an ideological construct. The admis-
sion of one campaigner that "apathy is more of a crime than exaggeration when dealing with this subject" deftly expressed the relationship the
white slave fiction bore to reality (Rosen, *The Lost Sisterhood*, 114). When
Teresa Billington-Grieg, a feminist critic of the National Vigilance
Association, challenged more than fifty "vice crusaders" and all British
and Irish chief constables to supply evidence of "any fully proved cases
of attempted trapping," she found not one could produce a single case

---

[17] Definition of "performer" as slang for "whoremonger" taken from McHugh,
Annotations to Finnegans Wake, 435. Compare Joyce's expression "vice crusaders" with the colorful rhetoric of William Coote, chairman of the National
Vigilance Association: "Our readers will naturally be anxious to know the
results of our legal *crusade against vice* in all its hydra-headed form" (italics
mine), in his memoirs, *The Romance of Philanthropy* (113).

of white slavery between 1895 and 1913 ("The Truth About White Slavery," 431). Her research undercut the assumption that for the last two decades Britain had been subject to a white slave epidemic with Buenos Aires at its center. As Coote was forced to acknowledge on an official visit to Argentina in 1913, "My enquiries led me to feel that the general opinion of Europe as to the moral standard of Buenos Aires is not quite justified" (*Romance of Philanthropy*, 82). Billington-Grieg publicized instead what she described as "an epidemic of terrible rumours," and, like most rumors, the white slave propaganda epidemic germinated from a seed of truth. During the peak years of emigration to Buenos Aires, between 1870 and 1914, the city gained a reputation for prosperity, tolerance, and a male surplus which made it a relatively attractive place for prostitutes to emigrate to (Guy, *Sex and Danger in Buenos Ayres*, 37, 41). Brothels were from 1875 state-registered legal enterprises, and British women were highly visible, as prostitutes had to register their country of origin on state records (14). Although a 1912 survey showed that most European prostitutes had sold sex before registering in Argentina, this visibility made the Argentine an ideal focus for white slave anxieties (73).

State records invited vice crusaders to find proof that the Argentinean sex industry led to the abduction of British women. They argued that one only had to look at the statistics to recognize that "the international traffic in women is fed by these houses that live off their sexual commerce."[18] Yet, state records failed to show how, or why, immigrant women came to be there. Rather than investigate the social and economic causes of prostitution, social purity workers preferred to theorize that the British prostitute in Buenos Aires was a whiter than white slave. They extrapolated a narrative accounting for her presence which connected female emigration to sexual slavery. One white slave pamphlet asserted:

> There are hundreds of wretched parents who do not know if their daughters are alive or dead, for they have suddenly vanished. Well, we can tell them where they have been brought. They are in Buenos Ayres. This trade is a very lucrative one, as the men in South America are of a very amorous disposition, and the fair merchandise soon finds buyers.
>
> (*The White Slave Traffic*, 18)

[18] Sir Percy Bunting, editor of *The Contemporary Review* and executive member of the National Vigilance Association, representing the association at the International Abolitionist Federation Meeting in 1908, quoted in Guy, *Sex and Danger in Buenos Ayres*, 63.

This crude yet potent cocktail of racial and sexual anxieties figured the white slave as a symbol of sullied national honor, a piece of "fair merchandise" to be rescued from the vile appetites of foreign men. She was the site of national contamination, and her rescue was a matter of English national pride. The National Vigilance Association located "nation" not only at the center of their name, but at the apex of their theories: if a woman had not crossed national boundaries to sell sex then she was not a white slave, but merely a prostitute. The white slave cautionary tale mapped imperialist fears of miscegenation on to the seduction and betrayal narrative by promoting an antiemigration fiction which encouraged all women to retreat from the dangers of "abroad" to the security of "home."

In "Eveline," then, Joyce appears to collide *Homestead* antiemigration fiction with a second, submerged fiction with broadly similar themes, the white slave cautionary tale. Joyce accomplished this collision by placing Buenos Aires at the center of his narrative, and allowing the city's various reputations – as a bygone center of Irish emigration, as, more recently, the site of Irish exploitation, as the capital of the White Slave Trade – to complicate his heroine's renunciation of it. Joyce's imbrication of the imperialist white slave cautionary tale within the context of nationalist antiemigration propaganda foregrounds the similarities between two ideologically divergent discourses. For the two fictions have the same purpose, to halt female emigration, and both produce a propaganda campaign constructing "abroad" as hollow yet dangerous, and "home" as a place of refuge. The rhetoric of national contagion promoted by the National Vigilance Association compares to Irish nationalist anxieties about the sexual vulnerability of Agnes O'Farelly's "poor little brown-haired Irish girls." When the National Vigilance Association sought to extend its campaign to Ireland through its satellite organization, the Dublin White Cross Vigilance Association, it was quick to exploit such a home-grown moral panic. The DWCVA defined itself as a group of "earnest, thoughtful men who love Ireland and Irish chastity" (*The Vigilance Record*, September 1902: 71), who understood social purity work to be "of national as well as international importance, as there is grave danger of Ireland losing her proud reputation for purity if the immoral tendencies which are at work in other countries are allowed to spread among our people" (*The Vigilance Record*, May 1893: 36). The National Vigilance Association was careful to map its form of nationalism, which placed the surveillance and protection of the nation's women at the heart of national identity, on to an Ireland where, in the words of Ellice Hopkins, the English evangelical founder of the DWCVA, "the purity which is so often quoted is evidently a matter of race" (*The Purity Movement*, 16).[19]

So glib a transference of an ideological construction of "nation" from England to Ireland was not untroubled by colonial implications, and the relationship between the Dublin satellite and its parent organization, the National Vigilance Association, further complicates Joyce's submersion of the white slave narrative within *The Irish Homestead*. The Dublin White Cross Vigilance Association preserved only a limited sense of separate identity, as the name's emphasis upon "Dublin" rather than "Ireland" placed the organization on a level with other local branches of the NVA. *The Vigilance Record* carried the reports from "our Dublin branch" alongside those from Southampton, Liverpool, and Hull, reinforcing this unionist assumption.[20] The NVA's complicity with British rule in Ireland was further consolidated by its choice of president, the Earl of Aberdeen, who was simultaneously the Lord Lieutenant of Ireland. The DWCVA's religious allegiances were firmly Protestant: it was supported by two successive Protestant archbishops of Dublin; and its rules required each member to be "recommended by the minister of whose congregation he is an accustomed member," and each meeting began with "united prayer and devotional exercises" (*The Vigilance Record*, April 1891: 18). It would seem that, despite the DWCVA's rhetorical insistence upon Irish national purity, the organization did little to smooth over sectarian tensions.

The organization responsible for importing propaganda about white slavery into Dublin was therefore eyed with a certain suspicion. Michael McCarthy's best-selling *Priests and People in Ireland* offers a glimpse of the contemporary tensions which might be expected to have existed between the evangelical Protestant unionism of the DWCVA and Catholic nationalism. McCarthy outlined Catholic hostility to the DWCVA as a perceived Protestant proselytizing organization: "They are the sort of people who are stoned in Phoenix Park on a Sunday,

[19] This pamphlet contains a critique of what Hopkins perceived as Roman Catholic apathy towards social purity work, and argues that the purity of the Irish is due to racial character, rather than "the influence of the priest." For an account of Hopkins's work in founding the Dublin White Cross Vigilance Association, see Bristow, *Vice and Vigilance*, 103–5.

[20] For example, see *The Vigilance Record*, May 1893: 36.

whom, forsooth, their stoners are taught to look on as worshippers of an apostate monk and a degenerate nun who lived together in a life of fornication" (293). This distrust was mutual, and strikingly underlined in *The Vigilance Record*'s report on the *Dresden* disaster, where the formation of the British Immigration Society in Argentina was read as a response to its own campaigns to halt white slavery, rather than as a measure to protect vulnerable Irish immigrants. The National Vigilance Association's displacement of the Irish in favor of the white slave as the focus of emigration anxieties was consolidated by scathing references to "the whiskey-loving character of the scum of Queenstown and Cork," implying that the Irish, unlike white slaves, were the authors of their own misfortune (*Vigilance Record*, February 1890: 10). The white slave cautionary tale, therefore, must be seen as an uneasy presence amid the emigration propaganda more usually found in *The Irish Homestead*. It may be a nationalist antiemigration fiction, but in the context of the DWCVA's self-identification as a regional branch of the National Vigilance Association, and furthermore in the context of the mutual hostility between the NVA and Irish Catholic nationalism, its nationalism is emphatically of the wrong kind.

The white slave cautionary tale can thus be seen to compromise the principles of national self-sufficiency which *The Irish Homestead*, as the official journal of the Irish cooperative movement, espoused. The white slave propaganda campaign was an ideological import, and Joyce, by using it as a submerged intertext in "Eveline," performs a radical act of cultural and creative "emigration." In smuggling this rival, English imperialist antiemigration narrative into the pages of *The Irish Homestead*, Joyce critiques the didactic nationalist purpose Plunkett's paper assigned to its fiction by highlighting the suggestive and compromising overlap between ideologically divergent propagandas. If Joyce, as I suggest, responded to George Russell's instructions that he "play to the common understanding for once" by corrupting the staple fictions of *The Irish Homestead*, then the corruption buried within "Eveline" is that the story masquerades as a simple antiemigration propagandist fiction along "Rose Brolley" lines, yet in fact interrogates the terms and function of the nationalist propaganda it supposedly embodies.

Joyce's semicolonial subversion in "Eveline" is, therefore, that he transforms a propagandist fiction of nation into a fiction about nationalist propaganda. For Joyce places his interrogation of propaganda at the center of "Eveline" by creating a heroine whose paralysis is imposed by her vulnerability to the persuasive fictions of others. Initial hints of Eveline's intertextual identity, or that she is a heroine plagiarized from other fictions, are contained in Joyce's suggestive choice of names which insinuate the latent sexual peril of her situation. In another concealed reference to the brothel, Eveline has two eponymous pornographic namesakes, the heroine of a mid-Victorian classic of the genre, *Eveline, or the Adventures of a Lady of Fortune who was Never Found Out*, and John Cleland's *Fanny Hill*, and the name of her lover also recalls the Victorian flagellant novel *Frank and I*.[21] Within the text, Eveline's story is similarly constrained by the conflicting fictions of Frank's "lass that loved a sailor," and Mr. Hill's tale of the sailor with a girl in every port. Eveline's yearning to imagine herself the heroine of other people's fictions is deeply implicated in her fantasy of marriage to Frank. "He would give her life" (*Dubliners*, 33), she thinks, the "life" of the lass called Poppens for fun who loves a sailor. Eveline's fantasy of entrance into this kind of romantic fiction most poignantly appears when she speculates upon the reaction of an implied readership to the page-turning gesture of elopement she contemplates: "What would they say of her in the Stores when they found out that she had run away with a fellow? Say she was a fool, perhaps; and her place would be filled up by advertisement" (30). Although the disapproval of her formidable superior, Miss Gavan, is contemplated in full, the hesitation on "perhaps," marked off by comma and semicolon into a separate phrase, hints at a host of alternative, elided responses Eveline dare not fantasize in full. What they would say of her in the Stores would depend upon the kind of framing narratives to her story "they" had read.

Eveline sits for most of her story with the evidence of her literacy, her two white letters of farewell, resting indistinct in her lap. Young, single, female, literate, and above all susceptible to the kinds of public fictions

---

[21] *Eveline* was partially rewritten at the turn of the century, and published in Paris in the first few months of 1904 as *The Modern Eveline* by "Charles Carrington," a well-known pseudonymous dealer in pornography who supplied Oscar Wilde. As R. B. Kershner (in *Joyce, Bakhtin, and Popular Literature*) and Cheryl Herr (in *Joyce's Anatomy of Culture*) have shown, Joyce was no stranger to pornography, and it is particularly tempting to speculate that he may have chanced upon Carrington's edition during his time in Paris, as *The Modern Eveline* carries a full-page advertisement for *Frank and I* on its rear flyleaf. Publication information from Mendes, *Clandestine Erotic Fiction*, 360–70. A copy of Carrington's edition, complete with flyleaf, is held in the Bodleian "Phi" collection.

my chapter has outlined, Eveline is the propagandist's sitting target. Buenos Aires' centrality to her story, as I have shown, brings into contest divergent potential readings of Eveline's emigration plans. One such reading might identify her with the pre-*Dresden* successful Irish pioneer in Argentina, another with the Irish migrants misled by the Argentinean government, a third with the Rose Brolleys in moral danger abroad, a fourth with the contemporary specter of the white slave. Eveline is doubly entrapped by her nation and her gender, as the emigration narratives surrounding both interact to produce a bewildering array of potential readings of her future. Joyce figures Eveline's entrapment between these fictions of her nation and her gender in terms of her paralysis at the North Wall, the point of her longed-for "escape." For, in pausing the narrative at the North Wall, the point at which such fictions would diverge from one another (and from the happy-ever-after narrative of women's magazines which Eveline so hopelessly yearns towards), Joyce endlessly defers the moment when Eveline's story must become conclusively identified with just one of these competing propagandas. If, as Hugh Kenner argues, Eveline will spend her life "regretting the great refusal," then her regret must take the form of the endless redraftings of that conclusion to her story which her paralysis suspends, redraftings which are inevitably influenced by her readings.

Eveline's mute anguish, her "silent fervent prayer," her white face set "passive like a helpless animal," together articulate the conditions of aphasia the competition between emigration propagandas have imposed upon her. She has no voice, and although her body might eloquently internalize her terror through her nausea, it can communicate nothing to Frank, as "her eyes gave him no sign of love of farewell or recognition." Tellingly, her paralysis places Frank beyond recognition: she cannot prioritize the different intertextual identities which may frame his character to discern who he is. Frank may be "saying something about the passage over and over again," but Eveline attends to other, more deeply embedded repetitions. In her desperation to privilege one form of propaganda over its rivals and thus navigate her "maze of distress," Eveline "prayed to God to direct her, to show her what was her duty" (33–34). What Eveline craves is the kind of monologic vision common to *Homestead* emigration narratives like "The Awakening of Brian Joyce," where a quasi-divine apparition teaches the protagonist his "duty to God and to Ireland," but she is permitted no such certainty. Instead, the closest approximation to a vision Eveline is granted is her glimpse of the steamer that is to carry her to Buenos Aires as a "black mass" (33), something vague, sinister, unholy, symbolically containing her impending sacrifice, a *trompe l'œil* of an emigration ship influenced by emigration scare stories. Eveline is embedded within such scare stories both in the way her imagination is so thoroughly colored by them, and through her debut in the pages of *The Irish Homestead*. Joyce's final subversion of Russell's plea that he "cater to the common understanding" takes the form of holding aloft his "nicely-polished looking glass" (*Letters* II, 64) to reflect back to his readers a mirror image of a fellow-reader of emigration propaganda. For Eveline, a woman paralyzed by her susceptibility to didactic fiction, chooses to experience city life from behind glass, in an atmosphere so saturated with propaganda that she must breathe it in along with the odor of dusty cretonne. Eveline is a victim, not of the nebulous perils of "abroad" described in *The Irish Homestead*, nor of the white slave trader disguised as Frank. Instead, she is a very private woman who succumbs to very public fictions of her proper place: home.

NOTE: I would like to thank my supervisor John Kelly for his support and help with earlier drafts.

Works cited

Anonymous. *The Modern Eveline*. Paris: Charles Carrington, 1904.
    The White Slave Traffic. London: C. Arthur Pearson, 1910.
    In the Grip of the White Slave Trader. By the Author of The White Slave Traffic. London: C. Arthur Pearson, 1912.
Billington-Grieg, Teresa. "The Truth About White Slavery." *English Review*, June 1913: 405–19.
Bulfin, William. *Tales of the Pampas*. London: Overseas Library, 1900.
Bristow, Edward. *Vice and Vigilance: Purity Movements in Britain Since 1700*. Dublin: Gill & Macmillan, 1977.
Coote, William, *A Vision and its Fulfilment*. London: National Vigilance Association, 1902.
    The Romance of Philanthropy. London: National Vigilance Association, 1916.
"Daedalus, Stephen." "Our Weekly Story: 'Eveline.'" *Irish Homestead*, 10 September 1904.
Diner, Hasia. *Erin's Daughters in America: Irish Immigrant Women in the Nineteenth Century*. Baltimore: Johns Hopkins University Press, 1983.
Dyer, Alfred. *The European Slave Traffic in English Girls: A Narrative of Facts*. London: Dyer Brothers, 1881.
Ellmann, Richard. *James Joyce*. Rev. edn. New York: Oxford University Press, 1982.

Fawcett, Millicent. *The White Slave Trade: Its Causes and the Best Means of Preventing It*. London: National Vigilance Association, 1899.

Graham-Yooll, Andrew. *The Forgotten Colony: A History of the English Speaking Communities in the Argentine*. London: Hutchinson, 1981.

Guy, Donna. *Sex and Danger in Buenos Ayres: Prostitution, Family and Nation in Argentina*. Lincoln: University of Nebraska Press, 1991.

Herr, Cheryl. *Joyce's Anatomy of Culture*. Urbana: University of Illinois Press, 1989.

Hopkins, Ellice. *The Purity Movement*. London: Hatchards, 1885.

Jackson, John Wyse, and Bernard McGinley. *James Joyce's "Dubliners": An Annotated Edition*. London: Sinclair Stevenson, 1993.

Jeune, Mary. "The Ethics of Shopping." *The Fortnightly Review*, o.s. 63 (1895): 120–25.

Joyce, James. *Dubliners*. Ed. Terence Brown. Harmondsworth: Penguin, 1992.
    The Index Manuscript: Finnegans Wake Holograph Workbook VI. B. 46. Ed. Danis Rose. Colchester: A Wake Newsletter Press, 1978.
    A Portrait of the Artist as a Young Man. Harmondsworth: Penguin, 1973.
    Selected Letters. Ed. Richard Ellmann. London: Faber & Faber, 1975.

Kenner, Hugh. "Molly's Masterstroke." *James Joyce Quarterly* 10 (1972): 17–30.
    The Pound Era. London: Pimlico, 1991.

Kershner, R. B. *Joyce, Bakhtin, and Popular Literature: Chronicles of Disorder*. Chapel Hill: University of North Carolina Press, 1989.

Kirby, Peadar. *Ireland and Latin America: Links and Lessons*. Blackrock: Trocaire, 1992.

Luddy, Maria. *Women and Philanthropy in Nineteenth-century Ireland*. Cambridge: Cambridge University Press, 1995.

Maddox, Brenda. *Nora*. London: Minerva, 1988.

McCarthy, Michael. *Priests and People in Ireland*. London: Hodder & Stoughton, 1908.

McHugh, Roland. *Annotations to Finnegans Wake*. Baltimore: Johns Hopkins University Press, 1991.

McKenna, Patrick. "Irish Migration to Argentina." *Patterns of Migration*. Ed. Patrick O'Sullivan. Leicester: Leicester University Press, 1992.

MacKirdy, Olive Christian, and W. N. Willis. *The White Slave Market*. London: Stanley Paul, 1912.

Mendes, Peter. *Clandestine Erotic Fiction in English, 1800–1930*. London: Scolar, 1993.

Morris, George. "Monica's Twin Sister." *Irish Homestead*, 6 February 1904.

National Vigilance Association. *Fourth Annual Report*. London: National Vigilance Association, 1889.
    Fourteenth Annual Report. London: National Vigilance Association, 1899.
    Sixteenth Annual Report. London: National Vigilance Association, 1901.
    Minutes. Callmark GB/ 106/ 4/ NVA. Fawcett Library Archive, London Guildhall University.

Nolan, Janet. *Ourselves Alone: Women's Emigration from Ireland, 1885–1920*.
    Lexington: University Press of Kentucky, 1989.
O'Donovan, Jeremiah. "An O'Growney Memorial Lecture." Gaelic League
    Pamphlets, 26. Dublin: Gaelic League, 1902.
    "The Awakening of Brian Joyce." *Irish Homestead*, Christmas Supplement,
    December 1901: 15–16.
    "Rose Brolley." *The Irish Homestead*, Christmas Supplement, December
    1902: 21–22.
O'Farelly, Agnes. "The Reign of Humbug." Gaelic League Pamphlets, 10.
    Dublin: Gaelic League, 1900.
Parliamentary Debates (Hansard). House of Commons Official Report.
    London: HMSO, 1889.
Parliamentary Papers. "Emigration: (III: Statistical Tables): Ireland"
    1886–1904 inclusive. Volumes and page numbers for each year
    provided in the Index to Parliamentary Papers.
    "Emigration from Ireland to Argentina." Vol. 76 (1889): 224–320.
    "Correspondence Respecting the International Conference on the White
    Slave Traffic." Vol. 137 (1907).
Partridge, Eric. *A Dictionary of Slang and Unconventional English*. London:
    Routledge, 1938.
Pearson, Michael. *The Age of Consent: Victorian Prostitution and its Enemies*.
    Newton Abbott: David & Charles, 1972.
Plunkett, Horace. *Ireland in the New Century*. London: Dublin, 1904.
Power, Mary. "'Eveline' and *The Weekly Freeman* Prize Stories." Paper given at
    the 1998 International Miami J'yce Conference.
Roe, Clifford G. *The Horrors of the White Slave Traffic*. London: n.p., 1912.
Rosen, Ruth. *The Lost Sisterhood: Prostitution in America, 1900–1918*. Baltimore:
    Johns Hopkins University Press, 1982.
Ryan, John F. "Gerald O'Donovan: Poet, Novelist and Irish Revivalist."
    Journal of the Galway Archaeological and Historical Society 48 (1996):
    1–47.
Travellers Aid Society. Minutes and Annual Reports, 1885–1904. Callmark 1/
    TAS/ Box 201. Fawcett Library Archive, London Guildhall
    University.
Verschoyle, John. "The Condition of Kerry." *Living Age* 171 (1886): 545–67.
Ward, Margaret. "Conflicting Interests: The British and Irish Suffrage
    Movements." *Feminist Review* 50 (1995): 129–40.

9

"Kilt by kelt shell kithagain with kinagain": Joyce and Scotland

WILLY MALEY

A specter is haunting Irish Studies – the specter of Scotland. All the established critical perspectives, old and new, have entered into a holy alliance to exorcise this specter: revisionist and nationalist, culturalist and politicist, historicist and postcolonialist. In this chapter, necessarily tentative and speculative since it touches on an unexplored aspect of Joyce's work, I want to trace the ghostly imprint of Scotland, and to suggest that this semicolonial neighbor nation, being both Celtic counterpart and British adjutant, can instructively be read alongside Ireland in order for their joint implication within a problematic "British" history to be grasped without succumbing to the equally anglocentric interpretations of Anglo-Irish and Anglo-Scottish history.[1] Joyce, I shall argue, offers a nuanced view of what historians of the early modern period are now calling the "British Problem," that process of conquest, plantation, and union that brought a multi-nation state into being (Bradshaw and Morrill, *The British Problem*). Literary critics have begun to respond to this historiographical shift, recasting the "English Renaissance" in terms of the emergence of a distinctive multiple monarchy, almost without parallel in Europe (Baker, *Between Nations*).

There is evidence in recent years of a growing interest in Scottish and Irish relations on a range of fronts – historical, political, cultural – that promises to undo the double bind implicit in traditional Anglo-Scottish and Anglo-Irish perspectives. The work of Murray Pittock on the eighteenth century, for example, suggests that the received version of early modern history – providential, progressivist, Protestant – that buys into the Tudor Myth of progress through expansion has to be read alongside a cautionary Stuart account that would reinscribe Catholic, Celtic, and

---

[1] My trawl for critical material on Joyce and Scotland while researching this chapter yielded scant reward, but after I had completed the final draft I came across Klein's "National Histories, National Fictions," which is an excellent example of the kind of detailed comparative study that is called for.

Gaelic narratives. Pittock advises against dissolving Scotland into a British identity which is problematic precisely because it has had a strong Irish input. Indeed, if Scotland is to blame for Ireland's present predicament then Ireland is responsible for Scotland's low profile. The former lies behind the modern Irish dilemma, while the latter, as England's first colony, underpins the history of expansion that led to the Ulster plantation. According to Pittock:

> Although Ireland's "Britishness" was perhaps less well developed than Scotland's, and coalesced at a later date, to write Ireland out of Britain is to risk serious misrepresentation of the nature of Britain and its identities, not least the identities of its élites, right into the twentieth century. James Joyce's short masterpiece, "The Dead," clearly indicates (as does the rest of the *Dubliners* collection in which it appears) that the paralysis of Dublin society to an extent derives from its role as a provincial British city racked by futile chauvinistic dreams of its own status as an Irish and Catholic metropolis, dreams which in their manifestation only confirm Dublin's provincialism: for to be provincial is to be chauvinistic about particularity without any wish to evaluate it through external reference.
>
> (*Inventing and Resisting Britain*, 133)

Academic periodization and the division of disciplines means that advances in one field of scholarship do not register immediately in another. Awareness of the complexity of the British Problem, and with it a four-nation historical perspective, is largely absent from those critical approaches that impinge most directly on Joyce's work. Neither Irish studies nor postcolonial theory have taken account of Scotland, preferring to let "English" and "British" remain interchangeable terms, but two recent departures – comparative studies of Scottish and Irish literature, and attempts to apply postcolonial theory to Scotland – promise to open up both fields.[2]

Cairns Craig has reminded us that English colonization has been much more successful in Ireland than in Scotland, hence the success of Irish literature this century, a preeminence paradoxically posited on its disconnection from its national roots (cited in Nicholson, *Poem, Purpose and Place*, 12). Joyce and Heaney are cases in point. The separateness of Scotland from the rest of Britain has, along with its affinities with Ireland,

---

[2] See Carter, "Women, Postcolonialism, and Nationalism"; Gardiner, "Democracy and Scottish Postcoloniality"; Horton, "'Bagpipe Music'"; Watson, "Postcolonial Subjects?"

been rendered invisible in much history and criticism. Ireland, it must be remembered, was a lordship of the English crown from the twelfth to the sixteenth centuries while Scotland enjoyed relative autonomy. As a consequence of the Ulster Plantation of the early seventeenth century, the English pale around Dublin became, in an act of upward displacement, a Scottish pale around Belfast, and the border between the North and South of "Britain" trans-shifted to become the border between the North and South of Ireland, thus laying the foundations of partition. The Ulster Plantation solved England's Scottish and Irish problems at a single stroke, and created deep-seated difficulties for future generations.

Any critique of the British state has to be thoroughgoing. It cannot stop at 1800, or at Ireland. All those whom Joyce called "fullstoppers and semicolonials" have to be prepared to change their punctuation, their periodization, their policing of borders. We must, again citing Joyce, learn to "think two thinks at the same time," to have it both ways. Some cultural margins remain marginalized in even the most theoretically sophisticated criticism. Cyclopean Joyceans holding to a singular vision of Ireland and Panoptic Joyceans wishing to cut him loose from any national moorings are ill-equipped to discern divisions within British identity. Joyce, on the other hand, is famously adept at seeing double.

Marilyn Reizbaum has pointed to an Irish–Scottish double cross. Major canonical authors from both cultures have been paradoxically marginalized by being decontextualized – genericized, regionalized, historicized, or globalized out of their particular national contexts:

> Burns is sentimentalized, remembered as little more than the author of "Auld
> Lang Syne" and "quaint" verse in dialect . . . Scott is regionalized, disinherited
> from his place in literary history as one of the originators of the historical novel
> (the *Waverley* novels) by virtue of the local(e) (his ambivalent treatment of that
> locale might account for the position he does hold) . . . Joyce has been
> internationalized, his Irishness often seen as primarily a rhetorical, or almost
> incidental, dimension of his work.
> ("Canonical Double Cross," 168–69)

It is Reizbaum's contention that related processes of critical reception have denationalized Scottish and Irish authors, and she justifies her comparative approach on the grounds of the shared colonial experience of two minority cultures struggling to be heard within a larger state.

Despite the efforts of Craig and Reizbaum, those engaged in Irish studies appear reluctant to enter into dialogue, or "proximity talks," with Scotland, and for good historical reasons, for their own standpoints depend upon an unproblematized Anglo-Irish relationship and a safe and smooth passage between "English" and "British" paradigms. The most significant works on Ireland in recent years have largely ignored the impact and influence of Scotland. Despite their differences, Irish critics are locked into an Anglo-Irish framework that fails to grasp the nettle of the British Problem/Irish Question. The strength of Joyce's writing, and of postcolonial criticism, ought to be an assiduous attention to context, in all its complexity, and to the local and regional and national milieux informed by, and informing, his work.

Gillian Carter has written of the paradoxical situation whereby "Scotland, Wales, and, to a lesser extent, Ireland, are viewed as part of England and denied their cultural specificity and difference: the very concepts the postcolonial critic is trying to establish in his or her country of interest" ("Women, Postcolonialism, and Nationalism," 65). The failure to distinguish between "British" and "English" in the work of critics otherwise obsessively attentive to difference is troubling. A few examples will have to stand for a whole tendency. Edward Said describes Joyce as an "Irish writer colonized by the British," but one suspects that the Irish are no more homogeneous than the British, if indeed these are exclusive categories, which is in a way the problem – the British Problem (*Culture and Imperialism*, 254). Robert Young is likewise lax in alluding to Linda Colley's monumental book on the making of the British state, *Britons: Forging the Nation* (1992), as a text on "Englishness" (*Colonial Desire*, 183). Young vacillates between "British" and "English" in most of his work, but in *Colonial Desire* he goes so far as to suggest that no distinction ought to be made since "'British' is the name imposed by the English on the non-English" (183). This is an astonishing claim coming from an expert on the language of colonialism. In another footnote, Young maintains the appropriateness of using "English" to refer to "English" literature, but on the page to which this note refers he mentions Scottish writers like John Buchan and Robert Louis Stevenson (3). Joyceans concur with this pressing together of "English" and "British." Colin MacCabe, in speaking of the gendering of the nation, cites "France's 'Marianne' and England's 'Britannia'" (*James Joyce and the Revolution of the Word*, 165).

In an essay on Shakespeare and Joyce, Richard Brown speaks of "English/British nationality" (Brown, "'Shakespeare Explained,'" 91). It is that stroke or slash that concerns me. Is it a positive stroke? Just as it gets lost in the hyphen of Anglo-Irish history, so Scotland slips through the slot that separates England and Britain. Taking account of Scotland opens up a potential "Third Space," and offers a way of undoing binaries and adulterating entrenched identities (Bhabha, "The Third Space").

How can Irish critics allow Scotland to interface with Irish culture and at the same time keep an all-embracing Britishness at bay? How can the Anglo-Celtic frontier be kept intact even as the Scottish–Irish border is crossed and traversed? In order to include Scotland we have to open up the hyphen between Anglo and Irish. Scotland is the skeleton in the closet of Anglo-Irish history, the missing link between Ireland and England, an in-between location that infringes accepted boundaries. Irish and Scottish critics are reluctant to compare notes. It is almost as though neither nation wishes to concede close kinship or common cause. Yet there are a number of points of comparison. Both have a vexed relationship with England, a problematic position within Europe as a result of this, and a long history of emigration, particularly with regard to North America. The twin realities of geographical proximity and the existence of a dominant Scottish planter culture in the eastern counties of Ulster and a significant Irish immigrant community in the west of Scotland has not been matched by critical concern. Yet it is precisely because of their different but related involvements with England that each has resisted comparison with the other. Anglo-Irish and Anglo-Scottish hyphens conceal an Irish–Scottish interface, with literature as a key crossover. Leaving aside the troubled issue of the Ossian controversy, it is worth noting that Scott learned the value of regional and historical narrative from Edgeworth, that Yeats regarded Burns as a model of a national poet, that Muir saw Yeats in the same light, that MacDiarmid regarded Joyce's writing as a blueprint for overcoming the tyranny of the English language, and, more recently, that the fiction of James Kelman and Janice Galloway can fruitfully be read alongside that of Roddy Doyle and Patrick McCabe.

There is another way in which Ireland and Scotland are closely linked. Each country has three literary languages – English, a "variety of English" (Scots and "Hiberno-English," or "Irish English"), and an older native language that has survived despite prosecution and proscription, Scots Gaelic and Irish Gaelic. Modern Irish literature, for a variety of reasons, has arguably parted company with Scottish literature, eschewing the latter's charged advocacy of a vernacular located between Gaelic and English. There is a missing middle in Irish writing which is only now beginning to be filled by writers like Roddy Doyle. The dramatic work of O'Casey and Synge, partly because of their Protestantism, partly because of a perception that they were reproducing aspects of stage Irishness in their representation of an urban or rural demotic, has been seen as a failed experiment. Ironically, even as Yeats's attempt to speak for the nation was being abandoned, Irish writers were becoming increasingly anglicized in their writing. Joyce is of course an exception. It is no coincidence that he offered a model for Hugh MacDiarmid in the Scottish poet's efforts to invent a synthesized Scots. Katie Wales has argued for Joyce's language as "Irish English," a more subtle standpoint than that which sees Joyce simply abandoning Irish for English (*James Joyce and the Forging of Irish English*).

For different historical reasons critics on all sides – nationalists, revisionists, and postcolonial theorists – resist seeing Scotland as in any way central to the making of modern Ireland. Scotland is a local and national referent that complicates a Britishness various critical factions do not wish to see unpacked. The present "British Problem," the problem of partition, cannot be fully comprehended without including the North, and in a double sense, both as Ulster and as Scotland (Longley, "Including the North"; Edwards, "Scotland, Ulster and You"). In a lecture delivered in Belfast in 1979, F. S. L. Lyons outlined four different cultures in modern Ireland – English, Anglo-Irish, Catholic/Gaelic, and Scottish Presbyterian ("The Burden of Our History," 95–98). Ten years later, the load was lightened considerably by Roy Foster, who named only three communities, excluding the Scots from his hugely influential history of modern Ireland ("Varieties of Irishness," 3–14). Lyons, though, had himself set the tone by declaring of the colonial experience in Ireland: "I call it English rather than British because, with the obvious exception of the Scottish influence in Ulster . . . English is essentially what it was" (Lyons, "The Burden of Our History," 95). This "obvious exception" is also a notable omission.

In the case of postcolonial critics, they have only recently begun to countenance Ireland's postcolonial status, and remain unwilling to accept that Scotland has a claim to the same territory. Ashcroft, Griffiths, and Tiffin, in *The Empire Writes Back* (1989), distinguish between "dominated" and "dominating" societies. Drawing on the work of Max Dorsinville, they discuss the constituent parts of the British state and conclude: "While it is possible to argue that these societies were the first victims of English expansion, their subsequent complicity in the British imperial enterprise makes it difficult for colonized peoples outside

Britain to accept their identity as postcolonial"(33). Leaving aside the problematic status of inside and outside, terms demanding to be deconstructed, what is meant by "complicity" here? And what is the relationship between that process of incorporation and subordination, union and plantation, conquest and colonization that saw the British state formed, and "the British imperial enterprise?" There are several things wrong with this argument. It ignores colonial legacies, mistakes a tyranny of the barracks and the factory for "complicity," and assumes that colonized peoples must be "outsiders." What about the complicity of postcolonial critics with a British state that their every word props up? What about the place of colonized peoples within a multi-nation state? Since when did providing ca(n)on fodder, literary and literal, amount to complicity? To refuse a postcolonial passport to Scotland, to deny Scots a boarding pass, is to betray a lack of historical understanding about the formation of the British state. This is not to suggest that Scotland did not play her part in establishing colonies, but to insist that she first yielded as one herself.

Even when Ireland is permitted access to the postcolonial field, it is through comparison with non-European colonial contexts. David Lloyd, who has done much to establish an international context for Irish Studies, complains in a recent issue of *Bullán* of a lack of attention to "larger global tendencies," which he says is "a fault as much of a tradition of insular scholarship within Ireland as of Anglo-American oversight." Lloyd argues for a broader perspective, and for the need for critics to look beyond Ireland for comparative models of colonial development, and insists that "we still have to learn from other locations and from non-western scholarship." He is right of course, but there is a risk of exoticism and orientalism implicit in this call, for there is a place East of Erin, one of Lloyd's "occluded spaces of cultural history," that may profitably be compared with Ireland, one which has had little attention from prominent opponents of revisionism such as Lloyd, Seamus Deane, and Terry Eagleton, all of whom appear happy to collapse England and Britain (Lloyd, "Cultural Theory and Ireland," 87, 92). In fairness it is worth noting that Seamus Deane has begun to accord space to Scotland, and indeed goes so far as to suggest that in certain respects "the Irish-English relation . . . was mediated through Scotland" (*Strange Country*, 108). It is precisely because I believe that Lloyd is correct to maintain that "what is currently being debated in Ireland has implications broader than its borders" that I have sought in my own work to open up the hyphen between Anglo-Irish history and insert Scotland into the equation (Maley, "Lost in the Hyphen of History," 1997).

If it has suited revisionists and postcolonialists to ignore Scotland, then Irish nationalists are similarly slow on the uptake. In his critique of the absence of Scotland from *The Field Day Anthology*, W. J. McCormack argues that if Ireland is seen "as a cultural entity," rather than "a geographical one,"

> then the culture of that geographical space known as Scotland should properly be treated because, for much of the historical period covered by the early pages of the *Anthology*, the oral or literary culture of the two places were interactive in a most intimate manner. Why then – considerations of expense, length etc., aside – is early Scottish literature omitted? Perhaps the implication that Gaelic Scotland constituted an instance (not wholly unique) of Irish colonizing activity was politically inadmissible. The counterargument, that events in the eighth century (or earlier) hardly compromise the integrity of twentieth-century independent Ireland, is forceful – suspiciously so, if one recalls that Yeats's first play about Cuchulain, *On Baile's Strand* (1904), crucially depends on kinship and antagonism bridging the North Channel . . . The nation, conceived historically, is no more and no less than a totality made up of all totalities subordinated to it and is (at the same time) overdetermined by totalities of a higher complexity. In contrast, any notion of Ireland as "self-identical whole" stems (whether it likes it or not) from the Prussian side of Hegel's system.
>
> (*From Burke to Beckett*, 445)

Joyce resisted any conception of Ireland as a "self-identical whole," opting instead for an Ireland that was pluralized and problematized. The trick is to maintain the demand for exclusion from incorporating totalities while at the same time voicing a desire for inclusion in a network of differential identities.

Neither Emer Nolan nor Vincent Cheng engage with Scotland in their respective studies of colonialism and nationalism in Joyce's work (Nolan, *James Joyce and Nationalism*; Cheng, *Joyce, Race, and Empire*). Nolan's is one of the most compelling and sustained engagements with Joyce's politics that I know of, but I am disappointed both by her resistance to theory, which she sees as implicitly antinationalist, and by the fact that she is not interested in unwrapping Britishness, and even has "British (English)" as an entry in her index (215). Compare Louis Mink's listing: "BRITAIN. See *England*" (*A "Finnegans Wake" Gazetteer*, 241).

The entry for England reads: "Strictly, it does not include Scot or Wales; but historically and politically, esp from the Ir point of view, it has often been regarded as equivalent to Brit, or the United Kingdom, which for convenience are included here" (306). Mink's mixing of history, politics, point of view and convenience is highly revealing, but the very next line complicates his editorial decision: "In both Ir and Scots Gaelic it is 'Sasana,' and Eng people are 'Sasanachs,' terms which have become pejorative." So much for the Scottish "point of view," which is no more Cyclops-like than the Irish. The anglocentrism and panopticism to which Joyce was opposed are at work here. Other critics are aware of Joyce's preoccupation with questions of union and sovereignty, but do not bring Scotland into the reckoning (Shloss, "Molly's Resistance to the Union"; Wollaeger, "Bloom's Coronation").

This oversight is arguably justified insofar as Scotland is rarely addressed head-on by Joyce in his work, but there are a sufficient number of tantalizing allusions to suggest a jaundiced perspective with regard to the Scottish dimension of Irish history. Scotland is there in Joyce as envoy, traitor, or apocalyptic vision. She figures as a sister subject nation who has, in order to curry favor with England, betrayed her Hibernian sibling. There is a subtle exposure of the competing efforts of successive British governments in the period, Liberal and Conservative, to enlist the non-English nations of the British state in the service of an imperial monarchy, and to turn the vice of Celtic encircle- ment into the virtue of colonial recruitment. Liberal efforts were argu- ably more insidious, since Liberals could not be accused of the obvious anglocentrism that characterized Conservative rule. A pan-Celticism that served British interests, rather than undoing English authority, was not something to which anti-imperialists could subscribe. Joyce was as skeptical of a pan-Celtic future as he was of "our ancient Panceltic fore- fathers" (12.906–7). He saw through efforts to integrate Scotland, Ireland, and Wales more fully into the British state through empire and monarchy, the cruces of British identity. Joyce's awareness of the com- plexity of the British Problem and the consequent poverty of anglocen- tric and hibernocentric perspectives is in stark contrast to the complacency of his critics.

Joyce's work is by no means Scot-free. There are several telling instances of Scottish interludes and interpolations in Joyce, selective hostings and hauntings, and I want to work my way through these towards the beginnings of an understanding of an eloquent silence punctuated by negative sound bites. The theme of betrayal that runs through all of Joyce's writing has a special Scottish inflexion. In the poem "Gas from a Burner" (1912), for example, he writes:

> I pity the poor – that's why I took
> A red-headed Scotchman to keep my book.
> Poor sister Scotland! Her doom is fell;
> She cannot find any more Stuarts to sell
>
> . . .
>
> My Irish foreman from Bannockburn
> Shall dip his right hand in the urn
> And sign crisscross with reverent thumb
> *Memento homo* upon my bum.
>
> (Levin, ed., *The Essential James Joyce*, 462–63)

The "Irish foreman from Bannockburn" is George Roberts, an Ulster Scot, and the manager of the printing firm which pulped and guillotined *Dubliners* (Ellmann, *James Joyce*, 339–49). Roberts, who also makes an appearance in *Ulysses*, certainly did nothing to change Joyce's negative perception of Scots, and may have contributed to it (9.301).

Joyce's references to Scotland are infrequent and generally uncomplimentary, and come back time and again to the question of Scotland's alleged or apparent complicity with England in the plantation of Ulster and the pursuit of empire. In *Ulysses* we learn that Shakespeare wrote "Hamlet and Macbeth with the coming to the throne of a Scotch philosophaster with a turn for witchroasting" (9.751–52). Since Joyce was familiar with major English authors like Bacon, Milton, and Spenser he must have known the extent to which Scotland figured in their work on Ireland (Maley, "The British Problem in Three Irish Tracts").

There is that peculiar moment in "The Dead" when Gabriel, bristling after Miss Ivors has called him a "West Briton," retreats "to a remote corner of the room where Freddy Malin's mother was sitting":

> Gabriel asked her whether she had had a good crossing. She lived with her married daughter in Glasgow and came to Dublin on a visit once a year. She answered placidly that she had had a beautiful crossing and that the captain had been most attentive to her. She spoke also of the beautiful house her daughter kept in Glasgow, and of all the nice friends they had there. While her tongue rambled on Gabriel tried to banish from his mind all memory of the unpleasant incident with Miss Ivors.
>
> (Levin, ed., *The Essential James Joyce*, 149)

If we set the above passage in its immediate context, the two references to "crossing" suggest a double cross, one that involves a West Briton and an East Hibernian. Our attention is drawn to "a remote corner of the room," and the figure of an old woman who is a "North Briton" by dint of dwelling in another provincial town that looks to London for patronage.

In "An Encounter" the man the boys meet recommends the works of Sir Walter Scott, and when Joyce has the boy in "Araby" read Scott's *The Abbot*, he is making a deliberate and informed choice, as Vincent Cheng and Harry Stone have illustrated, since that novel was a piece of Mariolatry, written in defense of Mary Queen of Scots (Cheng, *Joyce, Race, and Empire*, 96; Stone, "'Araby' and the Writings of James Joyce"). Neither Cheng nor Stone wants to emphasize more than Mary's status as a Catholic queen, but the fact that she was a Scottish sovereign executed by an English monarch mattered to Scott and matters to Scottish readers. It mattered to Joyce, too, for in *Finnegans Wake* we hear of "Marely quean of Scuts" (245.28).

Elsewhere, a Scottish sell-out is hinted at. In *Ulysses*, Mr Deasy has on his sideboard a "tray of Stuart coins, base treasure of a bog: and ever shall be . . . dead treasure, hollow shells. A sovereign fell, bright and new, on the soft pile of the tablecloth" (2.201, 215–17). The Stuarts are invoked always as part of a theme of betrayal, a theme that runs through Joyce's work: " – Ay, says John Wyse. We fought for the royal Stuarts that reneged us against the Williamites and they betrayed us" (12.1379–80). The Scots are not only treacherous, but teleological. Bloom overhears someone with the same initials as the Prince of Wales – "A. E." (George Russell) – speak of "the two headed octopus" and "the ends of the world with a Scotch accent" (8.520, 529–30). Don Gifford has speculated that the "Scotch accent" belongs to the most notorious Scot of the day, Arthur Balfour, the Scottish Conservative who was chief secretary for Ireland from 1887 to 1901, and British Prime Minister in 1904. He was nicknamed by the Irish "Bloody Balfour" for his harsh policies. Gifford oddly styles him "Conservative prime minister of *England*" (*sic*). Hugh Kenner has argued that the "two heads" refer to London and Edinburgh (cited in Gifford, ed., *Ulysses Annotated*, 173). The notion of an apocalyptic Scottish dimension to Irish politics would fit well with the turbulent history of the Ulster Plantation, one instance of Scotland serving to extend English colonial power. Finance capital in Edinburgh would be another arm or orb. According to William Drummond, Ben

Jonson saw the Scottish capital as a lookout post for empire: "In a poem
he calleth Edinburgh 'The heart of Scotland, Britain's other eye'"
(Parfitt, *Ben Jonson*, 472). In the same passage in *Ulysses*, the line
"Coming events cast their shadows before" is taken from a Jacobite
ballad in which a wizard foretells the doom of Bonnie Prince Charlie at
Culloden in 1745, and the effective end of the Stuart cause (Gifford, ed.,
Ulysses Annotated, 173).

In an early moment in *Ulysses*, the contradictions of Britishness, and
the strategies of containment that keep them in check, are beautifully
parceled out, as Mr Deasy betrays an identity politics of easy inclusiveness:

> Do you know what is the pride of the English? . . .
>
> Mr Deasy stared sternly for some moments over the mantelpiece at the
> shapely bulk of a man in tartan filibegs: Albert Edward, prince of Wales . . .
> – I have rebel blood in me too, Mr Deasy said. On the spindle side. But I am
> descended from sir John Blackwood who voted for the union. We are all Irish,
> all kings' sons.   (2.243, 265–67, 278–80)

The "pride of the English" is set against the backdrop of a British
monarch who bears the title "Prince of Wales" and dresses in traditional
Scottish costume, and against a claim for an all-inclusive Irishness. The
speaker is descended from both rebels and unionists. Joyce is constantly
dismantling and displaying "Britishness" as a multinational construct, a
patchwork quilt that folds under questioning.

Recent work on the coronation of Edward's son, George V, and the
investiture of his son as Prince of Wales in 1911, suggests that there was a
concerted effort to address "the relationship between the British nation-
state and the Celtic peoples of the United Kingdom" (Ellis, "Reconciling
the Celt," 392). Joyce's deconstruction of Britishness – itself a Celtic
myth, whose origins lie in Ireland and Scotland as much as in Wales – has
to be set in this context, the context, that is, of a British state desperate to
comb its Celtic fringe, grooming itself in the face of calls for home rule
from its three non-English ("Celtic") constituent parts.

In another significant passage, walking along the shoreline, Stephen
muses on the failed saviors of Irish history:

> Pretenders: live their lives. The Bruce's brother, Thomas Fitzgerald, silken
> knight, Perkin Warbeck, York's false scion, in breeches of silk of whiterose
> ivory, wonder of a day, and Lambert Simnel, with a tail of nans and sutlers, a
> scullion crowned. All kings' sons. Paradise of pretenders then and now.
> (*U*3.313–17)

Most English readers would be familiar with Warbeck and Simnel, the former through John Ford's play. Both had bases in Ireland – Warbeck was declared Richard IV there. Silken Thomas, who led the first of the Anglo-Irish rebellions against Henry VIII in 1534, would be well known to Irish readers. But what of "The Bruce's Brother?" Edward Bruce was brother of the more famous Robert, the Scottish king who defeated the English at Bannockburn in 1314, temporarily securing Scotland's independence in the process. Edward invaded Ireland the following year, 1315, and in alliance with Irish forces swept the English down and out of the North of Ireland. In fact, according to Edmund Spenser, Edward Bruce was the first king of Ireland, and the English pale was carved out by this Scottish monarch (*A View of the State of Ireland*, 26). Later murdered by the Irish as a pretender, Edward Bruce is an example of an historical effort at *rapprochement* between Scotland and Ireland. In this allusion, and in the mention in *Finnegans Wake* of the "two Bruces" and the word wild web of a "scotch spider" (108.15), Joyce is touching on the bruises of history, and the braces holding the legacies of Scotland and Ireland together, or as he puts it in *Finnegans Wake*: examining the pict pockets of "scoutsch breeches" (204.6).

"Mr Allfours (Tamoshant. Con.)" (*U* 12.865) is one of many references to Arthur Balfour. "Tamoshanter" is not a place, one annotation of this line tells us, but refers both to a Scottish wool cap and a poem by Burns. The same annotation observes that "'Con,' short for Conservative, is appropriate not only with respect to Balfour but also because the Irish assumed that Scots were Protestant-Conservative" (Gifford, ed., *Ulysses Annotated*, 341). There are two points worth making here. One is to suggest that "con" also suggests a double-cross or sleight of hand, and that "Allfours" is both "all force" and a quadruped, which is an apt characterization of the four-nation British state. The use of Burns in this context does appear to fit in with a mocking or ironic attitude, though Joyce's references to "Bobby Burns," as he is called in *Finnegans Wake*, also suggests a familiarity with, even a fondness for, the great bard of Scottish literature (520.26). Citing at least nine songs in *Ulysses* implies more than a passing acquaintance.

The reference to "Crotthers of Alba Longa" is also intriguing (*U* 14.233). Crotthers is the Scottish student in the maternity hospital mentioned several times in "Oxen of the Sun." "Alba" is the Irish word for Scotland. It is unlike Joyce to typecast, to speak of someone as representative of a nation, to speak of a Scot, for example, in terms of "the land for which he stood," as he does of Crotthers, "the Caledonian envoy" (14.988–90). The name is an odd one, suggesting "rotters" (Caledonian Rotters, perhaps). It may be that Joyce is playing with the name of one of George Russell's intellectual adversaries, the "wild professional Scot," and apocalyptic visionary, S. Liddell MacGregor Mathers (Gifford, ed., *Ulysses Annotated*, 173). The word "crott," according to the *OED*, means "dung" or "dirt," while "crottle" is Scots Gaelic for "a species of lichen used in dyeing," which would chime with "Mat." The fact that Crotthers is described as "a little fume of a fellow" suggests that Joyce may have had this etymology in mind (14.738–39). The description of Crotthers "at the foot of the table in his striking Highland garb, his face glowing from the briny airs of the Mull of Galloway," is hardly complimentary (14.1204–6). Joyce's most sustained piece of Scots dialect, a vernacular spectacular, also occurs in "Oxen of the Sun," where the Scottish speech of Crotthers is parodied: "Hurroo! Collar the leather, youngun. Roun wi the nappy. Here, Jock braw Hielentman's your barleybree. Lang may your lum reek and your kailpot boil!" (14.1488–91). Gifford, sourcing this passage in a chorus of Burns's "The Jolly Beggars" and that of another of Burns's songs, "Willie Brew'd a Peck of Maut [Malt]," gives the following gloss to a colloquialism: "*Lang may your lum reek* [*sic*] *and your kailpot boil!* – Scots dialect: 'Long may your chimney smoke and your soup pot boil'" (444). "Kail" has more specific connotations, and it would be all too easy to see this passage as a critique of "kailyard" or "cabbage-patch" literature, just as critics have seen the colloquialisms of "Cyclops" as merely a source of comic parody or satire, but recent work on Joyce's language would guard against such a straightforward reading.[3]

The status of Burns in an Irish national context can perhaps be gauged from the fact that in 1904 Yeats described Synge as "truly a National writer, as Burns was when he wrote finely" (*Explorations*, 157). Yeats defended Lady Gregory's Kiltartanese, "as true a dialect of English as the dialect that Burns wrote in" (Flanagan, "Yeats, Joyce, and the Matter of Ireland," 54). Yeats's insistence on representing the nation, spurned by subsequent Irish authors, was – perhaps paradoxically, perhaps appropriately – a notion that found favor in Scotland, the home of Burns.

[3] See Nolan, *James Joyce and Nationalism*, 85–119; Wales, *James Joyce and the Forging of Irish English*.

The allusion to "Fingal's Cave" – located in the Scottish Hebrides – in the list of key Irish place-names in "Cyclops" suggests an acknowledgment of a deep historical Scottish dimension in Irish identity formation (12.1461). Finally, when Joyce declared in *Finnegans Wake* that "Kilt by kelt shell kithagain with kinagain," he was putting the matter in a nutshell (594.3–4). Did Joyce anticipate a kind of "Kinagains Wake," one that would reconcile Ireland and Scotland, or at least peel them from an English kernel? As well as being the name of a garment synonymous with Scotland, "kilt" is also the past tense of kill in Scots and in Irish English, as in "You've kilt me." In her glossary to *Castle Rackrent*, Maria Edgeworth writes: "[Kilt] This word frequently occurs in the following pages, where it means not *Killed*, but much *hurt*. In Ireland, not only cowards, but the brave 'die many times before their death.' There *Killing is no murder*" (114). As for "kelt," as well as being a variation of "Celt," it refers to a noun for "salmon or sea-trout after spawning," and thus continues a theme of dissemination and cross-fertilization.

What sense, finally, do we make of Joyce's silence with regard to Scotland, and the stereotypes he employs, apparently without the undercutting irony he usually reserves for such national characterizations? Given the historical centrality of Scotland with respect to Irish history, how can Joyce be so slight and slighting in his citations? Although he had first-hand experience of Scotland, having visited Glasgow with his father in 1894, aged twelve, there is little direct evidence of its impact in his writing (Ellmann, *James Joyce*, 41). When he does refer to Scotland, it tends to be to imperial or literary Scotland, to Edinburgh or the Highlands. Joyce knew Scottish literature, and drew on Hogg and Stevenson as well as Burns and Scott. Louis Mink has argued that James Hogg's *Confessions of a Justified Sinner* is a structural book for *Finnegans Wake* (*A "Finnegans Wake" Gazetteer*, 41–42). Both Hogg's work and Stevenson's *Jekyll and Hyde* offer crucial instances of what critics have called "Caledonian antisyzygy," the splitting of identity caused by Scotland's divided heritage and vexed position within the Union.

How could an Irish author of such deep learning and possessed of a cultivated European and world view overlook Scotland, especially given that the so-called "Irish Question" in its modern form, from plantation to partition, is posed first and foremost by Scotland? How could someone with such an encyclopedic knowledge of Irish history gloss over the role of Scotland in the formation of that country, especially since the key to the present state of Ireland, then and now, lay in the use of Scotland by England to drive a wedge between both countries by planting some of the troublesome Scots on its border in the North of Ireland, thus killing two birds with one stone? How could a writer like Joyce, obsessed with fringes and hinges, pass over such a double-cross in silence? How could someone all too aware of double-yokes – the Roman and British ones being the most obvious – appear unaware of the double-bind of the Anglo-Scottish legacy? These are questions that remain for the future. My own impression, tinged with sadness, is that Joyce appears to have shared the prejudice of those Irish of the time who assumed that all Scots were incorrigibly Protestant, Conservative, and Unionist. Certainly, in Arthur Balfour they had a prime example of that type. In *Finnegans Wake* a reference to a "scotobrit sash" reminds readers that the origins of Orangeism and its continuing influence in the North of Ireland has a distinct Scottish dimension (387.5). Other histories, other possibilities, remain hidden. Twice in *Ulysses* Joyce cites the song "Scotland's Burning," substituting "London" and "Dublin" respectively (15.172; 15.4660). In Joyce's texts, Scotland remains a burning issue smoldering beneath the blanket terms of Anglo-Irishness.

NOTE: this chapter is based on a paper entitled "Jockularity: Joyce and Scotland," presented to the Joyce Research Seminar, School of English, University of Leeds, 21 November 1997. I am grateful to Richard Brown for inviting me to speak on that occasion. I am also grateful to Alex Benchimol, Philip Hobsbaum, and Andrew Hook for reading and commenting on an earlier draft, and to Alasdair Gray for a lively discussion of the issues.

Works cited

Ashcroft, Bill, Gareth Griffiths, and Helen Tiffin. *The Empire Writes Back.* London: Routledge, 1989.

Atherton, James S. *The Books at the Wake: A Study of Literary Allusions in James Joyce's "Finnegans Wake."* London: Faber, 1959.

Baker, David J. *Between Nations: Shakespeare, Spenser, Marvell, and the Question of Britain.* Stanford: Stanford University Press, 1997.

Bhabha, Homi K. "The Third Space: Interview with Homi Bhabha." *Identity: Community, Culture, Difference.* Ed. Jonathan Rutherford. London: Lawrence & Wishart, 1990. 207–21.

Bradshaw, Brendan, and John Morrill, eds. *The British Problem, c. 1534–1707.* London: Macmillan, 1996.

Brown, Richard. "'Shakespeare Explained': James Joyce's Shakespeare from Victorian Burlesque to Postmodern Bard." *Shakespeare and Ireland: History, Politics, Culture*. Ed. Burnett, Mark Thornton, and Ramona Wray. London: Macmillan, 1997. 91–113.

Carter, Gillian. "Women, Postcolonialism, and Nationalism: A Scottish Example." *SPAN* 41 (1995): 65–74.

Cheng, Vincent J. *Joyce, Race, and Empire*. Cambridge: Cambridge University Press, 1995.

Colley, Linda. *Britons: Forging the Nation, 1707–1837*. New Haven: Yale University Press, 1992.

Deane, Seamus. *Strange Country: Modernity and Nationhood in Irish Writing Since 1790*. Oxford: Clarendon Press, 1997.

Edgeworth, Maria. *Castle Rackrent*. Ed. George Watson. Oxford: Oxford University Press, 1995.

Edwards, Owen Dudley. "Scotland, Ulster and You." *Scotland and Ulster*. Ed. Ian S. Wood. Edinburgh: Polygon, 1994. 172–82.

Ellis, John S. "Reconciling the Celt: British National Identity, Empire, and the 1911 Investiture of the Prince of Wales." *Journal of British Studies* 37 (1998): 391–418.

Ellmann, Richard. *James Joyce*. New York: Oxford University Press, 1959.

Flanagan, Thomas. "Yeats, Joyce, and the Matter of Ireland." *Critical Inquiry* 2 (1975): 43–67.

Foster, Roy. "Varieties of Irishness." *Modern Ireland, 1600–1972*. London: Allen Lane, 1988. 3–14.

Gardiner, Michael. "Democracy and Scottish Postcoloniality." *Scotlands* 3.2 (1996): 24–41.

Gifford, Don, ed. *Ulysses Annotated: Notes for James Joyce's "Ulysses."* With Robert J. Seidman. 2nd edn. Berkeley: University of California Press, 1974; 1988.

Horton, Patricia. "'Bagpipe Music': Some Intersections in Scottish and Irish Writing." *Scotlands* 4.2 (1997): 66–80.

Jonson, Ben. *The Complete Poems*. Ed. George Parfitt. Harmondsworth: Penguin, 1974.

Klein, Scott W. "National Histories, National Fictions: Joyce's *A Portrait of the Artist as a Young Man* and Scott's *The Bride of Lammermoor*." *ELH* 65 (1998): 1017–38.

Levin, Harry, ed. *The Essential James Joyce*. St. Albans: Granada, 1977.

Lloyd, David. "Cultural Theory and Ireland." *Bullán* 3.1 (1997): 87–92.

Longley, Edna. "Including the North." *Text & Context* 3 (1988): 17–24.

Lyons, F. S. L. "The Burden of Our History." *Interpreting Irish History: The Debate on Historical Revisionism, 1938–1994*. Ed. Ciarán Brady. Dublin: Irish Academic Press, 1994. 87–104.

MacCabe, Colin. *James Joyce and the Revolution of the Word*. London: Macmillan, 1979.

McCormack, W. J. *From Burke to Beckett: Ascendancy, Tradition and Betrayal in Literary History*. Cork: Cork University Press, 1994.

Maley, Willy. "Lost in the Hyphen of History: The Limits of Anglo-Irishness." *Irish Review* 20 (1997): 23–29.

Mink, Louis A. *A "Finnegans Wake" Gazetteer*. Bloomington: Indiana University Press, 1978.

Nicholson, Colin. *Poem, Purpose and Place: Shaping Identity in Contemporary Scottish Verse*. Edinburgh: Polygon, 1992.

Nolan, Emer. *James Joyce and Nationalism*. London: Routledge, 1995.

Parfitt, George. *Ben Jonson: Public Poet and Private Man*. London: J. M. Dent, 1976.

Pittock, Murray. *Inventing and Resisting Britain: Cultural Identities in Britain and Ireland, 1685–1789*. London: Macmillan, 1997.

Reizbaum, Marilyn. "Canonical Double Cross: Scottish and Irish Women's Writing." *Decolonizing Tradition: New Views of Twentieth-century "British" Literary Canons*. Ed. Karen R. Lawrence. Urbana: University of Illinois Press, 1992. 165–90.

Said, Edward W. *Culture and Imperialism*. London: Vintage, 1993.

Shloss, Carol. "Molly's Resistance to the Union: Marriage and Colonialism in Dublin, 1904." *Modern Fiction Studies* 35 (1989): 529–41.

Spenser, Edmund. *A View of the State of Ireland (1633): from the first printed edition*. Ed. Andrew Hadfield and Willy Maley. Oxford: Blackwell, 1997.

Stone, Harry. "'Araby' and the Writings of James Joyce." *"Dubliners": Text, Criticism, and Notes*. Eds. Robert Scholes and A. Walton Litz. New York: Viking, 1969. 344–67.

Wales, Katie. *James Joyce and the Forging of Irish English*. London: British Library, 1993.

Watson, Roderick. "Postcolonial Subjects? Language, Narrative Authority and Class in Contemporary Scottish Culture." *European English Messenger* 7.1 (1998): 21–31.

Wollaeger, Mark A. "Bloom's Coronation and the Subjection of the Subject." *James Joyce Quarterly* 28 (1991): 799–808.

Yeats, W. B. *Explorations*. London: Macmillan, 1962.

Young, Robert J. C. *Colonial Desire: Hybridity in Theory, Culture, and Race*. London: Routledge, 1994.

Phoenician genealogies and oriental geographies: Joyce, language and race

ELIZABETH BUTLER CULLINGFORD

Analogy – the discovery of a likeness between two apparently discrete things – is the imaginative process by which metaphors are constructed. Genealogy – the claim that a likeness is inherited – is often equally imaginative, despite its historical pretensions. In this chapter I explore genealogies of language and race in the writings of James Joyce, and situate him in an Irish cultural continuum that reaches back to *The Book of Invasions* and forward to the historical geographer Estyn Evans and the independent filmmaker Bob Quinn. In the process, I explore the aptness of this volume's title, "Semicolonial Joyce," and its relation to the contested postcolonial celebration of hybridity.

Joyce's ambivalent attitude towards Ireland's colonial status informs the pseudo-historical genealogy of the Irish language elaborated in his 1907 Trieste lecture, "Ireland, Island of Saints and Sages." Joyce argues that the Irish language "is oriental in origin, and has been identified by many philologists with the ancient language of the Phoenicians" (*CW* 156). The politics of this assertion need decoding. What is the ideology of a linguistic map that connects Ireland with the Semitic Orient and Arab North Africa rather than with "mainland" Britain?

While Edward Said defines Orientalism as "a Western style for dominating, restructuring, and having authority over the Orient" (*Orientalism*, 3), Lisa Lowe suggests that orientalist strategies are "not exclusively deployed by European or colonial rule, but articulated . . . by a variety of dominant and emergent positions on the critical terrain" (*Critical Terrains*, 12). But is Ireland a dominant or an emergent culture? Postcolonial critics privilege the negative impact of British imperialism as the determining factor in Ireland's history, and encourage analogical links between the Irish and other "emergent" ethnic groups (see Kiberd, *Inventing Ireland, passim*). Revisionists, however, assert that Ireland was a beneficiary as well as a victim of empire, and that geographical proximity, common language and skin color, and shared prosperity link the Irish more closely with their "dominant" British neighbors than with other postcolonial societies.[1] Ireland is, in David Lloyd's phrase, an "anomalous" state (*Anomalous States*, 3).

Bell hooks's response to Neil Jordan's *The Crying Game* provides an exemplary illustration of this anomaly. Jordan places Fergus the white IRA man in parallel with Jody the black British soldier: though enlisted in opposing armies, both are "emergent" products of British colonialism. Fergus's repressed homoerotic desire for both Jody and his black "girlfriend" Dil suggests an emotional analogy between "Paddies" and "wogs" (*Outlaw Culture*, viii). As Fergus tells Dil Jody's parable of the scorpion and the frog, we understand that Jody and Fergus share the same "nature": they are trusting frogs, not predatory scorpions. hooks, however, reads Fergus's story as a "dominant" rhetorical move:

> As the film ends, Fergus as white male hero has not only cannibalized Jody, he appropriates Jody's narrative and uses it to declare his possession of Dil . . . This paradigm mirrors that of colonialism. It offers a romanticized image of the white colonizer moving into black territory, occupying it, possessing it in a way that affirms his identity.
>
> (*Outlaw Culture*, 59)

For the black feminist hooks, the power differentials between white and black, masculine and feminine, obscure the power differential between Brits and Paddies. Fergus is not a member of an "emergent" ethnic group, just plain "white folks" (*Outlaw Culture*, 62). But for Jordan and the actor Stephen Rea, Fergus is a portrait of the IRA man as human being, alienated by the colonial presence of the British in Northern Ireland (Rea, interviewed in the *Los Angeles Times*, 9).

Analogies, then, are slippery things: one man's sympathetic identification is another woman's "cannibalistic" appropriation, and the construction of aesthetic parallels that elide historical differences or asymmetries of power may appear racist or falsely totalizing. Nevertheless, imaginative connections between oppressed groups demonstrate that the postcolonial condition is widely shared, destabilize essentialist conceptions of national identity, and increase the potential complexity of literary metaphors. Joyce's transnational and transhistorical "orientalist" analogies are formal strategies that express his rejection of "the old pap of racial hatred" (*Letters* II, 167).

---

[1] For this debate, see Brady, ed., *Interpreting Irish History*.

In the bad old days, when Joyce was an apolitical Modernist, "Ireland, Island of Saints and Sages," source of the Phoenician genealogy, was rarely cited. Now that he has become an Irishman once again, it is ubiquitous. But the lecture is an anomalous, even a "semicolonial" document, claimed by some critics as evidence that Joyce was fed up with Irish politics, by others as testimony of his political extremism. Herring uses it to prove that "the plight of Ireland left him cold and somewhat bored" ("Joyce's Politics," 6); MacCabe to argue that by 1907 "Joyce's interest in Irish politics [had] waned" (*James Joyce and the Revolution of the Word*, 165). But Costello claims that all Joyce's Trieste writings evince "extreme" nationalism, and show that "even in distant Austria he remained true to the politics of his father and John Kelly, the politics that still impose upon unhappy Ulster the burden of revolutionary violence and community hatred" (*James Joyce*, 273). Vincent Cheng cites anti-British passages to demonstrate that Joyce is not "an apolitical colonial author" (*Joyce, Race, and Empire*, 6), but omits his bitter reflections on Irish self-betrayal, emblematized by Dermot McMurrough's invitation to Strongbow and the Irish parliament's vote for the Union. "From my point of view," Joyce writes, "these two facts must be thoroughly explained before the country in which they occurred has the most rudimentary right to persuade one of her sons to change his position from that of an unprejudiced observer to that of a convinced nationalist" (*CW* 162–63). Only Emer Nolan emphasizes his "ambiguities and hesitations" as evidence of "the uncertain, divided consciousness of the colonial subject" (*James Joyce and Nationalism*, 130).

In 1906/7 Joyce was feeling warmer than usual about Ireland (Ellmann, *James Joyce*, 239), and the lecture demonstrates his desire to mitigate the harshness of *Stephen Hero* and the earlier stories of *Dubliners*. Yet he remains skeptical about Revivalist claims for Ireland's Catholic virtue and Celtic purity, and about the practical effectiveness of her revolutionary organizations. He condemns the British Empire, and considers rebellion justifiable; but cannot see "what good it does to fulminate against the English tyranny when the Roman tyranny occupies the palace of the soul" (173). We might call this political position indifferent, balanced, or confused – or we might call it "semicolonial."

Joyce's Orientalist genealogy of the Irish language undermines the "Roman tyranny" by challenging Catholic religious primacy in Ireland. His tendentious linguistics subverts the pious patriotic cliché embodied in his title, "Island of Saints and Sages":

This language is oriental in origin, and has been identified by many philologists with the ancient language of the Phoenicians, the originators of trade and navigation, according to historians. This adventurous people, who had a monopoly of the sea, established in Ireland a civilization that had decayed and almost disappeared before the first Greek historian took his pen in hand. It jealously preserved the secrets of its knowledge, and the first mention of the island of Ireland in foreign literature is found in a Greek poem of the fifth century before Christ, where the historian repeats the Phoenician tradition. The language that the Latin writer of comedy, Plautus, put in the mouth of Phoenicians in his comedy *Poenulus* is almost the same language that the Irish peasants speak today, according to the critic Vallancey. The religion and civilization of this ancient people, later known by the name of Druidism, were Egyptian. The Druid priests had their temples in the open, and worshipped the sun and moon in groves of oak trees. In the crude state of knowledge of those times, the Irish priests were considered very learned, and when Plutarch mentions Ireland, he says that it was the dwelling place of holy men. Festus Avienus in the fourth century was the first to give Ireland the title of *Insula Sacra*; and later, after having undergone the invasions of the Spanish and Gaelic tribes, it was converted to Christianity by St. Patrick and his followers, and again earned the title of "Holy Isle." (156)

Ireland's "Saints and Scholars" are usually identified as the monks who kept Christian piety and learning alive in Europe during the Dark Ages. Joyce's "Sages," on the other hand, are Egyptianized Phoenicians (Phoenicia was a client state of Egypt) who got to Ireland a century ahead of St. Patrick and the Saints, and subsequently metamorphosed into Druids. The genealogical question of who first sanctified Ireland, though apparently abstruse, carries an ideological charge. In the 1930s Yeats justified the unorthodox sexual and religious views of his heretical Irish hermit Ribh with the conjecture that "Saint Patrick must have found in Ireland, for he was not its first missionary, men whose Christianity had come from Egypt, and retained characteristics of those older faiths that have become so important to our invention" (*Variorum Poems*, 837). Yeats needs "those older faiths" as allies against the Catholic theocracy of the newly founded Free State; he therefore uses Egypt, and his Egyptianized sage Ribh, to dispute the axiomatic primacy of St. Patrick. But why would Joyce, who claimed that he had left Ireland in order to fly by the nets of nationality, language, and religion, use Phoenicia to reproduce – albeit with a subversive twist – the familiar nationalist topoi of Ireland's superior antiquity, literacy, and sanctity? Is his deadpan promulgation of Vallancey's long-exploded linguistic theories serious or tongue-in-cheek?

Joyce's attitude to the language fluctuates, even as he celebrates its putative oriental ancestry. In *Stephen Hero* he satirizes Hughes, Stephen's Gaelic League instructor (modeled on Joyce's teacher, Padraic Pearse); and in 1906 he told Stanislaus that his distaste for the language revival prevented him from calling himself a nationalist (*Letters* II, 187). But the next year, delivering "Ireland, Island of Saints and Sages" to an Irredentist Triestine audience, who were Italian speakers unwillingly marooned in the Teutonic desert of the Austro-Hungarian empire, he represents the Gaelic League with only a touch of his usual irony: "The members of the League write to each other in Irish, and often the poor postman [is] unable to read the address" (156).[2] Perhaps in deference to the Italian nationalist politics of his listeners, Joyce is uncharacteristically positive about the language. He even effects a geographical reversal by which the Aran Islands, usually depicted as the backward fringes of the continental landmass, become what he calls the "pickets of the vanguard of Europe, on the front of the eastern hemisphere" (155). This remapping of the Aran Islands as the frontline rather than the backyard of Europe resonates with Molly Ivors's invitation in "The Dead": "Will you come for an excursion to the Aran Isles this summer? . . . It will be splendid out in the Atlantic" (*Dubliners*, 189).

The Atlantic ocean may be construed as a barrier or an opportunity: the end of a continent or the beginning of a sea journey. Joyce occasionally praised the "ingenuous insularity" of the Irish (*Letters* II, 166), but usually saw the ocean as an impediment to intellectual advancement. In *Stephen Hero* he describes his protagonist as "living at the farthest remove from the centre of European culture, marooned on an island in the ocean" (199). Stanislaus agreed: he called the Irish "The lying, untrustworthy, characterless inhabitants of an unimportant island in the Atlantic" (*Dublin Diary*, 64). Despite nationalist laments about Ireland's loss of population, Joyce's story "Eveline" endorses emigration: better Buenos Aires (even though "Buenos Aires" may be code for the life of an expatriate prostitute)[3] than a celibate existence at the mercy of an abusive father, the life of a "passive . . . helpless animal." Not to get on the boat is to refuse both the risk and the promise of living fully: "All the seas of the world tumbled about her heart. He was drawing her into them: he would drown her" (*Dubliners*, 34). Bolder than Eveline, Joyce "sailed" to

---

[2] For Joyce and Triestine politics, see Manganiello, *Joyce's Politics*, chapter 2.

[3] *Dubliners*, ed. Brown, 254n. See the chapter by Katherine Mullin in this volume.

Trieste, metaphorically retracing the route from the Mediterranean first traveled by the Phoenicians, an "adventurous people, who had a monopoly of the sea" (156).

But in 1907 Britannia ruled the waves. In the face of imperialism, nationalists defined Ireland's insularity not as a condition of deprivation and isolation, but as a God-given physical indicator of her right to independence. The ideological importance of being surrounded by water is manifest in the recently deleted Article 2 of the Constitution: "The national territory consists of the whole island of Ireland, its islands and the territorial seas" (*Bunreacht*, 4). Yet in *The Personality of Ireland* (1973) the influential Belfast geographer Estyn Evans challenges "the naïve conception of geography's place in history apparently held by some pious nationalists who see Ireland as a God-given island which was predestined to be the home of a single nation" (xii). Evans rejects the nationalist interpretation of Irish history as the story of a racially pure Celtic people reclaiming from their conquerors a nation tidily contained within a sea-bound physical territory. In *Ulysses* Leopold Bloom is also skeptical about the politics of natural boundaries: he swiftly expands his initial definition of "a nation" as "the same people living in the same place" to encompass the same people "living in different places" (12.1428): an elastic approach to geography dictated by his diasporic Judaism.

Like Joyce, Evans often equates insularity or "islandness" with narrow-minded isolationism. But he also points out that insularity can mean exactly the opposite: islanders use boats, and sea travel used to be easier than travel across a large landmass. In the past, Ireland's insularity meant openness to other cultures, since "islands are accessible from all directions" (20). Joyce's Phoenician model depends on a "diffusionist" theory of cultural development, which posits the physical migration of languages and peoples, usually from East to West. The alternative model, "autochthonous" or independent development of cultures, is more attractive to romantic nationalists, who prefer the idea of nations uncontaminated by the genetic material of their neighbors. The idea that insularity signals not the "autochthonous development" of an indigenous civilization, but rather accessibility and receptivity to foreign influences, is antithetical to the concept of Celtic racial purity promulgated by such Irish-Irelanders as Moran, Pearse, and Corkery. In "Ireland, Island of Saints and Sages," Joyce adopts the diffusionist position that the Irish were hybrids, "compounded of the old Celtic stock and the Scandinavian, Anglo-Saxon, and Norman races . . . with the various elements mingling and renewing the ancient body" (161).

Joyce's Orientalist assertion of exotic (and factually dubious) Phoenician–Semitic and Egyptian–African origins, whether it is serious or strategic, balances his condemnation of Irish insularity, and complicates the Unionist view that Ireland's geographical proximity to Britain must determine its political destiny. The western and southwestern coasts of Ireland have excellent harbors, and an "Atlantean" geography, which connects the Irish with the seafaring coastal peoples of Morocco and Spain, challenges the idea of Ireland as West Britain, a small island in the shadow of its larger neighbor, through which all continental influences must be mediated. In this geography of the margins, Ireland is not an "insular" backwater whose cultural retardation is a function of its situation "behind" Britain and its distance from a single metropolitan–imperial center, but is linked by the Atlantic ocean with many other, and older, cultures.

Though Phoenicians make no appearance in Joyce's story, Cheng correctly argues that we must relate "Ireland, Island of Saints and Sages" to "The Dead," composed in the same year (*Joyce, Race, and Empire*, 130). Like the lecture, "The Dead" foregrounds questions of antiquity, geography, and language. Cheng reads both texts as indictments of the failures of empire and patriarchy (128–47), but if his stimulating interpretation ignores some striking passages from the essay, it also removes some of the "ambiguities and hesitations" that make the story "semi" rather than "post" colonial. Gabriel's interaction with Miss Ivors, for example, complicates any univocal reading of the language politics of "The Dead."

Molly Ivors is introduced, through Gabriel's eyes, as "a frank-mannered talkative young lady, with a freckled face and prominent brown eyes. She did not wear a low-cut bodice and the large brooch which was fixed in the front of her collar bore on it an Irish device" (187). Gabriel stereotypes her as a New Woman: verbally bold but prudish and forbiddingly plain (those "prominent" brown eyes become "rabbit's" eyes later in the story). Though he first describes her as a "young lady," her assertive language politics confound Gabriel's traditional gender categories: "Of course the girl or woman, or whatever she was, was an enthusiast" (191).[4]

---

[4] For a feminist reading of "The Dead" that does not focus on Molly Ivors, see Norris, "Stifled Back Answers."

Miss Ivors's twice-repeated insistence that because Gabriel writes for the *Daily Express* he is a "West Briton" frames their encounter in geographical terms. In between, their conversation fluctuates abruptly between cordiality and hostility. After attacking its place of publication, she admits to liking the offending review, and extends her invitation to Aran, a move that would translate Gabriel from West Britain to the West of Ireland. Gabriel's refusal, however, elicits a stern public "cross-examination" about his holiday preferences, culminating with the pointed question, "Haven't you your own language to keep in touch with – Irish?" Gabriel is so stung by this interrogation that he declares, "Irish is not my language," and exclaims that he is "sick of my own country" (188–90). Whether or not publication in the *Daily Express* is a reliable indicator of West Britonism, Miss Ivors's initial indictment of Gabriel has gained in credibility.

All the negative diction applied to Miss Ivors as a woman who dares to be frank, opinionated, and talkative (she has "critical quizzing eyes," she is full of "propagandism," and her manner is "heckling" [191–92]) is mediated through Gabriel's limited consciousness. Gabriel does not know much about women, especially New ones. His famous speech in praise of Irish hospitality is initially conceived as a hypocritical riposte to Miss Ivors and "*the new and very serious and hypereducated generation that is growing up around us . . .* Very good: that was one for Miss Ivors. What did he care that his aunts were only two ignorant old women?" (193). Miss Ivors's credit is strengthened by Gretta's longing to accept her invitation, and by Gabriel's discourteous rejection of his wife's desire to revisit Galway. If it were not for her precipitous departure from the party, Gabriel's negative assessment would be enough to establish Molly Ivors as a minor heroine of "The Dead," the first person to point out that, in geographical terms at least, "The time had come for him to set out on his journey westward" (225).

But she does leave the party early, and in defiance of the conventions of hospitality refuses even "a pick" of the Morkans' food, wounding the sensibilities of her youngest hostess: "I am afraid you didn't enjoy yourself at all, said Mary Jane hopelessly." After her departure, "Mary Jane gazed after her, a moody puzzled expression on her face" (196). Miss Ivors's rejection of Gabriel's pseudo-chivalric offer to accompany her home and her breezy exit, punctuated by laughter and the pointedly Irish valediction, "*Beannacht libh*," conflate feminist independence with linguistic politics; but she snubs another woman who has sacrificed herself in order to become the "main prop" of her elderly aunts. In the dispute between the New Woman, the "old maid" and the wife-and-mother (for Gretta too attempts to uphold the conventions by persuading Molly Ivors to stay) our sympathies are divided. When Gabriel makes his speech celebrating "the tradition of genuine warm-hearted courteous Irish hospitality" (a tradition Joyce felt he had neglected in his earlier stories),[5] the thought that Miss Ivors "had gone away discourteously" gives him renewed self-confidence; and this time he is not represented as a hypocrite (204).

Joyce's attitude towards the standard-bearer of the Irish language in "The Dead" is therefore not easy to decode. Cheng sees her as "something [Gabriel] fears and has repressed, denied, or sold out: his 'Irishness,' that unruly, romantic, wilder, less cultured, less civilized, and uncolonizable self which . . . seems to be represented here by Gretta and Michael Furey and the West of Ireland" (138). But Cheng's rapturously Yeatsian representation of "Irishness" as wild, romantic, uncultured, and uncivilized ignores the fact that the journey westward could also symbolize regression.[6] In this reading Michael Furey's death, the pathetic self-immolation of a dying boy from the unromantic gasworks suggests the futility of sacrifice for Kathleen ni Houlihan, and his ghost signifies the dead hand of the past (Foster, *Fictions of the Irish Literary Revival*, 160–61). Moreover Miss Ivors, a hypereducated, sexless, and urban young woman, makes an odd representative of the wild romance of the uncultured West, and her proposed "excursion" suggests cultural tourism rather than a return to authentic, "uncolonizable" origins. Her traveling companion Kathleen Kearney, the daughter of "A Mother," epitomizes the manipulative pretensions of Miss Ivors's Gaelic League milieu:

> When the Irish Revival began to be appreciable Mrs. Kearney determined to
> take advantage of her daughter's name and brought an Irish teacher to the house
> . . . Soon the name of Miss Kathleen Kearney began to be heard often on
> people's lips. People said that she was very clever at music and a very nice girl
> and, moreover, that she was a believer in the language movement.
>
> (*Dubliners*, 135)

---

[5] "I have reproduced (in *Dubliners* at least) none of the attraction of the city . . . I have not reproduced its ingenuous insularity and its hospitality" (*Letters* II, 166).
[6] See Cheng's contribution to this collection for a rather different account of "Irishness."

Joyce satirizes this Revivalist culture in *Stephen Hero*, when Stephen takes up Irish at the behest of Emma Clery, whom he worships physically but despises intellectually. He joins her Gaelic League class, but fails to command her exclusive attention, and when he is feeling particularly lonely, discovers that "Emma had gone away to the Isles of Aran with a Gaelic party" (167). Here the journey westward is undertaken by a young woman whose "distressing pertness and middle-class affectations" (72) irritate Stephen so much that he tries to persuade her to sleep with him once and then part with him for ever (203). The Aran Islands are the tourist destination of both the flirt and the prude: Miss Ivors is Emma Clery turned inside out. If "the ladies" are "the best helpers the language has" (*A Portrait*, 239), their journey westward invites conflicting interpretations.

Indeed, the end of "The Dead" is a political Rorschach blot for Joyceans. Joep Leerssen agrees with John Wilson Foster that the journey westward is deathly, Michael Furey another Count Dracula, and the past a nightmare from which no one can escape (Foster, *Fictions of the Irish Literary Revival*, 142–74; Leerssen, *Remembrance and Imagination*, 228, 288n). But Seamus Deane endorses the views of Cheng, Gibbons (*Transformations*, 144–45), and Nolan (*James Joyce and Nationalism*, 34–36) when he claims that "an actual space for liberation open[s], in the west of Miss Ivors and Michael Furey" (*Strange Country*, 95).[7] If we look to "Ireland, Island of Saints and Sages" for help, Joyce's apparent pride in the ancient Oriental provenance of the Irish language seems to bear Deane out, but in closing Joyce dismisses antiquity: "If an appeal to the past . . . were valid, the fellahin of Cairo would have all the right in the world to disdain to act as porters for English tourists." But they do not, because "Ancient Ireland is dead just as ancient Egypt is dead" (173).

There is, however, a geographical key to Joyce's Protean ability to have it both ways: not Miss Ivors's Aran, but Gretta's Galway: the seaport in the West that leads back East, via Spain and Gibraltar, to the Mediterranean from which the Phoenicians came, and to which Joyce himself had fled. In "Ireland, Island of Saints and Sages" Joyce sketches a preliminary map that disturbs the topographical essentialism of the Irish–English dialectic and anticipates the cultural hybridity of *Ulysses*, a text which imaginatively superimposes the Mediterranean basin upon

---

[7] For a somewhat different response to the ending of "The Dead" by Deane, see his chapter in this volume.

Dublin. Both Bloom and Stephen prefer "a continental to an insular manner of life, a cisatlantic to a transatlantic place of residence" (*U* 17.21–22). In Friel's *Translations*, Hugh tells the English mapmaker Yolland that he has never heard of Wordsworth, poet of the English landscape: "I'm afraid we're not familiar with your literature, Lieutenant. We feel closer to the warm Mediterranean. We tend to over-look your island" (41). This neglect of the proximate in favor of the exotic follows the same analogical reasoning as Joyce's Phoenician story, and depends on a similar appeal to the distant past. Evans argues that, "The land that was to become Ireland . . . lay near the edge of another ocean in far geological time, for it was never far from the fluctuating margins of that warm mediterranean ocean (Tethys) of which the Mediterranean Sea is a remnant" (*The Personality of Ireland*, 21). Geology is metaphorically related to linguistics, for in *Translations* the Irish can speak the languages of the warm Mediterranean, Latin and Greek: the English speak only English, and are themselves regarded as "insular."

In "Ireland, Island of Saints and Sages," Joyce emphasizes the Mediterranean connection by stressing Ireland's historically well-attested relationship with Spain, first mentioned in the pseudo-histories of the twelfth-century *Book of Invasions*. This mythical native account of how Ireland was peopled provides the opening chapters of many pre-twentieth-century antiquarian and historical texts and, as Maria Tymoczko has convincingly demonstrated, Joyce did not have to know the original in order to know its contents (*The Irish "Ulysses,"* 24–36). Although *The Book of Invasions* was used by anti-imperialists to privi-lege Ireland's distinctive history and superior antiquity it is, ironically, a record of successive military conquests by Mediterranean peoples. Joyce's assertion that, via its clients the Phoenicians, Egypt was one of the matrices of Irish culture derives from the Irish origin myth of the sons of Milesius. The ancestors of Milesius moved from their native place, Scythia, to Egypt, where their leader Niul married Scota, the Pharaoh's daughter. They were expelled from Egypt for helping the Jews to make their Red Sea getaway, and subsequently migrated through Greece into Spain. "If the Jews are on their way back to Palestine, could not the Irish be prevailed on *antiquam exquierer matrem* [to seek their ancient mother] and emigrate in search of Scota, Pharaoh's daughter?" asked Bishop Stubbs (quoted in Curtis, *Anglo-Saxons and Celts*, 82). Leopold Bloom, who is associated throughout *Ulysses* with Masonic signs and insignia,[8] belongs to a brotherhood that derived much of its symbolism (including the pyramid with the eye at its apex that still appears on the American dollar bill) from Egypt. Accused in "Circe" of sexual assault by the maid Mary Driscoll, Bloom is defended by J. J. O'Molloy on the grounds that "such familiarities as the alleged guilty occurrence [are] quite permitted in my client's native place, the land of the Pharaoh" (15.945–47). Bloom is dubbed "that bloody freemason" by the nationalist Citizen (12.300), and vilified by his Irish–Ireland antagonists as a foreigner; but in the light of *The Book of Invasions*, his Masonic connections suggest that the shortest way to Tara is via the Great Pyramid of Giza.

Joyce's "Egypt," however, is a sliding political signifier. In J. F. Taylor's famous allegory of the Irish as Israelites in the house of bondage, the Egyptians represent the British. The Egyptian high priest sneers, "You are a tribe of nomad herdsmen: we are a mighty people" (7.845), and the "Circe" episode shows the English King Edward VII "robed as a grand elect perfect and sublime mason with trowel and apron" (15.4454–55). Yet Egypt's place in the ancient Irish genealogy, its status as the origin of Druid wisdom, and its present abject state ("The masters of the Mediterranean are fellaheen today" [7.911]) make it a sympathetic colonial analogy. The paradox by which Egypt can stand either for the British oppressor (the high priest) or the victim of British oppression (the fellahin) demonstrates the protean slipperiness of the analogical method, and underlies Joyce's mischievous play with J. F. Taylor's nationalist allegory. Bloom's twice-repeated misquotation of his father's prayer, "brought us out of the land of Egypt and into the house of bondage" (7.208–9, 13.1158–59) hints that the house of bondage is Ireland itself, and that the ancestors of Milesius should have stayed with the Pharaoh (Tymoczko, *The Irish "Ulysses,"* 32).

Instead, after spending many years in the Iberian peninsula, the Milesians left Spain for Ireland and banished the Tuatha de Dannaan to their fairy forts. With a straight face Joyce told his Trieste audience how the Irish churchman Sedulius was sent to Spain to settle an ecclesiastical dispute,

---

[8] *U* 5.75, 8.184, 8.958–76, 15.450–51, 15.590–91, 15.758–60, 15.2011–12, 15.2724, 15.2854, 15.4298–99, 15.4951–56. See Nadel, *Joyce and the Jews*, 211, and Davidson, *James Joyce*, 54–57.

but when he arrived there, the Spanish priests refused to listen to him, on the grounds that he was a foreigner. To this Sedulius replied that since he was an Irishman of the ancient race of Milesius, he was in fact a native Spaniard. This argument so thoroughly convinced his opponents that they allowed him to be installed in the bishop's palace at Oreto.

(*CW* 159)

Spaniards are usually considered European, but until the end of the Middle Ages most of Spain was controlled by Moors from North Africa, who were dark-skinned and of mixed Arab and Berber descent. As Joyce's portrait of Molly Bloom emphasizes, the Moorish and Sephardic Jewish presence in Southern Spain has left exotic oriental traces: Gibraltar-born Molly has a "jewess looking" mother, from whom she inherited her Moorish blood and "Moorish" eyes (18.1184).

The Moorish–Iberian–Irish connection evoked during Molly's reminiscences of Gibraltar is historical rather than mythic. Yeats's great-great-grandfather, "trading out of Galway into Spain," and his great-grandfather, the "Old merchant skipper who leaped overboard / After a ragged hat in Biscay Bay" (*Collected Poems*, 101), were following an ancient shipping route, memorialized today by the Spanish Arch on the quays in Galway. But the Phoenician–Semitic and Egyptian–African connections that Joyce posits in his lecture and develops in *Ulysses* are less susceptible of proof. From Carthage, Phoenicia's North African colony, an explorer named Himilco sailed through the Pillars of Hercules (of which Molly's Gibraltar was supposedly one), along the Atlantic coasts of Spain and France, and maybe reached the British Isles. But even if it could be established that Carthaginian sailors carrying Egyptian cultural baggage came over the sea to Irish harbors, it is impossible to determine whether they stayed, or what they left behind. Contemporary Irish archaeologists seldom mention them. Until the era of historical revisionism, however, almost everyone relied on the Phoenicians to get the story of Ireland off the ground. As late as 1922 the Oxford University Press published a book that asserts, "Everything points to the conclusion that Ireland was discovered by the Phoenicians," and claims Dun Aengus as a Phoenician settlement (Dunlop, *Ireland*, 8–9).

Joyce attributes his Phoenicianism to an appropriately semicolonial source: the eighteenth-century antiquarian and philologist General Charles Vallancey, a British army engineer who was, paradoxically, one of the leading figures of the first Celtic Revival. Vallancey's theories correspond roughly with the story of the Milesians from *The Book of Invasions*. Armed with innumerable false etymologies, he argues that the Irish language originated with Noah's son Japhet in Scythia and was disseminated via the Semitic Phoenician cities of the eastern Mediterranean (Lebanon) to Carthage (Tunis). Carthaginian merchants brought the language to Spain, and then to Ireland. Vallancey's theory provided the Irish tongue with a Semitic, oriental, and North African pedigree that distinguished it from Indo-European, and more specifically from the Teutonic languages from which Anglo-Saxon, the language of the colonizer, was derived (Leerssen, "On the Edge of Europe," 95–102). Moreover, Phoenicians were credited with the invention of the alphabet, which accorded with ancient Ireland's reputation for book-learning; and the destruction of Carthage by Rome paralleled the conquest of Ireland by the British.[9] Leerssen comments on the "strong . . . anti-English subtext" of the Phoenician model (*Remembrance and Imagination*, 74).

Vallancey's ideas, discredited in the philological community by the rise of the Indo-European paradigm, were still a part of the *Zeitgeist* in late nineteenth-century Ireland. They predisposed Joyce towards Victor Bérard's theory, advanced in *Les Phéniciens et l'Odyssée* (1902–3), that although Homer was Greek, his mariner Ulysses was a Semitic Phoenician (Seidel, *Epic Geography*, 4–8). In his *Handbook of Homeric Study*, Father Henry Browne, one of Joyce's teachers at University College, Dublin (Costello, *James Joyce*, 217–19), emphasizes the contemporary racial significance of Bérard's theory: "The Phoenicians were the Semites of the West, and . . . to discuss the history and the importance of Phoenician activity in early times is to enter upon the question as to the debt we Aryans owe to a people whom we are naturally inclined to hate" (182). Despite Browne's enthusiasm for the Phoenician hypothesis, orthodox Homeric scholars regard it as eccentric: in picking Vallancey and Bérard as his authorities, Joyce situates himself within an appropriately heretical tradition. Martin Bernal, whose Afrocentric *Black Athena* argues that the influence of Nubian Egypt and Semitic Phoenicia on Greece was played down by nineteenth-century German philologers, sees the neglect of Bérard as an anti-Semitic academic conspiracy (1, 337–66).

Leopold Bloom, a peripatetic Jew whose ethnic identity is uncertain (his mother was a Gentile; he is uncircumcised and has been baptized),

[9] See Cullingford, "British Romans and Irish Carthaginians," passim.

who fantasizes about the Orient, and who is subjected to the racial hatred of Irish nationalists, embodies (among many other things) Joyce's affirmation of cultural hybridity through the myth of wandering Ulysses, the Semitic Phoenician. Bloom and Stephen compare Hebrew with Irish:

> What points of contact existed between these languages and between the peoples who spoke them?
>
> The presence of guttural sounds, diacritic aspirations, epenthetic and servile letters in both languages: their antiquity, both having been taught on the plain of Shinar 242 years after the deluge in the seminary instituted by Fenius Farsaigh, descendant of Noah, progenitor of Israel, and ascendant of Heber and Heremon, progenitors of Ireland. (17.745–51)

The political point of this arcane parody of Vallancey's linguistics emerges in the final parallel between the Jews and the Irish: "the restoration in Chanah David of Zion and the possibility of Irish political autonomy or devolution" (17.759–60).

Analogical, genealogical, and linguistic connections between the Irish and the Jews were, of course, commonplace. In *Ulysses*, J. F. Taylor's speech "advocating the revival of the Irish tongue" evokes Moses *"bearing in his arms the tables of the law, graven in the language of the outlaw"* (7.795–96, 868–69). But although the Irish Famine and the Holocaust have been equated, contemporary Israel is no longer an appropriate model of "the outlaw," so the artistic and theoretical stock of alternative genealogies of "bondage" has risen. The Milesian hegira is reinflected to stress its North African sectors, emphasizing the connection of the Irish with Islamic Moors, and by a longer and more imaginative associational stretch, with black Africans and their descendants the American slaves (see O'Toole, "Going Native").

Several nineteenth-century Irish history books assert that Ireland's shores were "the resort of Vikings, not from Scandinavia, but Africa" (Ferguson, *The Story of the Irish Before the Conquest*, 1–3), and that these Africans were Carthaginian pirates known as the Formorians (Conyngham, *Ireland Past and Present*, 20).[10] In Yeats's play *Deirdre* (1907), the treacherous King Conchubar's messenger, executioner, and soldiers are Libyans, described as physically sinister "dark men, / With

---

[10] Historians cite Geoffrey Keating's 1633 *History of Ireland* as the originator of this tale; Keating's own source was *The Book of Invasions*.

murderous and outlandish-looking arms" (*Collected Plays*, 175). Yeats's negative depiction of his Libyan mercenaries reminds us that representational connections between Ireland and the "darkness" of Spaniards, Moors, Arabs, Egyptians, or Africans are double-edged.

Nineteenth-century colonial commentators found it inconvenient that, despite their African pedigree and prognathous facial angles, the Irish remained stubbornly white. Charles Kingsley said of the inhabitants of Sligo: "To see white chimpanzees is dreadful; if they were black, one would not feel it so much" (Kingsley, ed., *Letters*, 111). Carlyle's solution to Kingsley's visual dilemma was simple: "Black-lead them and put them over with the niggers" (quoted in Hackett, *Ireland*, 227); and English cartoonists attempted to follow his prescription by turning the native Irish origin myth against itself (Curtis, *Apes and Angels, passim*). Milesian Spain is the crucial link in the genealogy that derives the Irish from African Negroes:

> The Iberians are believed to have been originally an African race, who thousands of years ago spread themselves through Spain over Western Europe ... The skulls are of low, prognathous type. They came to Ireland, and mixed with the natives of the South and West, who themselves are supposed to have been of low type and descendants of savages of the Stone Age, who, in consequence of isolation from the rest of the world, had never been outcompeted in the healthy struggle of life, and thus made way, according to the laws of nature, for superior races.
>
> (Quoted from *Harper's Weekly* in Bornstein, "Afro-Celtic Connections," 176a)

The geographical progression from Africa through Spain to Ireland "blackens" the Irish by association (see Bornstein, "Afro-Celtic Connections").

In *Ulysses*, however, Stephen's meditation on the Moorish origins of mathematics reverses the Christian image of the Redeemer as a "light shining in darkness" to affirm two "dark men": the Jewish philosopher Moses Maimonides and his Islamic contemporary Averroes, who both worked in Spain:

> Across the page the symbols moved in grave morrice, in the mummery of their letters, wearing quaint caps of squares and cubes. Give hands, traverse, bow to partner: so: imps of fancy of the Moors. Gone too from the world, Averroes and Moses Maimonides, dark men in mien and movement, flashing in their mocking mirrors the obscure soul of the world, a darkness shining in brightness which brightness could not comprehend. (2.155–60)

Joyce revalued both the Spanish and the African associations of the word "Moor" in order to assert the Irish claim to intellect and civility against the pejorative "barbaric" stereotype promulgated by the English press. His brother Stanislaus accepted the prognathous slur: "It is annoying that I should have a typically Irish head; not the baboon-faced type, but the large, square low fronted head of O'Connell" (*Dublin Diary*, 21), and Joyce had noticed "the baboon faced Irishman that we see in *Punch*" (*Stephen Hero*, 69). In "The Dead," the drunken Freddy Malins resembles Kingsley's "white chimpanzee": "His face was fleshy and pallid, touched with colour only at the thick hanging lobes of his ears and at the wide wings of his nose. He had coarse features, a blunt nose, a convex and receding brow, tumid and protruded lips" (184–85). Freddy may look like a loser, but his emotional appreciation of Aunt Julia's song suggests his capacity for empathy (Norris, "Stifled Back Answers," 497). In a subtle associational move, Joyce gives Freddy his finest moment when he praises "a negro chieftain singing in the second part of the Gaiety pantomime who had one of the finest tenor voices he had ever heard," and defends him against Bartell D'Arcy's indifference: "And why couldn't he have a voice too? asked Freddy Malins sharply. Is it because he's only a black?" (199).[11]

Since 1968, when the Irish civil rights movement took some of its inspiration and its anthem, "We Shall Overcome," from the civil rights crusade in America, there have been many efforts to reproduce Freddy Malins's imaginative solidarity with the musical Negro chieftain. In his 1983 television documentary *Atlantean: An Irishman's Search for North African Roots*, independent filmmaker Bob Quinn revives Joyce's Phoenician story to assert that the Irish are not Celts, but part of an "ignored culture of maritime peoples" from the Atlantic seaboard who "owe more to the immense artistic and religious traditions of North Africa and the Middle East than to any European tradition."[12] Like Joyce, Quinn works by analogy: *sean nos* singing sounds like Moroccan or Nubian music; Irish illuminated manuscripts resemble Islamic ones; certain grammatical and lexical features of the Irish language suggest not

---

[11] Cheng notes their symbolic connection, but not the physical description of Freddy Malins (*Joyce, Race, and Empire*, 140).

[12] One of Quinn's Irish-language film projects was funded by Official Sinn Fein (who in 1970 split from the Provisionals in pursuit of a nonviolent neo-Marxist agenda): this anti-Celtic theory of origins is also anti-Provo.

the Indo-European family but the Hamito-Semitic group. In his eager-
ness to undermine the myth of Celtic racial purity, Quinn adopts the
eccentric theories of General Vallancey, for whom a spurious etymological resemblance was enough to prove that "Pat's language sprung from
the same clime / With Hannibal, and wears the Tyrian tunic / Of Dido's
alphabet" (Byron, *Don Juan*, canto 8, 756).

Quinn also pillages more respectable authorities, including Heinrich
Wagner, professor of Celtic philology at University College, Dublin,
who argues that "many peculiar features of Insular Celtic, rarely trace-
able in any other Indo-European language, have analogies in Basque,
Berber, Egyptian, Semitic and even in Negro-African languages"
(Quinn, *Atlantean*, 85–89). Linguistic affinities slide almost impercept-
ibly into ethnic identifications, as Quinn notes that the Irish phrase "fir
gorm" or blue man, means native of Africa; a little-known fact that also
appears in Stuart Gilbert's book on *Ulysses*. Gilbert cites an early Irish
chronicle that describes a group of Moorish prisoners who were brought
to Ireland as "the blue men of Erin," and notes the numerous references
to Moors in Joyce's novel, from *Othello* to Morris (or Moorish) dances
and Molly's Moorish eyes (73–74).

Ethnic hybridity threatens Celtic enthusiasts like the Citizen, who
calls Bloom a "whiteeyed kaffir" (12.1552). The Cyclops chapter contains
a horrific newspaper description of the real-life consequences of such
racist rhetoric: "*Black Beast Burned in Omaha, Ga*. A lot of Deadwood
Dicks in slouch hats and they firing at a Sambo strung up in a tree with his
tongue out and a bonfire under him. Gob, they ought to drown him in the
sea after and electrocute and crucify him to make sure of their job"
(12.1324–28). Though the anonymous narrator is not particularly sympathetic to the "Sambo," the word "crucify" connects the black lynching
victim with Christ, anticipating Bloom's assertion: "Christ was a Jew like
me" and the Citizen's threat to "crucify" him (12.1812). Bloom himself
notes that Jews are being "sold by auction in Morocco like slaves or
cattle" (12.1471–72), underscoring the analogical connection between
his people and black Americans.

Although his analogies between subjugated cultures and ethnicities
are literary rather than literal, sympathetic rather than substantive, Joyce
sends his Semitic hero and his "Moorish" heroine on what Luke Gibbons
has called "lateral journeys along the margins which short-circuit the
colonial divide" (*Transformations*, 180). On these imaginative journeys
the Phoenicians, legendary voyagers along Mediterranean and Atlantic

margins, provide a mythical map of the route to ethnic hybridity. As Joyce says in "Ireland, Island of Saints and Sages," "What race or what language . . . can boast of being pure today? And no race has less right to utter such a boast than the race now living in Ireland. Nationality . . . must find its reason for being rooted in something that surpasses and transcends and informs changing things like blood and the human word" (*CW* 165–66).

Works cited

Atlantean: An Irishman's Search for North African Roots. Dir. Bob Quinn. Carraroe, Co. Galway: Cinegael, n.d.

Bernal, Martin. *Black Athena: The Afroasiatic Roots of Classical Civilization*. 2 vols. New Brunswick: Rutgers University Press, 1987.

Bornstein, George. "Afro-Celtic Connections." *Literary Influence and African-American Writers*. Ed. Tracy Mishkin. New York: Garland, 1996. 171–88.

Brady, Ciaran, ed. *Interpreting Irish History*. Dublin: Irish Academic Press, 1994.

Browne, Henry. *Handbook of Homeric Study*. Dublin: Browne & Nolan, 1905.

Bunreachht na hÉireann. Dundalk: Dundalgan Press, n.d.

Byron, George Gordon, Lord. *Poetical Works*. Rev. edn, ed. John Jump. London: Oxford University Press, 1970.

Cheng, Vincent J. *Joyce, Race, and Empire*. Cambridge: Cambridge University Press, 1995.

Conyngham, David Power. *Ireland Past and Present*. New York: Sheehy, 1884.

Costello, Peter. *James Joyce: The Years of Growth, 1882–1915*. Schull, West Cork: Roberts Rinehart, 1992.

Cullingford, Elizabeth Butler. "British Romans and Irish Carthaginians: Anticolonial Metaphor in Heaney, Friel, and McGuinness." *PMLA* 111 (1996): 222–39.

Curtis, L. P. *Anglo-Saxons and Celts: A Study of Anti-Irish Prejudice in Victorian England*. Bridgeport, Conn.: University of Bridgeport Press, 1968.

Apes and Angels: The Irishman in Victorian Caricature. Washington, DC: Smithsonian Institution Press, 1971.

Davidson, Neil. *James Joyce, "Ulysses," and the Construction of Jewish Identity*. Cambridge: Cambridge University Press, 1996.

Dunlop, Robert. *Ireland from the Earliest Times to the Present Day*. Oxford: Oxford University Press, 1922.

Deane, Seamus. *Strange Country*. Oxford: Clarendon Press, 1997.

Ellmann, Richard. *James Joyce*. Oxford: Oxford University Press, 1959.

Evans, Estyn. *The Personality of Ireland*. 1973. Dublin: Lilliput Press, 1992.

Ferguson, M. C. *The Story of the Irish Before the Conquest*. London: Bell & Daldy, 1868.

Foster, John Wilson. *Fictions of the Irish Literary Revival*. Syracuse: Syracuse University Press, 1987.

Friel, Brian. *Translations*. London: Faber, 1981.

Gibbons, Luke. *Transformations in Irish Culture*. Cork: Cork University Press, 1996.

Gilbert, Stuart. *James Joyce's "Ulysses."* New York: Alfred A. Knopf, 1952.

Hackett, Francis. *Ireland: A Study in Nationalism*. New York: Huebsch, 1919.

Herring, Phillip F. "Joyce's Politics." *New Light on Joyce*. Ed. Fritz Senn. Bloomington: Indiana University Press, 1972. 3–14.

hooks, bell. *Outlaw Culture*. New York: Routledge, 1994.

Jordan, Neil. *The Crying Game*. London: Vintage, 1993.

Joyce, James. *Dubliners*. Ed. Terence Brown. Harmondsworth: Penguin, 1992.

A Portrait of the Artist as a Young Man. Ed. Seamus Deane. Harmondsworth: Penguin, 1992.

Stephen Hero. London: Cape, 1969.

Joyce, Stanislaus. *The Complete Dublin Diary*. Ed. George H. Healey. Ithaca: Cornell University Press, 1971.

Kiberd, Declan. *Inventing Ireland: The Literature of the Modern Nation*. London: Cape, 1995.

Kingsley, Francis, ed. *Charles Kingsley, His Letters and Memories of His Life*. Vol III. London: Macmillan, 1901.

Leerssen, Joep. "On the Edge of Europe: Ireland in Search of Oriental Roots, 1650–1850." *Comparative Criticism* 8 (1986): 91–112.

Remembrance and Imagination: Patterns in the Historical and Literary Representation of Ireland in the Nineteenth Century. Cork: Cork University Press, 1996.

Lloyd, David. *Anomalous States: Irish Writing and the Post-Colonial Moment*. Durham: Duke University Press, 1993.

Lowe, Lisa. *Critical Terrains*. Ithaca: Cornell University Press, 1991.

MacCabe, Colin. *James Joyce and the Revolution of the Word*. London: Macmillan, 1979.

Manganiello, Dominic. *Joyce's Politics*. London: Routledge & Kegan Paul, 1980.

Nadel, Ira. *Joyce and the Jews*. London: Macmillan, 1989.

Nolan, Emer. *James Joyce and Nationalism*. London: Routledge, 1995.

Norris, Margot. "Stifled Back Answers: The Gender Politics of Art in Joyce's 'The Dead.'" *Modern Fiction Studies* 35 (1989): 479–503.

O'Toole, Fintan. "Going Native." *Black Hole Green Card*. Dublin: New Island Books, 1994. 55–69.

Quinn, Bob. *Atlantean: Ireland's North African and Maritime Heritage*. London: Quartet, 1986.

Rea, Stephen. "Actor Stephen Rea Relishes the Ambiguity of Irish Life." *Los Angeles Times*, 4 January 1993: 9.

Said, Edward. *Orientalism*. New York: Vintage, 1979.

Seidel, Michael. *Epic Geography: James Joyce's "Ulysses."* Princeton: Princeton University Press, 1976.

Tymoczko, Maria. *The Irish "Ulysses."* Berkeley: University of California Press, 1994.

Yeats, W. B. *Collected Plays*. London: Macmillan, 1952.

Collected Poems. Ed. Richard Finneran. London: Macmillan, 1989.

Variorum Poems. Ed. Peter Allt and Russell Alspach. New York: Macmillan, 1940.

Authenticity and identity: catching the Irish spirit

VINCENT J. CHENG

In the opening pages of *Ulysses*, the Englishman Haines, visiting Ireland in order to study its native culture and folk customs, tries speaking Gaelic – as a linguistic marker of genuine Irish identity – to the old milkwoman, a presumably "authentic" Irish figure. What is it, after all, that defines Irishness? The speaking of Gaelic? Old age and peasant status? But the old milkwoman does not understand, and Mulligan comments wryly that "He's English . . . and he thinks we ought to speak Irish in Ireland" (*U* 1.431–32). According to Haines's view, then, the milkwoman does not pass muster, is not sufficiently and authentically Irish.

But who or what *is* "Irish?" What defines Irishness? Is it Irish blood (a tautological concept in itself)? Is it residence in Ireland (but then how about all the wild geese and emigrants)? What are the essentials or essences needed to qualify as "Irish?" And who gets to say what qualifies as genuinely Irish? The issue of defining "Irishness" was a central one in Joyce's time, witnessing the attempts by a nationalist movement to forge a national identity – and is still a visceral and urgent issue in Ireland today, with the continuing debates about the positions of North and South, Catholic and Protestant, republican and unionist, citizen and emigrant, the place of Irish Americans, and so on. Is perhaps the best we can do Leopold Bloom's vague and hapless vacillation that "A nation is the same people living in the same place . . . Or also in different places" (*U* 12.1417–31)? – a position which, one might add, seems less hapless and rather more viable since the 22 May 1998 referendum on Northern Ireland.

Recently I received in the mail an advertisement for an Irish American publication, the *Irish Voice Newspaper*: "CATCH THE IRISH SPIRIT!" the ad urged me in big bold lettering. Catch the Irish Spirit: well, at one level – at the level of popular culture – America has indeed, of late, been catching the Irish spirit. Witness the popularity and omnipresence of Irish culture in American cultural life today: popular films (everything from *Michael Collins* and *The Crying Game* to *The Secret of Roan Inish*, *A Circle of Friends*, *The Boxer*, *Waking Ned Devine*, and so on); popular music and dance (Enya, Clannad, U2, Cranberries, Sinead O'Connor, the Riverdance craze, and so on); even literature, with the growing popularity of numerous Irish poets and novelists, capped in 1997 by the surprising *Angela's Ashes* phenomenon. Even *TV Guide* and *Newsweek* both recently pointed out that one of the most notable trends in the new TV season was the number of new shows featuring Irish folks.[1] One might well speculate why this is so: what are the reasons for this phenomenon in contemporary American culture, what I call "Irish chic"; what is the "cultural work" being performed? Whatever the reasons, in America today, Irishness is clearly "in" – in striking contrast to the pejorative cultural valence of "Irishness" throughout most of American history. And, if you subscribe to the *Irish Voice Newspaper*, presumably you, too, can catch the Irish spirit.

But the seemingly straightforward formulation – "Catch the Irish Spirit" – masks some not-so-straightforward implications. First of all: what *is* "the Irish spirit?" Is there any such thing? Can we even know what it is? And secondly, how does one *catch* it? Can it even be caught – and presumably transferred or adopted? Or can it only be inherited and innate, "native" and "natural" only to those who are already authentically Irish – and thus a quality or essence *not* subject to acquisition or subscription or belated membership?

I daresay that we each carry with us certain personal assumptions about the Irish spirit, such as: Gaelic inflections and influences; the rural and peasant West; the Connemara hills; folk traditions; pub culture and a communal life of bibulous, even drunken, joviality; music, dance, and

---

[1] The 12 September 1998 issue of *TV Guide* (page 11) notes that "Irish culture has swept the dance world ('Riverdance') and the book industry (*Angela's Ashes*), so why should TV be any different?" Quoting a TV executive's opinion that "Irish families make for good drama," the feature cites the new shows *Turks* (a drama in Chicago about a family of Irish cops) and *To Have and to Hold* (more families of Irish cops, but in Boston, featuring – among others – Irish actress Fionnula Flanagan), both on CBS; Fox's sitcom *Costello* (about a foul-mouthed Boston-Irish barmaid named Sue Costello); and NBC's drama *Trinity*. That same week, *Newsweek* (14 September 1998, page 70) previewed the Fall television season with the storyline "A season of testosterone, ambiguous gayness and way too many Irish people" – similarly citing "Riverdance," *Angela's Ashes*, and the same group of new television programs.

the arts; the gift of gab; an emotional and temperamental, sometimes sentimental, mindset; a brooding and poetic imagination; a quality of mists, fairies, spirits, and an ineffable mystique or otherworldliness. All of these and more are perhaps part of the cultural baggage we take with us on our travels to Ireland, looking for the real, the authentic, the hidden Ireland; armed with our Fodors and Michelins the way English tourists (like Haines) were armed, a century ago, with travel guides like Mr. and Mrs. S. C. Hall's *Ireland: Its Scenery, Character, etc.* (1841–43) and Mrs. Hall's *Tales of Irish Life and Character* (1909), or Clifton Johnson's *The Isle of the Shamrock* (1901), we arrive on the emerald shores intent on catching the real Ireland, the true "Irish spirit."

As a tourist coming from the center of empire, Haines in *Ulysses* reflects one discourse – that of the colonizer – that fashions Irish character and identity as one of "otherness" – in that process of racialized "othering" so familiar now to scholars of colonial and imperial discourses. The Irish were depicted as ineradicably "other" from the English, defined through their difference, their very alter-ity. Haines's opinion – "he thinks we ought to speak Irish in Ireland" – thus smacks of the same hegemonic cultural needs as the desire of white American culture to construct the "authentic" Native American Indian, to view the Indian (or Irish) other as Other, as quaint, primitive, "wild Irish" – as dead stereotype of an absolute difference. Controlling the dissemination of popular images, the conquering culture was able to fashion a hegemonic discourse about the conquered people as distinctively and ineluctably Other, a discourse frequently used to justify and even encourage brutal domination and violence against the conquered culture.

For a nationalist movement, then, the issue of wresting back the power to define oneself and one's own national identity is understandably of paramount importance. But there is a perilous dilemma in such a national project of self-definition: in order to combat the pejorative labels of an imperialist English discourse of Irishness, in response to the anxiety of a loss of subjectivity and self-representation, and in order to prove that the Irish are indeed a very particular people distinct and different from all other peoples, it is an almost irresistible urge to define oneself (one's national identity) in terms of one's specific distinctiveness – that is, and once again, in terms of one's specific "otherness" (even sometimes one's otherworldliness, what Cheryl Herr has called the Irish "elsewhere"). That is to say, ironically, that both projects – that of a racialist imperial discourse and that of a nationalist self-definition –

are, although emanating from very different political positions, both engaged in defining Irishness as distinctively "other" and different; in this way, the two projects sometimes merge in a parallel attempt to find or define an authentic "otherness" known variously as the Irish self, the Irish mystique, the Irish soul, the Irish spirit, the Irish mind. Describing the views of Yeats and his circle at the end of the nineteenth century, Declan Kiberd writes: "If [nationalist intellectuals] were to create an *authentic movement*, . . . If they were to invent Ireland, they must first invent the Irish" (*Inventing Ireland*, 100, 136; my emphasis). This leads to the striking but inescapable paradox at the heart of the project of national self-definition: the *invention* of an "authentic" self.

As Kiberd's reference to "an authentic movement" exemplifies, discussions about national identities by even the most scrupulous scholars repeatedly circle around what the folklorist Regina Bendix calls the "A-word": after all, what is an "authentic movement" – as opposed to, say, an "inauthentic" one? Emer Nolan points out that "authenticity" remains an important theme in the work of certain Irish scholars (such as Richard Kearney and Declan Kiberd), "whereas the [poststructuralist] theorists to which they are occasionally indebted attack the very idea of a self to which one might be true or false" (*James Joyce and Nationalism*, 17).

As Bendix argues, in her groundbreaking study of folkloric and ethnographic theory entitled *In Search of Authenticity*:

> European nationalism was part of the effort to cast off monarchical government and establish democratic institutions. Yet the notion of national uniqueness harbors a conservative ethos of the past. Because of the insistence on national purity or authenticity inherent in the idea of a unique nation, the notion of authenticity ultimately undermines the liberating and humanitarian tendencies from which it grew. The universalist aspirations implicit in casting out the old order are contradicted by the particularist emphasis that each nation constructs to distinguish itself from all other nations. In emphasizing the authentic, the revolutionary can turn reactionary, a process all too vividly played out in global political movements of the late twentieth century. (8)

Bendix suggests that it was the notion of authenticity (and "the rhetoric of authenticity") which legitimated folklore and ethnography as scientific disciplines in post-Enlightenment Western culture (5). This notion of, and desire for, a national uniqueness embodies, for many national mythologies, the Romantic legacies of the sublime and the transcendent: "Original, genuine, natural, naïve, noble and innocent, lively, sensuous, stirring – the string of adjectives could be continued" (15) – all adjectives which have also been frequently used to describe "authentic" Irish folk culture. In short, national "authenticity" functions as a quasi-religious locus of transcendence, in much the same way that the concept of "nation" itself operates, as Benedict Anderson has so skillfully demonstrated.

The pressure to define a unique and authentic national character and identity, one that is distinct from all others (and preferably originary and premodern, an always already-manifest destiny), may indeed be growing even more urgent with the globalization of our own postmodern era – the world of global markets, global media, and neocolonial economies – where cultural and natural distinctness and distinctions are fading, and cultures all grow increasingly to resemble, not distinct and separate uniquenesses, but predictable simulacra of millennial inauthenticity, complete with CNN and a McDonald's in every village. "Behind the assiduous documentation and defense of the authentic lies an unarticulated anxiety of losing the subject" (Bendix, *In Search of Authenticity*, 10).

It is here, perhaps, that we may glimpse a hint of the cultural forces behind the continuing reification of "authenticity" and ethnic identitarianism in the world today – at a time when one might be tempted to imagine the need for such militant identity politics to be less necessary, with distinct cultures gradually melding into a transnational global culture: for rather than needing now to depend less on cultural differences and identities, previously distinct cultures suffer an anxiety about the perceived loss of identity and subjectivity, thus requiring the continuing construction and maintenance of fantasmatic identities and authenticities, so as to continue to be able to assert difference and superiority (rather than global sameness and what Seamus Deane calls the "harmony of indifference" [*Heroic Styles*, 15]) – whether in the forms of World Cup soccer competitions, sectarian politics, or ethnic warfares.

In the particular case of the "Irish Chic" in American culture, what is still identifiable (at least to a popular American audience) as a distinct and "authentic" ethnic/cultural identity – Irishness – can thus function within American culture as a still-legitimate way to deal with ethnicity, and even class and race, without actually having to stray from the familiar (i.e., whiteness): indeed, this seems to be how Irishness functioned in the monster-hit movie *Titanic*, in which Irish/Gaelic music (at least of the Enya-influenced New Age variety) would well up whenever darker ethnicities and lower-class people were being represented, eliding all specificities and difference into a generic otherness-as-Irishness; when the heroine wants to leave her stuffy upper-crust company up there in First Class, she goes down below to Third Class and whoops it up by pulling up her skirts and doing an Irish jig. In America today, Irishness may be both popular and comfortable precisely because it remains an identifiable (and presumably authentic) ethnicity that is nonetheless unthreatening and familiar; in both academia and in popular culture, one can have the ideological justification of doing ethnic studies or "performing ethnicity" simply by doing Irish studies – while actually still working within the familiar and with whiteness, and without having to actually venture into the more threatening theatres of racial and Third World otherness.[2]

In order to convince ourselves of our uniqueness and authenticity in a world of increasingly global sameness, we have created a booming "market of identifiable authenticities" (Bendix, *In Search of Authenticity*, 3) – especially in the combined and closely related markets known as folklore studies, museum collecting, cultural anthropology, and tourism. Thus, the "authentic" Aran sweater or the thatched-roof cottage become markers or talismans for the authentic Irish experience. That exuberant search for what the great eighteenth-century theologian and folklorist Johann Gottfried Herder called the "soul of the people" is a seductive but troubling and complex quest to "pinpoint the ineffable". "Folklore," as Bendix points out, "has long served as a vehicle in the search for the authentic, satisfying a longing for an escape from modernity. The ideal folk community, envisioned as pure and free from civilization's evils, was a metaphor for everything that was not modern." Taking advantage of this ideal, "the most powerful modern political movement, nationalism, builds on the essentialist notions inherent in authenticity, and folklore in the guise of native cultural discovery and rediscovery has continually served nationalist movements since the Romantic era" (*In Search of Authenticity*, 7).

However, there is an intrinsic, structural paradox to this quest to locate the authentic, to "catch" the soul or spirit of an authentic Irishness. Over fifty years ago Walter Benjamin delineated the dilemma of authenticity in the age of mechanical reproduction: "Precisely because authenticity cannot be reproduced," Benjamin writes, "the arrival of certain

[2] On this last point, see also my essay "Of Canons."

techniques of reproduction . . . has provided the means to differentiate *levels of authenticity*" (*Das Kunstwerk*, 52n.3; my emphasis). Previous to the age of mechanical reproduction, Benjamin argues, art existed in the world of *cult*, seducing us through its aura – which depends precisely on inaccessibility and remoteness. In an age of mechanical reproduction, aura becomes tarnished by reproduction, and as a result "secularization affords authenticity the place previously held by cult value" (53n.8; see Bendix, *In Search of Authenticity*, 6). Our own contemporary world of color xeroxes, lip-synching contests, and Elvis look-alikes has perfected the art of the copy (is it Ella or is it Memorex?), making a mockery of the notion of an "original" or an "authentic" copy; if imitation is the highest form of flattery, nowadays such flattery also robs the original of its exclusive aura. In a world where we can no longer clearly distinguish between Ella and Memorex, between a photocopy and an original document (even faxed signatures are now accepted as legal documents), between a Rembrandt and a skillful forgery – the "authentic" item hovers somewhere between a transcendent talisman with sacred powers and a shabby trinket from the Araby bazaar.

This process of degradation – from authenticity to its material reproduction or textual representation – involves a further paradox. Once a cultural commodity has been identified as "authentic," its market value rises, as does the demand for it. Unlike, say, Rembrandts or Cézannes, folkloric items *can* be endlessly replicated: any member of the group (say, residents of the West of Ireland) can start making them and declaring them to be authentic cultural goods – thus again devaluing each separate item as well as the very notion of the genuine and the authentic.

These paradoxes end up forcing the range of the authentic (and the very essence of authenticity) further and further into the past: as Bendix points out, "Declaring a particular form of expressive culture as dead or dying limits the [possible] number of authentic items, but it promotes the search for not yet discovered and hence authentic folklore" (*In Search of Authenticity*, 9). Or, in Baudrillard's terms: "In order for ethnology to live, its object must die, by dying, the object takes its revenge for being 'discovered' and with its death defies the science that wants to grasp it" (*Simulacra and Simulation*, 7). The search for the authentic, then, is an intrinsically hopeless quest to "catch" and pin down something already defined as ungraspable.

This quest for authenticity, in a nationalist politics, frequently takes the familiar form of a national nostalgia for origins, a yearning for a premodern and uncontaminated past that somehow authorizes and defines the authenticity and essence of the cultural present. Bendix notes that, in the history of folklore studies, ever since the time of Herder and the Sturm und Drang Romantics, "the verbal art of the peasantry became [the primary] means for humanity at large to get in touch with authenticity" – especially in the activities of "pilgrimage, and its commodified form, travel" as "loci of transcendence" (*In Search of Authenticity*, 17). The latter is certainly true of the familiar rite of passage of Irish Americans "returning" across the Big Pond to "rediscover" the authentic homeland – as it is equally true of Haines's passage to Ireland in search of authentic Irish folklore.

Playing native informant to Haines's imperial ethnography, Buck Mulligan understands the paradoxes of commodification and the ethnographic mentality, as he entertains the Englishman with a bawdy story about "old mother Grogan": " – That's folk, he said very earnestly, for your book, Haines. Five lines of text and ten pages of notes about the folk and the fishgods of Dundrum. Printed by the weird sisters in the year of the big wind" (*U* 1.365–67). Mulligan's own self-consciously nonsensical parody of Irish "folk"lore reflects his understanding of exactly what the ethnographic discourse is looking for (and its structural indistinguishability from reproducible parody): having trotted out some morose local color and verbal wit in the person of Stephen Dedalus, he now tells colorful stories about "fishgods" in "the year of the big wind" ("Can you recall, brother, is mother Grogan's tea and water pot spoken of in the Mabinogion?"), and then unveils his most promising local specimen, the old milkwoman.

The entire scene with the milkwoman is a wonderful parody of the ethnographic encounter with a tribal culture, with Mulligan acting as interpreter/informant. " – The islanders, Mulligan said to Haines casually, speak frequently of the collector of prepuces" (1.393–94). Mulligan's self-consciously parodic orchestration and manipulation of the scene manages actually to engage Haines's ethnographic interest in both Stephen's Irish wit and in the milkwoman as an essentialized specimen of Irish folksiness. What Mulligan knows Haines is looking for are the comfortably static images of an essentialized stage Irishness, such as colorful verbal wit (Stephen) and primitive, folksy backwardness (old milkwoman). Such images are not only marketable commodities, but in their more insidious implications "could be used to justify any aspect of the colonial enterprise" (Webb, "Manipulated Images," 5). For "primitive" peoples have repeatedly functioned within what William Simmons calls "anthropological fictions," "the purist notions that native cultures resist history, or that they disappear in its presence" ("Culture Theory in Contemporary Ethnohistory," 7) – in what James Axtell describes sarcastically (in discussing Native American history) as "the short 'pathetic' story of the 'inevitable' triumph of a 'booming' white 'civilization' over a 'fragile' 'primitive' culture" (*The European and the Indian*, 7); all of these attempts to freeze a static backwardness on to a native culture collude to construct a European–imperial sovereignty of self in what James Clifford calls "master narratives of cultural disappearance" ("Four Northwest Coast Museums," 214).[3]

In this way Haines's quest parallels the project of what Declan Kiberd calls "narrow-gauge nationalists" in Joyce's time: both attempted to define an Irish uniqueness and authenticity as a static otherness already frozen in the past. As David Lloyd points out in his chapter in this volume, the nationalist agenda constructed an identity that "writes out" some of the actual realities of its contemporary present (such as the feminist and labor movements) in order to facilitate the construction of a dead but authenticating past. Which is to suggest that an "authentic" folk culture is so only if it in fact no longer exists, and thus can be reified and sentimentalized. As Lloyd goes on to write: "A Celticist nationalism engages in a revalorization of social or cultural traits whose material conditions of possibility it in fact seeks to eradicate" (above, p. 132); in short, Gaelicness is of greatest use to Celtic nationalists when it can be construed as dying, archaic, and premodern – and thus of sentimental and nostalgic value in constructing and authenticating an invented national identity. As a result, both the English imperial discourse of Irish Otherness and the narrow-gauge nationalist construction of a distinct and unique Gaelic otherness collude in the process that Renato Rosaldo has succinctly coined "imperialist nostalgia."

Declan Kiberd describes this process thus:

> Part of the modernization process was the emergence of nation-states, which often arose out of the collapse of the old ways of life and so were badly in need of legitimation: this was afforded by the deliberate invention of traditions, which allowed leaders to ransack the past for a serviceable narrative. In this way, by recourse to a few chosen symbols and simple ideas, random peoples could be

---

[3] The previous two paragraphs are adapted from my book on *Joyce, Race, and Empire*, chapter 6.

transformed into Italians or Irish, and explain themselves by a highly-edited
version of their history.

(*Inventing Ireland*, 140).

For such a mythologizing/authenticating function, Gaelic culture was
almost perfectly, indeed frighteningly, tailor-made: after all, it was
already a dying culture (brutally eradicated by both the English and the
Famine) whose records of its own traditions and culture had been
systematically destroyed for centuries by the English; in this cultural
vacuum the "invention of traditions" could take place relatively unhin-
dered. "Gaelic Ireland," Kiberd writes, "had retained few institutions or
records after 1601 to act as a brake on these tendencies: all that remained
were the notations of poets and the memories of the people.
[Consequently] these played a far greater part in [Douglas] Hyde's
remodelled Ireland than they did in many of the other emerging
European countries" (*Inventing Ireland*, 140) – where the invention of
authentic traditions at least still had to face *some* on-going reality checks.

What resulted is a construction of Irish national identity around the
idealization of a rural and primitive West: "Like other forms of pastoral," Kiberd notes in a recent essay, "this complex of ideas was a wholly
urban creation, produced by such artists as W. B. Yeats and George
Russell and by such political thinkers as Eamonn de Valera and Michael
Collins. They were, to a man, the urbanized descendants of country
people, and they helped to create the myth of a rural nation" ("The
Periphery and the Center," 5). And the emerging Irish Catholic middle
class embraced this sentimentalized national mythology about rural
Ireland as the authentic Ireland.

One critical problem with such a discursive logic is that the concept of
authenticity implies and mandates the existence of its opposite, the inauthentic, the fake, the nonauthorized: it is here that the violence of discourse (in Derrida's sense) takes place – and where Joyce parted
company with a Gaelic nationalism weaned, as he put it, on "the old pap
of racial hatred" (Ellmann, *James Joyce*, 237). For by valorizing some
things as authentic or essential one necessarily brands other things – a
feminine oral tradition, say, or Protestants, Italians, and Jews – as ines-
sential, illegitimate, un-Irish. Kiberd has remarked that "the ludicrous
category *un-Irish* was among [the] weird achievements" of the narrow-
gauge nationalists (*Inventing Ireland*, 337). Various forms of sport, literature, dance, and so on – as well as ethnic or racial heritages (Jewish,

Italian, Anglo-Irish, black) – thus risked being denounced as "un-Irish."
Yet what does it really mean to be an "inauthentic" Irish person, or an
"un-Irish" Irish citizen? It *is* a positively bizarre category, that of the
inauthentic Irishman (a category Oscar Wilde embraced with relish). It
is one thing to have urban guilt – as with Gabriel Conroy's *seoninism* –
over not being sufficiently in touch with the rural West. But it is another
thing when the folkloric rhetoric of authenticity is used by ethnic nationalisms to discriminate against an Irish Jew born in Ireland, or – as we
have seen too often in this century – used to justify acts of "ethnic cleans-
ing." As Bendix argues:

> A very thin line separates the desire for individual authenticity and the calling to
> convince others of the correctness of a particular rendering or localization of
> the authentic. The most powerful and lasting example of this double legacy in
> folklore's disciplinary history is the (ethno-)nationalist project. Textualized
> expressive culture such as songs and tales can, with the aid of the rhetoric of
> authenticity, be transformed from an experience of individual transcendence to
> a symbol of the inevitability of national unity ... [Such a rhetoric] could
> legitimate its collectivized corollary of cultural authenticity and serve in the
> unambiguous exclusion and annihilation of all who could not or would not
> belong.   (*In Search of Authenticity*, 20–21)

If the English imperial discourse had sought a primitive Celtic Other as
the foil to Englishness, the Gaelic Revival now searched for many of the
same elements in "the true Celtic other within." "The Gaelic *Ur-
ground*," as the anthropologist Lawrence J. Taylor calls it, "was to be
sought on such outposts as the Arans, west of Galway, or the Blaskets, off
the southwest Kerry coast"; it was there that both anthropologists and
the public came to look for "'authentic' voices . . . of a pure western,
primitive wisdom" ("Two Things that People Don't Like to Hear," 216).
    In fashioning such an "authentic" Irish spirit, the Revivalists needed
to be selective and inventive, purging some of the folk legends of their
more sordid, vulgar, or obscene elements, under the urging of such historians as Samuel Ferguson and Standish O'Grady. As T. W. Rolleston
wrote in 1887, "We *want* the Irish spirit, certainly, in Irish literature . . .
but we want its gold, not its dross" ("Shamrocks," 19; quoted in Gibson,
"History, All That," 58). O'Grady intended these idealized legends to be
a safe haven to which "the intellect of man" could turn "for rest and recuperation" when "tired by contact with the vulgarity of actual things"

(*History of Ireland*, I, 22). This sentimentalized whitewashing of sordid and vulgar realities was certainly at odds with Joyce's attempt to make the Irish take a good look at themselves in his nicely polished looking glass. (Though, to be sure, there were also other Revivalists – D. P. Moran, for instance – who, like Joyce, objected to this very selective, laundered version of Irish history and literature.)

But it was embraced by much of the movement, with the Revivalists and the nationalists collaborating in purveying the idealized image of "a generic, ahistorical peasantry" (Kiberd, "The Periphery and the Center," 11) in the Blasket or Aran islanders – while ignoring the fact that their world was one actually riven with class snobberies and other dissensions. On this issue even the usually pragmatic Michael Collins wore rose-tinted lenses:

> Impoverished as the people are . . . the outward aspect is a pageant. One may see processions of young women riding down on island ponies to collect sand from the seashore, or gathering turf, dressed in their shawls and in their brilliantly-coloured skirts made of material spun, woven and dyed by themselves . . . their cottages also are little changed. They remain simple and picturesque. It is only in such places that one gets a glimpse of what Ireland *may become again.*
> (Quoted in Kiberd, "The Periphery and the Center," 10; emphasis added)

The sentimentalized images here are indistinguishable from those in imperialist ethnographies or in Mrs. Hall's sentimental, ethnographic tour books. The striking opening line "Impoverished as the people are" suggests, as Kiberd has noted, an elision of material poverty, a willing investment in, and acceptance of, an imagined Irishness that is defined as necessarily backward and poor. As Kiberd goes on to argue:

> in subsequent Irish politics: rural Ireland was real Ireland, the farmer the moral and economic backbone of the country. That myth was given a further lease on life in each generation . . . [as] Dublin was overrun by unanticipated numbers of rural immigrants, who had no sooner settled in than they were consumed by a fake nostalgia for a pastoral Ireland they had "lost."
> ("The Periphery and the Center," 16)

Joyce, as an urbanized Dubliner, both felt and saw through the invented pressure of such a romantic–pastoral authenticity. The tension is represented in "The Dead," for example, when Miss Ivors plays the authenticity-card with Gabriel, inviting him to vacation in the Aran Islands – and Gabriel is discomfited by her accusation that he is not sufficiently interested in his own country (that is, in the authentic, rural, and primitive

West). The Gaelic Revival was funneling tour groups to the Gaeltacht, to learn Gaelic language and dancing and music, to study its folk poetry. Nearly a century and several generations later, the West continues to be the critical marker of Irishness for both Irish citizens and people of Irish descent; it is also where most anthropologists have repeatedly gone to study the Irish. As Taylor, one such anthropologist, reminds us: "In the *Gaeltachts* . . . the 'Irish colleges,' which are not unlike the ethnic summer camps one finds in America, still welcome children from the north and the east, teaching them the language, as well as Irish dancing and singing, in the places where these cultural icons are supposed to be enshrined" ("Two Things that People Don't Like to Hear," 217). "Retribalization centers," he calls them. I am reminded by how the Irish spirit is catching on in America, too, with "retribalization centers" now moving on to American college campuses – such as the summer camps at Boston College, or Syracuse University, or Notre Dame.

Unfortunately, the cumulative effect of such "invented traditions" and authenticities often merely serves to further reify or shore up sentimental or stage-Irish stereotypes, such as those so influentially disseminated by Matthew Arnold. Basing his ideas on the theories of Ernest Renan, who had found the quintessential Celtic mind to be dreamy and politically ineffectual, Arnold wrote: "The Celtic genius had sentiment as its main basis . . . with love of beauty, charm and spirituality for its excellence, ineffectualness and self-will for its defect" (Kiberd, *Inventing Ireland*, 31) – a general description still believed by many and offered up in many contemporary guidebooks. Arnold suggested that the Celt was unduly susceptible to emotion and excitement – "he is truly . . . sentimental" – and, with predictable logic, he thus also argued that "the sensibility of the Celtic nature, its nervous exaltation, have something feminine in them, and the Celt is thus peculiarly disposed to feel the spell of the feminine idiosyncrasy; he has an affinity to it; he is not far from its secret" ("On the Study of Celtic Literature," 344, 347). This is a kind of "gendered" othering that has similarly been applied to Jews and to "Orientals," as a way to distinguish them from the sovereign (read masculine) imperial European subject.

We find elements of such stereotypes of a sentimentalized otherness reflected in, say, the ideas of Yeats, when he writes of "men born into our Irish solitude, of their curiosity, their rich discourse, their explosive passion, their sense of mystery" (Johnston, "Cross-Currencies," 56). Or, in the words of another Yeates, Ray Yeates, writing in a book published as recently as 1997 – a collection of essays about the Famine:

"Deep down . . . I think I have always known that to be Irish meant to be a lovable loser" ("My Famine," 195); such widespread beliefs echo Renan's and Arnold's ideas of Irish ineffectualness – what Arnold callously referred to as "nations disinherited of political success" in his "On the Study of Celtic Literature," with its suggestive epigraph from Ossian, "They went forth to the war, but they always fell" (a line which Yeats also borrowed). Such images only encourage and reinforce an already internalized Irish creed of noble failure and martyrdom.

We see traces everywhere of such beliefs in a brooding, ineffectual, dreamy Irish spirit. The Irish-American editor of that recent collection of essays entitled *Irish Hunger*, Tom Hayden (yes, he of sixties activism fame and Jane Fonda's ex-husband) writes about the dark and brooding Robert F. Kennedy as "a raw Celtic spirit" who made him realize that "there was such a thing as an Irish soul" (287). Even in contemporary Irish cultural studies we find the continued traces of the reification of Irish otherness, as in Terry Eagleton's description of Irish writing as "the home of a brooding, isolated subjectivity confronting a recalcitrant world" ("Form and Ideology," 18).

No intelligent person would, of course, dispute the danger of stereotypes. And yet we cannot seem to get beyond stereotypes; as one well-meaning and intelligent senior colleague commented to me after I delivered a paper several years ago on the English discourse about the Irish: "But isn't there some truth to those stereotypes? They *are* often slovenly, drunken, sentimental, poetic, and so on." Or, as Donald S. Connery writes in his chapter on "National Character" in his 1968 book on *The Irish*: "The trouble is that every time I am solemnly told in Ireland that the stage Irishman does not exist I meet one the next day" (91; quoted in Gupta, "'What Colour's Jew Joyce,'" 64).

The trouble is not that the stereotyped traits may exist; the trouble is our confusion, our inability to distinguish, between essence and circumstance. The comic vein in Irish literature, for example, may be very real and very particular, very specific to an Irish cultural history – as is, say, the scatological vein in Irish literature (what Lloyd calls "writing in the shit"); but these are frequently the complex and symptomatic results – and sometimes even coping strategies – developed (individually and communally) in reaction or response to external circumstances *imposed* on a people, and not a measure of innate essences or racial character. Irish pub culture and drinking, for example, can be interpreted variously as a response to the hopelessness of the poverty and destitution wrought on the Irish by the English; or also – as Lloyd argues – as a populist and potentially subversive set of practices which could not be governed by English modes of order and discipline, including the activities of collective treating on the round system, oral traditions and musical performances, and a premodern, communal valuation of the individual.

Unfortunately, there is a long tradition of such "authentic" stereotyping of the Irish spirit in academia, too, and I am going to focus briefly (and very selectively) on Joyce studies.[4] In 1932 Charles Duff wrote in *James Joyce and the Plain Reader*: "[Joyce's] mind is abnormally Irish – that is to say, he has the qualities that make up the typically Irish mind" – which Duff enumerates as "a restless and often fantastic imagination, a keen sense of realism and the comic, a tendency to somber, mystical brooding, which often finds compensation in either genial or sardonic wit" (23). Such a description turns Joyce into the typical stage Irishman, since it is based on a stage-Irish otherness. Similarly, Joyce's early biographer Herbert Gorman wrote that the "Irishman has been so coloured by romance" and is "a creature of emotions" – and that, although it might not be immediately obvious, Joyce is "essentially Irish" (*James Joyce*, 62). Finally, Frank Budgen, as Gupta has convincingly demonstrated, was – in spite of his loyalty and friendship to Joyce – a believer in biogenetically predetermined racism; among other rather repulsive comments, Budgen wrote: "We must suppose that part of Stephen's physical recoil was due to their difference in race. The Jew sometimes hates the Gentile, and the Gentile occasionally hates the Jew but, religious and political differences apart, there exists also a physical chemical repulsion and this is felt only by the Gentile for the Jewish man" (*James Joyce*, 255). It is in such a discursive context and intellectual history that the turn in Joyce studies, in the past few years, towards investigating multiple discourses of Irishness, race, and coloniality – and this volume seems a healthy example – presents a welcome and overdue corrective.

After its founding in 1922, the Irish Free State instituted a Gaelic language revival, in correspondence with the ideology of the Gaelic League, as government policy, an authenticating nationalist effort "to help establish its legitimacy" (Brown, *Ireland*, 47). This officially authenticated the notion of a narrowly definable Irishness – in tandem with the "Irish Ireland" movement, led by Daniel Corkery among others.

[4] I am indebted here to Suman Gupta's article, "'What Colour's Jew Joyce.'"

Corkery, in his influential study of *The Hidden Ireland* (1924), encouraged the Irish "to seek their cultural heritage in an exclusively Gaelic past" (Foster, *Modern Ireland*, 167), evolving the notion of an "Irish mind." Ireland, Corkery claimed, was "a land dark, scorned, and secretly romantic" – and the real, hidden "Irish Ireland" was "a peasant nation, with no urban existence and no middle class, oppressed by an alien gentry" (Foster, *Modern Ireland*, 195). For Corkery, the "Irish mind" was characterized by Catholic religion, republican nationalism, and a deep connection to the land.[5] Consequently, the Irish Ireland movement tended to exclude anything or anyone that lay outside the pale of its categories of Irishness – as un-Irish.

This legacy is reflected in subsequent Irish literary history, including Joyce criticism. For example, in 1961 Vivian Mercier's important study of *The Irish Comic Tradition* endorses the notion of an "Irish mind" by associating the supposedly Irish traits of fantastic humor and verbal wit with a history of magic and mythology, an essential mindset that supposedly worked its way into a writer's sensibility without his or her awareness; Mercier argued that Joyce was essentially Irish in this sense. In response to Mercier's book, Conor Cruise O'Brien insisted on distinguishing between circumstance and essence, arguing that "Irish wit is a political contingency as words are the weapons of the disarmed" – rather than an innate essence of the Irish mind: "The idea," O'Brien wrote further, "that there is 'an Irish mind' . . . with its own peculiar quirks, not shared even by other Europeans, from medieval times to the days of Samuel Beckett, seems to me implausible . . . There is probably no continuous and distinctive 'Irish mind,' but there has been since the sixteenth century at least an Irish predicament: a predicament which has produced common characteristics in a number of those who have been involved in it" (*Writers and Politics*, 104). The distinction lies between innate essences and historical–political circumstances.[6]

---

[5] Corkery thus summarily dismissed both Yeats and Joyce (the latter for being too vulgar and impure) as anti-Irish; no Ascendancy or Anglo-Irish writer, according to Corkery, could write authentic Irish literature because "Synge's class have always been reared on an alien porridge" (*Synge*, 240).

[6] Recently, W. J. McCormack has commented on a debate between Declan Kiberd and Kevin Barry regarding the intellectual histories of Protestant culture and of Catholic culture, a distinction (based on such blanket terms as "Catholic" and "Protestant" that assume essential differences) whose very assumptions McCormack questions:

So is there an "Irish spirit?" Rather than endorse any such notion of an inherent Irishness, I would prefer to cite Stuart Hall's definition of "cultural identity": "Far from being grounded in a mere 'recovery' of the past, which is waiting to be found, and which once found, will secure our sense of ourselves into eternity, identities are the names we give to the different ways we are positioned by, and position ourselves within, the narratives of the past" ("Cultural identity," 70). Such a definition allows for analyses of the discursive processes by which identities are formed in response to real-world situations and political contingencies. A number of Irish literary scholars have recently worked fruitfully with just such a discursive understanding of cultural identity. For example, David Lloyd reminds us of Frantz Fanon's distinction between "culture" and "custom," in which Fanon makes the important point, as I understand it, that colonial cultures are teeming, complex, and perpetually in motion, while custom and tradition construct static and oversimplified essentialisms that only hint at the multifarious complexities of the hidden life of a people. What ensues and survives over time are cultural forms that carry both the traces of the violence and trauma of the colonial encounter, as well as countermechanisms of survival and adaptation; as Lloyd concludes, "This unevenly distributed relation of damage and survival forges the recalcitrant grain of cultural difference" (see above, p. 141).

Luke Gibbons has also argued that we should be skeptical of simple generalizations about a cultural identity: "It is important not only to re-think but to *re-figure* Irish identity, to attend to those recalcitrant areas of

footnote 6 (*cont*)

> When "protestant culture" and "Catholic culture" are set up by Kiberd and Barry, their phrases require more concise definition. For, if culture is used in its anthropological sense, then it would be required of them to show that Catholics and Protestants ploughed in different ways, ate different food, harnessed their horses differently, bought clothes at different times, and instilled different values in their children ... Undoubtedly, certain activities – the eating of fish, the consumption of alcohol, the use of Sunday – do distinguish Catholics from members of the reformed churches – but other factors including social class, prosperity and poverty, climate and geographical variety are at work. Some attention to the vast, supportive web of cultural practices held in common by Irish Catholics, protestants, and persons not coming under those headings, might be timely.
>
> ("Convergent Criticism," 97)

expertise which simply do not lend themselves to certainty, and which impel societies themselves towards indirect and figurative discourse" (*Transformations*, 18) – for "there is no prospect of restoring a pristine, pre-colonial identity," Gibbons writes; "instead of being based on narrow ideals of racial purity and exclusivism, identity is open-ended and heterogeneous" (179). Gibbons argues that Irishness, indeed, rather than being characterizable as essentially premodern, is in fact modern before its time due to the circumstances of its history, one "seared as the record is by the successive waves of conquest and colonization, by bloody wars and uprisings, by traumatic dislocations, by lethal racial antagonisms, and indeed, by its own nineteenth-century version of a holocaust" (6). As a result, Gibbons argues, "Irish society did not have to await the twentieth century to undergo the shock of modernity: disintegration and fragmentation were already part of its history so that, in a crucial but not always welcome sense, Irish culture experienced modernity before its time. This is not unique to Ireland, but is the common inheritance of cultures subjected to the depredations of colonialism" (6). And Joyce, Declan Kiberd argues, was in touch with this "modernity" in the Irish experience: "[Joyce] did not become modern to the extent that he ceased to be Irish; rather he began from the premise that to be Irish was to be modern anyway . . . It was the politicians who, in cleaving to tired, inherited forms, failed to be modern and so ceased being Irish in any meaningful sense" (*Inventing Ireland*, 267). Joyce himself had written that "To tell the truth, to exclude from the present nation all who are descended from foreign families would be impossible" (*CW* 166); "In the face of such variousness," Kiberd concludes, "a unitary racial nationality could never be [for Joyce] more than 'a convenient fiction'" – and Joyce tried, instead, to develop in his fiction open-ended forms "hospitable to the many strands that made up Irish experience" (337).

Quite a few scholars lately, in Irish studies, have been at work demonstrating how Joyce's texts in fact do just that, and how they reflect symptomatically the various grains of influence and heritage in Irish history. Lloyd, for example, has argued that *Ulysses* "circulates not only thematically but also stylistically around adulteration [as opposed to purity] as the constitutive anxiety of nationalism" and that an episode like "Cyclops" "dramatizes adulteration as the condition of colonial Ireland at virtually every level" (*Anomalous States*, 106). *Ulysses*, Lloyd contends, refuses to fulfill the narrative demands consistent with the socializing functions of national identity formation, and its radicality comes from its insistence "on a deliberate stylization of dependence and *in*authenticity, a stylization of the hybrid status of the colonized subject as of the colonized culture, their internal adulteration and the strictly parodic [and hybrid] modes that they produce in every sphere" (110; emphasis added). And, in a compelling set of readings of the "Circe" episode, Andrew Gibson has demonstrated how that episode is full of English idiom and Anglicized voices, English forms revealing a cultural desire for Englishness, exposing "the anglicized or imported nature of Irish popular culture": in this way, the episode dramatizes the reality that "the characters in 'Circe' are necessarily divided against themselves" ("Strangers in My House," 197), a self-dividing doubleness that is at the very heart of an Irish culture long dominated by the hegemony of English discourse and desire. As Gibson concludes: "Joyce's point has to do with a culture caught in a specific historical configuration . . . It remains adulterate, compromised – 'infected,' to use one of Seamus Deane's terms. It fails to move beyond the anglicized nature of the context from which it sprang . . . This particular colonized culture is inevitably a culture of imposture" (201).

In other words, and in conclusion, rather than based on a narrow "authenticity," the specific culture of a late-colonial Ireland might be theorized indeed as a mongrel culture – even a culture of imposture, adulteration, and inauthenticity: modern and diverse in its variety and complexity – rather than primitive, premodern, and ineluctably Other by virtue of a narrowly defined, authentic otherness. As Joyce himself wrote: "Our civilization is a vast fabric, in which the most diverse elements are mingled . . . In such a fabric, it is useless to look for a thread that may have remained pure and virgin without having undergone the influence of a neighbouring thread" (*CW* 165–66).

In his recently published study *Remembrance and Imagination*, Joep Leerssen has suggested that *Ulysses* marks the end of the Irish nineteenth century precisely because Joyce "dared to describe an Irish setting in terms of its *normalcy*" (231) – rather than its ineradicable alienness. Leerssen punctuates this point by noting that the last word of *Ulysses* is not, in fact, "Yes" – but rather, "Trieste–Zurich–Paris 1914–21." In this way, "Joyce carefully situates the fictional universe of Dublin, 16 June 1904, not in a Celtic never-never land or in a stagnated out-of-the-way backwater, but squarely in the space-time of the Joyce family and its vagaries across Europe" (231). In spite of Joyce's efforts, however, Leerssen can only ruefully conclude that "the acknowledgment of normalcy is still very rare in Ireland-related discourse" – a discourse still deeply enmeshed in a rhetoric of authenticity and in a narrow effort to catch, pin down, and codify into national dogma an authentic "Irish spirit." Nevertheless, Leerssen's own efforts, as well as those by many others involved in contemporary Irish cultural studies, suggest that the portals of Irishness are beginning to open up.

Works cited

Anderson, Benedict. *Imagined Communities: Reflections on the Origin and Spread of Nationalism*. Rev. edn. London: Verso, 1991.

Arnold, Matthew. "On the Study of Celtic Literature." *The Complete Prose Works of Matthew Arnold*, vol. IX, *English Literature and Irish Politics*. Ed. R. H. Super. Ann Arbor: University of Michigan Press, 1973.

Axtell, James. *The European and the Indian: Essays in the Ethnohistory of Colonial North America*. New York: Oxford University Press, 1981.

Baudrillard, Jean. *Simulacra and Simulation*. Trans. Sheila Faria Glaser. Ann Arbor: University of Michigan Press, 1994.

Bendix, Regina. *In Search of Authenticity: The Formation of Folklore Studies*. Madison: University of Wisconsin Press, 1997.

Benjamin, Walter. *Das Kunstwerk im Zeitalter seiner technischen Reproduzierbarkeit*. Frankfurt: Suhrkamp, 1963.

Brown, Terence. *Ireland: A Social and Cultural History, 1922–79*. Glasgow: Fontana, 1981.

Budgen, Frank. *James Joyce and the Making of "Ulysses."* Bloomington: Indiana University Press, 1960.

Cheng, Vincent J. "Of Canons, Colonies, and Critics: The Ethics and Politics of Postcolonial Joyce Studies." *Cultural Critique* 35 (winter 1996–97): 81–104.

   Joyce, Race, and Empire. Cambridge: Cambridge University Press, 1995.

Clifford, James. "Four Northwest Coast Museums: Travel Reflections." *Exhibiting Cultures: The Poetics and Politics of Museum Display*. Ed. Ivan Karp and Steven D. Lavine. Washington, DC: Smithsonian Institution Press, 1991. 212–54.

Connery, Donald S. *The Irish*. London: Eyre & Spottiswoode, 1968.

Corkery, Daniel. *The Hidden Ireland: A Study of Gaelic Munster in the Eighteenth Century*. Dublin: Gill, 1925.

   Synge and Anglo-Irish Literature. London: Longmans, Green, 1931.

Deane, Seamus. *Heroic Styles: The Tradition of an Idea*. Derry: Field Day pamphlet no. 4, 1984.

Duff, Charles. *James Joyce and the Plain Reader*. London: Desmond Harmsworth, 1932.

Eagleton, Terry. "Form and Ideology in the Anglo-Irish Novel." *Bullán* 3.1 (1997): 17–26.

Ellmann, Richard. *James Joyce*. Rev. edn. New York: Oxford University Press, 1982.

Foster, R. F. *Modern Ireland, 1600–1972*. Harmondsworth: Penguin, 1988.

Gibbons, Luke. *Transformations in Irish Culture*. Cork: Cork University Press, 1996.

Gibson, Andrew. "'History, All That': Revival Historiography and Literary Strategy in the 'Cyclops' Episode in *Ulysses*." *Essays and Studies: History and the Novel*. Ed. Angus Easson. Bury St. Edmunds: D. S. Brewer, 1991. 53–69.

—— "'Strangers in My House, Bad Manners to Them!': England in 'Circe.'" *Reading Joyce's "Circe."* Ed. Andrew Gibson. *European Joyce Studies*. Amsterdam: Rodopi, 1994.

Gorman, Herbert S. *James Joyce: His First Forty Years*. New York: B. W. Huebsch, 1924.

Gupta, Suman. "'What Colour's Jew Joyce...': Race in the Context of Joyce's Irishness." *Bullán* 1.2 (1994): 59–72.

Hall, A. M. *Tales of Irish Life and Character*. Edinburgh: Foulis, 1910.

Hall, S. C. and A. M. *Ireland: Its Scenery, Character, etc.* 3 vols. London: How & Parson, 1841–43.

Hall, Stuart. "Cultural Identity and Cinematographic Representation." *Frameworks* 36 (1989): 68–81.

Hayden, Tom, ed. *Irish Hunger: Personal Reflections on the Legacy of the Famine*. Boulder: Roberts Rinehart Publishers; Dublin: Wolfhound Press, 1997.

Herr, Cheryl. "The Silence of the Hares: Peripherality in Ireland and in Joyce." *Joycean Cultures/Culturing Joyces*. Ed. Vincent J. Cheng, Kimberly J. Devlin, and Margot Norris. Newark, Del.: University of Delaware Press, 1998. 216–40.

Hobsbawm, Eric, and Terence Ranger, eds. *The Invention of Tradition*. Cambridge: Cambridge University Press, 1983.

Irish Voice Newspaper. Sicklerville, New Jersey.

Johnson, Clifton. *The Isle of the Shamrock*. London: Macmillan, 1901.

Johnston, Dillon. "Cross-Currencies in the Culture Market: Arnold, Yeats, Joyce." Waters, *Ireland*, 45–78.

James Joyce. *Dubliners: Text, Criticism, and Notes*. Ed. Robert Scholes and A. Walton Litz. New York: Viking, 1969.

Kiberd, Declan. *Inventing Ireland: The Literature of the Modern Nation*. Cambridge, Mass.: Harvard University Press, 1995.

—— "The Periphery and the Center." Waters, *Ireland*, 5–22.

Leerssen, Joep. *Remembrance and Imagination: Patterns in the Historical and Literary Representation of Ireland in the Nineteenth Century*. Cork: Cork University Press, 1996.

Lloyd, David. *Anomalous States: Irish Writing and the Post-Colonial Moment.* Durham: Duke University Press, 1993.

———. "Cultural Theory and Ireland." *Bullán* 3.1 (1997): 87–92.

McCormack, W. J. "Convergent Criticism: *The Biographia Literaria* of Vivian Mercier and the State of Irish Literary History." *Bullán* 2.1 (1995): 79–100.

Mercier, Vivian. *The Irish Comic Tradition.* Oxford: Oxford University Press, 1962.

Moran, D. P. *The Philosophy of Irish Ireland.* Dublin: James Duffy, 1905.

Nolan, Emer. *James Joyce and Nationalism.* London: Routledge, 1995.

O'Brien, Conor Cruise. *Writers and Politics.* London: Chatto & Windus, 1965.

O'Grady, Standish. *History of Ireland.* 2 vols. London, 1878–80.

Rolleston, T. W. "Shamrocks." *The Academy* (9 July 1887): 19.

Rosaldo, Renato. *Culture and Truth: The Remaking of Social Analysis.* Boston: Beacon Press, 1989.

Simmons, William S. "Culture Theory in Contemporary Ethnohistory." *Ethnohistory* 35.1 (1988): 1–14.

Taylor, Lawrence J. "'There Are Two Things that People Don't Like to Hear About Themselves': The Anthropology of Ireland and the Irish View of Anthropology." Waters, *Ireland*, 213–26.

Waters, John Paul, ed. *Ireland and Irish Cultural Studies.* Special issue of *South Atlantic Quarterly* 95.1 (winter 1996).

Webb, Virginia-Lee. "Manipulated Images: European Photographs of Pacific Peoples." *Prehistories of the Future.* Ed. Elazar Barkan and Ronald Bush. Stanford: Stanford University Press, 1994.

Yeates, Ray. "My Famine." Hayden, *Irish Hunger*, 191–200.

Index

Act of Union, 6, 106, 221
Acton, Lord, 102
Adams, James Eli, 97, 99
Adams, Robert M., 23n
Adrian IV, Pope, 2
Aesop, 2
African-American studies, 9, 11
Ahmad, Aijaz, 9n, 90
Anderson, Benedict, 10, 62–3, 66–7, 70, 74, 244
Anglo-Irish treaty, 5, 55
anthropology, 43–55 *passim*, 64, 248, 250, 252, 256n; *see also* ethnography
Aquinas, Thomas, 146
Archer, William, 153n
Arensberg, Conrad, 64
Argentine League for the Protection of Young Women, 189–90
Arnold, Matthew, 33, 102, 105, 115, 133–4, 252–3
Arnold, Thomas, 102
Ashcroft, Bill, 6n, 206
Attridge, Derek, 15
Augé, Marc, 44–55 passim
Axtell, James, 248

Bachelard, Gaston, 43
Bacon, Francis, 210
Baker, David J., 201
Bakhtin, Mikhail, 46, 153–4
Balakrishnan, Gopal, 11n
Balfour, Arthur, 211, 213, 216
Barnacle, Nora, 78, 168, 189
Barry, Kevin, 255n
Barta, Peter, 41n
Baudelaire, Charles, 44

Baudrillard, Jean, 246
Beckett, Samuel, 46, 53–4, 56, 255
Bendix, Regina, 243–7
Benjamin, Walter, 43, 47, 140, 245–6
Benstock, Bernard, 66
Bérard, Victor, 232
Bernal, Martin, 232
Bhabha, Homi, 8n, 58, 60–1, 66, 106, 205
Billington-Grieg, Teresa, 191–2
Book of Invasions, The, 219, 229, 232, 233n
Borges, Jorge Luis, 46
Bornstein, George, 234
Bourdieu, Pierre, 34n
Bourke, Angela, 158, 159n, 160n, 164
Boxer, The, 241
Boyce, George, 6, 63
Bradshaw, Brendan, 201
Braque, Georges, 46, 53
Breakspeare, Nicholas, 2
Brecht, Bertolt, 147
Breuilly, John, 78n
Bristow, Edward, 183, 194n
British Immigration Society, 182, 189–90, 195
Brown, Richard, 204
Brown, Terence, 68, 223n, 254
Browne, Father Henry, 232
Bruce, Edward, 212–3
Bruce, Robert, 213
Buchan, John, 204
Budgen, Frank, 254
Buenos Ayres Standard, 177–8
Bulfin, William, 176
Bullán, 207
Bullock, Frederick, 190

Bunting, Percy, 192n
Burns, Robert, 203, 205, 213, 214, 215
Butt, Isaac, 104
Byron, George Gordon, Lord 236

Cairns, David, 101, 111
Carlyle, Thomas, 102, 234
Carter, Gillian, 202n, 204
Celticism, 21, 60, 65–6, 102, 105, 115,
    132, 158, 231, 248; *see also* Irish
    Revival
Cézanne, Paul, 246
Chakrabarty, Dipesh, 83n, 87–8, 92
Charcot, Jean-Martin, 155, 157
Chartism, 101
Chatterjee, Partha, 78–9, 80, 88, 131,
    133
Cheng, Vincent J., 16, 23n, 54n, 59, 68,
    78n, 144n, 208, 211, 221, 225, 227,
    228, 245n, 248n
Ciaran, Brady, 220n
Circle of Friends, A, 241
Cixous, Hélène, 157
Clannad, 241
Cleary, Bridget, 158–9, 164
Cleary, Joe, 90n
Cleland, John, 196
Clément, Catherine, 157
Clifford, James, 248
Colley, Linda, 204
Collins, Michael, 249, 251
Connery, Donald S., 253
Connolly, James, 86
Contemporary Review, The, 192n
Conyngham, David Power, 233
Coote, William, 190, 191n, 192
Corkery, Daniel, 224, 254–5
Costello, Peter, 221, 232
Craig, Cairns, 202, 203–4
Cranberries, 241
Croke, Archbishop, 139
Croke Park Massacre, 115
Crying Game, The, 220, 241

Cubism, 46
Curtis, L. P., 102, 105, 134n, 229, 234
Curtis, Liz, 102n
Cusack, Mary Francis, 160n
Cusack, Michael, 104, 106

Daily Express, The, 226
Daily News, The, 183n
Daly, Mary, 156n
Darwin, Charles, 102, 105
Davidson, Neil, 230n
Davis, Kathleen, 11n
Davis, Thomas, 103, 114
Day, Robert Adams, 45
Deane, Seamus, 15, 16, 64, 73, 102n,
    105n, 107n, 207, 228, 244, 258
De Certeau, Michel, 50
Derrida, Jacques, 12, 36n, 120n, 249
De Valera, Eamon, 150, 249
Diner, Hasia, 180
Dinneen, Michael, 177
Dirlik, Arif, 7n
Döblin, Alfred, 41
Dorsinville, Max, 206
Doyle, Sir Arthur Conan, 47–8
Doyle, Roddy, 205
Drummond, William, 211–2
Dublin Review, 113
Dublin White Cross Vigilance
    Association, 193–5
Duff, Charles, 254
Duffy, Charles Gavan, 103
Duffy, Enda, 16, 38n, 59, 64, 69, 78n,
    82n, 107n, 108, 119, 166n
Dunlop, Robert, 231
Dunne, Tom, 8, 12n
Durkheim, Emile, 50
Dyer, Alfred Stace, 183

Eagleton, Terry, 9n, 12, 15, 16, 61, 62,
    89–90, 207, 253
Easter Rising, 4, 37–41, 119
Edgeworth, Maria, 205, 215

Edward VII, King of Great Britain, 21, 27–31 *passim*, 230
Edwards, Owen, Dudley, 206
Elias, Norbert, 153–4
Eliot, T.S., 14, 40, 41
Ellis, John S., 212
Ellmann, Richard, 14, 15, 151n, 153n, 172, 210, 215, 221, 249
Emmet, Robert, 50, 54, 115
Envoy, 14
Enya, 241, 244
ethnography, 133–4, 243–50 *passim*; see also anthropology
Euclid, 43
European Joyce Studies, 16
Evans, Estyn, 219, 224, 229
Eveline, or the Adventures of a Lady of Fortune who was Never Found Out, 196
External Relations Act, 5

Fairhall, James, 16, 64
famine, 62, 104, 137, 142, 151, 153–7, 163, 168, 233, 249, 252–3
Fanon, Franz, 11, 51, 53, 78, 84, 86, 90, 131, 148, 256
Fawcett, Milicent, 190
feminism, 9, 11, 12, 34, 81, 85, 86–7, 96, 220, 226
Fenianism, 21, 28, 29, 31, 67, 104, 105, 113, 115, 134, 136, 141
Ferguson, Francis, 38
Ferguson, M. C., 233
Ferguson, Samuel, 250
Fitzgerald, Thomas, 212–3
Flanagan, Thomas, 214
Flaubert, Gustave, 34n
Foley, Timothy, 8
Fonda, Jane, 253
Ford, John, 213
Foster, John Wilson, 227, 228
Foster, Roy, 6n, 158, 206, 255
Foucault, Michel, 42–3, 51

Frank and I, 196
Fraser's Magazine, 160n
Freud, Sigmund, 121, 155, 157, 168
Friedman, Alan, 163n
Friel, Brian, 229
Froude, J. A., 102

Gaelic Athletic Association, 104, 106, 113, 114, 115, 139
Gaelic League, 118, 135, 136, 139, 174, 180, 223, 228, 254
Galloway, Janice, 205
Gardiner, Michael, 202n
Garvey, Johanna, 53n
gay studies, 9
Gellner, Ernest, 40n
George V, King of Great Britain, 212
Gilbert, Stuart, 236
Gibbons, Luke, 9n, 10n, 16, 61, 63, 67, 78, 81n, 131n, 158n, 180n, 228, 236, 256–7
Gibson, Andrew, 250, 258
Gifford, Don, 60, 211, 212, 213, 214
Gilroy, Paul, 10n, 65n
Gogarty, Oliver St. John, 176
Goldstein, Jan, 155
Good Friday Agreement, 90
Gorman, Herbert, 254
Graham, Brian, 59n
Graham, Colin, 6n, 10, 12n
Gramsci, Antonio, 81
Gregory, Augusta, Lady, 60, 158, 160, 214
Griffith, Arthur, 104, 119, 176n, 181
Griffiths, Gareth, 6n, 206
Guha, Ranajit, 79n, 81n
Guinan, Reverend J., 165–6
Guinness, Arthur, 185n
Gupta, Suman, 253, 254
Guy, Donna, 192

Hackett, Francis, 234
Hall, A. M., 242, 251

Hall, Donald, 101
Hall, S. C., 242
Hall, Stuart, 256
Halpin, Father J., 138
Harper's Weekly, 234
Hayden, Tom, 253
Healy, Tim, 178
Heaney, Seamus, 202
Hecter, Michael, 8, 61
Hegel, G. W. F., 208
Heidegger, Martin, 43
Henry II, King of England, 2
Herder, Johann Gottfried, 245,
    247
Herr, Cheryl, 42, 196n, 242
Herring, Philip, 221
Hobsbawn, Eric, 10
Hofheinz, Thomas, 38
Hogg, James, 215
Home Rule, 31, 103, 104
hooks, bell, 220
Hopkins, Ellice, 194
Horton, Patricia, 202n
Howes, Marjorie, 102n, 136n
Hughes, Robert, 53
Hughes, Thomas, 98–9, 113–4
Hugo, Victor, 37
Hyde, Douglas, 132, 136n, 249

Ibsen, Henrik, 33, 34
Irish constitution, 5, 90, 135, 224
Irish Homestead, The, 152, 165,
    172–83, 193, 195, 197, 198
Irish Ireland, 224, 230, 255
Irish National Theatre, 139
Irish Parliamentary Party, 31
Irish Republican Brotherhood, 104,
    113, 115
Irish Revival, 105, 108, 135, 136, 139,
    140, 158, 221, 227–8, 250–3
Irish studies, 4–13, 89–90, 201, 202,
    207, 245, 253, 257–9
Irish Voice Newspaper, 240, 241

Jackson, John Wyse, 175n
Jameson, Fredric, 15, 42, 48–9, 64,
    90n
JanMohamed, Abdul, 8n
Jenner, George, 178
Jeune, Mary, 184n
Johnson, Clifton, 242
Johnston, Dillon, 252
Jones, Ellen Carol, 16
Jonson, Ben, 212–2
Jordan, Neil, 220
Jordi, M., 179
Joyce, James, works by
    Critical Writings, 59, 61, 67, 68–9,
        117, 120–1, 160, 210, 219,
        221–31 *passim*, 237, 257, 258
    Dubliners, 21, 33, 35–6, 146, 147,
        151–2, 167, 168, 202, 221
    "After the Race," 21–4, 25–6, 34,
        144n
    "Araby," 184n, 211
    "Boarding House, The," 167
    "Clay," 161–4
    "Counterparts," 128–9, 133,
        143–5, 167–8
    "Dead, The," 22, 33–6, 59,
        65–70, 74–5, 147, 151n, 202,
        210–1, 223, 225–8, 235, 250,
        251–2
    "Encounter, An," 167–8, 211
    "Eveline," 164–7, 172–98
        passim, 223
    "Grace," 26, 27, 29, 30–1, 33,
        150, 160, 167
    "Ivy Day in the Committee
        Room," 27–33, 167–8
    "Little Cloud, A," 167–8
    "Mother, A," 26, 29, 227
    "Painful Case, A" 21, 24–7, 29
    "Sisters, The," 152
    "Two Gallants," 69, 150
    Finnegans Wake, 1–3, 4, 33, 38, 59,
        85, 184, 190–1, 211, 213, 215, 216

Joyce, James, works by (*cont.*)
    Letters, 147, 151n, 152n, 168, 172,
      176n, 198, 220, 223, 227n
    Poems and Shorter Writings, 152n
    *Portrait of the Artist as a Young
      Man, A,* 27, 33, 59, 65, 69,
      70–5, 113, 166, 168, 228
    Stephen Hero, 146–7, 151–3, 163,
      166–7, 221, 223, 228, 235
    Ulysses, 32–3, 37–8, 40–56, 69,
      83–6, 145, 151, 153, 169, 184n,
      209, 210, 211–6 *passim*, 224,
      228–30, 232–4, 240, 257–8
      "Circe," 93, 230, 258
      "Cyclops," 38, 58–60, 65, 79–83,
      96, 106–25, 214, 215, 236, 257
      "Eumaeus," 110–1
      "Hades," 37–8, 49
      "Ithaca," 45, 93
      "Lestrygonians," 37
      "Lotus Eaters," 53
      "Nausicca," 53
      "Nestor," 113
      "Oxen of the Sun," 213–4
      "Penelope," 33, 85, 93, 231
      "Sirens," 139–40, 184n
      "Telemachus," 240, 242, 247–8
      "Wandering Rocks," 37, 49, 52,
      53
Joyce, Stanislaus, 158n, 162n, 176n,
    223, 235

Kafka, Franz, 40, 41
Kain, Richard M., 151n
Kaplan, Karen, 45n
Kaul, Suvir, 7n
Kearney, Richard, 16, 243
Keating, Geoffrey, 233n
Kelman, James, 205
Kennedy, Liam, 8
Kennedy, Robert F., 253
Kenner, Hugh, 14, 45, 177, 182, 190,
    197, 211

Kershner, Brandon, 151n, 163, 196n
Kiberd, Declan, 9n, 10n, 16, 59, 118,
    219, 243, 248–9, 251, 252, 255n, 257
Kimball, Solon T., 64
Kingsley, Charles, 98, 100, 102, 234,
    235
Kipling, Rudyard, 24n
Kirby, Peadar, 176, 177
Klein, Scott W., 201n

labor studies, 9
Lacan, Jacques, 15, 96, 117
Land League, 104, 118, 141
Land War, 38
Law, Jules David, 167
Lazarus, Neil, 86n, 88–9
Lecky, W. E. H., 154–5, 157
Le Corbusier, 43
Leerssen, Joep, 16, 64, 66, 228, 232,
    258–9
Lefebvre, Henri, 42–4, 53, 54
Levin, Harry, 210
Livesey, James, 13
Lloyd, David, 8, 16, 78, 79–93, 131n,
    136n, 142n, 146n, 207, 220, 248,
    253–4, 256, 257–8
Longley, Edna, 206
Loos, Adolf, 43
Lowe, Donald, 142n
Lowe, Lisa, 219
Lowe–Evans, Mary, 153n
Luddy, Maria, 182n
Luftig, Victor, 16
Lukács, Georg, 83
Lyons, F. S. L., 62, 206

MacCabe, Colin, 15, 204, 221
MacLeod, Christine, 9n
MacDiarmid, Hugh, 205, 206
MacDonagh, Oliver, 58, 63
MacKirdy, Olive, 184, 190
Maddox, Brenda, 189n
Magalaner, Marvin, 151n

Mahaffey, Vicky, 71
Malcolm, Elizabeth, 141n
Maley, Willy, 208, 210
Mangan, J. A., 113
Manganiello, Dominic, 15, 54n, 78n, 223n
Mann, Thomas, 48
Markievicz, Constance, Countess, 86
Mary, Queen of Scots, 211
Marx, Karl, 42, 48
Marxism, 9, 11, 79
Mathers, MacGregor, 214
Matthew, Father, 47
Maxwell, Grenfell, 182–3
McCabe, Patrick, 205
McCannell, Dean, 52
McCarthy, Michael J. F., 157–60, 168, 194–5
McClintock, Anne, 5n
McCormack, W.J., 8, 208, 255n
McCourt, Frank, 241
McGinley, Bernard, 175n
McGrath, William, 155
McHugh, Roland, 191n
McKenna, Patrick, 176
McLoughlin, Dympna, 156
McManus, Seumas, 173n
Mendes, Peter, 196n
Mercier, Vivian, 255
Michael Collins, 241
Mill, J. S., 99
Miller, Kerby, 64
Milton, John, 210
Mink, Louis, 208–9, 215
Mitchel, John, 84
Modern Eveline, The, 196n
modernism, 11, 34, 40–54 *passim*, 221
Molly Maguires, 118
Moore, Thomas, 50
Moore-Gilbert, Bart, 82n
Moran, D. P., 224, 251
Morrill, John, 201
Morris, George, 173n

Mosse, George, 98, 103
Muir, Edwin, 205
Mulhern, Francis, 85
Mullin, Katherine, 165, 223n
Murphy, Cliona, 9n
Murray, Stuart, 13
Musil, Robert, 41

Nadel, Ira, 230n
Nandy, Ashis, 103
Nation, The, 38
National Vigilance Association, 183–95 *passim*
New Criticism, 14
Newland, Ellen, 183
Newsweek, 241
Nicholson, Colin, 202
Nietzsche, Friedrich, 21, 25, 33
Nolan, Emer, 2, 11n, 16, 23n, 40, 54n, 59, 66–7, 82n, 85n, 107n, 117, 119, 208, 214n, 221, 228, 243
Nolan, Janet, 180
Norris, Margot, 161–2, 225n, 235

O'Brien, Conor Cruise, 255
O'Brien, Joseph V., 64
O'Casey, Sean, 206
O'Connell, Daniel, 47, 63, 104, 235
O'Connor, Charles, 38
O'Connor, John, 178
O'Connor, Sinead, 241
O'Day, Alan, 6
O'Doherty, Michael, 104
O'Donovan, Connor, 38
O'Donovan, Jeremiah, 173–4, 180–2, 185
O'Farelly, Agnes, 180, 185, 193
O'Grady, Standish, 250–1
O'Keefe, F. A., 178
O'Meara, Mr. 178, 179
O'Nolan, Brian, 14
Ordinance Survey, 38
O'Suilleabhain, Sean, 156n, 162

O'Toole, Fintan, 233
Owens, Cóilín, 67

Pall Mall Gazette, 183n
Parfitt, George, 212
Parnell, Charles Stewart, 21, 27–32
  passim, 49–50, 73
Parry, Benita, 5n, 7n, 8n, 88
Partridge, Eric, 189
Pascal, Blaise, 120
Paulin, Tom, 15
Pearse, Patrick, 137, 223, 224
Pearson, Michael, 183n
Petrie, Sir George, 38
Picasso, Pablo, 43
Pittock, Murray, 201–2
Plunkett, Horace, 173, 179, 195
postmodernism, 12, 44, 50
poststructuralism, 12, 15
Pound, Ezra, 14, 15
Power, Arthur, 14
Power, Mary, 175
Prasad, Madhava, 87
Presley, Elvis, 246
Proust, Marcel, 44
Pynchon, Thomas, 46

Quinn, Bob, 219, 235–6

Rea, Stephen, 220
Reizbaum, Marilyn, 203–4
Renan, Ernest, 252–3
revisionism, 6, 8–9, 9, 10, 12, 89–90,
  201, 206, 207, 208, 219–20
Richards, Grant, 151
Richards, Shaun, 101, 111
Rimmon-Kennan, Shlomith, 163n
Riverdance, 241
Roberts, George, 210
Robbins, Bruce, 89
Roche, Joseph, 104
Rockett, Kevin, 139n
Rolleston, T. W., 250

Rosaldo, Renato, 248
Rosen, David, 96–7
Rosen, Ruth, 191
Rosenzweig, Roy, 139n, 142
Rossa, O'Donovan, 104
Rousseau, Jean-Jacques, 88
Russell, George, 118, 172, 173, 174,
  176, 195, 198, 211, 214, 249
Ryan, John, 14, 174n

Said, Edward, 6, 90, 92–3, 101, 204,
  219
Sangari, Kumkum, 134n
Scott, Sir Walter, 203, 205, 211, 215
Secret of Roan Inish, The, 241
Seidel, Michael, 59, 232
Shakespeare, William, 204, 210
Shell, Mark, 145n
Shloss, Carol, 209
Shohat, Ella, 5n
Simmel, Georg, 41
Simmons, William, 248
Simnel, Lambert, 212–3
Sinfield, Alan, 110
Sinn Fein, 103, 104, 118–9, 121
Sinn Fein, 176n
Smiles, Samuel, 98
Smith, Neil, 61, 63
Smyth, Gerry, 7n
socialism, 24, 26–7, 81, 85, 86
Southern Cross, The, 176, 177, 178
Spenser, Edmund, 210, 213
Spierenburg, Pieter, 154n
Spivak, Gayatri Chakravorty, 9n, 82,
  88
Spoo, Robert, 16
Stallybrass, Peter, 154n
Standard, 183n
Starobinski, Jean, 44
Steiner-Scott, Elizabeth, 168
Stephens, James, 104
Stevenson, Robert Louis, 204, 215
Stone, Harry, 211

Stubbs, Bishop, 229
subaltern studies, 9, 9n, 78–9, 80–91
Synge, John Millington, 206, 214, 255n

Taylor, John F., 230, 233
Taylor, Lawrence J., 250, 252
Tennyson, Alfred, Lord 102
Thom's Dublin Directory, 49, 179n
Thomas, Paul, 80, 88–9
Tiffin, Helen, 6n, 206
Tifft, Stephen, 119
Titanic, 244
Tóibín, Colm, 4, 6
Tone, Wolfe, 73
Torchiana, Donald, 163
Tratner, Michael, 11n
Travellers Aid Society, 185n
Trench, W. Steuart, 153
TV Guide, 241
Tymoczko, Maria, 229, 230

U2, 241
Ulrichs, Karl, 110
United Irishman, 84
United Irishmen, 136

Vaid, Sudesh, 134n
Valente, Joseph, 16, 69, 102n, 111n, 134n
Vallancey, Charles, 222, 231–3, 236
Verschoyle, John, 180, 185
Vidor, Charles, 172

Wagner, Heinrich, 236
Waisbren, Burton, 152n
Waking Ned Devine, 241
Wales, Katie, 206, 214n
Walzl, Florence, 152n
Warbeck, Perkin, 212–3
Ward, Margaret, 87n, 181
Watson, Roderick, 202n
Watt, Stephen, 166n
Webb, Virginia-Lee, 247
Weber, Max, 33
Weekly Freeman, The, 175, 176n
Williams, Trevor, 72n
Wills, Clair, 69, 155–6
Whelan, Kevin, 142n
White, Allon, 154n
White Slave Traffic, 182–98
Wilde, Oscar, 158, 250
Wollaeger, Mark, 16, 209
Wordsworth, William, 229

Yeates, Ray, 252–3
Yeats, W. B., 41, 136, 137, 146, 158–9, 205, 208, 214, 222, 227, 231, 233–4, 243, 249, 252, 255n
Young, Filson, 150–2, 156–7, 168
Young Ireland, 103, 104, 135, 136
Young, Robert, 12, 81, 204

Ziarek, Ewa, 36n
Žižek, Slavoj, 92, 122